FREE Test Taking Tips DVD Offer

To help us better serve you, we have developed a Test Taking Tips DVD that we would like to give you for FREE. **This DVD covers world-class test taking tips that you can use to be even more successful when you are taking your test.**

All that we ask is that you email us your feedback about your study guide. Please let us know what you thought about it – whether that is good, bad or indifferent.

To get your **FREE Test Taking Tips DVD**, email freedvd@studyguideteam.com with "FREE DVD" in the subject line and the following information in the body of the email:

a. The title of your study guide.

b. Your product rating on a scale of 1-5, with 5 being the highest rating.

c. Your feedback about the study guide. What did you think of it?

d. Your full name and shipping address to send your free DVD.

If you have any questions or concerns, please don't hesitate to contact us at freedvd@studyguideteam.com.

Thanks again!

US History Smart Review Complete Prep Guide Book with Practice Test Questions

[Include Detailed Answer Explanations]

Joshua Rueda

Written and edited by TPB Publishing.

ISBN 13: 9781637758267
ISBN 10: 163775826X

Table of Contents

Quick Overview

As you draw closer to taking your exam, effective preparation becomes more and more important. Thankfully, you have this study guide to help you get ready. Use this guide to help keep your studying on track and refer to it often.

This study guide contains several key sections that will help you be successful on your exam. The guide contains tips for what you should do the night before and the day of the test. Also included are test-taking tips. Knowing the right information is not always enough. Many well-prepared test takers struggle with exams. These tips will help equip you to accurately read, assess, and answer test questions.

A large part of the guide is devoted to showing you what content to expect on the exam and to helping you better understand that content. In this guide are practice test questions so that you can see how well you have grasped the content. Then, answer explanations are provided so that you can understand why you missed certain questions.

Don't try to cram the night before you take your exam. This is not a wise strategy for a few reasons. First, your retention of the information will be low. Your time would be better used by reviewing information you already know rather than trying to learn a lot of new information. Second, you will likely become stressed as you try to gain a large amount of knowledge in a short amount of time. Third, you will be depriving yourself of sleep. So be sure to go to bed at a reasonable time the night before. Being well-rested helps you focus and remain calm.

Be sure to eat a substantial breakfast the morning of the exam. If you are taking the exam in the afternoon, be sure to have a good lunch as well. Being hungry is distracting and can make it difficult to focus. You have hopefully spent lots of time preparing for the exam. Don't let an empty stomach get in the way of success!

When travelling to the testing center, leave earlier than needed. That way, you have a buffer in case you experience any delays. This will help you remain calm and will keep you from missing your appointment time at the testing center.

Be sure to pace yourself during the exam. Don't try to rush through the exam. There is no need to risk performing poorly on the exam just so you can leave the testing center early. Allow yourself to use all of the allotted time if needed.

Remain positive while taking the exam even if you feel like you are performing poorly. Thinking about the content you should have mastered will not help you perform better on the exam.

Once the exam is complete, take some time to relax. Even if you feel that you need to take the exam again, you will be well served by some down time before you begin studying again. It's often easier to convince yourself to study if you know that it will come with a reward!

Test-Taking Strategies

1. Predicting the Answer

When you feel confident in your preparation for a multiple-choice test, try predicting the answer before reading the answer choices. This is especially useful on questions that test objective factual knowledge. By predicting the answer before reading the available choices, you eliminate the possibility that you will be distracted or led astray by an incorrect answer choice. You will feel more confident in your selection if you read the question, predict the answer, and then find your prediction among the answer choices. After using this strategy, be sure to still read all of the answer choices carefully and completely. If you feel unprepared, you should not attempt to predict the answers. This would be a waste of time and an opportunity for your mind to wander in the wrong direction.

2. Reading the Whole Question

Too often, test takers scan a multiple-choice question, recognize a few familiar words, and immediately jump to the answer choices. Test authors are aware of this common impatience, and they will sometimes prey upon it. For instance, a test author might subtly turn the question into a negative, or he or she might redirect the focus of the question right at the end. The only way to avoid falling into these traps is to read the entirety of the question carefully before reading the answer choices.

3. Looking for Wrong Answers

Long and complicated multiple-choice questions can be intimidating. One way to simplify a difficult multiple-choice question is to eliminate all of the answer choices that are clearly wrong. In most sets of answers, there will be at least one selection that can be dismissed right away. If the test is administered on paper, the test taker could draw a line through it to indicate that it may be ignored; otherwise, the test taker will have to perform this operation mentally or on scratch paper. In either case, once the obviously incorrect answers have been eliminated, the remaining choices may be considered. Sometimes identifying the clearly wrong answers will give the test taker some information about the correct answer. For instance, if one of the remaining answer choices is a direct opposite of one of the eliminated answer choices, it may well be the correct answer. The opposite of obviously wrong is obviously right! Of course, this is not always the case. Some answers are obviously incorrect simply because they are irrelevant to the question being asked. Still, identifying and eliminating some incorrect answer choices is a good way to simplify a multiple-choice question.

4. Don't Overanalyze

Anxious test takers often overanalyze questions. When you are nervous, your brain will often run wild, causing you to make associations and discover clues that don't actually exist. If you feel that this may be a problem for you, do whatever you can to slow down during the test. Try taking a deep breath or counting to ten. As you read and consider the question, restrict yourself to the particular words used by the author. Avoid thought tangents about what the author *really* meant, or what he or she was *trying* to say. The only things that matter on a multiple-choice test are the words that are actually in the question. You must avoid reading too much into a multiple-choice question, or supposing that the writer meant something other than what he or she wrote.

5. No Need for Panic

It is wise to learn as many strategies as possible before taking a multiple-choice test, but it is likely that you will come across a few questions for which you simply don't know the answer. In this situation, avoid panicking. Because most multiple-choice tests include dozens of questions, the relative value of a single wrong answer is small. As much as possible, you should compartmentalize each question on a multiple-choice test. In other words, you should not allow your feelings about one question to affect your success on the others. When you find a question that you either don't understand or don't know how to answer, just take a deep breath and do your best. Read the entire question slowly and carefully. Try rephrasing the question a couple of different ways. Then, read all of the answer choices carefully. After eliminating obviously wrong answers, make a selection and move on to the next question.

6. Confusing Answer Choices

When working on a difficult multiple-choice question, there may be a tendency to focus on the answer choices that are the easiest to understand. Many people, whether consciously or not, gravitate to the answer choices that require the least concentration, knowledge, and memory. This is a mistake. When you come across an answer choice that is confusing, you should give it extra attention. A question might be confusing because you do not know the subject matter to which it refers. If this is the case, don't eliminate the answer before you have affirmatively settled on another. When you come across an answer choice of this type, set it aside as you look at the remaining choices. If you can confidently assert that one of the other choices is correct, you can leave the confusing answer aside. Otherwise, you will need to take a moment to try to better understand the confusing answer choice. Rephrasing is one way to tease out the sense of a confusing answer choice.

7. Your First Instinct

Many people struggle with multiple-choice tests because they overthink the questions. If you have studied sufficiently for the test, you should be prepared to trust your first instinct once you have carefully and completely read the question and all of the answer choices. There is a great deal of research suggesting that the mind can come to the correct conclusion very quickly once it has obtained all of the relevant information. At times, it may seem to you as if your intuition is working faster even than your reasoning mind. This may in fact be true. The knowledge you obtain while studying may be retrieved from your subconscious before you have a chance to work out the associations that support it. Verify your instinct by working out the reasons that it should be trusted.

8. Key Words

Many test takers struggle with multiple-choice questions because they have poor reading comprehension skills. Quickly reading and understanding a multiple-choice question requires a mixture of skill and experience. To help with this, try jotting down a few key words and phrases on a piece of scrap paper. Doing this concentrates the process of reading and forces the mind to weigh the relative importance of the question's parts. In selecting words and phrases to write down, the test taker thinks about the question more deeply and carefully. This is especially true for multiple-choice questions that are preceded by a long prompt.

9. Subtle Negatives

One of the oldest tricks in the multiple-choice test writer's book is to subtly reverse the meaning of a question with a word like *not* or *except*. If you are not paying attention to each word in the question, you can easily be led astray by this trick. For instance, a common question format is, "Which of the following is...?" Obviously, if the question instead is, "Which of the following is not...?," then the answer will be quite different. Even worse, the test makers are aware of the potential for this mistake and will include one answer choice that would be correct if the question were not negated or reversed. A test taker who misses the reversal will find what he or she believes to be a correct answer and will be so confident that he or she will fail to reread the question and discover the original error. The only way to avoid this is to practice a wide variety of multiple-choice questions and to pay close attention to each and every word.

10. Reading Every Answer Choice

It may seem obvious, but you should always read every one of the answer choices! Too many test takers fall into the habit of scanning the question and assuming that they understand the question because they recognize a few key words. From there, they pick the first answer choice that answers the question they believe they have read. Test takers who read all of the answer choices might discover that one of the latter answer choices is actually *more* correct. Moreover, reading all of the answer choices can remind you of facts related to the question that can help you arrive at the correct answer. Sometimes, a misstatement or incorrect detail in one of the latter answer choices will trigger your memory of the subject and will enable you to find the right answer. Failing to read all of the answer choices is like not reading all of the items on a restaurant menu: you might miss out on the perfect choice.

11. Spot the Hedges

One of the keys to success on multiple-choice tests is paying close attention to every word. This is never truer than with words like almost, most, some, and sometimes. These words are called "hedges" because they indicate that a statement is not totally true or not true in every place and time. An absolute statement will contain no hedges, but in many subjects, the answers are not always straightforward or absolute. There are always exceptions to the rules in these subjects. For this reason, you should favor those multiple-choice questions that contain hedging language. The presence of qualifying words indicates that the author is taking special care with their words, which is certainly important when composing the right answer. After all, there are many ways to be wrong, but there is only one way to be right! For this reason, it is wise to avoid answers that are absolute when taking a multiple-choice test. An absolute answer is one that says things are either all one way or all another. They often include words like *every*, *always*, *best*, and *never*. If you are taking a multiple-choice test in a subject that doesn't lend itself to absolute answers, be on your guard if you see any of these words.

12. Long Answers

In many subject areas, the answers are not simple. As already mentioned, the right answer often requires hedges. Another common feature of the answers to a complex or subjective question are qualifying clauses, which are groups of words that subtly modify the meaning of the sentence. If the question or answer choice describes a rule to which there are exceptions or the subject matter is complicated, ambiguous, or confusing, the correct answer will require many words in order to be expressed clearly and accurately. In essence, you should not be deterred by answer choices that seem excessively long. Oftentimes, the author of the text will not be able to write the correct answer without offering some qualifications and modifications. Your job is to read the answer choices thoroughly and completely and to select the one that most accurately and precisely answers the question.

13. Restating to Understand

Sometimes, a question on a multiple-choice test is difficult not because of what it asks but because of how it is written. If this is the case, restate the question or answer choice in different words. This process serves a couple of important purposes. First, it forces you to concentrate on the core of the question. In order to rephrase the question accurately, you have to understand it well. Rephrasing the question will concentrate your mind on the key words and ideas. Second, it will present the information to your mind in a fresh way. This process may trigger your memory and render some useful scrap of information picked up while studying.

14. True Statements

Sometimes an answer choice will be true in itself, but it does not answer the question. This is one of the main reasons why it is essential to read the question carefully and completely before proceeding to the answer choices. Too often, test takers skip ahead to the answer choices and look for true statements. Having found one of these, they are content to select it without reference to the question above. Obviously, this provides an easy way for test makers to play tricks. The savvy test taker will always read the entire question before turning to the answer choices. Then, having settled on a correct answer choice, he or she will refer to the original question and ensure that the selected answer is relevant. The mistake of choosing a correct-but-irrelevant answer choice is especially common on questions related to specific pieces of objective knowledge. A prepared test taker will have a wealth of factual knowledge at their disposal, and should not be careless in its application.

15. No Patterns

One of the more dangerous ideas that circulates about multiple-choice tests is that the correct answers tend to fall into patterns. These erroneous ideas range from a belief that B and C are the most common right answers, to the idea that an unprepared test-taker should answer "A-B-A-C-A-D-A-B-A." It cannot be emphasized enough that pattern-seeking of this type is exactly the WRONG way to approach a multiple-choice test. To begin with, it is highly unlikely that the test maker will plot the correct answers according to some predetermined pattern. The questions are scrambled and delivered in a random order. Furthermore, even if the test maker was following a pattern in the assignation of correct answers, there is no reason why the test taker would know which pattern he or she was using. Any attempt to discern a pattern in the answer choices is a waste of time and a distraction from the real work of taking the test. A test taker would be much better served by extra preparation before the test than by reliance on a pattern in the answers.

FREE DVD OFFER

Don't forget that doing well on your exam includes both understanding the test content and understanding how to use what you know to do well on the test. We offer a completely FREE Test Taking Tips DVD that covers world class test taking tips that you can use to be even more successful when you are taking your test.

All that we ask is that you email us your feedback about your study guide. To get your **FREE Test Taking Tips DVD**, email freedvd@studyguideteam.com with "FREE DVD" in the subject line and the following information in the body of the email:

- The title of your study guide.
- Your product rating on a scale of 1-5, with 5 being the highest rating.
- Your feedback about the study guide. What did you think of it?
- Your full name and shipping address to send your free DVD.

Introduction

Purpose of this Guide

The purpose of this guide is to help students from grades six to twelve review and practice concepts from exploration of the United States to its modern day. The guide includes review material that covers appropriate topics in chronological order, skills needed for reading historical texts, three practice tests, and an essay prompt. The practice tests are thirty-five questions each and contain reading passages; illustrations, graphs, and tables; and multiple-choice questions. A long essay prompt is included at the end of the practice tests so that students may practice writing historical analysis and synthesizing historical material.

Alignment Topics

This guide is an overview of U.S. History from its beginning to its current state, so many key events and persons throughout history will be revisited. This guide also aligns with common core standards, as it includes sections specifically dedicated to reading for meaning in social studies, analyzing historical events and arguments, and using numbers and graphs. The practice questions are similar to questions that are given to students in the common core standards, as they also deal with assessing knowledge through multiple-choice questions, reading comprehension, and illustrations.

Skills Assessed

The following points are skills that should be developed by the completion of this guide:

- Historical Events and People
    - Reviewing U.S. History from exploration to modern times
    - Assessing political ideas and principles
    - Learning about events and people who have significantly affected history
- Finding the Central Idea and Supporting Details
    - Citing evidence
    - Acknowledging primary and secondary sources
    - Reading summaries
    - Evaluating authorial explanations
- Determining a Text's Craft and Structure
    - Finding a word's meaning
    - Assessing the makeup of a passage
    - Evaluating different points of view
- Analyzing and Synthesizing New Ideas and Knowledge
    - Evaluating multiple sources of information in diverse formats
    - Integrating information from various sources
- Reading Comprehension of a Text
    - Developing critical thinking skills
    - Comprehending historical texts

Section 1: Exploration (1491–1607)

Native American Societies Before European Contact

Maize Cultivation in the Southwest

Maize (corn) is a cereal grain, and it played a significant role in the development of American settlements. Indigenous tribes first domesticated maize approximately 10,000 years ago in present-day Mexico. Eventually, human migration and cultural interactions resulted in the spread of maize from Central America and Mexico to the present-day American southwest. Eventually, nearly all North American indigenous agricultural societies relied on maize in some way, either through production or trade.

The cultivation of maize triggered dramatic changes in many indigenous societies. Compared to other crops, maize could be produced at a relatively larger scale with fewer resources. Additionally, maize was rich in calories and dynamic in its application to a wide variety of recipes. As such, the cultivation of maize helped agricultural societies generate a food surplus, facilitating the establishment of permanent settlements and diversification of socioeconomic classes. Furthermore, diversification spurred more dynamic economic development, complex trade patterns, and sophisticated urbanization. For example, the cultivation of maize led to societies discovering advanced irrigation techniques through the pursuit of more consistent and robust production. Lastly, the size of indigenous militaries increased as more males were freed from providing agricultural labor, and the rise of permanent settlements led to more competition over resources.

Mobile Lifestyles in the Great Basin and Great Plains

Indigenous societies living in the Great Basin and Great Plains didn't engage in agricultural development; instead, they developed complex hunter-gatherer societies to adapt to the climate and open space. The **Great Basin** is an enormous watershed with a relatively arid climate, and it's primarily located in present-day eastern California, southeastern Oregon, Nevada, and western Utah. Because much of the climate was generally incompatible with permanent large-scale agricultural production, the indigenous societies tended to travel based on the movement of wildlife and freshwater. The Great Plains had a more hospitable climate for agriculture, but indigenous societies specialized in hunting buffalo across the Great Plains' unusually flat land located in present-day eastern Wyoming, eastern Colorado, Nebraska, and Kansas.

Spanish expeditions into South America introduced pack animals, such as donkeys and horses, to the Great Basin and Great Plains during the late sixteenth and seventeenth centuries. The arrival of domesticated horses strongly complemented Great Plain Native Americans' hunter-gatherer societies by enhancing mobility and expediting travel times. Mobile societies living in teepees didn't have the luxury of storing materials, so Great Plains Native Americans learned to use every part of the animals they killed. For example, the fur, skin and bones of buffaloes provided everything from teepees to cooking tools.

The Development of Permanent Villages in the East

Many indigenous societies blended characteristics of agricultural and hunter-gatherer societies. Within the present-day United States, many indigenous nations with mixed forms of development were established in the Mississippi River Valley, Atlantic Coastal region, and Northeast due to the temperate climate and availability of plentiful fish, wildlife, and fertile soil. When British and French expeditions arrived in the sixteenth century, they expected to find mines of gold and silver like the Spanish encountered in South America. Instead, much of the eastern portion of the present-day United States had an abundance of natural resources, like waterways, timber, and arable land. In addition, the relatively temperate climate and rich soil allowed for consistent agricultural production. Agriculture provided a consistent source of food, bringing stability and permanence to settlements.

The combination of agricultural productivity and hunter-gatherer lifestyles produced powerful and enduring indigenous confederations across the Mississippi Valley and Atlantic region of the present-day United States and Canada. Indigenous confederations in these areas constructed permanent villages, facilitating the rise of more complex political organizations. As a result, many European colonies in New England and along the Atlantic seaboard struggled mightily to initially gain a foothold and expand frontier borders in this region throughout the seventeenth century.

Hunter-Gatherer Societies in the West

Indigenous societies in present-day California and the North American Northwest were primarily hunter-gatherer societies with some notable exceptions along the Pacific coastline. As with indigenous nations in the Great Basin region, the climate was mostly incompatible with large-scale agriculture. So, most nations from northern California to the Pacific Northwest favored transient settlement patterns that mirrored the migratory path of natural resources. Permanent settlements in this region were, significantly, built within fertile valleys, especially in present-day southern California, and areas with direct access to the Pacific Ocean.

Pacific Northwest indigenous communities stood apart from the rest of the region. Increased access to waterways facilitated expansion by expediting travel times and reducing the burden of moving supplies across long distances. These settlements were also unique in the sense they established permanence without a stable agricultural system; instead, fishing functioned as the primary method of acquiring food, and fish were plentiful enough to support significant population growth. Pacific Northwest regions especially prized and revered salmon as nature's greatest bounty. For example, many indigenous cultures incorporated the worship of deities tied to salmon. Salmon also had long-distance seasonal migration patterns, which resulted in the natural growth of shared cultural and economic characteristics across the region.

European Exploration in the Americas

European Nations' Motives to Conquer the New World

When examining how Europeans explored what would become the United States of America, one must first examine why Europeans came to explore the New World as a whole. In the fifteenth century, tensions increased between the Eastern and Mediterranean nations of Europe and the expanding Ottoman Empire to the east. As war and piracy spread across the Mediterranean, the once-prosperous trade routes across Asia's Silk Road began to decline, and nations across Europe began to explore alternative routes for trade. Italian explorer Christopher Columbus proposed a westward route. Contrary to popular lore, proving that the world was round was not the main challenge that Columbus faced in finding backers. In fact, much of Europe's educated elite knew that the world was round; the real issue was that they rightly believed that a westward route to Asia, assuming a lack of obstacles, would be too long to be practical. Nevertheless, Columbus set sail in 1492 after obtaining support from Spain, and arrived in the West Indies three months later.

Spain launched further expeditions to the new continents and established **New Spain**. The colony consisted not only of Central America and Mexico, but also the American Southwest and Florida. France claimed much of what would become Canada, along with the Mississippi River region and the Midwest. In addition, the Dutch established colonies that covered New Jersey, New York, and Connecticut. Each nation managed its colonies differently, and thus influenced how they would assimilate into the United States. For instance, Spain strove to establish a system of Christian missions throughout its territory, while France focused on trading networks and had limited infrastructure in regions such as the Midwest. Even in cases of limited colonial growth, the land of America was hardly vacant, because a diverse array of Native American nations and groups were already present.

Throughout much of colonial history, European settlers commonly misperceived native peoples as a singular, static entity. In reality, Native Americans had a variety of traditions depending on their history and environment, and their culture continued to change through the course of interactions with European settlers; for instance, tribes such as the Cheyenne and Comanche used horses, which were introduced by white settlers, to become powerful warrior nations. However, a few generalizations can be made: many, but not all, tribes were matrilineal, which gave women a fair degree of power, and land was commonly seen as belonging to everyone. These differences, particularly European settlers' continual focus on land ownership, contributed to increasing prejudice and violence.

News of success sparked a number of other expeditions and the British, French, Dutch, Spanish, and Portuguese all eventually laid claim to lands in the New World. Columbus himself made three more voyages to the Americas. The French and Dutch focused mostly on the lucrative fur trade in North America. The Spanish and Portuguese sought gold in Central and South America but also tried to convert Native Americans to Christianity. British settlers also sought economic opportunity and created the first British colony at Jamestown, Virginia, in 1607. However, the Puritans, who landed at Plymouth Rock in 1620, left for the New World in order to establish their ideal religious community.

Columbian Exchange, Spanish Exploration, and Conquest

The Columbian Exchange

European exploration in North America dates back to around 1000 AD when Scandinavian Vikings, led by **Leif Eriksson**, first made their way to Greenland and then journeyed on to modern-day Newfoundland. They settled briefly in an area now known as L'Anse Meadows. However, clashes with the Native American people living nearby caused them to return to Greenland a few years later. The first permanent settlements in North America began after Italian sailor Christopher Columbus landed in the Caribbean in 1492. This was a significant breakthrough since most Europeans did not know that this huge landmass even existed. It initiated a period of discovery, conquest, and colonization of the Americas by the Europeans. Often referred to as the **Columbian Exchange**, this period allowed people who had been cut off from each other for 15,000 years to share knowledge, ideas, culture, food, plants and animals, technology, and religion. This led to significant changes and enhancements for both regions. The population in Europe grew, largely due to the benefits imparted by the new crops, which diversified and enriched the diet over time. Additionally, new sources of mineral wealth contributed to the shift in much of Europe from feudalism to capitalism.

Maritime Technological Advancements and Joint-Stock Companies

European powers leveraged technological, political, and economic innovations to colonize the Americas. During the fifteenth century, European explorers adopted and improved several types of existing **maritime technologies**, including lateen sails, magnetic compasses, and cartography. European engineers created significantly larger versions of Indian dhows, such as galleys, and outfitted the ships with cannons to achieve maritime superiority. Portugal and Spain were the early European maritime powers during this period, but by the late sixteenth century, the Iberian powers faced stiff competition from the Dutch, English, French, and Swedes.

During the late sixteenth and seventeenth centuries, European powers established joint-stock companies to facilitate colonization. **Joint-stock companies** consisted of a public-private partnership in which the government granted property rights and legal authority over colonies to private companies, and the parties shared the necessary capital investments and potential profits in accordance with a formalized agreement. In effect, joint-stock companies allowed governments to mitigate the risk and subsidize the cost of colonization. In the Americas, European settlements experienced exponential expansion due to the injection of capital investments and consolidation of resources. Overall, this expansion led to a colossal transfer of wealth from indigenous to European societies. Wealth transfers especially facilitated the beginning stages of European textile manufacturing and industrialization.

Diseases Spread to Native Americans

Native Americans were vulnerable to diseases to which the Europeans had developed immunity. These diseases included bubonic plague, cholera, chicken pox, pneumonic plague, influenza, measles, scarlet fever, typhus, smallpox, and tuberculosis. These diseases killed millions of Native Americans and were sometimes used as a biological weapon. Historians estimate that as much as 80 percent of the Native American population died through disease and warfare.

Labor, Slavery, and Caste in the Spanish Colonial System

The Encomienda System

Initially, Spain enforced the ***encomienda* system** in the Americas to meet its labor needs. Under this labor system, the Spanish crown allowed conquistadors to enslave people they conquered, so as to incentivize territorial expansion. More specifically, the Spanish crown sought to expand profitable economic opportunities, such as large-scale plantation (***haciendas***) agriculture and mining precious metals. In theory, enslaving indigenous people was more efficient than importing Africans, but the encomienda system failed spectacularly for two reasons. First, it was ineffective. Indigenous populations resisted enslavement, and the Spanish elites killed indigenous workers at an unsustainable rate. Second, the horrific working conditions and massive death toll shocked the Spanish crown and broader public. Due to these reasons, the Spanish crown implemented the **New Laws of 1542** to abolish the encomienda system in the Americas. This reform didn't quite free indigenous workers from forced labor; instead, the New Laws replaced the encomienda system with a policy known as the ***repartimiento* system**.

Repartimiento placed indigenous population under the monarchy's direct authority. As a result, the Spanish crown allotted labor to plantation owners and regulated working conditions. Despite this effort to reduce overt abuses, indigenous populations continued to suffer staggering death tolls until the system collapsed at the end of the seventeenth century.

The Beginnings of the Transatlantic Slave Trade

The **transatlantic slave trade** involved European merchants acquiring slaves from West Africa and transporting them to the Americas. During the early sixteenth century, Portugal and Spain were the dominant powers in West Africa, and as a result, they played an outsized role in shaping the transatlantic slave trade in its early stages. However, by the beginning of the seventeenth century, Dutch, English, and French merchants had become significantly more involved in the slave trade. The competition was fierce due to the immense value of African slaves because they were the most profitable source of labor for plantation-based agriculture and mining in the Americans.

Slavery had been practiced in West Africa for many centuries prior to the arrival of Europeans, and most slaves were prisoners of war. European merchants originally worked within this traditional framework; however, when demand for labor increased in the Americas, European merchants sought to increase the supply of slaves. Consequently, the merchants allied themselves with individual tribes and financed military expeditions for the explicit purpose of enslaving the conquered people. These tribal conflicts also benefited the Europeans by sowing chaos and preventing the consolidation of political power under a united African kingdom.

The Spanish-Imposed Caste System

To increase socioeconomic stability, Spain instituted a highly unique and complex racial caste system in its American colonies. The **caste system** classified the colonial population based on residents' ancestry and purity of blood. These racial classifications functioned as the foundation of a rigid social system that determined residents' legal status, rights, and obligations within the Spanish Empire.

The highest classes had the closest connections to Spain and the most Spanish blood. As such, Spaniards born in Spain (***peninsulares***) occupied the highest tier in the caste system. Slightly below the *peninsulares* were the American-born Spaniards (***criolles***). Mixed-race classes were significantly below these two European classes, but they occupied the middle tiers of the caste system. Examples of mixed-race classes included: Spanish and indigenous (***mestizo***), Spanish and mestizo (***castizos***), Spanish and African (***mulatto***), and Spanish and mulatto (***moriscos***). Despite the severe restrictions Spain placed on mixed-race residents' property and legal rights, they were still above two classes—African slaves (**negros**) and indigenous peoples (***indios***). African slaves effectively had no rights, while indigenous societies enjoyed some very limited protections under the ***repartimiento* system**. Given the dramatic disparities in class status, people in the Spanish Empire often attempted to forge ancestral histories and pass as a member of a different class.

Cultural Interactions Between Europeans, Native Americans, and Africans

Divergent Worldviews Between Europeans and Native Americans

The conflict between Europeans and Native Americans was largely the product of their different worldviews on major issues, including land use, power, religion, and family dynamics.

Compared to Native Americans, Europeans were far less likely to consider the long-term sustainability of land-use practices. North America is Native Americans' ancestral homeland, but colonization was a for-profit venture for Europeans. Likewise, although Native Americans regularly consolidated power at the expense of their rivals, their conquests were far more regionally based and limited in scope. Europeans held a much more global attitude. European powers were already fighting all over the globe before they arrived in North America. As such, they didn't just want to make a tidy profit; they wanted to monopolize power and conquer as much territory as they possibly could.

Europeans were almost universally Christian, and many leaders believed non-Christians were condemned to eternal damnation. So, European colonizers often believed it was their moral duty to convert Native Americans by any means necessary. In contrast, Native American groups rarely proselytized and practiced a diverse array of traditional religions, ranging from nature-based monotheism to polytheistic animism. Furthermore, Native American family dynamics were relatively egalitarian, with women and elders assuming key leadership roles in many groups. Europeans were far more hierarchical, with men serving as the head of the household and holding undisputed authority. Native Americans also valued kinship and revered elders, whereas aggressive young men with few family ties dominated European colonial expeditions and early settlements.

Interactions Between Native Americans and Europeans

Native Americans played an important role in the early history of Britain's North American colonies. Some Native American tribes were friendly towards the colonists and traded with them. **Squanto** was an Algonquian Indian who helped English settlers in Massachusetts survive by teaching them how to plant native crops. However, Native Americans and Europeans often came into conflict, frequently over land disputes. The Native Americans and Europeans had very different concepts of land use and ownership. Native Americans did not understand the concept of landownership or sale. When they entered into agreements with the colonists, Native Americans thought they were allowing the settlers to farm the land temporarily, rather than retain it in perpetuity. On the other hand, colonists were frustrated when Native Americans continued to hunt and fish on lands they had "sold." These, and other disagreements, eventually led to bloody conflicts that gradually weakened Native American tribes.

Although the early years of their interactions were often marked by mutual misunderstandings, over time, Europeans and Native Americans did adopt some aspects of one another's culture that proved useful. For example, European technology, such as hatchets, weapons, and kettles, were adopted by some Native American tribes. A Native American agricultural technique, known as **companion planting**, for crops such as the **Three Sisters** (maize, winter squash, and climbing beans), was adopted by Europeans who had settled in New England and the Chesapeake areas. Because these three crops, when planted together, benefited one another, Europeans were able to have a reliable food source and stay alive.

Native Americans' Efforts to Preserve Their Way of Life

The arrival of Europeans in the Americas quickly posed an existential challenge to indigenous people's way of life. Europeans seized vast swathes of indigenous territory and violated indigenous peoples' **political sovereignty**, meaning the ability to self-govern without external interference. Similarly, European enslaved indigenous people and disrupted ancient patterns of trade, effectively stunting indigenous economic development. Indigenous cultural values also came under attack through forced conversions to Christianity and limitations placed on the role of women in tribal leadership.

Indigenous peoples adopted a variety of diplomatic and military strategies to resist European colonization between 1491 and 1607. Some indigenous tribes, like those encountered by **Hernan de Soto** during his expedition across the present-day southeastern United States, provided European explorers with gifts and guides as a sign of friendship. Other tribes, like the **Powhatan** in present-day Virginia, initially accepted European colonies' boundaries and graciously traded maize to prevent the newly arrived colonists from starving. However, many historians believe that when English colonists massacred a Powhattan village, the tribe wiped out the entire Roanoke colony. The Araucanians successfully turned back Pizzaro's forces after they conquered the Inca Empire in the mid-sixteenth century and held out against Spanish colonization for centuries.

"Justifications" for the Subjugation of Non-Europeans

Europeans propagated a host of arguments to justify and encourage their subjection, persecution, and domination of Africans and Native American populations. The foundation was the idea that Africans and Native American were sub-human "savages" with self-evidently inferior cultures. Some arguments even took it a step further, saying it was not only natural but also the Europeans' duty to spread their more advanced technological and supposedly superior cultural characteristics to Africa and the Americas. Likewise, Christian leaders viewed it as their sacred duty to save the souls of these populations, especially in Catholic Spain and Portugal. Broadly speaking, the "savagery" of Africans and Native Americans was treated as a settled truth across Europe throughout the sixteenth century, with few exceptions.

Due to the overwhelming popular support of these theories, few Europeans publicly called for the abolition of slavery or an end to colonization, and dissidents who did so were relentlessly persecuted. Still, in the aftermath of particularly horrific massacres, some Europeans called for limited reforms. For example, Spanish religious and political leaders pushed for the **New Laws of 1542** to categorize indigenous populations as the monarchy's property; mostly, the leaders hoped to secure some oversight authority over how the colonists exploited the indigenous labor force.

Practice Quiz

Questions 1–5 are based on the following passage:

2. Chap.

Of their departure into Holland and their troubls ther aboute, with some of the many difficulties they found and mete withall.

Being thus constrained to leave their native country, their lands and livings, and all their friends and familiar acquaintance, it was much, and thought marvellous by many. But to go into a country they knew not, but by hearsay, where they must learn a new language, and get their livings they knew not how, it being a dear place, and subject to the miseries of war, it was by many thought an adventure almost desperate, a case intolerable, and a misery worse than death; especially seeing they were not acquainted with trades nor traffic, (by which the country doth subsist) but had only been used to a plain country life and the innocent trade of husbandry. But these things did not dismay them, (although they did sometimes trouble them,) for their desires were set on the ways of God, and to enjoy his ordinances. But they rested on his providence, and knew whom they had believed. Yet this was not all. For although they could not stay, yet were they not suffered to go; but the ports and havens were shut against them, so as they were fain to seek secret means of conveyance, and to fee the mariners, and give extraordinary rates for their passages. And yet were they oftentimes betrayed, many of them, and both they and their goods intercepted and surprised, and thereby put to great trouble and charge; of which I will give an instance or two, and omit the rest."

"There was a great company of them purposed to get passage at Boston, in Lincolnshire; and for that end had hired a ship wholly to themselves, and made agreement with the master to be ready at a certain day, and take them and their goods in, at a convenient place, where they accordingly would all attend in readiness. So after long waiting and large expenses, though he kept not the day with them, yet he came at length, and took them in, in the night. And when he had them and their goods aboard, he betrayed them, having beforehand complotted with the searchers and other officers so to do; who took them and put them into open boats, and there rifled and ransacked them, searching them to their shirts for money, yae, even the women, further than became modesty; and then carried them back into the town, and made them a spectacle and wonderment to the multitude, which came flocking on all sides to behold them. Being thus by the catchpole officers riffled and stripped of their money, books and much other goods, they were presented to the magistrates, and messengers sent to inform the Lords of the Council of them; and so they were committed to ward. Indeed the magistrates used them courteously, and showed them what favor they could; but could not deliver them until order came from the Council table. But the issue was, that after a month's imprisonment the greatest part were dismissed, and sent to the places from whence they came; but seven of the principal men were still kept in prison and bound over to the assizes."

In the spring of 1608 another attempt was made to embark and another Dutch shipmaster engaged. This second party assembled at a point between Grimsby and Hull not far from the mouth of the Humber. The women and children arrived in a small bark which became grounded at low water and while some of the men on shore were taken off in the ship's boat they were again apprehended. And to quote again:

"But after the first boat-full was got aboard, and she was ready to go for more, the master espied a great company, both horse and foot, with bills and guns and other weapons: for the country was raised to take them."

"But the poor men which were got on board were in great distress for their wives and children, which they saw thus to be taken, and were left distitute of their helps, and themselves also not having a cloth to shift them with, more than they had on their backs, and some scarce a penny about them, all they had being on the bark. It drew tears from their eyes, and anything they had they would have given to have been on shore again. But all in vain; there was no remedy; they must thus sadly part.

Excerpt from History of Plymouth Plantation by William Bradford, written between 1630 and 1651

1. Which of the following was NOT a difficulty faced by the group of travelers?
   a. They didn't know the new country's language.
   b. They weren't allowed to bring their wives or children to the new country.
   c. They didn't know how to make a living in the new country.
   d. Ships charged exorbitant rates for the voyage to the new country.

2. What type of passage is this?
   a. Historical memoir or journal
   b. Passage from a textbook
   c. Poem or Epic Poem
   d. An instructional/technical document

3. What went wrong with the ship hired at Boston in Lincoln-shire?
   a. The women got sick due to the rough seas.
   b. The men were separated from their wives and children.
   c. The group couldn't get out of jail in time to board the ship.
   d. The shipmaster betrayed them.

4. Based on the passage, why did the men leave their wives and children?
   a. Armed government officials arrived on the shore.
   b. The government refused to let them out of prison.
   c. The sea was too rough to risk going back for them.
   d. The women were too sick to make the voyage.

5. Ships charged the group of travelers extra fees because:
   a. they were a vulnerable minority group.
   b. the voyage was particularly long and dangerous.
   c. the government outlawed their departure.
   d. they were wealthy enough to afford it.

Answer Explanations

1. B: The first paragraph explains the difficulties facing the group of travelers. Language and making a living are listed in the second sentence, so Choices *A* and *C* are both incorrect. Extra fees and exorbitant rates are described in the first paragraph's final sentence; therefore, Choice *D* is incorrect. Although the men were later separated from their wives and children, that separation was due to a problem with logistics. There was no prohibition specifically against bringing their wives and children. The entire group was legally barred from leaving the country.

2. A: We can see that this text records parts of history, so this is most likely a historical memoir or the author's personal journal retelling an event that happened. We see a brief summary of the event before the passage begins.

3. D: The ship hired at Boston in Lincoln-shire is the group's first attempt to flee their homeland, and it's described in the second paragraph. After the group reached an agreement with the shipmaster, he betrayed them to the government, which led to government officials arresting the group. The women didn't become sick or get separated until their second attempt at fleeing, so Choices *A* and *B* are both incorrect. Following the first shipmaster's betrayal, the group did go to jail, but their imprisonment occurred after their first attempt to leave went wrong; therefore, Choice *C* is incorrect. Thus, Choice *D* is the correct answer.

4. A: After the men boarded the ship, armed government officials arrived on the shore. Rather than risk everyone getting caught, the Dutch shipmaster raised the anchor, hoisted the sails, and took off. So, even though the men were moved to tears by the separation, there was nothing they could do. The government refused to let some of the group's member out of prison, but that's not what caused the separation; therefore, Choice *B* is incorrect. Choices *C* and *D* are factually incorrect based on the information contained in the third paragraph. Thus, Choice *A* is the correct answer.

5. C: Ships charged the group of travelers extra fees because the government outlawed their departure. The first paragraph says that the government barred them from the ports and havens, so they needed to find a secret passage out of the country. As helping the group was illegal, ships charged them extra fees in exchange for taking on that risk. The passage doesn't state why the group is being persecuted; therefore, Choice *A* is incorrect. Choice *B* is incorrect because the passage doesn't mention whether the voyage was particularly long or dangerous. While the government does seize property from the group, it's unclear whether the group is particularly wealthy; therefore, Choice *D* is incorrect.

Section 2: Colonization (1607–1754)

European Colonization

Spanish Colonization Efforts

Spain largely pursued colonization to maintain its status as a European and global power; and once Spain discovered large deposits of precious metals in the Americas, it implemented policies to maximize the extraction of wealth from its colonies. The pursuit of profit necessitated the seizure of strategic and valuable territory and the acquisition of a cheap labor source. So, Spain pressed its military advantages, deadly diseases, and political infighting to conquer powerful indigenous confederations, such as the Inca Empire and Aztec Empire.

The Spanish crown initially allowed ***conquistadores*** to fully enslave the Native Americans, but over time, they sought to better incorporate indigenous populations into colonial society. Religion played a major role in this transformation, including both missionary work and forced large-scale conversions after Spanish conquests. Additionally, reforms introduced through the *repartimiento* system protected some aspects of indigenous societies as well, assuming they fulfilled Spanish demands for labor or tribute. Recall that within territories directly under the colonial system, Spain enforced a strict racial caste system, which granted freedoms and opportunities based on blood purity. In a practical sense, the racialization of the caste system served to maintain Spanish superiority in the colonies by formalizing the limitations on mixed-race individuals, Native Americans, and African slaves.

French and Dutch Colonization Efforts

French and Dutch colonization efforts were unique because they relied on maintaining economic relationships with indigenous societies to a far greater degree than Spanish and English colonies. During the sixteenth century, Dutch colonies were generally limited to the northeastern United States, and France mostly colonized eastern Canada. Because these regions couldn't support large-scale mining or agriculture, they mostly extracted wealth through fur trapping and trade with the Native Americans. Oftentimes, a colonial government would control a city or central region, and then joint-stock companies would establish trading posts in the outlying wilderness. Because geographic separation restricted the extent to which French and Dutch colonial governments could protect remote trading posts, they were often motivated to maintain peaceful diplomatic relations with indigenous confederations.

French settlements later developed more permanent structures to support the booming fur trapping trade, which ratcheted up tensions with the Iroquois confederation. The French and Iroquois fought a prolonged series of conflicts, collectively known as the **Beaver Wars**, from 1629 to 1701. The conflict ended in a stalemate with the French consolidating control over present-day eastern Canada, and the Iroquois tribe established itself as the hegemonic power in the Great Lakes region and wilderness surrounding New England.

English Colonization Efforts

English colonies attracted relatively more European migrants than their competitors for several reasons. England's thirteen colonies in the present-day United States featured a wide array of different climates and ecosystems. As a result, the colonies offered many different types of prosperous economic opportunities, such as plantation agriculture, family farming, fur trapping, manufacturing, fishing, and shipping. More broadly, the sheer amount of cheap land offered migrants hope of socioeconomic mobility. Several major groups of Christian dissidents migrated to British North America to secure religious freedom, which further increased British colonial diversity.

Economies also attracted different European immigrant groups based on different labor demands. For most of the seventeenth century, the southern Atlantic colonies' plantations mostly relied on African slaves, as did the British West Indies. So, the overwhelming bulk of European immigrants, those lacking the resources to invest in a plantation, sought to settle further north on the Atlantic Coast where there were more economic opportunities. Northern colonies also attracted more indentured servants compared to other colonial systems. **Indentured servitude** involved farmers paying a European male's immigration and living costs in exchange for a designated future period of free labor. The practice was most cost effective for small-scale farming.

Overall, the English colonies were characterized by their agricultural focus on the lands they had taken from Native Americans.

The Regions of British Colonies

Situated on the Atlantic Coast, the Thirteen Colonies that would become the United States of America constituted only a small portion of North America. Even those colonies had significant differences that stemmed from their different origins. For instance, the Virginia colony under **John Smith** in 1607 started with male bachelors seeking gold, whereas families of Puritans settled Massachusetts. As a result, the Thirteen Colonies—Virginia, Massachusetts, Connecticut, Maryland, New York, New Jersey, Pennsylvania, Delaware, Rhode Island, New Hampshire, Georgia, North Carolina, and South Carolina—had different structures and customs that would each influence the United States.

The Chesapeake and North Carolina Colonies

Colonial economies in the **mid-Atlantic** (present-day North Carolina and southern Virginia) and **Chesapeake Bay** (present-day Maryland, Delaware, and northern Virginia) regions primarily engaged in tobacco and family farming. Compared to New England, there was less centralization, smaller urban centers, and minimal industrial production. In contrast, North Carolina and Virginia disproportionately relied on producing a single cash crop, **tobacco**, with family farming accounting for the region's only other vibrant economic sector.

Despite their common reliance on agricultural and similar rural settlement patterns, colonial North Carolina and Virginia were strikingly different than the **southern Atlantic colonies** (South Carolina and Georgia). Unlike the southern Atlantic colonies' plantation-based agriculture, farming occurred on smaller plots of land. Tobacco was less compatible with large-scale production, and environmental conditions prevented the near-continual production that occurred deeper south.

Chesapeake and mid-Atlantic agriculture also uniquely relied more heavily on European indentured servitude than African slavery for its labor demands from the outset. Consequently, colonies in present-day North Carolina and Virginia had much more ethnic and religious diversity than the more universally British southern Atlantic colonies. However, African slaves gradually overtook indentured servitude as the dominant labor system, largely because the ever-increasing supply of African slaves in the southern Atlantic led to major cost reductions.

The New England Colonies

Connecticut, New Hampshire, Massachusetts, and Rhode Island were considered the "**New England colonies.**" The settlements in New England were based around an economy focused on fishing and lumber. These colonies maintained puritanical and Congregationalist religious beliefs, and developed around family farms situated in small towns. Political power was also distributed differently among the colonies. Some colonies, such as New York and Virginia, were royal colonies ruled directly by the king. Pennsylvania was a **proprietary colony**—the king allowed William Penn to appoint officials and govern the colony as he saw fit. **Corporate colonies**, such as Rhode Island and Connecticut, were administered by a group of investors. But, by the early 1700s, the king had revoked the charters of most proprietary and corporate colonies and assumed direct control himself.

The Middle Colonies

While English Puritans mostly settled in New England, a wide variety of colonists settled in the mid-Atlantic region. English, Scottish, Dutch, and Swedish settlers came to Delaware, New York, New Jersey, and Pennsylvania. As a result, the mid-Atlantic colonies were more religiously diverse and tolerant than the settlements in New England. Because the land in the region was so fertile, agriculture was the foundation of the economy in mid-Atlantic colonies, with the primary output of **cereal crops**, such as wheat, rye, and corn. For this reason, the Middle Colonies were also known as the **Bread Basket colonies**. Shipbuilding and lumbering were also common because of the abundant forests. Settlements were more dispersed, and government and administration were based on counties instead of towns.

Southern Atlantic Coast and the British West Indies Colonies

Southern Atlantic and British West Indies' tropical climate, long growing seasons, and rich soil supported the development of plantation-based economies. Agricultural production had a sizable effect on these colonies' economic development and demographic makeup. Because land was divided into plantations under the control of societal elites, there was minimal commercial growth and few employment options. As such, the European population of plantation-based economies often consisted of only an elite cadre of ultra-wealthy landlords and a small managerial class to support operational logistics.

Unlike most other English colonies, plantation agriculture primarily relied upon African slaves as a labor force. In many instances, Africa slaves accounted for the majority of the population in England's plantation-based colonies. Fearing a slave insurrection, plantation owners attempted to enforce slave codes that were designed to be as draconian, dehumanizing, and profitable as possible. To keep the races more firmly separated by skin color, Southern Atlantic and British West Indian slave codes emphasized and sought to preserve the purity of race. The codes enforced prohibitions on interracial relationships and enslaved all descendants of African mothers. Eventually the plantation-based colonies transitioned into using "**one drop**" racial policies, meaning that anyone with any African ancestry was subject to enslavement.

Governing in the Colonies

The thirteen colonies formed when royal charters were granted, either to individuals or corporations, and the colonies were allowed limited **self-rule**. A governor for the colonies was appointed by England, but each colony could rule by its own laws enacted by colonial assemblies. The method in which these men were appointed, and the laws of each colony, differed based on the type of charter each had, if any. In **royal colonies**, those of Virginia, Massachusetts, New Hampshire, New York, New Jersey, North

Carolina, South Carolina, and Georgia, the king of England was the direct authority of the colony and chose the governor, among other things. **Proprietary colonies**, which included Pennsylvania, Delaware, and Maryland, were under the authority of the owner of the colony, while Rhode Island and Connecticut were self-governing and had no direct authority. They elected members to their legislatures.

Transatlantic Trade

The Triangular Trade

European exploration and colonization laid the foundation for a truly global trade network. The transatlantic portion of this network, commonly referred to as the **triangular trade**, consisted of interconnected and economic relationships between Europe (mainly England), Africa, and the Americas.

All of the major European powers adhered to **mercantilist** economic policies, which prioritized extracting wealth from colonies and developing domestic industries through the erection of strategic trade barriers. Aside from securing access to valuable commodities and cheap labor, American colonies and African trading posts functioned as markets for European consumer goods and manufactured products. African nations typically exchanged enslaved captives for European goods, such as guns and cloth. Likewise, Europeans sought American colonies to extract commodities, such as sugar, cotton, and tobacco, and exploit labor to an unprecedented degree.

Mercantilism was inarguably transformative. Within a relatively short time span, Europeans depleted South American mines, seized stockpiles of commodities, decimated animal populations, and installed large-scale agriculture of cash crops. Colonial domestic economies benefited from the run-off of the staggering production of wealth, but European political and economic power centers were the clear-cut victors, as intended. Consequently, European powers were able to maintain a firm grip on the fledgling global trade network, ensuring they had a consistent supply of cheap labor and access to raw commodities.

Impact of Trading with Europeans on Native Americans

Extended contact with Europeans produced many transformative cultural, economic, and political changes across indigenous societies. Horses enhanced indigenous societies' mobility and cavalry tactics. Likewise, steel and gunpowder revolutionized warfare. Commerce led to more cultural exchanges, including Christian proselytizing and the evolution of syncretic blends of Christianity, African Vodun, and traditional indigenous beliefs.

At the same time, European contact ultimately devastated and nearly eradicated most indigenous communities and confederations due to the spread of disease. Indigenous populations suffered staggering population loss in massive waves due to the lightning-fast spread of epidemics, many of which struck communities shortly before Europeans made formal contact. Europeans had developed genetic immunities to these diseases, like smallpox, plague, and flu varieties, for many centuries prior to their arrival in the Americas. On the other hand, indigenous populations had no genetic resistance to the diseases, and they had a genocide-like effect on indigenous societies.

The destabilizing impact unchecked epidemics had on indigenous political structures cannot be overstated. Indigenous militaries were certainly terrified by cavalry and gunpowder, but more importantly, Europeans were attacking societies suffering an apocalyptic crisis. Some previously powerful indigenous tribes didn't have the male labor to gather food, let alone the military strength and resiliency to fend off an invasion.

British Mercantilist Efforts in the Colonies

Like the other major European powers, Britain pursued mercantilist goals in terms of economic development. **Mercantilism** aims to maximize resource extraction, develop domestic industries, and centralize the state's authority. European powers sought to implement mercantilist policies through the establishment of a relatively centralized imperial government based on a top-down, hierarchical command structure with the monarchy at the very top. European powers had tremendous success at destabilizing Native American confederations, subjugating indigenous populations, and exercising absolute authority over the colonial government. The only slight exception to this general trend was British North America.

As a multinational representative government, Britain was uniquely flexible in granting some autonomy and authority to popularly elected colonial governments. British leaders viewed local autonomy as an advantage because it improved how colonial governments responded to immediate threats; rather than waiting for specific instructions from across the Atlantic, British colonial governments could adjust to, leverage, and exploit current happenings. However, conditions on the ground also forced Britain to go further than they otherwise would have preferred. Unlike most other colonial systems, Britain struggled in subduing their strongest indigenous military rivals, like the Powhatan, Algonquin, and Iroquois confederations. As a result, Britain couldn't always defend frontiers or enforce imperial laws, which granted legitimacy to colonial power structures.

Interactions Between American Indians and Europeans

Conflicts and Alliances Between Europeans and American Indians

Indigenous groups regularly sought and secured military alliances with European groups to gain an advantage in regional conflicts with indigenous nations. Naturally, Native Americans adjusted to the initial stages of colonization by incorporating European groups into the traditional diplomatic and military system, treating them like an ascendant and powerful indigenous nation. Europeans routinely exploited this opportunity to carry out its divide-and-conquer strategy. Overall, European powers and indigenous groups acted in their self-interest, resulting in a fluid system of shifting military alliances.

Given the deep and complex regional rivalries within indigenous communities, it was common for colonial conflicts to have alliances of Native American groups aligned on both sides. The rise of the Iroquois confederation during the seventeenth century is indicative of European and indigenous alliances. During the **Beaver Wars**, the French established alliances with numerous Algonquian societies, including the Erie, Huron, and Mahican. The Algonquians believed they would be rewarded for their support of the rising French power, and any losses suffered by the Iroquois would automatically be their gain. On the other side, the Dutch and English supported the Iroquois to undermine the French. However, once the Iroquois emerged as the clear-cut indigenous power, they began to threaten the British North American frontier.

Military Conflicts Between the British and American Indians

British colonies' aggressive territorial expansion, broad consolidation of resources, and wanton violation naturally resulted in near-constant conflicts with many Native American nations.

By the late seventeenth century, most British colonies had survived starvation-like conditions, established a consistent agricultural food supply, and commanded well-armed and robust military units featuring a strong mix of imperial troops and more informal citizen militia-type forces. At this point, most indigenous leaders viewed Europeans as rising regional competitors, not as an existential threat to indigenous societies. Although Britain was generally less successful than its European rivals at decimating local indigenous power centers, the British fiercely protected their territory and engaged in incremental expansion.

Metacom's War (1675–1678) was one of the most influential conflicts with an indigenous confederation in British colonial history. **Metacom** was a Wampanoag chief who occasionally went by his Anglicized name, King Philip, and he formed an alliance with New England-based indigenous tribes, such as the Narragansetts and Podunks. The New England colonies barely survived Metacom's War. Approximately half of New England colonial villages were attacked during the conflict, and more than a dozen towns totally collapsed. Despite the heavy losses, Metacom's War forged an American identity because it marked the first time the colonists fought any imperial support.

American Indians' Resistance to Spanish Colonizing Efforts

Prior to the arrival of Europeans, the **Pueblo** confederation had a large population, centralized urban centers, and influence across much of present-day northern Mexico and the southwestern United States. During the late sixteenth and early seventeenth centuries, Spanish Franciscans sought to subjugate indigenous populations under a totalitarian and coercive theocracy. Combined with successive poor harvests and famines, tensions reached a boiling point in the summer of 1680. Shortly after his release from prison for resisting colonial policies, a mythical Pueblo leader known as **Popé** organized a covert insurrection. Popé skillfully forged alliances with other indigenous regional powers, such as the Apache and Navajo, to support his well-armed militias. Following a decisive victory, Spain retreated and Popé assumed leadership over the ancestral Pueblo territory.

On August 10, 1680, Spanish Franciscans returned offering protection and increased autonomy in exchange for the Pueblos willingly submitting themselves to the Spanish crown. The Pueblos ultimately accepted the arrangement due to increased foreign threats, reviving Spanish colonial efforts in the American southwest. Although it didn't secure long-term freedom, the **Pueblo Revolt** led to meaningful cultural accommodations, such as tolerance for traditional religions and access to legal assistance while navigating the colonial legal system.

Slavery in the British Colonies

Slavery in the British Colonies

Slavery was pervasive across British North America. The New England economies attracted religiously and ethnically diverse groups of Europeans. Because the dominant economic sector was commerce, New England's African slave population never reached southern levels due to slavery's limited application and associated costs. New England areas with the highest concentration of slaves were the ports because transporting and processing cargo was labor intensive.

Chesapeake colonies' slave populations steadily increased throughout the seventeenth and early eighteenth centuries. These colonies primarily developed around small family and tobacco farms. Such types of small-scale agriculture primarily relied on indentured servitude and cheap labor contracts with landless immigrants. However, as the scales of these operations increased and labor shortages arose, Chesapeake farmers purchased larger quantities of African slaves.

Southern Atlantic colonies were most similar to European colonies in South America. The tropical climate and longer growing seasons supported the development of a plantation-based agricultural system designed for large-scale agricultural production.

Because the British West Indies had the highest concentration of plantations, it also had the largest cumulative and per capita slave people. The slaves condemned to the West Indies suffered a staggering, genocidal-like death rate due to the physical labor demands and abominable working conditions.

Slave Codes and Racial Laws

During the latter half of the seventeenth and early eighteenth centuries, southern Atlantic plantation-based economies began to resemble the British West Indies more strongly in their utter dependence on **chattel slavery**, wherein slaves were considered the owner's personal property to be bought and sold. Under this system, even the children of the purchased slave were automatically inherited by the owner as property. Southern colonial government also went much further than nearly all other historical systems of slavery. Because the population of African slaves exceeded the white population, southern governments developed a particularly totalitarian system of chattel slavery.

The British West Indies and Southern Atlantic colonies enacted brutal slave codes to enforce white supremacy and purity of blood through prohibitions on interracial relationships. Some codes even went so far as to classify anyone with one drop of African ancestry as a slave. Overall, the British colonies' hyper-racial and generational enslavement of Africans actively sought to beat down, physically and emotionally, the humanity of the people it ensnared.

British colonial slave codes were especially dehumanizing because African slaves had dramatically different cultural, linguistic, and historical backgrounds. During the sixteenth and seventeenth centuries, the West African political system was incredibly decentralized with dozens of regional rival nations, making it relatively easier for European powers to manipulate. Consequently, African slaves struggled to communicate and navigate cultural differences among themselves, greatly undermining the establishment of an Afro-American community.

Africans' Resistance to Slavery

Despite their physical isolation and persecution of chattel slavery, Africans still found ways to overtly and covertly resist chattel slavery's most dehumanizing and domineering effects.

African slaves developed a complex Afro-American culture that relied on numerous resistance strategies to survive. One tactic involved incorporating aspects of European culture under a **syncretic model**. For example, the ancient religious practice of Vodun influenced myriad syncretic religions with regional differences, including British West Indian Obeah, Haitian Vodou, and Hoodoo folk magic systems. All of these syncretic religions adapted to Christianity in order to survive forced conversions and blanket prohibitions. For example, many Afro-American religions characterized the worship of saints in the same way as traditional African deities. Other private cultural practices remained mostly intact, like the traditional leadership role African women played within families.

Some acts of cultural preservation appealed to Europeans' desire for profits, like African slaves being allowed to cultivate traditional food crops, such as yams and okra. Covert actions against labor exploitation were also incredibly common, including work slowdowns and intentional sabotage. In some instances, slaves overtly rebelled, most commonly by fleeing. One of the strongest motivations behind the desire for escape was to reunite with loved ones.

Colonial Society and Culture

Pluralism and Intellectual Exchange

British colonies had significant religious and ethnic diversity. Unlike the Catholic French and Spanish monarchies, Britain's state-sanctioned Anglican Church tolerated the presence of minority Protestant denominations to varying degrees. When the Anglican Church began persecuting and expelling some of these denominations during the seventeenth century, they typically migrated to the Americas. British colonies' ethnic diversity was the product of Britain's rise as a truly global empire and its rising status as the undisputed global maritime power. As such, British merchants and manufacturing leaders maintained close commercial relationships throughout Europe. Finally, the British colonies' climate, geography, and economic development influenced the establishment of sprawling large-scale permanent settlements. As a result, Britain was much more aggressive in attracting mainland European indentured servants.

Enlightenment philosophy and the First Great Awakening stimulated intellectual exchange and cultural interactions across British North America. **The Enlightenment** (1687–1789) argued the importance of civil liberties, including the free exercise of religion and some separation of church and state. British colonists seized on these arguments to preserve their religious freedom in the Americas. **The First Great Awakening** (1730-1750) was a grassroots evangelical movement that swept across British North America. Unlike more establishment Christian denominations, **evangelicalism** emphasized an individualized, active, and spiritual relationship with the divine.

Despite their relatively dynamic ethnic and religious diversity—as compared to other American colonial systems—the British colonies still underwent extensive **Anglicization** during the sixteenth and seventeenth centuries. Specifically, the British colonies adopted their home country's political and legal systems. The common law legal society increased the British colonies' uniformity, while representative government fueled colonists' demands for the right to more autonomy and self-government. Commercial ties between the British colonies also played a unifying role, especially as their economic differences strongly complemented each other. For example, southern Atlantic agricultural products were often shipped to New England where they were exchanged for timber and manufactured goods.

The First Great Awakening further unified British North America through a uniquely American cultural and religious experience. **Colonial evangelicalism** differed from British-based Protestantism, including dissident sects, because it prioritized individualism and the power of direct revelations. Religious and political movements were able to rapidly spread across the Americas due to the growth of **print culture**, including the publication of pamphlets and newsletters. The American-based print culture also established ties across the Atlantic. So, British colonists generally kept abreast of major European events and cultural movements despite the vast physical separation from their ruler's seat of power.

Colonists' Dissatisfaction with European Leaders

The most influential and powerful American-based economic groups generally strove for more autonomy. In Spanish colonies, plantation owners and mine operators deeply resented the Spanish crown's role in the acquisition of indigenous labor. Likewise, Dutch and French merchants objected to profit sharing and their limited involvement in high-level decision making in colonial policies. Wealthy British colonists resisted numerous imperial policies concerning political boundaries, frontier protection, self-government, and mercantilist trade policies.

Many factors contributed to British colonists being uniquely dissatisfied and mistrustful of the imperial government. Perhaps the greatest challenge was the proximity and resistance of North American indigenous confederations. Other European colonial systems thoroughly dismantled regional indigenous rivals, such as Spain's strangling of the Aztec and Inca confederations. In contrast, the Iroquois regularly and successfully challenged British North America's territorial integrity and resisted expansionist military expeditions. As a result, British colonies struggled to expand and protect their frontier regions.

Widespread insecurity also contributed to the legitimization of colonial self-government in British North America. Oftentimes, Britain would be unable or unwilling to reinforce frontier areas, placing territorial matters squarely within the purview of colonial governments. Over time, colonial desire for self-rule spread from military decision making to economic development.

British North America's Resistance to Imperial Control

British North America had a uniquely independent and dynamic political culture for four major reasons.

First, the British constitutional monarchy and parliamentary system drew a sharp contrast with European absolute monarchies. Out of all the European powers, the British system was by far the most flexible in delegating political authority because they viewed the flexibility as a developmental advantage.

Second, Enlightenment philosophers popularized concepts of universal equality among men and the model of popular sovereignty in which the people legitimize government authority. So, Enlightenment thought directly provided colonial authorities legal and ethical arguments for independence, fanning the flames of an ascending independence movement.

Third, the British colonies had partially been settled to secure the free exercise of religion, so they were naturally more independent-minded and hostile to British meddling in domestic affairs. The lack of a majority religion also helped preserve religious freedom because there was no central religious authority to ally with state actors.

Fourth, the British colonists condemned the actual and perceived corruption within the colonial system. While corruption undoubtedly hampered the governance of British North America, colonists took a radical approach to taxation. Even when British taxes specifically funded frontier defenses, colonists regularly characterized the practice as imperial coercion.

Slavery in the English Colonies

Slavery is believed to be as old as civilization itself, likely beginning during the First Agricultural Revolution nearly ten thousand years ago. The enslavement of human beings was integral to such early civilizations as Egypt, China, the Mayan Empire, Greece, and Rome. Nevertheless, race did not become the primary driving force behind human captivity and forced labor until the so-called Age of Exploration. Previously, slaves were held captive as prisoners of war. In the case of Egypt, the Jews were enslaved because of their ethnic origins and religious beliefs, but not their "race." **Race** is a construct that did not develop fully until the Early Modern period of world history. Once the Europeans made contact with the New World, they developed a new system of slavery in the Atlantic World that categorized black and indigenous persons as naturally inferior. The so-called **Atlantic Slave Trade** was built upon the foundations of racial constructs and racism. Slavery in the Americas became a hereditary phenomenon during the peak centuries of the Atlantic Slave Trade. This slave trade was also economic in origin: The sugar and tobacco plantations of the Americas demanded an excess of cheap or free labor. Initially, Europeans looked to Native Americans as their enslaved labor supply. Quickly, however, millions of Native Americans died because of the spread of unfamiliar diseases. As a result, the Atlantic Slave Trade reared its ugly head in history, and millions of Africans were uprooted to work the fields in the Thirteen Colonies, the Caribbean, and Brazil in place of their Native American brethren. This slave trade lasted from the 1400s well into the late nineteenth century.

Practice Quiz

Questions 1–3 refer to the passage below:

> I come now to the Pyrates that have rose since the Peace of Utrecht; in War Time there is no room for any, because all those of a roving advent'rous Disposition find Employment in Privateers, so there is no Opportunity for Pyrates; like our Mobs in London, when they come to any Height, our Superiors order out the Train Bands, and when once they are raised, the others are suppressed of Course; I take the Reason of it to be, that the Mob go into the tame Army, and immediately from notorious Breakers of the Peace, become, by being put into order, solemn Preservers of it. And should our Legislators put some of the Pyrates into Authority, it would not only lessen their Number, but, I imagine, set them upon the rest, and they would be the likeliest People to find them out, according to the Proverb, set a Thief to catch a Thief. To bring this about, there needs no other Encouragement, but to give all the Effects taken aboard a Pyrate Vessel to the Captors; for in Case of Plunder and Gain, they like it as well from Friends, as Enemies, but are not fond, as Things are carry'd, of ruining poor Fellowes, say the Creoleans, with no Advantage to themselves.

Excerpt from A General History of the Pyrates by Charles Johnson, 1724

1. According to the historian, which of the following groups of people would be the most effective at capturing pirates?
   a. Creolans
   b. Mobs
   c. Pirates
   d. Privateers

2. Which of the following did the historian propose as an incentive for capturing pirates?
   a. Crews that captured pirates received a military promotion.
   b. Crews that captured pirates were allotted territory in the Caribbean.
   c. Crews that captured pirates were given legal permission to plunder merchant ships.
   d. Crews that captured pirates were allowed to keep the treasure they found onboard.

3. According to the historian, what caused the rise in piracy?
   a. The Mobs in London funded piracy to increase their profits.
   b. The government refused to prohibit privateering.
   c. Many sailors were left unemployed after the Peace of Utrecht.
   d. The English Royal Navy stopped patrolling in the Caribbean.

Questions 4 and 5 refer to the diagram below.

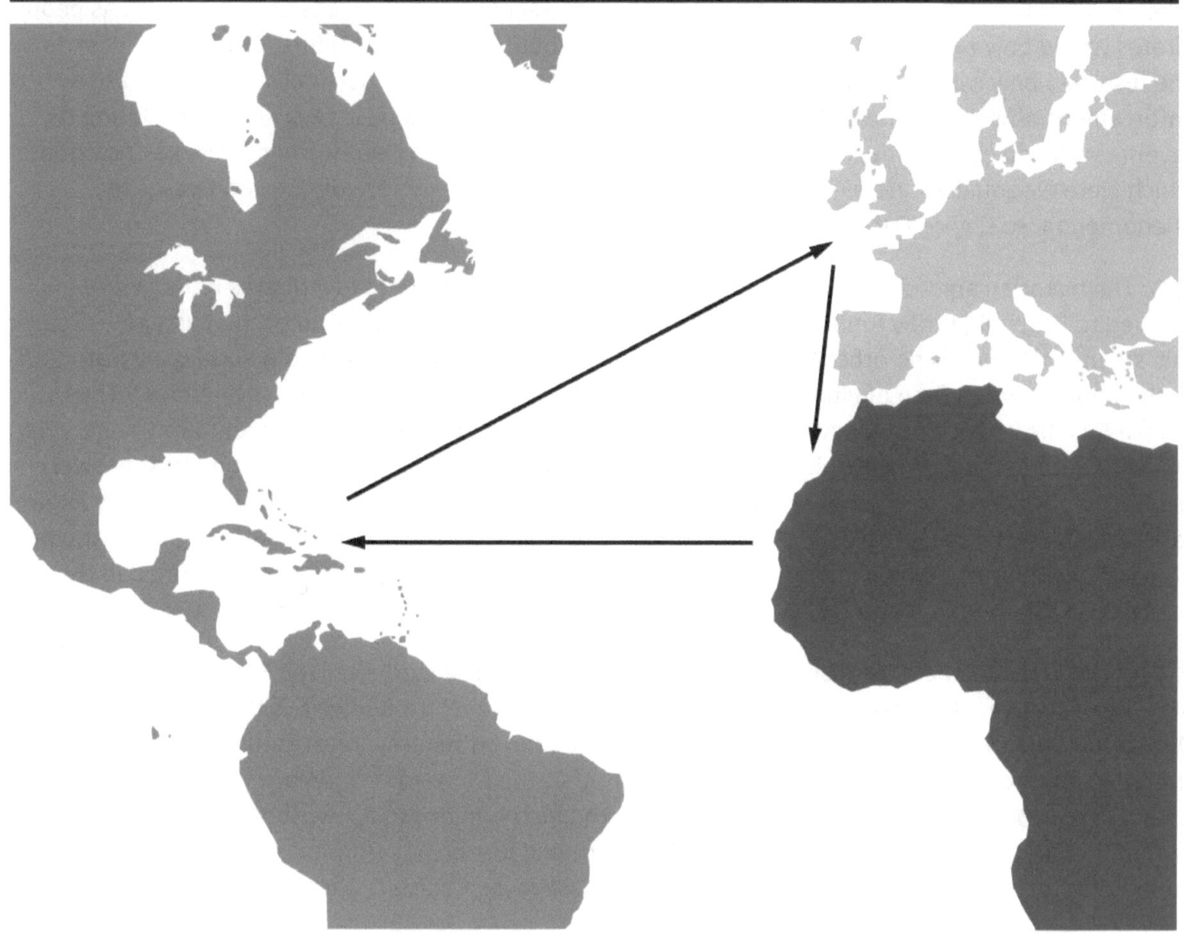

4. The diagram most likely illustrates which of the following patterns of diffusion?
   a. Columbian Exchange
   b. Contemporary global supply chain
   c. Free-trade network
   d. Green Revolution

5. Which of the following most accurately describes the consequence of this pattern of diffusion?
   a. The pattern of diffusion led to the corporatization of agricultural production, resulting in economic catastrophe for small family farms.
   b. The pattern of diffusion resulted in the spread of the Norfolk crop rotation techniques and new iron swing ploughs.
   c. The pattern of diffusion generated new employment opportunities, disproportionately benefiting low-income communities.
   d. The pattern of diffusion triggered groundbreaking global diffusion of agricultural products.

Answer Explanations

1. C: The historian argues granting pirates with legal authority to capture their fellow pirates because it takes a "Thief to catch a Thief." Thus, Choice *C* is the correct answer. Creolans are mentioned as people pirates would only rob when it was financially advantageous to do so; therefore, Choice *A* is incorrect. The historian only references the Mobs in London in a metaphor to support enlisting pirates as law enforcement officers, so Choice *B* is incorrect. Choice *D* is the second best answer choice. During the seventeenth and eighteenth centuries, governments occasionally enlisted former pirates as privateers, which were essentially state-sanctioned pirates. However, Choice *C* more directly addresses this phenomenon, so Choice *D* is incorrect.

2. D: The historian argued that pirates would be motivated to capture fellow pirates if they were allowed to keep what they found aboard. The relevant line appears at the end of the passage—"To bring this about, there needs no other Encouragement, but to give all the Effects taken aboard a Pyrate Vessel to the Captors; for in Case of Plunder and Gain, they like it as well from Friends, as Enemies." Thus, Choice *D* is the correct answer. Military promotions and territorial allotments are not mentioned anywhere in the passage, so Choices *A* and *B* are both incorrect. Choice *C* is the second best answer. Governments often tasked privateers with capturing pirates, and privateers were also generally allowed to attack enemy merchant ships. However, Choice *C* is too broad because it doesn't specify what types of merchant ships could be plundered. In addition, attacking merchant ships isn't mentioned in the passage. So, Choice *C* is incorrect.

3. C: In the first sentence, the historian mentions that piracy increased after the Peace of Utrecht because sailors could no longer find employment as privateers. Thus, Choice *C* is the correct answer. During the seventeenth and eighteenth centuries, European criminal syndicates funded piracy and shared in the profits, but the historian doesn't claim that the Mobs in London are funding piracy. So, Choice *A* is incorrect. Choice *B* is incorrect because the historian doesn't describe or support a prohibition on privateering; in fact, the historian is arguing for the government to hire pirates as privateers. The Royal Navy is not mentioned in the passage, so Choice *D* is incorrect.

4. A: The diagram has a series of arrows pointing from the Americas to Europe, Europe to Africa, and Africa to the Americas. This pattern is consistent with the Columbian Exchange. During the colonization of the Americas, Europeans transported African slaves to the Americas, extracted raw resources from the Americas, and exported manufactured goods to Africa. Choice *B* is incorrect because the title of the map says it represents a pattern of diffusion that was active in the seventeenth century, and the contemporary global supply chain includes Asia and Australia. Similarly, Choice *C* is incorrect because free-trade networks weren't active in the seventeenth century. Choice *D* is incorrect because the Green Revolution involved the diffusion of high-yield crops and technological innovations during the mid-twentieth century.

5. D: The pattern of diffusion can be identified as the Columbian Exchange due to the time period and emphasis on Europe, Africa, and the Americas. The Columbian Exchange included a significant diffusion of agricultural products. For example, merchants exported the American potato to Europe, and it quickly became a staple crop. Choice *A* is incorrect because small family farms thrived during the Columbian Exchange, and the corporatization of agricultural production didn't occur until the latter half of the twentieth century. Choice *B* is incorrect because the Norfolk crop rotation and iron swing plough spread from England to the Americas during the Second Agricultural Revolution in the eighteenth century.

Choice *C* is incorrect because although the Columbian Exchange did generate new employment opportunities in international commerce, the economic activity enriched states and wealthy investors.

Section 3: American Revolution (1754–1800)

The Seven Years' War (The French and Indian War)

The Beginnings of the Seven Years' War

In the mid-eighteenth century, conflict between the French and British North American colonial systems intensified within the broad historical context of a decades-long rivalry between global superpowers. Tensions between France and Britain erupted in the **Seven Years' War** (1756–1763), and both superpowers marshaled together powerful coalitions in a contest for economic and military superiority. The Seven Years' War had an unprecedented global scope with military theaters in the Americas, Europe, West Africa, India, and Southeast Asia. In North America, the conflict was referred to as the **French and Indian War** because British colonists were pitted against French Canada and its indigenous allies, including the mighty Iroquois confederacy.

Colonial rivalries over land, resources, and trade networks ratcheted up tensions prior to the outbreak of the Seven Years' War. French Canadian and Iroquois leaders categorically opposed British settlers creeping north toward Nova Scotia and westward over the Appalachian Mountains, which threated both the autonomy of American Indian populations and the French-Indian trade networks. With the fate of the colonies on the line, much of present-day eastern Canada and northeastern United States quickly became engulfed in war. The French and Indian War was a transformative experience for the British colonists. Despite living in proximity to active frontlines, the conflict was relatively popular because the colonists assumed they would be able to seize northern and western lands.

Britain achieved a major expansion of its territorial holdings by defeating the French, but at tremendous expense, setting the stage for imperial efforts to raise revenue and consolidate control over the colonies.

Britain's victory in the Seven Years' War was a transformative achievement. Under the terms of the **Treaty of Paris** (1763), British gained control over the entirety of French territory in present-day Canada and the fortress of Minorca.

On the losing side, the Seven Years' War grievously injured the French economy and national pride. While Britain had overextended itself financially, France had risked triggering a complete financial meltdown in leveraging itself to fund the conflict. Afterward, France chose to keep its more profitable Caribbean colonies at the cost of all its Canadian territory. Furthermore, Spain annexed French Louisiana. As a result, Britain established itself as the undisputed colonial power in northern North America with Spain remaining as its only major competition to the south.

Although Britain certainly fared much better than France in the late 1760s, it still needed to service its own significant debts. From the British perspective, it was more than reasonable to expect the British colonists to repay some of those debts because Britain's global empire had enriched and protected the colonies. However, British colonists viewed new restrictions and imperial taxes as a slap in the face given what they'd sacrificed and contributed to the French and Indian War. The financial expense of the war served as the root of Britain's subsequent imperial efforts to raise increased revenue from the colonies.

Imperial Efforts to Prevent Westward Expansion in the Colonies

Following its decisive victory in the Seven Years' War, Britain struggled to balance conflicting promises it had made to indigenous allies and colonists. Britain had not formally promised to back the colonists' expansion, but the British military had heavily relied on colonial militias during the conflict. One of the shining stars of the British officer corps was **George Washington**, and he standardized colonial military units to fight alongside citizen militias. Given their invaluable role in Britain's victory, many colonists naturally assumed they'd be allowed to take share in the spoils. Unfortunately, all of the above directly contradicted British agreements with its indigenous allies, like the Iroquois.

The **Royal Proclamation of 1763** forbade British colonization west of the Appalachian Mountains, and it reserved all eastern lands for the Iroquois and associated indigenous allies. While the indigenous people gained the short-term benefit of legal protection for tribal lands and continued access to colonial markets, the Proclamation was a major factor in the American independence movement. Believing they were betrayed, the colonists exploded in anger and widespread organized protests occurred for the first time across many of the colonies. Combined with the new imperial taxes, the Proclamation served as the breaking point and rallying cry for the **Patriot Movement**.

Taxation Without Representation

Competition among several imperial powers in eastern areas of North America led to conflicts that would later bring about the independence of the United States. The **French and Indian War** from 1754 to 1763, which was a subsidiary war of the **Seven Years' War**, ended with Great Britain claiming France's Canadian territories as well as the Ohio Valley. The same war was costly for all the powers involved, which led to increased taxes on the Thirteen Colonies. In addition, the new lands to the west of the colonies attracted new settlers, and they came into conflict with Native Americans and British troops that were trying to maintain the traditional boundaries. These growing tensions with Great Britain, as well as other issues, eventually led to the American Revolution, which ended with Britain relinquishing its control of the colonies.

As the colonies grew in population, they began to develop local institutions and a separate sense of identity. For example, it became common for ministers to receive their education at seminaries in North America rather than Britain. Newspapers also began to focus on printing more local news as well. Perhaps most importantly, the colonies began to exercise more control over their own political affairs. The British government retained control over international issues, such as war and trade, but the colonists controlled their own domestic affairs. Colonies began to form their own political assemblies and elect landowners who represented local districts. In addition, communications between the colonies and Britain were very slow because it took months for a ship to cross the Atlantic and return with a response.

Taxes were imposed in an effort to help reduce the debt Britain amassed during the French and Indian War. In 1764, Parliament passed the **Sugar Act**, which reduced the tax on molasses but also provided for greater enforcement powers. Some colonists protested by organizing boycotts on British goods. One year later, in 1765, Parliament passed the **Quartering Act**, which required colonists to provide housing and food to British troops. This law was also very unpopular and led to protests in the North American colonies.

The **Stamp Act** of 1765 required the colonists to pay a tax on legal documents, newspapers, magazines and other printed materials. Colonial assemblies protested the tax and petitioned the British government in order to have it repealed. Merchants also organized boycotts and established correspondence committees in order to share information. Eventually, Parliament repealed the Stamp Act but simultaneously reaffirmed the Crown's right to tax the colonies.

In 1767, Parliament introduced the **Townshend Acts**, which imposed a tax on goods the colonies imported from Britain, such as tea, lead, paint, glass, and paper. The colonies protested again and British imperial officials were assaulted in some cases. The British government sent additional troops to North America to restore order. The arrival of troops in Boston only led to more tension that eventually culminated in the **Boston Massacre** in 1770, where five colonists were killed and eight were wounded. Except for the duty on tea, most of Townshend Act taxes were repealed after the Boston Massacre.

Parliament passed the **Tea Act** in 1773 and, although it actually reduced the tax on tea, it was another unpopular piece of legislation. The Tea Act allowed the British East India Company to sell its products directly, effectively cutting out colonial merchants and stirring more Anglo-American anger and resentment. This resulted in the **Boston Tea Party** in 1773, an incident in which colonial tea merchants disguised themselves as Indians before storming several British ships that were anchored in Boston harbor. Once aboard, the disguised colonists dumped more than 300 chests of tea into the water.

Because the British government was unable to identify the perpetrators, Parliament passed a series of laws that punished the entire colony of Massachusetts. These acts were known as the **Coercive** or **Intolerable Acts**. The first law closed the port of Boston until the tea had been paid for (an estimated $1.7 million in today's currency). The second act curtailed the authority of Massachusetts' colonial government. Instead of being elected by colonists, most government officials were now appointed by the king. In addition, the act restricted town meetings, the basic form of government in Massachusetts, and limited most villages to one meeting per year. This act angered colonists throughout the thirteen colonies because they feared their rights could be stripped away as well. A third act allowed for British soldiers to be tried in Britain if they were accused of a crime. The fourth act once again required colonists to provide food and shelter to British soldiers.

Colonists responded by forming the **First Continental Congress** in 1774, and all the colonies except for Georgia sent delegates. The delegates sought a compromise with the British government instead of launching an armed revolt. The First Continental Congress sent a petition to King George III affirming their loyalty but demanding the repeal of the Intolerable Acts. The delegates organized a boycott of imports from and exports to Britain until their demands were met.

The colonists began to form militias and gather weapons and ammunition. The first battle of the revolution began at Lexington and Concord in April 1775 when British troops tried to seize a supply of gunpowder and were confronted by about eighty Minutemen. A brief skirmish left eight colonists dead and ten wounded. Colonial reinforcements poured in and harassed the British force as they retreated to Boston. Although the battle did not result in many casualties, it marked the beginning of war.

A month later, the Second Continental Congress convened in Philadelphia. The delegates formed an army and appointed George Washington as commander in chief. Delegates were still reluctant to repudiate their allegiance to King George III and did not do so until they issued the **Declaration of Independence** on July 4, 1776. The Declaration drew on the ideas of the Enlightenment and declared that the colonists had the right to life, liberty, and the pursuit of happiness. The Declaration stated that the colonists had to break away from Britain because King George III had violated their rights.

After the Battle of Lexington and Concord, British troops retreated to Boston and the colonial militias laid siege to the city. Colonists built fortifications on Bunker Hill outside the city and British troops attacked the position in June 1775. The colonists inflicted heavy casualties on the British and killed a number of officers. However, the defenders ran out of ammunition and British troops captured Bunker Hill on the third assault. Although it was a defeat for the colonists, the Battle of Bunker Hill demonstrated that they could stand and fight against the disciplined and professional British army.

The British army initially had the upper hand and defeated colonial forces in a number of engagements. The Americans did not achieve a victory until the **Battle of Trenton** in December 1776. Washington famously crossed the Delaware River on Christmas Day and launched a surprise attack against Hessian mercenaries. They captured more than 1,000 soldiers and suffered very minimal casualties. The victory at Trenton bolstered American morale and showed that they could defeat professional European soldiers.

The **Battle of Saratoga** in New York in the fall of 1777 was an important turning point in the American War for Independence. American troops surrounded and captured more than 6,000 British soldiers. This victory convinced the French king to support the revolutionaries by sending troops, money, weapons, and ships to the American continent. French officers who fought alongside the Patriots brought back many ideas with them that eventually sparked a revolution in France in 1789.

Unification of Colonists

The aftermath of the Seven Years' War triggered renewed calls for more political representation and autonomy from colonial patriot groups. With Britain weighed down fighting and financing a global conflict, the colonies provided the manpower and resources to defend British North America, so colonists naturally assumed they would share in the spoils of victory. In contrast, Britain expected the colonists to help repay the imperial wartime debt through nominal tax increases on consumer goods.

Many American Patriots rejected the tax increases, arguing that Britain's denial of political representation meant the colonists hadn't consented to imperial authority. In addition, the **Royal Proclamation of 1763** sparked intense anger all across the American colonies for its prohibitions on westward expansion. The Patriots responded by rallying public support for independence, organizing boycotts, and carrying out public demonstrations of anger, like the **Boston Tea Party** (1774). Britain refused to be cowed and passed a series of punitive measures widely referred to as the **Intolerable Acts** (1774). The **Quebec Act** of 1774 was especially provocative because it allowed the Province of Quebec to annex territory previously reserved for indigenous populations under the Royal Proclamation of 1763. By early 1775, the American colonists were fed up and prepared to escalate.

The concept of colonial unity originated with the famous publisher and political leader Benjamin Franklin's **Albany Plan of Union** (1754). The Albany Plan proposed a unified colonial government that would work with the British Crown to increase cooperation and coordination. Although it was ultimately rejected, the Albany Plan marked the beginning of a larger discussion about unity and self-government in the colonies.

Following the French and Indian War, colonial unity increased out of shared opposition to perceived and real issues with British rule. The British government claimed the colonies cost approximately four times as much to defend and govern than they generated in tax revenue. Consequently, British Parliament passed the **Stamp Act** of 1765, its first direct tax on the colonies, to help repay wartime debts. Colonial leaders admitted the tax was relatively minor, but they objected to being taxed without representation. In response, an anonymous separatist group, the **Sons of Liberty**, organized mass protests, acts of vigilante violence, and boycotts of British goods. Parliament refused to be bullied and passed the

Townshend Act (1767) and the **Tea Act** (1773) to implement more aggressive mercantilist economic policies. This only hardened the resolve of American Patriots, and requests for more political rights quickly became demands for independence.

Colonial Arguments to Resist British Rule

The **Patriot Movement** was predicated on a revolutionary ideology steeped in Enlightenment ideals about equality, and American Patriots developed a series of arguments to rally resistance to British policies and support for American independence.

Americans Patriots claimed that because the colonists paid taxes as British subjects, they should be entitled to the same rights as citizens living in the British homelands. When Britain not only rejected those demands but also increased taxes as a punishment for civil unrest, the American Patriots asserted that it was their natural right to revoke the social contra and revolt against tyranny. The Patriot Movement also greatly benefited from the colonies' tradition of self-rule, particularly the political infrastructure and large class of experienced public servants. The colonies' experience navigating and winning the chaotic French and Indian War was also critical because it arguably demonstrated that the colonies could survive and prosper as an independent state.

Historians continue to debate the American Patriots' intentions, especially in regard to the meaning of universal human rights, civic liberties, and popular sovereignty. Regardless of intent, the **American Revolution** ultimately ushered in a new era for the historical development of secular and representative government.

Leaders in the American Independence Movement

The American independent movement enjoyed strong support from across a diverse cross-section of the colonial population. At the top of the rebel hierarchy were societal and economic elites. Among other professions, this class of patriots generally owned plantations, farms, shipping companies, and law firms. Colonial elites developed Enlightenment-based and common law arguments to justify their rebellion. Some of the more influential elite colonial leaders were the military officer George Washington, writer Thomas Paine, and lawyers John Adams and Thomas Jefferson.

During the initial stages of the American Revolution, these colonial elites leveraged their local influence to energize and organize the independence movement. **Benjamin Franklin** was especially prolific at disseminating revolutionary works, and he continued in this role as the inaugural United States Postmaster General during the war.

The groundswell of support for independence also came from various grassroots movements. Laborers and artisans deeply resented British taxes on consumer goods and the Crown's mercantilist restrictions on trade. The lower classes were also the people most devastated by the Proclamation of 1763 because they viewed western expansion as their chance to own land and secure the American dream. Colonial women also contributed in diverse ways to the war effort, ranging from nurses to seamstresses.

Popular Support for the Patriot Movement

Obtaining and maintaining widespread popular support was essential to the Patriot movement. Armed conflict resulted in widespread economic shortages due to the British naval blockade, and British forces seized and stockpiled resources in regions they occupied. Additionally, the Patriots lacked a political system capable of levying taxes and distributing resources along the front lines. As a result, the Patriots depended on the financial support of private citizens.

The Patriots' military strategy similarly relied on leveraging popular support amongst the broader public. American armies and militias required a steady flow of volunteers to stay afloat in the struggle against a military and economic superpower. Furthermore, the Patriot militias regularly carried out irregular, asymmetric strikes against British forces, and adopted guerillas tactics like launching surprise strikes on nontraditional military targets and blending into the civilian population. Like modern-day American generals fighting Iraqi militias in urban environments during the **Iraq War** (2003–2011), British generals viewed the Patriots as terrorists because American militias refused to "honorably" fight battles on open battlefields where their weaker forces surely would've been annihilated. As such, maintaining popular support was essential to the Patriots' asymmetric warfare, particularly in the context of taking active measures against high-value targets behind enemy lines.

Philosophical Foundations of the American Revolution

Enlightenment Ideals Influenced the Patriot Movement

The Enlightenment was far and away the greatest intellectual, philosophical, and political influence on the Patriot movement. Enlightenment philosophers, like Thomas Hobbes and Jean-Jacques Rousseau, popularized the concept of social contract theory, which later developed into the political model of popular sovereignty. Under **social contract theory** and **popular sovereignty**, citizens collectively grant legitimacy and authority to the government, and that delegation could all be withdrawn at the public's will. Likewise, the Enlightenment popularized theories about universal rights and liberty, which later became the revolutionaries' rallying cry. Consequently, Enlightenment ideals inspired Americans to push even more civil liberties, religious protections, and property rights. Overall, colonial rebel leaders wielded Enlightenment philosophy to legally justify and inspire their rebellion.

Religion also increased national unity and the public's desire for independence. Many of the British colonies, such as Rhode Island and Maryland, had been founded for the explicit purpose of protecting the free exercise of religion. As a result, these colonies were predisposed to support the independence movement to further cement their freedom. In addition, the First Great Awakening crested a shared spiritual connection across the colonies, and evangelicalism combined with the Enlightenment to create a more individualistic colonial culture.

Documents that Shaped American Ideals

The majority of colonists believed that republican forms of government were ideal. Several groundbreaking documents played an outsized role in popularizing universal natural rights and representative government. These documents served as the foundations for what became generalized American ideals.

The dissemination of democratic documents was facilitated through the colonial **printing press** culture, which mass-produced revolutionary leaflets and newsletters in the run-up to the conflict. Some of the most important revolutionary pamphlets were Thomas Paine's ***Common Sense*** (1776) and ***The American Crisis*** (1776). Both pamphlets popularized and inspired the independence movement with its emphasis on civic virtue, the natural rights of people, and denunciations of King George III.

Based on its legal, moral, and rhetorical arguments, the **Declaration of Independence** is widely regarded as one of the most influential political documents in modern history. Mostly written by **Thomas Jefferson**, the Declaration of Independence stated the colonists' grievances against Britain, such as taxation without representation, and argued that Britain had violated Americans' unalienable rights of "life, liberty, and the pursuit of happiness." On July 4, 1776, the **Second Continental Congress** unanimously adopted and signed the Declaration of Independence, marking the official establishment of an independent United States.

Without a long national history, liberty and independence functioned as the American identity. This foundational legacy has endured through to the present day, especially in many Americans' hostility to government intervention in the economy, society, and daily life.

The American Revolution

Colonial Upset in the American Revolution

The Patriot movement suffered several glaring and large-scale disadvantages at the outset of the **American Revolutionary War** (1775–1783). Britain was the undisputed European superpower due to its hegemonic naval superiority and influence over global trade. Furthermore, Britain enjoyed a significant amount of loyalist support within the colonies. While the rebel forces worked to present the struggle as a united, patriotic effort, the colonies remained divided throughout the war. Thousands of colonists, known as **Loyalists** or **Tories**, supported Britain. Even the revolutionaries proved to be significantly fragmented, and many militias only served in their home states. The **Continental Congress** was also divided over whether to reconcile with Britain or push for full separation. These issues hindered the ability of the revolutionary armies to resist the British, who had superior training and resources at their disposal. Despite these long odds, the Patriots stunned the world through their ideological strength, asymmetric warfare, brilliant military leadership, and foreign assistance.

The Patriots' ideological emphasis on liberty helped generate a steady supply of volunteers and popular support for the American war effort. American militias terrorized British supply lines and defense positions throughout the conflict. The militias refused to wear uniforms and violated traditional norms of warfare, like conducting surprise attacks on lightly defended targets and targeting British officers in battle. This asymmetric warfare stretched the British military's resources to a breaking point, and the **Continental Army**, under General **George Washington**, gradually built up a force that utilized Prussian military training and backwoods guerrilla tactics to make up for their limited resources. Although the British forces continued to win significant battles, the Continental Army gradually reduced Britain's will to fight as the years passed. Furthermore, Americans appealed to the rivalry that other European nations had with the British Empire. The support was initially limited to indirect assistance, but aid gradually increased. For example, French loans and training also helped transform the Continental Army into a modern military, and Dutch and Spanish merchants broke the British blockade to supply the Americans with supplies and weapons. After the American victory at the **Battle of Saratoga** in 1777, France and other nations began to actively support the American cause by providing much-needed troops and equipment.

In 1781, the primary British army under **General Cornwallis** was defeated by an American and French coalition at Virginia, which paved the way for negotiations. The **Treaty of Paris** (1783) ended the war, recognized the former colonies' independence from Great Britain, and gave America control over territory between the Appalachian Mountains and Mississippi River. However, the state of the new nation was still uncertain.

The Influence of Revolutionary Ideals

Revolutionary Ideals of Equality and Slavery

The American Revolution's elaborate intellectual justifications for what amounted to an armed insurrection raised questions about the true meaning of equality, liberty, and representative government. Compared to Britain and other European states, the American Revolution was dramatic in terms of enhancing the political rights and economic freedom of common citizens; rather than recreating opaque aristocracy, the American Revolution genuinely sought to form a more meritocratic and representative government. However, concepts like equality were only ever intended for male Europeans, especially those wealthy enough to own land.

During the latter half of the eighteenth century, people of color faced enslavement in southern states. While most northern states abolished slavery between 1780 and 1804, racial discrimination was rampant. African Americans regularly faced economic barriers, and slave traders routinely kidnapped and enslaved people of color. Indigenous populations fared little better under the American legal system due to lax and/or nonexistent enforcement of treaty rights. Women were also politically disenfranchised and subjugated under a patriarchal socioeconomic system. However, there were some limited calls for more direct democracy in the state and federal political systems. In particular, property qualifications for white male suffrage were abolished during the late eighteenth century, beginning with Kentucky in 1792.

Republican Motherhood

American women gained newfound influence during and after the American Revolution, though the bulk of the revolution's victories didn't extend across gender lines. Women played an indispensable role during the American Revolutionary War. Without the widespread and unshakeable support of women, the Patriots would have had an impossible time turning American households into shelter for clandestine troops and centers of economic production. Following the American Revolution, the American home retained its status as the cradle of democracy, and women continued to function as the embodiment of **republican motherhood**. This motherhood sought to entrust women with the role of teaching their family republican values. As a result, women held considerable political power due to their informal role as civic teachers and patriotic leaders.

At the same time, women were systematically disenfranchised and generally barred from participating in the system they championed. The **Confederation Congress**, and its successor—the United States Congress—restricted women's property rights and economic opportunities. Consequently, women were often dependent on their fathers and husbands for material support. As a result, early American societies typically upheld traditional gender norms with women serving as housewives and men as breadwinners. Gender roles were more fluid on the frontier out of necessity due to these areas' smaller and less dense populations.

The American Revolution Inspired Other Independence Movements

Putting aside the American Revolution's historical impact as the birth of an economic and military superpower, the American Revolution was an earth-shattering historical moment in real time. The American Revolution marked the first time a colony successfully overthrew a European power and gained the right to self-government. Although far from perfect, the American political system protected an unprecedented number of political rights and civil liberties. As a result, the American victory inspired a variety of revolutionary movements in France, Haiti, and Latin America.

Along with Enlightenment thought, the American Revolution served as a major catalyst for the **French Revolution** (1789–1799). Inspired by the Americans' victory over the British imperial constitutional monarchy, revolutionaries overthrew the French absolute monarchy and installed a republican system of government. In turn, African slaves in the French colony of Haiti cited the American Revolution and French Revolution to legitimize their rebellion. In August 1789, the National Constituent Assembly, a democratic assembly formed during the French Revolution, passed the Declaration of the Rights of Man and of the Citizen, which defined the natural right of men to be free and equal under the law.

Fueled by the successful American Revolution, Napoleon's rise to power, and the writings of the Enlightenment, a spirit of revolution swept across the Americas. The French colony in Haiti was the first major revolution occurring in 1791. The **Haitian Revolution** was the largest slave uprising since the Roman Empire, and it holds a unique place in history because it is the only slave uprising to establish a slave-free nation ruled by nonwhites and former slaves. In 1804, the Haitians achieved independence and became the first independent nation in Latin America. When Napoleon conquered Spain in 1808, Latin American colonies refused to recognize his elder brother, Joseph Bonaparte, as the new Spanish monarch and advocated for their own independence. Known as the **Latin American Wars of Independence**, Venezuela, Colombia, Ecuador, Argentina, Uruguay, Paraguay, Chile, Peru, and Bolivia all achieved independence between 1810 and 1830. In 1824, Mexico declared itself a republic when, after several attempts by the lower classes of Mexico to revolt, the wealthier classes joined and launched a final and successful revolt. When Napoleon overtook Portugal, King John VI fled to Brazil and set up court. Later he left his son Pedro behind to rule. Pedro launched a revolution that saw him crowned emperor.

By the mid-1800s, the revolutions of Latin America ceased, and only a few areas remained under European rule. The U.S. President James Monroe issued the **Monroe Doctrine**, which stated that the Americas could no longer be colonized. It was an attempt to stop European nations, especially Spain, from colonizing areas or attempting to recapture areas. England's navy contributed to the success of the doctrine, as they were eager to increase trade with the Americas and establish an alliance with the United States.

The Articles of Confederation

State Constitutions

Following the American Revolutionary War, the newly freed British colonies each adopted state constitutions to establish a government and delineate its powers. Like the Declaration of Independence, the state constitutions were steeped in Enlightenment thought. As such, state constitutions provided for extensive civil liberties, legal rights, and private property protections. Shared historical and cultural experiences also shaped how state constitutions enacted relatively limited governments with exceptionally weak executive branches. While governors and courts enjoyed some influence, state legislatures generally wielded the overwhelming majority of political power because they were theoretically more representative of the people and responsive to their needs.

At the same time, early state constitutions were oppressive documents and essentially functioned as a means of maintaining elite power structures. Early state constitutions placed limits on both voting rights and citizenship, typically in the form of property qualifications. So, the state government generally represented the views of an elite class of landowners, merchants, and religious leaders. Over time, low-income Europeans gained political equality, but people of color suffered systemic discrimination until at least the **Civil War** (1861–1865). For indigenous populations, the development and centralization of state power historically came at their expense, and state constitutions were no different.

The Articles of Confederation

American states signed the **Articles of Confederation** soon after the end of colonial rule. The Articles broadly sought to retain and maintain some degree of unity between the former British colonies and avoid destructive European-like regional rivalries.

The Articles of Confederation established a formal agreement or confederation between the original thirteen states. The Articles of Confederation established a central government composed of a unicameral legislative assembly in which each state was granted a single representative. Passing a bill required votes from nine of the thirteen representatives. Under the Articles of Confederation, the centralized government, the Continental Congress, was granted very limited powers, rendering it largely ineffective. Those powers included:

- Borrowing money from states or foreign government
- Creating post offices
- Appointing military offices
- Declaring war
- Signing treaties with foreign states

The Articles of Confederation established a central government, but given the colonial experience with a centralized constitutional monarchy, it was comically weak. The central government essentially consisted of a unicameral legislature. Right from the outset, the **Confederation Congress** was severely undermined by states' reservation of robust powers. For example, states held the power to print currency, assume debt, and pursue independent foreign trade deals; the central government couldn't implement a uniform economic agenda under this power-sharing scheme. In addition, states enjoyed veto power over the central government, effectively allowing minority opinions to override the entire confederation. The central government also lacked an executive branch because political leaders believed it would lead to tyrannical rule. As a result, even when the Confederation Congress passed laws, enforcement was close to impossible.

The early American political system deteriorated rapidly. Domestic unrest and border conflicts sapped the central government of its legitimacy and forced American political leaders to realize they needed to revamp the entire system.

The Northwest Ordinance

A driving force behind the American Revolution was overwhelming opposition to British restrictions on westward expansion. Once Americans gained independence, settlers streamed across the Appalachian Mountains and settled in land between the Ohio River and Great Lakes. During the nineteenth century, the Northwest Territories became the states of Ohio (1803), Indiana (1816), Illinois (1818), Michigan (1837), Wisconsin (1848), and Minnesota (1858).

The Confederation Congress passed a series of land ordinances to disentangle states' claims to the land and directly oversee its development during the transition to statehood.

The **Northwest Ordinance** of 1789 was very arguably the Confederation Congress' most impactful piece of legislation passed, marking one of the few times they successfully centralized political power. This legislation established federal conservatorship over territories as public domain until they qualified for statehood, effectively denying states the power to expand their internal boundaries. As such, the federal government enjoyed the power to enforce property rights and direct the development of civic institutions, such as a public education system. Additionally, the Northwest Ordinance enacted one of the few federal prohibitions on slavery, and the area between the Appalachian Mountains and Mississippi River became an extension of the **Mason-Dixon Line**, which later divided free and slave states.

The Constitutional Convention and Debates over Ratification

The Constitutional Convention

The **Constitutional Convention** (1787) met in Philadelphia a few months after the rebellion in order to create a stronger federal government. However, delegates disagreed over how to structure the new system. The **Virginia Plan** was one proposal that included a bicameral legislature where states were awarded representation based on their population size. This would benefit more populous states at the expense of smaller states. The other main proposal was the **New Jersey Plan**, which retained many elements of the Articles of Confederation, including a unicameral legislature with one vote per state. This plan would put states on an equal footing regardless of population. Eventually, delegates agreed to support the **Connecticut Compromise** (also known as the **Great Compromise**), which incorporated elements from both the Virginia and New Jersey Plans, and embodied federalism. Under the new Constitution, Congress would be a bicameral body. In the House of Representatives, states would be allocated seats based on population, but in the Senate each state would have two votes. The Constitution also included a president and judiciary that would each serve to check the power of other branches of government. In addition, Congress had the power to tax and had more enforcement powers.

Slavery and the Constitutional Convention

Even more than political representation and separation of powers, disputes over slavery threatened the Constitutional Convention. From the very beginning, overt limitations on chattel slavery were a political nonstarter, carrying the risk of a complete withdrawal of southern Atlantic state delegations. With the legalization of slavery being a foregone conclusion, the founding fathers eventually reached two pivotal compromises over slavery.

First, the **Three-Fifths Compromise**, which, in an effort to appease both the South states who wanted slaves to be counted as part of the population for the purpose of representation but not counted for the purpose of taxes, and the North, who demanded slaves be counted for taxes but not representation, determined that three-fifths of the slave population of each state would be counted for the purpose of both taxes and representation. This generally worked to the benefit of large slave-holding states because it inflated their populations by counting nonvoters while still giving a massive tax cut to slave owners who treated Africans purely as a commodity.

Second, the southern states agreed to a future federal prohibition on the international slave trade. The prohibition, called the **Commerce and Slave Trade Compromise**, would take effect in 1808, so southern states knew they had thirty years to safeguard slavery. This eased Southerners' fears that if the Northern states controlled the federal government, then they could enforce antislavery policies. Shortly after ratification, the importation of African slaves increased exponentially, partially due to the booming cotton industry. So, by 1808, domestic slave populations had become self-sustainable, and the domestic slave trade easily kept pace with demand. The southern states also accepted the future prohibition because they, correctly, assumed it would be impossible to enforce.

Debates Over Ratifying the Constitution

Once the Constitution had been drafted, nine of the thirteen states had to ratify it. Vigorous debate erupted over whether or not the Constitution should be approved. Two different political factions emerged. The **Federalists** supported the Constitution because they felt a stronger central government was necessary in order to promote economic growth and improve national security. Several leading federalists, including Alexander Hamilton, John Jay, and James Madison, published a series of articles urging voters to support the Constitution. However, the **Anti-Federalists**, including Thomas Jefferson and Patrick Henry, felt that the Constitution took too much power away from the states and gave it to the national government. They also thought there weren't enough protections for individual rights and lobbied for the addition of a **Bill of Rights** that guaranteed basic liberties.

The debates between these two parties continued for two years and inspired a series of essays known as the **Federalist Papers** and **Anti-Federalist Papers** authored anonymously by leaders of their respective party.

Notable Federalists and authors of the **Federalist Papers** include:

- **Alexander Hamilton**: founder of the Federalist Party and advocate for a centralized financial system
- **George Washington**: commander-in-chief of the Continental Army and future first president of the United States
- **James Madison**: one of the primary drafters of the Constitution and the future fourth president of the United States
- **John Jay**: president of the Continental Congress and future first chief justice of the United States
- **John Adams**: future second president of the United States

Notable anti-Federalists and authors of the **Anti-Federalist Papers** include:

- **Thomas Jefferson**: primary author of the Declaration of Independence and future third president of the United States
- **Patrick Henry**: governor of Virginia (1776-1779, 1784-1786)
- : governor of Massachusetts (1794-1797), lieutenant governor of Massachusetts (1789-1794), and president of the Massachusetts Senate (1782-1785, 1787-1788)
- **George Mason**: one of only three delegates who did not sign the Constitution at the Constitutional Convention and author of Objections to This Constitution of Government (1787) and the Virginia Declaration of Rights of 1776, which served as the basis for the Bill of Rights

The first state to ratify the Constitution was Delaware in a unanimous vote on December 7, 1787. Several other states followed, and eventually, after ten months, New Hampshire became the ninth state to ratify the Constitution in June 1788. However, some states still remained divided between Federalist and anti-Federalist sentiments and had yet to approve the document, including the two most populous states, Virginia and New York. To reconcile their differing views, the Federalists agreed to include a bill of rights if anti-Federalists supported the new Constitution. Federalist sentiment prevailed, and the remaining states approved the document. On May 29, 1790, the last holdout, Rhode Island, ratified the Constitution by two votes. As promised, the **Bill of Rights**—the first 10 amendments to the Constitution—was added in 1791, providing expanded civil liberty protection and due process of law.

The Constitution

Separation of Powers in the Constitution

To strengthen the central government, while still appeasing the individual states who preferred to remain sovereign over their territories, the framers of the Constitution based the new government upon the principles of **Federalism**—a compound government system that divides powers between a central government and various regional governments. The Constitution clearly defined the roles of both the state governments and the new federal government, specifying the limited power of the federal government and reserving all other powers not restricted by the Constitution to the states in the Tenth Amendment to the Constitution, commonly referred to as the **Reservation Clause**.

The Constitution establishes the specific powers granted to the federal and state governments.

- **Delegated powers**: the specific powers granted to the federal government by the Constitution
- **Implied powers**: the unstated powers that can be reasonably inferred from the Constitution
- **Inherent powers**: the reasonable powers required by the government to manage the nation's affairs and maintain sovereignty
- **Reserved powers**: the unspecified powers belonging to the state that are not expressly granted to the federal government or denied to the state by the Constitution
- **Concurrent powers**: the powers shared between the federal and state governments

The Constitution would delegate the following expanded powers to the federal government:

- Coin money
- Declare war
- Establish lower federal courts
- Sign foreign treaties
- Expand the territories of the United States, and admit new states into the union
- Regulate immigration
- Regulate interstate commerce

The following powers were reserved for the states:

- Establish local governments
- Hold elections
- Implement welfare and benefit programs
- Create public school systems
- Establish licensing standards and requirements
- Regulate state corporations
- Regulate commerce within the state

The **concurrent powers** granted to both the federal and state governments in the Constitution include:

- The power to levy taxes
- The power to borrow money
- The power to charter incorporations

Shaping a New Republic

Initiatives Addressing Continued European Colonial Powers

The United States took a variety of actions to mollify and usurp European colonial powers during the late eighteenth century.

British Canada had remained loyal during the American Revolutionary War, and even taken up arms against the Americans when they invaded Quebec in 1775. Consequently, Britain continued to be a major force in the Americas even after America gained independence. American expansion across the Appalachian Mountains poured fuel on the fire, igniting frontier conflicts all across the Great Lakes region. The federal government negotiated numerous ceasefires, but the border skirmishes continued until Washington signed the Jay Treaty in 1794.

Spain held some of the most strategically valuable territory in North America, but most of it was lightly populated and underdeveloped. American settlers regularly violated the Spanish territorial border in northern Florida, which was a haven for escaped slaves and indigenous military units. Angered by the Americans' encroachment, Spain revoked American merchants' access to the port city of New Orleans in 1798. This was unacceptable for the Americans, who used the port to send supplies up the Mississippi River to territories west of the Appalachian Mountains. So, once Spain secretly ceded much of its American territory to France, the Jefferson administration purchased the entire Louisiana territory from Napoleon in 1803.

The Impact of War Between France and Britain on the United States

The **French Revolution** created a pressing challenge for the United States. France had been American Patriots' first and most important European benefactor. Without French loans, training, supplies, and troops, the Americans likely would have lost the fight for independence. Furthermore, the American Revolution partially inspired the French Revolution, which overthrew King Louis XVI and established a revolutionary representative government. Thus, when Britain formed a coalition of European powers to oust the French revolutionaries, many Americans demanded it was their moral obligation to support their ally and repay the revolutionary debt they owed.

Other Americans viewed the conflict through clear eyes and realized an intervention was squarely against their national self-interest. The Constitution had been written, but not ratified, when the French Revolution began. Consequently, the United States lacked the political strength, financial resources, and military power to wage war on foreign soil against multiple world powers. The British Royal Navy also occupied the status of a global hegemonic naval power, and American foreign policy experts understood supporting France would come at the cost of British blockades. Given its precarious political and economic situation at the end of the eighteenth century, a steep decline in international trade posed a direct threat to the long-term stability of the United States.

Spanish Colonization in California

Spanish colonization in California expanded throughout the eighteenth century. Franciscan friars migrated from Spanish colonies further south in present-day Mexico and western South America, founding **mission settlements** in coastal California. Mission settlements often began with a group of friars backed by a small retinue of laborers and/or soldiers, and the friars led a theocratic colonial system.

The mission settlements implemented the same policies toward indigenous populations as other Spanish colonies. The friars used forced conversions and persuasive proselytizing to gain some degree of cultural and societal control over the local population, and actively pursued alliances with influential groups and leaders. Once they were in a position to carry out enforcement, the friars instituted the ***repartimiento*** **labor system**, which required indigenous populations to provide free labor in exchange for some limited legal rights and protections.

Combined with a massive amount of undeveloped land and an abundance of natural resources, the region's relatively small population of Spanish soldiers and migrants enjoyed more social mobility than nearly anywhere else in the world. Greater accommodation of indigenous culture and Europeans led to considerable cross-cultural interactions, including the development of syncretic religious beliefs and interracial family blending.

Struggles Between the Federal Government and American Indian Tribes

The United States had a contentious and, in some cases, ambiguous relationship with Native American tribes. Frontier groups played the more active role in pressing into tribal lands, so westward expansion was a continual source of conflict due to the resulting displacement of indigenous populations. In many instances, the federal government was forced into the role of mediator between tribes, states, and settlers.

The federal government signed dozens of agreements with Native American tribes during the late eighteenth century, but the **Treaty of Harmar** (1789) illustrates what ultimately occurred under almost all the agreements. The Americans had agreed to limit settlers and reduce violence in the Great Lakes territories, but even if it desperately wanted to, the federal government lacked the authority and power to enforce the treaty on frontier communities. In response, indigenous regional powers, including the Huron and Delaware tribes, formed the **Western Confederation**. The West Confederation inflicted some of the worst defeats in American military history, but the Americans ultimately recovered and achieved a decisive victory at the **Battle of Fallen Timbers** (1794). Capitalizing on this victory, the federal government agreed to split the Northwest Territories with the Western Confederation under the **Treaty of Greenville** (1795), which was similarly violated in short order.

George Washington and John Adams' Presidential Terms

The first several presidential administrations developed political institutions and precedents to legitimize the Constitution.

George Washington was unanimously elected as America's first president in 1789, and he reluctantly agreed to serve two terms to stabilize the constitutional regime. Consequently, two terms served as an informal precedent for future presidential administrations. Washington's Treasury Secretary, **Alexander Hamilton**, established the **United States Mint** to print and regulate the new national currency, and oversaw the passage of an excise tax on liquor to raise revenue. When distillers launched the **Whiskey Rebellion** (1791–1794), Washington personally led a militia to shut it down, setting a precedent for the enforcement of federal laws.

John Adams won the presidential election of 1796, establishing the precedent of peaceful and democratic regime change, and he was the first president to govern from the permanent capital city of Washington, D.C. Unlike Washington, Adams wasn't a war hero with widespread popular support. Thus, to protect federal authority, Adams passed the controversial **Alien** and **Sedition Acts**. This series of acts allowed the federal government to deport noncitizens and criminalize slanderous criticism of the federal government. Adams also spearheaded the formation of a large standing army and navy to defend against French warships harassing American merchants.

The Formation of Political Parties

American political leaders held conflicting views on numerous critical issues. Following the ratification of the Constitution, **Federalists** dominated the Washington administration, and enacted policies designed to centralize political power. Washington's Treasury Secretary Alexander Hamilton was an especially fierce advocate for free trade, central banking, federal taxes, and economic interventions. More broadly, the Federalists valued an organized and efficient government more than maximizing the protection of personal freedoms.

Organized opposition to the Federalists increased during Washington's second term through the formation of the **Democratic Republican Party** during the late 1790s. The Democratic Republicans favored limited government, civil liberty protections, and decentralized banking. In addition, the Democratic Republicans were less committed to free trade and an isolationist foreign policy. Many Democratic Republican leaders, including Thomas Jefferson and James Madison, viewed the **Jay Treaty** as a betrayal of Republican values for its concessions to Britain in exchange for reduced tensions on the frontier.

The Democratic Republicans nominated a presidential candidate, **Thomas Jefferson**, for the first time in 1796. Although Jefferson lost to the Federalist John Adams, he was victorious in the presidential election of 1800. Democratic Republicans then proceeded to control the executive branch until Andrew Jackson won the presidential election of 1828.

George Washington's Farewell Address

George Washington's **Farewell Address** is one of the most famous speeches in American history. While Washington reluctantly served as president, he had near-unanimous popular support. Washington realized that future American presidents would not enjoy that luxury, and he hoped the country wouldn't fracture when divisive issues arose. The revolutionary hero turned first president felt it was his duty to impart some words of wisdom to the country as it embarked on its first regime change.

Washington primarily warned of the dangers of **factionalism**. He argued that the United States would be safe and prosperous as long as it was uniform, and then proceeded to give a number of warnings about factionalism. He believed political factionalism would grind the new constitutional system to a halt and possibly lead to state disintegration. To prevent partisan bickering, Washington cautioned against the establishment of political parties, believing that private parties would consolidate power and dissolve the core tenets of representative government. The Farewell Address is also famous for Washington cautioning America against getting entangled in European rivalries, foreign disputes, and permanent foreign alliances. Washington pointed to the benefits of America's isolation, and urged the government to continue developing prosperous and peaceful relations with foreign powers whenever possible.

Developing an American Identity

New Forms of National and Regional Culture

The development of a national culture transformed the United States over the latter half of the twentieth century. A cohesive national culture first formed in the aftermath of the French and Indian War (1754–1763) as American colonists increasingly established militias and self-governing political institutions to defend their land. During the 1770s and 1780s, Enlightenment philosophies popularized the concepts of civil liberties, private property rights, and limited government. A robust publishing industry helped disseminate these ideas across the country, which led to the inclusion of **Enlightenment ideas** in the US Constitution (1789) and Bill of Rights (1791). These ideas laid the foundation for a capitalist economic system and shaped government policies, especially in terms of promoting individual liberties.

The new national culture was relatively diverse for its time. Although British culture played an outsized role in American culture, the presence of other European immigrants and a wide variety of Christian denominations resulted in considerable multiculturalism. However, white Europeans dominated the national identity by forcibly excluding African slaves and American Indians from mainstream society.

Early American culture also had significant regional variance. Northern states tended to place greater emphasis on economic and social freedom due to their larger urban centers of trade, technological investments, and immigrant populations. In contrast, Southern states were more conservative and hierarchical, largely due to their greater reliance on slavery and a plantation-based agricultural system. After Eli Whitney invented the **cotton gin** in 1793, the cultural and economic divide deepened as Southern states invested more heavily in large-scale agricultural production.

The Depiction of National Identity in Art

Given its relatively short and disjointed history, American-based artistic movements inspired and expressed the development of a uniquely American identity. American architects, artists, and writers all supported the revolutionary cause with works highlighting the twin virtues of patriotism and independence.

Americans tweaked the traditional British colonial architectural style after gaining independence. The new Federalist architectural style retained some colonial elements, like Georgian columns, but it added Classical Greek and Roman elements to link America with ancient democracies.

The American art movement primarily produced patriotic portraits of founding fathers and military triumphs. Artists also depicted everyday life of merchants and farmers, such as John Singleton Copley's famous *Paul Revere* (1768). Additionally, American artists created British-style landscape paintings that depicted nature's abundance, open land, and frontier life to emphasize America's divine blessing and unlimited opportunities.

American literature grew out of political writings, incorporating themes from the Declaration of Independence, *Common Sense*, and the Federalist Papers. At the tail end of the eighteenth century, American literary writers adopted the modern novel as a form of patriotic expression. Many early American novels were sentimental and idealistic, underscoring the importance and values of the American experiment. Other novels were satirical, such as Philip Freneau's mockery of British colonization.

Movement in the Early Republic

The Dynamic Relationships Between Native Americans and Others

Native American tribes responded with dynamic and ever-changing efforts to maintain political autonomy and economic prosperity against a creeping tide of European colonization. Both European settlers and Native American tribes pursued the same divide-and-conquer strategy of military alliances to isolate key rivals. Smaller indigenous tribes pursued alliances to establish more unified confederations, and regional powers sought alliances with other powerful indigenous confederations and European groups. For example, the Iroquois confederation incorporated smaller indigenous societies, and allied with the British first against the French and then later to push back the American frontier.

Wars were common between indigenous and European societies, especially in frontier areas that were outside the control of central governing authority. The **Northwest Indian War** (1785–1795) was the United States' first prolonged conflict with indigenous societies. With the support of British forts in the present-day American Midwest, the Delaware and Miami tribes led the Western Confederation to decisive victories over the United States before the **Jay Treaty** (1795) temporarily stopped the bloodshed. Britain's continued support of indigenous confederations not only undermined the United States' foreign policy ambitions, but it bred political controversy as more Americans pushed for more aggressive actions to be taken against Britain during the **French Revolutionary Wars** (1792–1802).

Westward Migration

Westward expansion across the Appalachian Mountains attracted a diverse group of migrants. The British colonies had rapidly increased in population density over the late seventeenth and eighteenth centuries, and migrants hoped to settle what they viewed as unclaimed lands. British colonists accounted for the vast majority of migrants, but there was considerable religious diversity as minority Christian sects sought even greater levels of independence. French, Spanish, and Dutch merchants also joined westward expeditions in the hopes of establishing a commercial presence in the early development of frontier settlements. Indigenous populations also had significantly more commercial and cultural interactions with frontier settlements, and it wasn't uncommon for indigenous people to live alongside frontier groups. Similarly, people of color often fled to the frontier due to the Northwest Territories' prohibitions on slavery, economic opportunities, and less traditional social institutions.

The clashing of cultures on the frontier often resulted in seething tensions and chilling violence. The diverse groups were interacting in a mostly lawless geographic area, and they often held conflicting values, beliefs, and economic interests. So, when political, social, and economic disputes arose, groups were quick to violence because they knew there was little hope of a central authority providing assistance or enforcing consequences.

Differing Regional Attitudes Toward Slavery

In the early 1800s, political and economic differences between the North and South became more apparent. Politically, a small but vocal group of abolitionists emerged in the North who demanded a complete end to slavery throughout the United States. **William Lloyd Garrison** edited the abolitionist newspaper *The Liberator* and vehemently denounced the brutality of slavery. His criticism was so vicious that the legislature of Georgia offered a $5,000 bounty to anyone who could capture Garrison and deliver him to state authorities. Other activists participated in the **Underground Railroad**—a network that helped fugitive slaves escape to the Northern United States or Canada.

Economic differences emerged as the North began to industrialize, especially in the textile industry where factories increased productivity. However, the Southern economy remained largely agricultural and focused on labor-intensive crops such as tobacco and cotton. This meant that slavery remained an essential part of the Southern economy. In addition, the North built more roads, railroads, and canals, while the Southern transportation system lagged behind. The Northern economy was also based on cash, while many Southerners still bartered for goods and services. This led to growing sectional tension between the North and South as their economies began to diverge further apart.

These economic differences led to political tension as well, especially over the debate about the expansion of slavery. This debate became more important as the United States expanded westward into the Louisiana Purchase and acquired more land after the Mexican-American War. Most Northerners were not abolitionists. However, many opposed the expansion of slavery into the western territories because it would limit their economic opportunities. If a territory was open to slavery, it would be more attractive to wealthy slave owners who could afford to buy up the best land. In addition, the presence of slave labor would make it hard for independent farmers, artisans, and craftsman to make a living, because they would have to compete against slaves who did not earn any wages. For their part, Southerners felt it was essential to continue expanding in order to strengthen the southern economy and ensure that the Southern way of life survived. As intensive farming depleted the soil of nutrients, Southern slave owners sought more fertile land in the west.

Practice Quiz

Questions 1–3 refer to the passage below:

> "The problem is to find a form of association which will defend and protect with the whole common force the person and goods of each associate, and in which each, while uniting himself with all, may still obey himself alone, and remain as free as before." This is the fundamental problem of which the *Social Contract* provides the solution.
>
> The clauses of this contract are so determined by the nature of the act that the slightest modification would make them vain and ineffective; so that, although they have perhaps never been formally set forth, they are everywhere the same and everywhere tacitly admitted and recognised, until, on the violation of the social compact, each regains his original rights and resumes his natural liberty, while losing the conventional liberty in favour of which he renounced it.

Excerpt from The Social Contract by Jean Jacques Rousseau, 1762

1. According to the passage, what happens after a "violation of the social compact"?
   a. The social compact resumes protecting rights and liberty as soon as possible.
   b. The social compact institutes reforms to serve the common good.
   c. The social compact dissolves and releases its constituent parties.
   d. The social compact reverts to the Social Contract between the state and citizens.

2. Social contract theory developed in which one of the following intellectual contexts?
   a. The Enlightenment
   b. Humanism
   c. Modernism
   d. The Renaissance

3. Which one of the following most accurately describes a consequence of social contract theory?
   a. Social contract theory incentivized imperial conquests and colonization.
   b. Social contract theory contributed to an intense period of revolutions.
   c. Social contract theory incentivized an expansion of international trade networks.
   d. Social contract theory led to the growth of state power.

4. Which of the following was NOT one of the compromises made in the Connecticut Compromise?
   a. A lower House of Representatives that is to be selected based on population size
   b. An Electoral College to give delegates a chance to intervene in the event of a wrong choice by the electorate
   c. A Senate consisting of two representatives from each state
   d. A Supreme Court with nine justices to prevent any ties during voting

5. Federalism is described as the contract between the federal government and which of the following?
   a. The people
   b. State governments
   c. The branches of government
   d. The Constitution

Answer Explanations

1. C: Social contract theory essentially involved a compromise where people sacrifice some individual freedom in exchange for mutual legal protection. If the social contract is violated, then people return to a state of complete natural freedom. This is not ideal because natural freedom encompasses the ability to inflict harm. After mentioning the "violation of the social compact," the passage describes how people regain original rights and natural liberty. This is referencing people returning to a state of complete natural freedom, meaning they are released from the dissolved social contract. Thus, Choice *C* is the correct answer. The social contract doesn't resume after a violation; in fact, the opposite happens. So, Choice *A* is incorrect. Choice *B* is incorrect because the passage doesn't mention reform. Choice *D* is a red herring. Although the passage refers to a social contract and social compact, contract and compact carry the same meaning—a mutual agreement. Nothing in the passage indicates otherwise, so Choice *D* is incorrect.

2. A: Social contract theory developed during the Enlightenment in the eighteenth and nineteenth centuries. Along with John Locke and Thomas Hobbes, Jean Jacques-Rousseau was a prominent Enlightenment philosopher and social contract theorist. Thus, Choice *A* is the correct answer. Choice *B* is the second best answer. Humanism is a philosophy that emphasizes individualism, human freedom, critical thinking, and rationalism, and Jean Jacques-Rousseau was heavily influenced by the humanist tradition. However, the Enlightenment better describes the intellectual context of the eighteenth and nineteenth centuries because humanism dates back to ancient times. So, Choice *B* is incorrect. Modernism is a philosophical and artistic movement that developed in the late nineteenth century based on the rejection of traditionalism, so Choice *C* is incorrect. The Renaissance was a cultural movement that revived humanism; however, the Renaissance lasted from the fourteenth century to the seventeenth century, which predates the Enlightenment. So, Choice *D* is incorrect.

3. B: Social contract theory directly contributed to an intense period of revolution. According to social contract theory, if the state fails to fulfill its obligations, then the contract is broken. Because the contract is broken, people are released and free to form a new state. For example, French revolutionaries claimed the monarchy had broken the social contract by denying citizens basic liberties and legal protections. In addition, in the Americas, more than a dozen new nation-states gained independence in the nineteenth century. Thus, Choice *B* is the correct answer. Social contract theory didn't incentivize imperialism or colonization; if anything, it did the opposite. So, Choice *A* is incorrect. International trade isn't directly related to social contract theory, so Choice *C* is incorrect. Although a firm social contract would theoretically strengthen the state, social contract theory didn't directly lead to the growth of power. So, Choice *D* is incorrect.

4. D: The Connecticut Compromise finally eased the tensions of the Constitutional Convention enough to get a deal on the table. Combining the better parts of all of the proposed deals, the compromise was able to get through to become the frame of the new Constitution. Choice *A* (a House of Representatives fixed to population size for representation), Choice B (an Electoral College), and Choice *C* (a Senate where each state has exactly two representatives) were all part of the Connecticut Compromise. Choice *D*, the number of justices that currently sit on the court, is not mandated by the Constitution. In reality, there can be as many or as few as Congress wants.

5. B: Federalism, at least how it was put forth by the Framers, is the union between the federal and state governments. While it incorporates the people and the Constitution, the true marriage is the independence of both the states and the federal government.

Section 4: Industrialization and Reform (1800–1848)

The Rise of Political Parties and the Era of Jefferson

Debates Between Political Parties in the Early 1800s

As American political parties developed during the early nineteenth century, partisanship and rancor over hotly debated issues increased dramatically. Most broadly, politicians fiercely debated the extent of federal powers, particularly when those powers conflicted with the states' autonomy. Federalists advocated for a robust federal government to oversee nationwide policies, such as a centralized banking system, heavy tariffs, and national infrastructure projects. In contrast, the **Democratic Republicans**—members of the Democratic Republican Party—prioritized civil liberties, local government, and state autonomy. Aside from their distrust of the federal government, Democratic Republicans aggressively condemned tariffs to protect American agricultural exports.

However, at times, some Democratic Republican leaders strayed away from their ideals about limited government, such as when Thomas Jefferson dramatically expanded federal powers to facilitate the **Louisiana Purchase** (1803). For $15 million, Jefferson bought French territory west of the Mississippi River that doubled the size of the United States. He then appointed Meriwether Lewis and William Clark to lead an expedition to explore the vast new territory and study its geography, vegetation, and plant life. Clark also brought his African-American slave, York, on the journey. York helped hunt and even saved Clark's life during a flood. The expedition was also aided by Sacagawea, a Shoshone woman, who acted as a guide and interpreter. The explorers also established relations with Native American tribes and set the stage for further western expansion in the 1800s.

Relations with European powers were another sharply contested political issue. George Washington and the leading Federalists wanted to remain neutral and consolidate American resources. In contrast, the Democratic Republicans advocated for defending France, America's first meaningful ally. Hostilities between the United States and Britain boiled over during the **Napoleonic Wars** (1803–1815), when British blockades impacted American commerce.

War between the United States and Britain broke out in 1812 because the United States was drawn into a conflict between Britain and France. Britain refused to stop interfering with American ships bound for France and had begun forcibly recruiting American citizens into the British navy. Furthermore, the British still occupied several forts near the Great Lakes and continued to encourage Indians to attack American settlements in the Northwest Territories. The resulting **War of 1812** was a military stalemate, and hostilities concluded with the **Treaty of Ghent** (1815), which returned Anglo-American relations to the status quo.

Supreme Court Decisions in the Early 1800s

The Supreme Court spent much of the early nineteenth century attempting to gain formal constitutional authority and expand federal power. Legislative powers were found in Article I. The sweeping authority granted to the executive branch was found under Article II. Article III created a Supreme Court and delegated control and oversight over the development of a judiciary system to Congress.

Marbury v. Madison (1803) was an important case for the Supreme Court. Chief Justice John Marshall's decision legitimized the power of judicial review, meaning that that the Supreme Court enjoyed the power to review and possibly overturn any American law. This was a power far beyond anything explicitly provided under the Constitution, though Marshall persuasively argued it was implied.

McCulloch v. Maryland (1819) similarly stands out as an unprecedented change to American law. Marshall again wrote the majority decision and ruled that the **Supremacy Clause** elevated federal law above any conflicting state law. Furthermore, Marshall cited the **Necessary and Proper Clause** to justify the existence of implied legislative powers. As a result, Congress gained broad power to pass laws necessary for the implementation of an express power, such as regulating interstate commerce.

Governmental Efforts to Control North America

Constant immigration meant that land prices in the eastern United States rose, and people sought new economic opportunities on the frontier where land was cheaper. The United States government tried purchasing land from Native Americans, but most refused to relinquish their territories. Native Americans continued to defend their land until Tecumseh was defeated in the **War of 1812**. This defeat helped secure the **Northwest Territory**, and more settlers began pouring in. After the Louisiana Purchase, Lewis and Clark paved the way for expansion into the Great Plains and further west.

By the mid-1800s, the revolutions of Latin America ceased, and only a few areas remained under European rule. The U.S. President James Monroe issued the **Monroe Doctrine**, which stated that the Americas could no longer be colonized. It was an attempt to stop European nations, especially Spain, from colonizing areas or attempting to recapture areas. England's navy contributed to the success of the doctrine, as they were eager to increase trade with the Americas and establish an alliance with the United States.

The concept of **Manifest Destiny** emerged during the 1800s and introduced the idea that God wanted Americans to civilize and control the entire continent. This led to conflict when the province of Texas declared its independence from Mexico and asked to be annexed by the United States. President James K. Polk tried to buy Texas, but when Mexico refused, he sent troops into the disputed territory. Mexican troops responding by attacking an American unit, which led to war in 1846. Manifest Destiny also sparked a desire to expand American influence into Central and South America. Adventurers launched several unsuccessful attempts to invade Nicaragua and Cuba.

Politics and Regional Interests

Leaders' Responses to Regional v. National Concerns

Regional interests heavily influenced politicians' economic policies and approach to the looming controversy over slavery. The economies of Southern states were highly dependent on slave labor. Without an immense supply of African slaves, plantations would face exponentially higher costs and lost profits. Given their disproportionate wealth and power, plantation owners dominated Southern state governments and their federal representatives. So plantation owners were able to leverage political power to undermine attempts at reforming slavery and regulating agriculture. Many Southern political leaders, like John Calhoun of South Carolina, claimed the right to nullify federal laws and secede from the union. Therefore, the continuation of slavery and plantation-based economies was never in doubt.

Northern states industrialized during the nineteenth century, and they relied on cheap immigrant labor rather than slaves. Therefore, Northern states were relatively quick to abolish slavery, and their state governments willingly permitted, if not outright encouraged, the **abolitionist movement**.

Politicians on the frontier were sometimes pro-slavery, sometimes anti-, depending on location. The American Midwest generally opposed slavery and pushed for the federal government to support industrialization efforts. In contrast, the southern portion of the frontier hoped to recreate the plantation-based economies as practiced in the American South.

The American System

In general, the **American System** was a direct byproduct of the grand economic vision of **Alexander Hamilton**, who was treasury secretary under President George Washington. During the first half of the nineteenth century, congressmen **Daniel Webster** and **Henry Clay** led the charge to unify America's regional economies. More specifically, Webster and Clay championed heavy tariffs to protect domestic industries, unified banking system to stabilize the country's fledgling financial system, and major infrastructure investments to develop the western frontier. The American System was highly ambitious in its attempt to unify the United States and integrate regional economies.

Despite its undeniable effectiveness in binding the states together and generating economic growth, the American System was extraordinarily controversial. The **Whig Party**, who asserted Congress' supremacy over the president and primarily focused on economic concerns, easily convinced Northern businessmen of the financial benefits related to unification, and western frontiersmen reluctantly supported the federal government's consolidation of power in order to finance large-scale infrastructure projects. However, the reaction of southern states ranged from seething hostility to vocal resistance. They viewed the American System as a handout to northern industrialists at the expense of agricultural production. In particular, southern states balked at tariffs because it was far more profitable to ship cotton and foodstuffs to European markets than northern states.

Congressional Attempts at Political Compromise

Both the North and South also feared losing political power as more states were admitted to the nation. For example, neither side wanted to lose influence in the United States senate if the careful balance of free and slave state representation was disrupted. Several compromises were negotiated in Congress, but they only temporarily quieted debate. The first such effort, called the **Missouri Compromise**, was passed in 1820, and it maintained political parity in the U.S. Senate by admitting Missouri as a slave state and Maine as a free state. The Missouri Compromise banned slavery in the portion of the Louisiana Purchase that was north of the 36°30′ parallel and permitted slavery in the portion south of that line as well as Missouri.

However, the slavery debate erupted again after the acquisition of new territory during the Mexican-American War. The **Compromise of 1850** admitted California as a free state and ended the slave trade, but not slavery itself, in Washington D.C., in order to please Northern politicians. In return, Southern politicians were able to pass a stronger fugitive slave law and demanded that New Mexico and Utah be allowed to vote on whether or not slavery would be permitted in their state constitutions. This introduced the idea of popular sovereignty where the residents of each new territory, and not the federal government, could decide whether or not they would become a slave state or a free state. This essentially negated the Missouri Compromise of 1820. The enhanced fugitive slave law also angered many Northerners, because it empowered federal marshals to deputize anyone, even residents of a free state, and force them to help recapture escaped slaves. Anyone who refused would be subject to a $1,000 fine (equivalent to more than $28,000 in 2015).

America on the World Stage

United States' Efforts to Create an Independent Global Presence

The United States encountered significant difficulties in competing with European powers on the world stage during the first half of the nineteenth century. As a result, the United States sharpened its focus on increasing foreign trade and expanding its North American territories, which were far more achievable goals.

The United States relied on foreign trade to stimulate economic growth and gain global influence. During the early nineteenth century, the United States primarily traded with Europe, and cotton represented its most valuable export. In particular, the United States leveraged its commercial power to navigate the Anglo-French rivalry. After fighting Great Britain to a stalemate in the War of 1812, the United States quickly established itself as an important ally and trade partner with its former colonizer. Furthermore, the United States sought and gained export markets for its manufactured goods in Latin America and China.

The United States greatly benefited from the tumultuous conditions of the **Napoleonic Era** (1799–1815). With incessant warfare drowning French finances, Napoleon decided to abandon much of his North American colonial project and sell France's vast Louisiana Territory to the United States. The Louisiana Purchase (1803) nearly doubled American territory, and over the next several decades, the United States subsidized exploratory missions, commercial enterprises, and pioneer settlements to populate its new territory. As the United States expanded, Americans increasingly claimed Manifest Destiny to justify further conquests as a divine right.

Governmental Efforts to Gain Control over the Western Hemisphere

The United States combined skillful diplomacy and military right to dominate the Western hemisphere during the first half of the nineteenth century.

Several presidential administrations skillfully deployed diplomacy to mitigate the threat posed by European powers operating in the Western hemisphere. President Thomas Jefferson exploited Napoleon's precarious financial and military situation when negotiating the Louisiana Purchase, and France's departure from continental North America shored up the United States' western border. President James Monroe similarly acquired Florida for cash in the **Adams-Onis Treaty** of 1819 and also issued the highly influential Monroe Doctrine (1823) to threaten retaliation against European interventions in the newly independent Latin American states. The United States likely couldn't have prevented such an intervention, but this public declaration resulted in the United States developing a near-exclusive sphere of influence in Central and South America. The United States also signed a multitude of border treaties with Great Britain. For example, the **Oregon Treaty** (1846) established the 49th parallel of north latitude as the American-Canadian border from present-day Minnesota to Washington.

In its dealings with competing regional powers, the United States heavily favored military action. Congress worked to pass the **Indian Removal Act** of 1830, and President Andrew Jackson enforced it by relocating more than sixty thousand American Indians from their ancestral homelands in the southeastern United States to lands west of the Mississippi River. This event is commonly referred to as the *Trail of Tears,* and it killed approximately ten thousand American Indians. Additionally, President

James K. Polk secured nearly all of the present-day American Southwest by annexing Texas (1845) and instigating the Mexican-American War (1846–1848).

Market Revolution: Industrialization

The Industrial Revolution

The **Industrial Revolution** transformed the relationship between producers and consumers in the marketplace. Prior to the development of large-scale industrial manufacturing, economies depended on specialized tradesmen to produce goods for trade. Following the creation of interchangeable parts and mechanized tools, industrial production output soared. American entrepreneurs were early adopters of these British innovations, and they spearheaded the establishment of novel forms of economic organization, such as company mills and factories.

Samuel Slater is widely regarded as the father of the American Industrial Revolution. During the late eighteenth century, Slater toured British textile mills, memorized their designs, and then emigrated to the United States, where he adapted British innovations to American conditions. Slater built the first textile mills and factory towns in the United States, with most of his commercial empire located in Massachusetts and Rhode Island. Like Slater, **Francis Cabot Lowell** famously financed an innovative company town in the present-day city of Lowell, Massachusetts. Lowell pioneered new methods of corporate financing to raise capital investments, and his Boston Manufacturing Company was one of the first to employ women as factory workers. Lowell had a lasting impact on American manufacturing due to the Waltham-Lowell system's application of textile machinery to boost production.

Industrial Revolution Innovations

The American Industrial Revolution was powered and accelerated by technological innovations. Of all the innovations, the concept of using interchangeable parts was arguably the most influential in its impact on myriad industries. With interchangeable parts, workers could be assigned specific and isolated tasks, rather than bearing responsibility for an entire finished product. This more efficient model of production both reduced the skill requirements for workers and increased total industrial output as factories implemented increasingly complex assembly lines.

Similar groundbreaking innovations occurred in agriculture, such as advancements to Eli Whitney's cotton gin and the invention of mechanized farming equipment. The resulting increase in cotton production directly supported the deployment of textile machinery, such as the spinning jenny and the water frame, in order to mass produce garments.

Other inventions increased the efficiency of transportation and communication, which contributed to more economic integration and unification. The steam engine increased the reliability and speed of maritime travel on the Atlantic Ocean as well as critical domestic waterways like the Mississippi River. Likewise, the telegraph provided an unprecedented form of expedited communication across vast distances. As a result, interrelated networks of commercial relationships between consumers, producers, and investors sprang up all across the United States and even extended overseas.

Transportation Advancements and Networks

Several important laws also stimulated western expansion during the second half of the 19th century. Congress passed the **Homestead Act** in 1862, which allowed citizens to claim 160 acres for only $1.25

per acre. The settler also had to live on the land for five years and make improvements. That same year, Congress also passed the **Pacific Railroad Act**, which supported the construction of a transcontinental railroad. The United States government provided land and financial support to railroad companies and the first transcontinental link was established in 1869. This facilitated trade and communication between the eastern and western United States.

The government also supported the development of additional roads and canals throughout the country, which helped build further-reaching transportation networks. However, not all regions were equally connected; the North and Midwest regions were more closely linked together than any region was connected with the South. Transportation networks and advancements enhanced the mobility of goods and people.

The Development of National Commercial Ties

National commercial ties were predicated on intertwined economic growth and specialization. Northern states functioned as the engine for ramping up economic growth. Industrialization resulted in a skyrocketing supply of consumer goods at unprecedentedly low prices. Furthermore, the establishment of the First Bank of the United States (1791–1811) and the Second Bank of the United States (1816–1836) provided the necessary capital for aggressive and ambitious industrial efforts.

Southern states were nearly as indispensable to the development of a capitalist economic system. Aside from generating a considerable amount of staple foods, cotton fed industrialization efforts in the Northern states. For example, textile mills turned cotton into a variety of finished products, ranging from clothes to household items. Northern shipping companies facilitated these commercial exchanges up and down the Atlantic seaboard; however, the Southern states sometimes resisted political pressure to engage in domestic trade due to the increased profitability of foreign markets.

Western frontier areas were a combination of Northern and Southern economies. Given the surplus of land they seized from indigenous populations, frontier communities were able to engage in large-scale agriculture as well as hunting and fishing. However, as their populations increased and territories were admitted as states, the former frontier regions slowly transitioned toward industrialization.

Market Revolution: Society and Culture

Immigration and Internal Migration

Immigration to the United States grew exponentially during the early nineteenth century. The bulk of early immigrants came from Britain and Ireland, especially in the wake of the deadly **Great Potato Famine** (1845–1849). However, diverse ethnic and religious groups also set sail for American shores to obtain civil liberties, economic opportunities, and religious freedom. Germans constituted one of the largest immigrant groups that settled outside of the original British colonies on the western frontier, located in the present-day Midwestern United States.

Frontier communities located near the Appalachian Mountains, the Ohio River Valley, and the Mississippi River were amongst the most diverse in the world. Given the British colonial history in the formally recognized states, the federal territories attracted international migrants at elevated rates. Appalachian communities especially experienced tremendous growth in the early nineteenth century due to their proximity to the states. Irish and German immigrants arrived en masse and established rural settlements, which strongly resembled urban immigrant communities except on a far wider territorial scale. American Indian and African cultural beliefs were also more likely to be incorporated within the Western frontier due to the general lack of manpower and resources. This desire for sustained growth is also why the frontier generally supported unification plans, such as the infrastructure promised under the American System.

Diverging Socioeconomic Classes

Manufacturing led to more intense class stratification in the United States. At the top of the hierarchy, manufacturing magnates and business elites joined plantation owners as the dominant powers in American socioeconomic life. The rise of manufacturing spurred industrialization and urbanization in a virtuous cycle. A **virtuous cycle** is a chain of events that recycles through a feedback loop that has favorable results. Furthermore, as the cost of production plummeted and supplies of goods increased, commercial interactions rose significantly and drove general improvements in the standard of living. For example, many American cities were built with sanitation systems and large marketplaces to support entrepreneurial economic growth.

During the early nineteenth century, the American middle class largely consisted of skilled professionals, factory managers, and investors. The expanded middle class functioned as the consumer class, especially in regard to the purchase of new manufactured products.

The new class of urbanized industrial and unskilled laborers occupied the very bottom position in American society, lower than just about everyone except for slaves. The laboring poor tangentially benefited from rising prosperity, but they worked for twelve to fifteen hours per day under extreme work conditions with nearly no days off and minimal pay. Additionally, a significant portion of the laboring poor had less access to food than subsistence farmers.

The Shift From Semi-Subsistence Agriculture to Manufacturing

American employment opportunities largely shifted from agriculture to the industrial sector. Prior to the Industrial Revolution, most Americans engaged in **semi-subsistence agriculture**, meaning they grew a sizable percentage of the food they consumed. Therefore, industrialization involved a major change since factory workers depended on wages for food. The type of work was also different in the sense that workers produced goods destined for distant marketplaces.

Northern factory workers produced a variety of goods. The use of interchangeable parts and mass assembly was originally applied to firearms during the American Revolution, and arms manufacturing continued to be big business in the decades afterward. Many of these guns were shipped to the frontier for conflicts against indigenous populations, but they were also a significant export to Europe. Factories also produced mechanized agricultural equipment for farms and plantations across the country, especially the Southern states. Manufactured textiles, including clothing and household items, were another major manufactured product. Tariffs resulted in most of these goods remaining in the United States, but there was also a significant export market to Europe and Latin America. Southern plantations often shipped cotton to northern states in exchange for manufactured textiles and mechanized agricultural tools.

Changes in Gender and Family Roles

Industrialization facilitated incredible diversification in the workforce. Assembly lines and interchangeable parts greatly reduced businesses' reliance on skilled labor. Therefore, fresh opportunities and coercive economic pressure drove women and children to join the market revolution. Overall, women and children worked the most dangerous and least desirable jobs in exchange for inferior compensation relative to adult male peers.

The introduction of women to the workforce had a mixed effect on traditional gender and family norms. On the one hand, women had slightly more independence within the public sphere due to their new source of income and commercial interactions. However, at the same time, American society definitively kept the public and private spheres separate. Women were still expected to bear full responsibility over child rearing and myriad household obligations.

Given pervasive pay inequality and lack of political rights, American society remained firmly within the grasp of patriarchal power structures during the nineteenth century. Many women, including the feminist heroes **Elizabeth Cady Stanton** and **Susan B. Anthony**, helped lead the abolitionist movement during the 1830s and 1840s to not only condemn the injustices of slavery, but also to demand numerous legal reforms related to childcare, divorce, property rights, education, and medical access.

Expanding Democracy

The Transition to a More Participatory Democracy

American democracy became significantly more equal in the early nineteenth century. States originally restricted the franchise to adult white males who owned some minimum amount of property. Between 1800 and 1830, nearly all states eliminated property ownership requirements, although some states continued to allow only taxpayers to vote. Although this electoral expansion received incredible popular support, the **Dorr Rebellion** (1841–1842) was a notable exception. In this insurrection, landless laborers and small farmers revolted against Rhode Island's ruling class of rural elites, and it resulted in the property requirement being replaced with a poll tax for all native-born male citizens regardless of race.

Democratization occurred alongside the development of **factionalism**. The **First Party System** (1792–1824) involved two political parties—the Federalist Party and Democratic-Republican Party—but it was an extremely one-sided contest, with the Democratic-Republicans winning every presidential election between 1800 and 1824. The mobilization of newly enfranchised white males ushered in the **Second Party System** (1828–1854), and it was dominated by the Democratic Party against the Whigs. Democrats added a Populist appeal to the Democratic-Republican principles about limited government, and Congressman Henry Clay formed the Whig Party to advocate for federally funded modernization programs.

Compared to its predecessor, the Second Party System featured significantly higher levels of vitriolic partisanship. For example, President Jackson vetoed the Whig-backed Second Bank of the United States, alongside a fiery statement that accused Congress of selling out Americans to financial elites. The debate over slavery eventually broke the Second Party System; however, factionalism has remained a defining characteristic of American democracy ever since.

Jackson and Federal Power

Democrats and Whigs

The Founding Fathers of the United States opposed the divisiveness they associated with political parties, and President George Washington railed against the evil of political parties in his Farewell

Address. However, the ratification of the Constitution led to the creation of the first two American political parties, the **Federalists** and the anti-Federalist **Democratic-Republican Party**. When Andrew Jackson became the seventh president of the United States as a **Democrat**, his opposition organized under the **Whig Party**. The Whigs asserted Congress' supremacy over the president and primarily focused on economic concerns, like banking and violations.

These political parties disagreed about various issues such as the national bank, federal government powers, and federally-funded improvement projects.

American Indian Resistance to Frontier Expansion

As Americans poured westward, conflict again broke out between settlers and Native Americans. The discovery of gold in the Black Hills of South Dakota caused prospectors to flood into the area although the U.S. government had recognized the territory belonged to the Sioux. **General George Armstrong Custer** brought in troops to try and take possession of the Black Hills. This led to disaster when Custer and more than 250 soldiers died at the **Battle of Little Big Horn** in 1876. The U.S. government continued its efforts to control Native American tribes. The **Dawes Act** of 1887 encouraged Native Americans to settle on reservations and become farmers in exchange for U.S. citizenship. **Chief Joseph** was a leader of the Nez Perce tribe who refused to live on a reservation and tried to flee to Canada. However, the U.S. captured Chief Joseph and his tribe and forced them onto a reservation. Reformers also required Native Americans to send their children to boarding schools where they had to speak English and dress like Caucasians instead of maintaining their traditional culture. The schools were often crowded, and students were also subjected to physical and sexual abuse. In 1890, the **Lakota** Indians tried to preserve their traditional beliefs by performing a special ceremony called a **Ghost Dance**. U.S. government officials felt threatened and sent soldiers to try and disarm the Lakota. This led to the **Massacre at Wounded Knee** in 1890 where at least 150 Lakota, including many women and children, were slaughtered. It was the last major conflict between Native Americans and U.S. forces.

The Development of an American Culture

A New National Culture

A new national culture developed combining European identities, Christian beliefs, and regional diversity. Once the United States began expanding westward and industrializing, European immigration diversified considerably with large groups coming from Germany, Ireland, and Scandinavia during the first half of the nineteenth century. Immigration rates also skyrocketed in this period. For example, compared to the rates between 1790 and 1820, immigration increased tenfold by the 1840s. As a result, American culture developed as a melting pot where cultural values and traditions fused together.

Likewise, the promise of religious freedom resulted in more Christian sects taking root in the United States than anywhere else in the world. Christian revivalist movements also contributed to the growth of uniquely American religious beliefs, such as the importance of personal spiritual connections to the divine.

Unlike other countries, an American national culture was heavily influenced by regional economic development. Northern economies featured large-scale industrialization, urbanization, and immigration, which resulted in a greater emphasis on commerce and more frequent interactions among people of different cultures. Wealthy owners of plantations and slaves dominated the Southern economy, resulting in a hierarchical society and culture. In the Western territories, the regional culture was optimistic and adventurous as frontiersmen sought prosperity in the wilderness.

Influences on Art

The **Enlightenment** and the **Romantic movement** both had a transformative impact on early American culture. Beginning in the late seventeenth century, European philosophers embraced Enlightenment thought to strive for societal perfection in terms of liberty, equality, and rule of law. The Enlightenment began in Europe during the late 17th century and made its way to America as a period dedicated to scientific reasoning in areas such as science, politics, and religion. Unlike much monarchical rule in Europe, the Enlightenment encouraged public discourse and valued how the public felt about critical issues. For example, the American publishing industry emerged prior to the American Revolution and exploded in its aftermath, a process that gave the public broad access to political and religious texts.

The European Romantic movement directly led to the United States' first homegrown artistic movement, the **American Romantic movement**. Like their European contemporaries, American artists broke with the Enlightenment to inject emotion and spirituality back into philosophical and artistic endeavors. While the Enlightenment sought to perfect government, Romanticism concerned itself with human perfectibility.

The American Romantic movement birthed other artistic movements. **Gothic Revival architecture** popularized medieval European architectural styles with an American twist, such as incorporating chimneys and stained glass in the construction of neoclassical homes. Similarly, **New England Transcendentalism** merged Enlightenment and Romantic philosophy to create art based on spirituality, morality, nature, individualism, and independence. Famous examples of New England Transcendentalism include Ralph Waldo Emerson, Henry David Thoreau, and Louisa May Alcott.

The Second Great Awakening

The Second Great Awakening

The **Second Great Awakening** occurred in the early 1800s in response to the increases in democratic and individualistic beliefs, rationalism, and the social and economic changes brought on by the Industrial Revolution. It urged Protestants to work not only for their own salvation but for the salvation of others as well. This helped fuel a social reform movement that promoted the abolition of slavery, temperance, and prison reform. The question of slavery caused schisms in the Baptist and Methodist churches during the 1840s. The Second Great Awakening, much like the First Great Awakening, inaugurated the creation of several **New Religious Movements** (NRMs) in the United States, especially in the southern states.

An Age of Reform

The Progressive Era

In the late 1800s and early 1900s, the forces of urbanization and industrialization combined to create rampant urban plight across the metropolitan centers of the United States of America. During this era, many progressive political leaders and groups rose to power, opening the door to urban-based reforms in labor, health care, education, women's rights, and temperance. These reforms coalesced in what is now referred to by historians as a "**Progressive Era**." This period included activists in both the Democratic and Republican parties. The Progressives wanted to use scientific methods and government regulation to improve society. For example, they advocated the use of initiative, referendum, and recall to make government more responsive to its citizens. Progressives also argued that it was necessary to breakup large monopolies (known as trust busting) in order to promote equal economic competition.

Abolitionist and Antislavery Movements

The **abolitionist movement**—which was driven by an antislavery sentiment—gained steam in the early to mid-1800s as the United States became increasingly sectionalized in character. The abolitionist movement was not a monolithic, static phenomenon, but rather changed over time as different groups created different visions for solving the United States' slave issue. The American Colonization Society (founded 1816), for instance, helped create the African colony of Liberia as a refuge for freed and enslaved blacks living in the United States. Even within this movement, reformers produced different visions. Some simply wanted to send black residents back to Africa for the benefit of creating a less diverse and conflicted society; others saw Liberia as a way to help blacks regain their cultures overseas. Other movements included the American Anti-Slavery Society, the Philadelphia Female Anti-Slavery Society, the Anti-Slavery Convention of American Women, and the Female Vigilant Society. Led and motivated by women, these organizations brought the abolitionist and women's rights movements closer together, planting the seeds of a coalition that would once again join together in American history during the heart of the civil rights movement of the 1950s and 1960s. Abolition was eventually achieved through President Lincoln's Emancipation Proclamation, thanks in part to the efforts of these reformers.

Overall, the abolitionist movement was more successful in the North, and resultantly, even though the rights of African Americans were restricted by many state governments, there was a marked increase in the free African American population. In the South, however, relatively unsuccessful slave rebellions characterized the antislavery efforts.

Antislavery Movements in the North

Public support for and opposition to slavery exhibited incredible regional variation. Abolitionism first emerged in the Northern states in the aftermath of the American Revolutionary War. Once it was clear true equality would not be achieved under the Articles of Confederation or the U.S. Constitution, the abolitionist movement was formed. In conjunction with African American abolitionists, **William Lloyd Garrison** established the influential **American Anti-Slavery Society**, and within the vehemently anti-slavery Quaker community, he organized collective actions to protest the institution's continuation.

Southerners strenuously objected to any and all limitations on slavery under the belief that any change would lead to a slippery slope. The overwhelming majority of Southerners owned few, if any, slaves due to costs. However, most Southerners worked in areas tangentially related to plantation-based agricultures. Some worked at the wholesale purchase of agricultural products, while others worked as field hands and overseers. Therefore, these workers had a vested economic interest in the continuation of exploitative labor practices. Lastly, the Southern politicians characterized slavery and plantations as a critical part of the region's culture. As a result, Southerners generally viewed abolitionism as "Northern aggression" and a constitutional violation of states' rights. However, the states' rights approach to slavery is somewhat disingenuous, given how Southern politicians obsessed over the singular right to own slaves.

The Women's Rights Movement

The Fourteenth Amendment specified equal treatment for all citizens; however, it did not establish women's right to vote in elections, known as women's **suffrage**. Although landowning women were allowed to vote in New Jersey in the late eighteenth century, the right was removed in 1807. The fight for women's suffrage continued in the middle of the nineteenth century. Famous women's rights activists include **Susan B. Anthony**, **Lucy Stone**, and Elizabeth **Cady Stanton**, who authored the *Declaration of Rights and Sentiments*, which demanded access to the civil liberties granted to all men.

The **Women's Rights Movement** in the U.S. ranged from 1848 to 1920. This movement called for a woman's right to vote, the right to bodily autonomy, freedom from sexual violence, the right to hold public office, the right to work, the right to fair wages and equal pay, and the right to own property and obtain an education.

In July 1848, the **Seneca Falls Convention** met for two days to discuss the current conditions and rights of women in social, civil, and religious realms. This convention was the first of several women's right conventions in the following few years.

The women's suffrage movement gained momentum in the early twentieth century after their increased participation in the economy during World War I when much of the workforce went overseas to fight. The National Women's Party picketed outside the White House and led a series of protests in Washington, resulting in the imprisonment of the party's leader, Alice Paul. In 1918, Woodrow Wilson declared his support for women's suffrage despite earlier opposition, and in 1920, Congress passed the Nineteenth Amendment, which made it illegal for states to withhold voting rights based on gender.

Women continue to demand change during the 21st century for reasons such as the gender wage gap, better resources for women's health, female reproductive rights, and for protection of basic human rights, such as bringing greater awareness to rape culture, violence against women, and protection against female sex trafficking.

African Americans in the Early Republic

African American Communities

African Americans resisted white supremacy in a variety of ways. Enslaved African Americans collectively struggled to preserve their humanity against the horrors of slavery. Although slaves were descended from different and culturally diverse West African tribes, they crafted unique Afro-American languages to communicate in and strengthen interpersonal relationships. Likewise, slaves maintained cultural traditions and family structures even while slave owners prohibited such activities. When faced with separation, slaves often escaped to reunite with loved ones, and former slaves established independently governed communities.

Free African Americans similarly established tight-knit communities in the North to collectively thwart kidnappers, and community leaders sparked a popular movement predicated on freedom and equality. **Frederick Douglass** pushed for equality of all people regardless of race and gender, and his *Narrative of the Life of Frederick Douglass, an American Slave* (1845) was an international bestseller. The brothers Charles Henry Langston and John Mercer Langston formed the **Ohio Anti-Slave Society** to protest the westward expansion of slavery. African Americans' personal anecdotes had the most remarkable impact in terms of persuading the public. For example, former slaves injected the deplorable conditions and sexual abuse of enslaved women into the public consciousness when such topics were flatly denied and widely considered taboo.

The Society of the South in the Early Republic

Southern Agricultural Economy

The Southern regional identity was steeped in agriculture. To maximize the profit potential of large-scale production, plantations primarily grew cash crops, such as sugar, tobacco, and most importantly, cotton. However, less wealthy family farms continued to produce traditional agricultural staple foods, such as rice, citrus fruits, wheat, and legumes. Southern plantation owners regularly struggled with the decision of where to export crops. While Northern markets were closer and had less onerous shipping costs, European markets generally offered higher prices.

Aside from protecting slavery, Southern politicians were most adamant about protecting their agricultural exports. For example, during the **Nullification Crisis** (1832–1833), South Carolina passed legislation to nullify the so-called "Tariff of Abominations." The crisis only ended in a compromise after Andrew Jackson vowed to send an army to enforce federal law, but South Carolina nullified the **Compromise Tariff** as a symbolic gesture.

The impact of agriculture on the Southern regional identity cannot be overstated. Southern lands were almost exclusively devoted to agricultural production, which curbed the development of major urban centers. Without alternatives, Southerners either worked in agriculture or migrated outside the region. People lived and died with each successive harvest, and they were united in opposition to anything that threatened their way of life.

Westward Expansion of Plantations

Early settlers in the Southeast had established sprawling plantations, leaving less open land than in other regions. In addition, plantation-based production methods extensively extracted nutrients from the soil, resulting in decreased agricultural output. As a result, many plantation owners sought to shift operations westward to western Georgia and Mississippi, and this type of economic production was supported by a source of cheap and coerced labor, namely, slavery. As in the Southeast, plantation owners west of the Appalachians sought to legalize and protect the institution of slavery because they felt the most comfortable brutalizing and dehumanizing Africans for cheap labor.

The legality of slavery on the western frontier represents one of the most controversial political issues in the history of American politics, requiring numerous compromises. For example, the **Missouri Compromise** of 1819 admitted Maine as a free state, Missouri as a slave state, and prohibited slavery in westward lands above the 36º 30′ parallel. Many abolitionists and Northern politicians condemned these compromises because they legitimized and safeguarded slavery. All the compromises eventually unraveled, and the issue of western slavery resulted in mass bloodshed during the run-up to the American **Civil War** (1861–1865).

Practice Quiz

1. What's the term for the ability of a ruling body to influence the actions, behavior, and attitude of a person or group of people?
   a. Politics
   b. Power
   c. Authority
   d. Legitimacy

2. Which of the following is NOT a shared characteristic sufficient to form a nation?
   a. Culture and traditions
   b. History
   c. Sovereignty
   d. Beliefs and religion

3. How did the outcome of the French and Indian War impact the life of American colonists?
   a. The colonies expanded west of the Allegheny Mountains.
   b. Great Britain imposed taxes on the colonies to pay off the British war debt.
   c. A lasting peace developed between the colonists and Native Americans.
   d. The power of self-government increased in the colonies.

Question 4 is based on the following passage:

> We hold these Truths to be self-evident: that all Men are created equal; that they are endowed by their creator with certain inalienable rights; that among these are life, liberty, and the pursuit of happiness: that to secure these rights, governments are instituted among men, deriving their just powers from the consent of the governed; that whenever any form of government becomes destructive of these ends, it is the right of the people to alter or abolish it, and to institute new government, laying its foundation on such principles, and organizing its powers in such form, as to them shall seem most likely to affect their safety and happiness.
>
> Prudence indeed will dictate that governments long established should not be changed for light and transient causes; and accordingly all experience hath shown that mankind are more disposed to suffer while evils are sufferable, than to right themselves by abolishing the forms to which they are accustomed. But when a long train of abuses and usurpations begun at a distinguished period and pursuing invariably the same object, evinces a design to reduce them under absolute despotism, it is their right, it is their duty to throw off such government, and to provide new guards for their future security

Declaration of Independence, adopted July 4, 1776

4. What is the main purpose of the excerpt?
   a. Provide a justification for revolution when the government infringes on "certain inalienable rights"
   b. Provide specific evidence of the "train of abuses"
   c. Provide an argument why "all Men are created equal"
   d. Provide an analysis of the importance of "life, liberty, and the pursuit of happiness"

Question 5 is based on the following diagram:

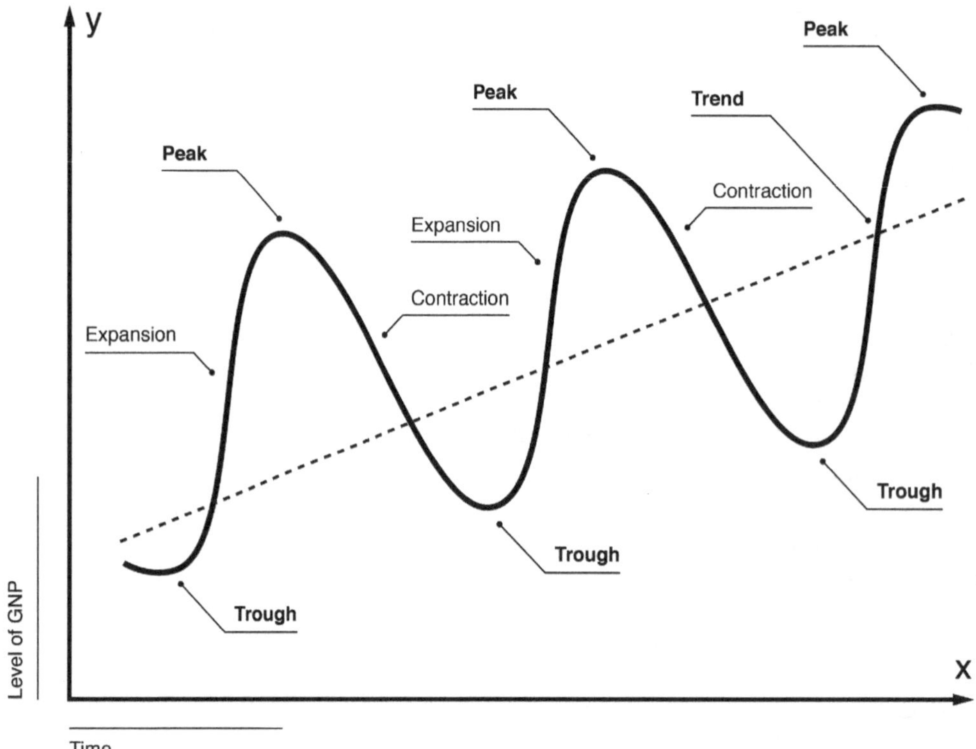

5. Which of the following phases of a business cycle occurs when there is continual growth?
   a. Expansion
   b. Peak
   c. Contraction
   d. Trough

Answer Explanations

1. B: Choice *B* is correct, as power is the ability of a ruling body to influence the actions, behavior, and attitude of a person or group of people. Choice *A* is incorrect, as politics is the process of governance typically exercised through the enactment and enforcement of laws over a community, most commonly a state. Although closely related to power, Choice *C* is incorrect, because authority refers to a political entity's justification to exercise power. Legitimacy is synonymous with authority, so Choice *D* is also incorrect.

2. C: Choice *C* is correct. There are no definitive requirements to be a nation. Rather, the nation only needs a group bound by some shared characteristic. Examples include language, culture, religion, homeland, ethnicity, and history. Choice *C* isn't a requirement to be a nation, though it is required to be a state.

3. B: Choice *B* is correct. Following the French and Indian War, the British government amassed an enormous war debt, and Great Britain imposed taxes on the colonists to generate more revenue. King George III argued that British resources defended the colonists from French and Native American forces, so the colonists should share in the expenses. The other choices are factually incorrect. The Royal Proclamation of 1763 prevented the colonies from expanding west of the Allegheny Mountains. No lasting peace ever occurred between the colonists and Native Americans. Self-government decreased in the colonies after the French and Indian War.

4. A: Choice *A* is correct. Heavily influenced by the Enlightenment, the Declaration of Independence repudiated the colonies' allegiance to Great Britain. The main purpose of the excerpt is to justify the colonists' revolutionary ambitions due to Great Britain's tyranny and the role of consent in government to protect the natural rights of citizens. Although the excerpt alludes to abuses, the purpose isn't to list specific evidence. This occurs later in the Declaration of Independence. Choices *C* and *D* are supporting evidence for the main purpose.

5. A: Choice *A* is correct. A business cycle is when the gross domestic product (GDP) moves downward and upward over a long-term growth trend, and the four phases are expansion, peak, contraction, and trough. An expansion is the only phase where employment rates and economic growth continually grow. Contraction is the opposite of expansion. The peak and trough are the extreme points on the graph.

Section 5: The Civil War Era (1844–1877)

Manifest Destiny

Westward Migration

In the mid-nineteenth century, people increasingly traveled west to pursue economic prosperity, natural resources, resources, and religious freedom.

Americans and newly arrived immigrants traveled westward where there were more economic opportunities and more land. Innovations like steamships and railways expedited travel times, but travel by caravans of covered wagons was also commonplace. The sudden influx of people and resources led to explosive urban population growth. For example, Chicago was officially established in 1833 with a population of 200, and by 1870 its population had reached nearly 300,000.

Many migrants sought to acquire and consolidate control over natural resources, with gold being the most prominent example. The **California Gold Rush** (1848–1855) attracted nearly 300,000 migrants and sped up its path to statehood. The acquisition of natural resources generated tremendous economic growth, but it devastated indigenous communities as settlers violently seized the land.

Several religious groups also traveled westward to proselytize and secure more independence. The Mormons were amongst the most organized and prolific migrant groups. **Mormonism** originated in upstate New York during the 1820s, and the movement quickly spread to the American Midwest. Following a series of conflicts in Illinois, Brigham Young led Mormon pioneers on a final migratory journey to the Utah Territory in the late 1840s.

Manifest Destiny and Expansion to the Pacific Ocean

The U.S. continued to seek out and acquire new lands, a tactic often referred to as **Manifest Destiny**. This practice led to the purchase of Alaska from Russia in 1867 and the annexation of Hawaii in 1898. The Spanish-American War in 1898 lasted just a few weeks, but helped Cuba gain its independence from Spain and helped the U.S. gain a strategic foothold in many distant locales that were formerly Spanish territories. These included Guam and the Philippines. Future president Theodore Roosevelt became a hero when his troops defeated the Spanish fleet at the Battle of San Juan Hill.

Alfred Thayer Mahan was a U.S. naval officer and historian who became famous after publishing a book titled *The Influence of Sea Power Upon History, 1600–1783* (1890). Mahan is famous for extending America's "Manifest Destiny" beyond its coasts and into the seas. Mahan believed that the future of world dominance and democratic hegemony rested upon the creation of a strong navy. He thus encouraged the United States to carry out its imperial dreams on the high seas, paving the way to the aggressive expansionist initiatives of the U.S. government in the late 1800s.

Legislation that Boosted Westward Migration

During the Civil War era, the federal government passed several laws to incentivize westward migration. During the early 1850s, Congress granted a charter for a national railway system and ordered a series of surveys to find a feasible and optimal route. After a decade of construction, the **First Transcontinental**

Railroad began its official operation in 1869. The national railroad revolutionized the American economy, particularly in facilitating the movement of goods and settlers from coast to coast.

To incentivize the settlement and economic development of western lands, the federal government passed a series of **homestead acts** during the latter half of the nineteenth century. The Donation Land Claim Act of 1850 offered large parcels of land to citizens who relocated to the Pacific Northwest. During the Civil War, President Lincoln oversaw the passage of the Homestead Act of 1862. The law provided plots of western land to citizens who promised to personally settle and develop the area. Citizens above the age of 21 were eligible to apply, including women, except for people who had waged war against the federal government. After the end of the Civil War, Congress passed additional homestead acts to enact land reform in the Southeast, plant forests, and support agriculture.

Increasing Ties with Asia

The United States sought closer ties and stronger commercial relationships with Asian nations during the latter half of the nineteenth century. The **Siamese-American Treaty of Amity and Commerce** (Roberts Treaty) was the first treaty between the United States and an Asian state. This treaty was mostly a symbolic victory to showcase American diplomacy, but it also increased commercial exchanges between the United States and Siam (Thailand). Following the Roberts Treaty, the United States attempted to develop a commercial network in China to gain access to the lucrative opium trade; however, Britain's monopoly on the Chinese market largely prevented American merchants from sustaining long-term commercial ties. During the latter half of the nineteenth century, the United States strengthened diplomatic ties to Japan, and San Francisco served as the cultural, diplomatic, and economic center for exchanges.

The United States' most successful initiative in Asia was missionary work. British missionaries had originally popularized Christianity in mainland China, and American evangelicals seized on this opportunity. While the American missionaries were not particularly successful at mass conversions, they did expand American influence in China by teaching English and introducing Western medicine. Back home, missionaries published novels and captivated audiences with stories about Chinese culture.

The Mexican–American War

The Mexican– American War

In the **Mexican-American War**, American troops won several battles although the Mexican army usually outnumbered them. The Mexican troops were poorly armed and trained, but, on the other hand, the Americans made use of their highly skilled artillery force. They eventually captured Mexico City and forced the Mexican government to sign the **Treaty of Guadalupe-Hidalgo** in 1848. The treaty recognized American control over Texas and also ceded California, Utah, Colorado, Arizona, New Mexico, and Nevada in exchange for $15 million. Tens of thousands of prospectors flooded into California when gold was discovered there in 1849. The prospectors often encroached on Native American lands, which led to further conflict. In 1854, the United States also acquired additional territories as part of the **Gadsden Purchase**. The acquisition of so much new territory sparked a debate over whether the land would be open or closed to slavery.

Governmental Conflict with Mexican Americans and American Indians

The United States' victory in the Mexican-American War (1846–1848) had a devastating effect on Mexican and indigenous culture. When the United States took control, the territory was home to approximately 75,000 Mexicans and several powerful indigenous nations, including the Apache, Navajo, and Puebloan. So the mass arrival of American settlers proved highly disruptive, especially in denying Mexican and indigenous communities the right to self-sufficiency and cultural preservation.

Although the **Treaty of Guadalupe-Hidalgo** had promised citizenship to the territories' current residents, there were significant obstacles and restrictions to citizenship. The United States refused to extend citizenship to all indigenous people, even though they'd been citizens under Mexican law. Mexicans living in the territories were offered American citizenship, but they also faced systematic discrimination. For example, California passed a series of so-called **Anti-Vagrancy Acts** to exact exorbitant taxes and implement punitive measures against Mexican and indigenous populations.

American settlers' economic activities, such as ranching and mining, frequently triggered conflicts due to settlers encroaching on indigenous nations' ancestral lands. Therefore, the United States military regularly intervened in the region. For example, the American military built permanent forts and coerced indigenous populations into reservations during the **Apache Wars** (1849–1886).

The Compromise of 1850

The Mexican Cession and Slavery

President John Tyler initiated an annexation bill in March 1845, which President James K. Polk officially signed in December 1845. The Republic of Texas officially revoked its sovereignty, lawfully agreeing to become the 28th state of the Union in February 1846. The Mexican-American War (1846-1848), in many ways, was a direct response to President Polk's annexation of Texas. The war ended in the Treaty of Guadalupe-Hidalgo, which resulted in a **Mexican Cession** that officially brought parts of Texas, New Mexico, Arizona, and California within the territory of the United States. One social impact of U.S. annexation and the Mexican-American War was increased political tensions over the role of slavery, and whether it was to be permitted, in new territories.

Attempts to Resolve the Issue of Slavery in the Territories

As mentioned, the **Compromise of 1850** admitted California as a free state and ended the slave trade, but not slavery itself, in Washington D.C., in order to please Northern politicians. In return, Southern politicians were able to pass a stronger fugitive slave law and demanded that New Mexico and Utah be allowed to vote on whether or not slavery would be permitted in their state constitutions. This introduced the idea of popular sovereignty where the residents of each new territory, and not the federal government, could decide whether or not they would become a slave state or a free state. This essentially negated the **Missouri Compromise** of 1820. The enhanced fugitive slave law also angered many Northerners, because it empowered federal marshals to deputize anyone, even residents of a free state, and force them to help recapture escaped slaves. Anyone who refused would be subject to a $1,000 fine (equivalent to more than $28,000 in 2015).

The debate over slavery erupted again only a few years later when the territories of Kansas and Nebraska were created in 1854. The application of popular sovereignty meant that pro- and anti-slavery settlers flooded into these two territories to ensure that their faction would have a majority when it came time to vote on the state constitution. Tension between pro- and anti-slavery forces in Kansas led to an armed conflict known as "**Bleeding Kansas**."

John Brown was a militant abolitionist who fought in "Bleeding Kansas" and murdered five pro-slavery settlers there in 1856. He returned to the eastern United States and attacked the federal arsenal at Harper's Ferry, Virginia, in 1859. He hoped to seize the weapons there and launch a slave rebellion, but federal troops killed or captured most of Brown's accomplices and Brown was executed. The attack terrified Southerners and reflected the increasing hostility between North and South.

The sectional differences that emerged in the last several decades culminated in the presidential election of 1860. Abraham Lincoln led the new Republican Party, which opposed slavery on moral and economic grounds. The question of how best to expand slavery into new territories split the Democratic Party into two different factions that each nominated a presidential candidate. A fourth candidate also ran on a platform of preserving the union by trying to ignore the slavery controversy.

Perhaps one of the strongest examples of unsuccessful attempts by abolitionists and anti-slavery leaders is the **Dred Scott** decision. In this 1857 case, the Supreme Court ruled that despite the fact that Dred Scott, who had been born into slavery but had lived with his master for a period of time in a "free" territory, was not a free man, but rather still the property of his master. Moreover, the Supreme Court essentially nullified the Missouri Compromise, stating that it was unconstitutional because it denied citizens of their property (as slaves were considered property).

Sectional Conflict: Regional Differences

Irish and German Immigration

Soaring immigration rates led to the development of ethnic communities across the United States. Between 1844 and 1877, German and Irish migrants were the largest migrant group, marking the first time Britain didn't account for the overwhelming majority of immigrants. German immigrants primarily came to the United States due to the economic and political turmoil in Germany prior to its unification in 1871. The **Great Famine** (1845–1849) prompted millions of Irish people to emigrate to the United States during the latter half of the nineteenth century and the early twentieth century.

German and Irish immigrants typically arrived in port cities on the Atlantic seaboard. Most of these immigrants initially settled in cities due to the superior economic opportunities on offer in urban and industrial centers like New York City and Boston. Urban ethnic communities helped assimilate newly arrived immigrants. In addition, the communities successfully preserved cultural traditions, including language, religious practices, and food. For example, German immigrants are widely credited with introducing kindergartens, Christmas trees, hamburgers, and hot dogs to the United States. When Northeastern urban environments became more crowded and expensive, immigrant communities often ventured westward, settling in the developing cities and establishing exclusive settlements to better protect their culture and history.

The Anti-Catholic Nativist Movement

Although Catholics were a minority during the colonial period of American history, Catholicism has become the largest religious denomination in the United States. Many colonial governments actually banned Catholicism, but the American Revolution brought more toleration. However, anti-Catholic sentiment renewed in the 1800s as immigrants from Ireland and Germany, many of whom were

Catholic, arrived in ever-increasing numbers. The arrival of Italian immigrants in the late 1800s and early 1900s also increased Protestant-Catholic tension in America. Many Americans feared that Catholic immigrants would be more loyal to Pope than they would be to the Constitution. This led to the creation of the **Know-Nothings** who sought to limit immigration and physically attacked Catholics. Anti-Catholic sentiment remained an issue even until the presidential election of 1960 when John F. Kennedy, a Catholic, won the Democratic nomination. Kennedy helped allay fears by promising to respect the separation of church and state. Since then, anti-Catholicism has largely disappeared.

The Free-Soil Movement

Many Northerners didn't view slavery as immoral; instead, they objected to the expansion of slavery into western territories because it suppressed the wages of white migrants, thus undermining the free-labor market. After President James K. Polk annexed Texas in 1845 and prepared to declare war on Mexico, Northern politicians rushed to pass a proposal known as the **Wilmot Proviso**, which would've outlawed slavery in all of the territory acquired in the upcoming conflict. Southerners shot down the Wilmot Proviso in the Senate, but Northern opposition to slavery's expansion triggered the formation of the **Free Soil Party** during the 1848 presidential election.

The Free Soil Party garnered significant support across most Northern states, especially in New England. By the late 1840s, manufacturing dominated the Northern economy, so there was little fear of economic fallout if slavery declined. Significant amounts of the working poor also hoped to pursue economic opportunities in Western territories, so they had a vested interest in preventing slavery from undermining the free-labor market. However, the Free Soil Party's cautious approach to abolitionism led to its dissolution in the 1850s. Following the Compromise of 1850 and a series of bloody territorial conflicts, the **free-soil movement** merged with the newly formed Republican Party, which more strongly denounced slavery in the United States.

Anti-Slavery Efforts by African Americans and White Abolitionists

African Americans and abolitionists resisted slavery in a variety of ways. Frederick Douglass and William Lloyd Garrison led the charge in building anti-slavery coalitions and spreading awareness about slavery's deep-rooted immorality. Anti-slavery activists often leveraged the extensive influence and reach of the American publishing industry. For example, Harriet Beecher Stowe's *Uncle Tom's Cabin* was the bestselling novel in the nineteenth century, only trailing the Bible in terms of total publication. While these moral arguments carried the Republican Party into national prominence, many anti-slavery activists pursued more direct action.

Abolitionists tirelessly worked to expand the **Underground Railroad**—a series of secretive networks across the United States—in defiance of federal Fugitive Slave Acts. Estimates vary but it's likely as many as 100,000 slaves escaped to Canada during the nineteenth century. Other direct actions were more controversial. Following the enactment of the **Kansas-Nebraska Act** of 1854, slave owners and slave-activists raced into Kansas, sparking a mini-civil war known as "Bleeding Kansas" (1854–1861). One abolitionist leader, John Brown, left the fighting in Kansas to organize a slave revolt in Virginia. Brown attempted to seize a federal weapons depot at Harpers Ferry prior to the planned revolt, but the plot was foiled.

Slavery Supporters

Slavery's supporters raised racial, moral, and legal arguments to defend its continuation. Racial arguments justified the enslavement of Africans based on beliefs about white supremacy. Generally speaking, slave owners believed might made right; so they characterized the enslavement of Africans as an expression of the natural order. White supremacy was also closely tied to moral arguments in claiming that slavery actually benefited Africans. Devout Christians were the most likely to adopt moral arguments because they genuinely believed the gift of eternal salvation outweighed the burden of enslavement. Furthermore, many plantation owners portrayed slavery as a social good since the institution boosted economic output and stabilized societal power structures.

While racial and moral arguments were commonly asserted to gain public support for slavery, legal arguments ensured that slavery would be protected from government interference. According to slave owners, the United States Constitution's references to slavery without expressing any reservations or limitations, except for a nominal compromise over the international slave trade, were conclusive proof of slavery's legality. In addition, slave owners relentlessly cited the Tenth Amendment to classify slavery as one of the rights reserved to the states. Although many Southerners sincerely believed in federalism, arguments about states' rights were almost always connected to slavery.

Failure of Compromise

The End of the Second Party System

During the 1850s, the **Second Party System** collapsed due to a host of intensely controversial issues, including anti-immigration nativism and controversies over slavery.

Nativism surged in the 1840s in response to rapidly rising rates of immigration, particularly in Northern cities. Nativists opposed all immigration, but they held a special disdain for Irish Catholics who were alleged to be part of a papal plot to overthrow the United States. When the Whigs and Democrats failed to limit immigration, nativists abandoned ship and formed their own political party, the **Know Nothings**. Although the Know Nothings never achieved mainstream political success, they severely undermined the Whigs and Democrats in Northern cities during the mid-1850s.

Slavery drove a stake through the heart of the Second Party System. To appease Southern voters and remain a viable national political party, the Whigs refused to meaningfully push back against slavery. So when the Free Soil Party merged with the more vigorously anti-slavery Republican Party, the Whigs lost nearly all their Northern support. In response to the rise of the Republicans (primarily in the North), Southerners flocked to the Democrats. By the late 1850s, the Republicans and Democrats functioned as regionally dominant parties, with the issue of slavery deciding where citizens stood politically.

Election of 1860 and Secession

Lincoln's Election and Southern Secession

As mentioned, the sectional differences that emerged culminated in the presidential election of 1860. Abraham Lincoln led the new **Republican Party**, which opposed slavery on moral and economic grounds. This party was particularly strong and represented in the North. The question of how best to expand slavery into new territories split the Democratic Party into two different factions that each nominated a presidential candidate. A fourth candidate also ran on a platform of preserving the union by trying to ignore the slavery controversy.

Lincoln found little support outside of the North; in fact, he did not earn any Southern electoral votes. However, Lincoln managed to win the White House since the Democratic Party was divided. Southern states felt threatened by Lincoln's anti-slavery stance and feared he would abolish slavery throughout the country. South Carolina was the first Southern state to secede from the Union and ten more eventually followed. Lincoln declared that the Union could not be dissolved and swore to defend federal installations. The **Civil War** began when Confederate troops fired on **Fort Sumter** in Charleston in 1861.

Military Conflict in the Civil War

Societal Mobilization and Opposition to the Civil War

The Union and the Confederacy both quickly adopted a total war military strategy during the American **Civil War** (1861–1865). Total war involved mass mobilization of economic and societal resources for military purposes. The Union and the Confederacy both instituted military drafts after a year of fighting discouraged volunteerism. Along with a draft, the Union granted immigrants' citizenship if they joined the military. As in the world wars, women achieved significant socioeconomic gains due to the wartime reduction in the workforce.

Mounting military costs eventually forced the Union and the Confederacy to alter economic policies. Both sides issued paper money backed by government credit rather than precious metals. Governments also regularly explicitly ordered or tacitly permitted the seizure of food, manufactured goods, and railway systems to support the war effort.

The Union and the Confederacy each faced considerable domestic resistance to the war. In the early stages of the conflict, President Lincoln suspended some civil liberties in Baltimore to quell rioting that threatened the capital. Many Northern cities also experienced violent draft riots. For example, President Lincoln diverted forces from the **Battle of Gettysburg** (1863) to suppress draft riots in New York City. Confederate leaders similarly moved to suppress slave insurrection that would have undermined agricultural production.

The Union Eventually Succeeds

The **First Battle of Bull Run** (also known as the **First Battle of Manassas**) in 1861 was the first major infantry engagement of the Civil War. Both the Northern and Southern troops were inexperienced and although they had equal numbers, the Confederates emerged victorious. Many had thought the war would be short, but it continued for another four years.

The Union navy imposed a blockade on the Confederacy and captured the port of New Orleans in 1862. The Union navy was much stronger than the Confederate fleet and prevented the Southern states from selling cotton to foreign countries or buying weapons.

In 1862, Union forces thwarted a Confederate invasion of Maryland at the Battle of Antietam. This engagement was the single bloodiest day of the war and more than 23,000 men on both sides were killed or wounded. Union troops forced the Confederates to retreat, and that gave Lincoln the political capital he needed to issue the **Emancipation Proclamation** in 1863. This declaration did not abolish slavery, but it did free slaves in Southern territory. It also allowed African Americans to join the Union navy and about 200,000 did so. The 54th Massachusetts Infantry was a famous unit of African American soldiers who led an assault on Fort Wagner in South Carolina in 1863. Although the attack failed, the 54th Massachusetts witnessed African American troops fighting bravely under fire.

The **Siege of Vicksburg** in 1863 was a major Union victory because they gained control of the Mississippi River and cut the Confederacy in half. This made it difficult the Confederacy to move troops around and communicate with their forces. Grant commanded the Northern forces in the siege and eventually became the Union army's top general.

The **Battle of Gettysburg** in 1863 marked the turning point of the Civil War. General **Robert E. Lee** led Confederate troops into Pennsylvania, but in three days of heavy fighting, the Union army forced them to retreat. The victory bolstered Northern morale and weakened Southern resolve. Never again would Confederate forces threaten Northern territory.

In 1864, Union general **William T. Sherman** captured Atlanta and then marched more than 200 miles to Savannah. Along the way, he destroyed anything that could support the Southern war effort, such as railroads and cotton mills. At this point, the Southern economy was beginning to collapse. The North had more manpower than the South and could afford to sustain more casualties. The North also had more industrial capacity to produce weapons and supplies and more railroads to transport men and equipment.

Eventually, Robert E. Lee surrendered to Ulysses S. Grant at Appomattox, Virginia, on April 9, 1865. Five days later, **John Wilkes Booth** assassinated Lincoln in Washington D.C. Vice President **Andrew Johnson**, a Democrat, succeeded him and soon came into conflict with Republicans in Congress about how to reintegrate Southern states into the nation. This process was known as **Reconstruction** and lasted from 1865 to 1877.

Government Policies During the Civil War

The Emancipation Proclamation's Role in the War

Although most Union supporters and President Lincoln began the Civil War with the goal of preserving the Union and preventing Southern Secession, this changed somewhat over the first couple of years. The **Emancipation Proclamation** represents the turning point in Lincoln's primary purpose of the Civil War, shifting it to the goal of abolishing slavery. Although the Emancipation did not abolish slavery, it did free slaves in Southern territory, and allowed African Americans to join the Union navy. This was crucial in the Union's ultimate triumph in the war because the 200,000 African Americans (many of whom were freed slaves from southern plantations) helped bolster the Union's forces and undermine the Confederacy.

The Gettysburg Address

Abraham Lincoln was inarguably one of the greatest politicians in American history in terms of how he nimbly balanced his support for reunification and arguments about the immorality of slavery.

Immediately upon the Southern states' secession, Lincoln chose to frame the conflict as a matter of national unity. Most historians believe Lincoln personally found slavery to be an abhorrent stain on the nation's character, but he publicly showed a willingness to negotiate with the Southern slave states to avoid a civil war. When peace failed, Lincoln moved quickly to secure the support of slave-owning border states—Delaware, Kentucky, Maryland, and Missouri—within the Union to avoid a military catastrophe. For example, if the Union lost Maryland, it would've needed to withdraw from Washington D.C. However, in private communications, Lincoln regularly placed pressure on the border states to abolish slavery on moral grounds.

Lincoln was a master of using strategic proclamations and speeches to secure his goals. Following a brutal bloodbath at the Battle of Antietam, Lincoln issued the Emancipation Proclamation (1863) to free the Confederacy's slaves as a wartime measure. Later that same year, Lincoln delivered the famously succinct **Gettysburg Address** to reaffirm the nation's commitment to reunification and moral ideals.

Reconstruction

Ideas of Citizenship and Federal and State Government Relationships

The **Reconstruction Era** (1865–1877) transformed the relationship between the federal government, states, and citizens. Despite the moderating forces within President Andrew Johnson's administration, the Radical Republicans successfully forced the federal government to take some unprecedented action.

Radical Republicans won the debate over citizenship for former slaves and people of color. After ratifying the Thirteenth Amendment to abolish slavery, they spearheaded the passage of the Fourteenth and Fifteenth amendments to guarantee due process under the law and universal male suffrage regardless of "race, color, or previous condition of servitude." Other minority groups, such as Chinese and Mexican immigrants, celebrated the Reconstruction amendments for the progress they made toward racial equality; however, the women's rights movement was much more divided. The Fourteenth Amendment added "male" to the US Constitution for the first time, and many suffragettes believed the use of gendered terminology would impede the fight for women's rights. The Fifteenth Amendment proved even more controversial because it only applied to men.

Federal forces conducted a large-scale occupation of states' territory for the first time in American history. This occupation was not strictly a punitive measure; the goal was to enforce the Reconstruction amendments in the former Confederate states. Consequently, African Americans gained new commercial opportunities and were elected to myriad public offices for the first time. However, white Southerners deeply resented this occupation and intervention, decrying it as yet another act of Northern aggression. Northern support for Reconstruction faded in the mid-1870s as white Southerners mounted more violent resistance, and President Rutherford B. Hayes officially withdrew federal forces in 1877. Immediately afterward, Southern states passed Jim Crow laws to legalize racial segregation and disenfranchisement, which obstructed the Reconstruction amendments' enforcement for nearly a century.

The Thirteenth, Fourteenth, and Fifteenth Amendments

The **Thirteenth Amendment** abolished slavery and involuntary servitude, except as punishment for a crime. The issue of slavery was no longer in the states' hands. Although the Emancipation Proclamation freed slaves in the Confederacy, the status of former slaves remained uncertain as the war neared its conclusion. Many Northerners did not hold strong views on slavery, but most wanted to punish the South and resolve the primary cause of the bloody Civil War. The Northern states all immediately ratified the amendment, and in December 1865, enough reconstructed Southern states ratified the amendment for it to be adopted into law.

The **Fourteenth Amendment** prohibited states from depriving life, liberty, or property without due process and from violating equal protection based on race, color, or previous condition of servitude. Now, all persons born or naturalized in the United States were considered legal citizens. Although revolutionary for the theoretical rights of all American citizens, newly freed or otherwise, the Fourteenth Amendment did not provide actual federally enforced equal protection until the **Civil Rights Act** of 1964.

The **Fifteenth Amendment** prohibits the government from denying a citizen the right to vote for reasons of race, color, or previous condition of servitude. Adopted in 1870, the last of the **Reconstruction Amendments**, the Fifteenth Amendment sought to protect newly freed slaves' right to vote. As discussed below, most states interpreted the amendment to only apply to male suffrage. In addition, Southern states passed a series of laws to systematically disenfranchise African Americans, like poll taxes, literacy tests, and residency rules. The use of violence and intimidation for political purpose was also common. Meaningful change did not occur until the Civil Rights Movement, nearly one hundred years later. In 1964, the **Twenty-Fourth Amendment** prohibited the states and federal government from charging a poll tax or fee to vote. Later, the **Voting Rights Act** of 1965 empowered the federal government to enforce the Fifteenth Amendment on the states for the first time.

The Women's Rights Movement

Debate over the Fourteenth and Fifteenth amendments sharply divided the women's rights movement. Suffragettes had strongly supported abolitionism to generate intersectional solidarity among oppressed Americans, and many women's rights leaders felt abandoned by the Reconstruction amendments' failure to address gender inequality.

Tensions within the women's rights movement reached a boiling point at the **American Equal Rights Association** (AERA) annual meeting in 1869, which was held during the run-up to the ratification of the Fifteenth Amendment. Two of the movement's preeminent leaders, Susan B. Anthony and Elizabeth Cady Stanton, stridently opposed this amendment, and Anthony went so far as to tell Frederick Douglass that white women were currently more oppressed than African Americans. In contrast, the majority of attendees and some important leaders, such as Lucy Stone and Julia Ward Howe, viewed the enfranchisement of African Americans as a positive step toward universal suffrage.

The AERA collapsed shortly after this meeting, and two competing organizations took its place. Anthony and Stanton formed the National Woman Suffrage Association, and Stone and Howe established the American Woman Suffrage Association. The organizations' relationship remained contentious until the formation of the National American Woman Suffrage Association in 1890.

Radical Republicans

Johnson opposed equal rights for African Americans and pardoned many Confederate leaders. However, many Congressional Republicans wanted to harshly punish Southerners for their attempts to secede from the Union. They were known as **Radical Republicans** because they also wanted to give former slaves equal rights.

Johnson vetoed bills that were designed to protect the rights of freed slaves, but Congress overrode his vetoes. This led to increasing conflict between Johnson and Congress, which eventually caused Radical Republicans to impeach him. Although Johnson was acquitted in 1868, he had very little power, and Radical Republicans took control of the Reconstruction process.

Republicans passed three important constitutional amendments as part of the Reconstruction process. The 13th amendment was ratified in 1865, and it abolished slavery throughout the country. The 14th Amendment was ratified in 1868 and gave equal rights to all citizens. The 15th Amendment was ratified in 1870 and specifically granted all men the right to vote regardless of race.

Failure of Reconstruction

Sharecropping

Policies enacted and implemented during the Reconstruction era failed to achieve long-term, meaningful land reform. While the Radical Republicans did greatly expand newly freed slaves' political rights and protections through the Reconstruction Amendments, economic measures missed the mark. At the tail end of the American Civil War, Union General **Tecumseh Sherman** had implemented orders to seize plantations and provide every former slave with "forty acres and a mule." However, President Andrew Johnson reversed Sherman's orders. This reversal allowed wealthy plantation owners to retain the vast majority of their land despite the material support they had provided to the traitorous Confederacy.

Once Reconstruction drew to a close, Southern state houses immediately passed legislation to obstruct African Americans and other people of color from exercising political rights as granted under federal law. The federal government refused to intervene, and disenfranchisement only compounded the already minimal economic opportunities available to African Americans.

Given the lack of open land and economic opportunity, poor whites and Africans Americans were forced into **sharecropping**, meaning they farmed small plots of land in exchange for a small portion of the harvest—the rest went to the landowner. Some sharecroppers lived on what little they could raise in subsistence farming, and some went into debt to their landlords so they could buy food and other goods. Additionally, sharecropping was incredibly exploitative since agricultural outputs steadily declined due to rapid soil degradation.

The Basis of Civil Rights in the Twentieth Century

After the much-disputed election of 1876, the Democrats offered to let the Republicans have the White House if they agreed to end Reconstruction. After the Republicans agreed, federal troops were withdrawn and African Americans in the South were subjected to discrimination until the Civil Rights movement of the 1960s. Scholars often consider the Reconstruction era the beginning of **Jim Crow** and a transition into a new form of "institutionalized racism" that still pervades much of modern U.S. society.

Practice Quiz

1. What was a consequence of the industrialization that followed the Civil War?
   a. Decreased immigration
   b. Increased urbanization
   c. Decreased socioeconomic inequality
   d. Increased rights for workers

2. Which of these is NOT a protection within the Bill of Rights?
   a. Right to due process
   b. Freedom of speech
   c. Right to privacy
   d. Right to a speedy and fair trial

3. The establishment clause deals with which of the following?
   a. The relationship between government and labor unions
   b. The relationship between government officials and lobbyists
   c. The relationship between government and the creation of new federal courts
   d. The relationship between government and religion

4. The Supreme Court has ruled that the federal government may limit a certain type of speech without violation of the First Amendment. What is an example of that type of speech?
   a. Students wearing black arm bands to protest a war
   b. A person writes a newspaper article using falsified quotes to attack a rival's character
   c. A student giving a speech outside of Congress protesting the passing of a bill that cuts school funding
   d. A citizen writes up a flier about the dangers of the government's new hunting regulations and hangs them up all over town

Question 5 is based on the following passage:

> Now, therefore I, Abraham Lincoln, President of the United States, by virtue of the power in me vested as Commander-in-Chief, of the Army and Navy of the United States in time of actual armed rebellion against the authority and government of the United States, and as a fit and necessary war measure for suppressing said rebellion...
>
> And by virtue of the power, and for the purpose aforesaid, I do order and declare that all persons held as slaves within said designated States, and parts of States, are, and henceforward shall be free; and that the Executive government of the United States, including the military and naval authorities thereof, will recognize and maintain the freedom of said persons.

President Abraham Lincoln, Emancipation Proclamation, January 1, 1863

5. How does President Lincoln justify freeing the slaves in designated areas of the South?
   a. Emancipation is necessary since slavery is evil.
   b. Emancipation is necessary to boost the morale of the North.
   c. Emancipation is necessary to punish for the South seceding from the Union.
   d. Emancipation is necessary to strengthen the war effort of the North.

Answer Explanations

1. B: Choice *B* is correct. Industrialization directly caused an increase in urbanization. Factories were located near cities to draw upon a large pool of potential employees. Between 1860 and 1890, the urbanization rate increased from about 20 percent to 35 percent. The other three choices are factually incorrect. Immigration increased during industrialization, as immigrants flooded into America to search for work. Socioeconomic problems plagued the period due to the unequal distribution of wealth and the social ills caused by rapid urbanization. Labor unrest was common as unions advocated for workers' rights and organized national strikes.

2. C: The Bill of Rights grants protections for almost all conceivable parts of life. The Framers were quite adamant that freedom was the ultimate right that the federal government could give to its people, and so they worked hard to ensure that that was exactly what the federal government gave them. Due process is one of those key pieces, guaranteeing every American gets equal protections under the law. Freedom of speech grants this protection too, as one of the more well-known guarantees of the Constitution. The right to a fair and speedy trial is also one of those crucial protections. Right to privacy, however, is not considered one of these protections. While some have recently argued that it is implied, this protection is not explicitly given in the Bill of Rights.

3. D: The term “establishment clause” refers to the part of the First Amendment that applies to freedom of religion. It says: “Congress shall make no law respecting an establishment of religion.”

4. B: Our first choice is the subject of another famous case. This one, students wearing bands to protest a war, saw the students winning their case against their school district, so this speech is definitely not restricted. Choice *C* is also incorrect, as you can protest whatever you want as long as it is peaceful and approved. Choice *D* is another action that's acceptable, as fliers are okay as long as you are not impeding a war effort. Choice *B*, however, is libel, and is outlawed as the type of speech that can be restricted and is even punishable by law.

5. D: Choice *D* is correct. President Lincoln issued the Emancipation Proclamation to free the slaves in the Confederacy, allowing the institution to continue in states and territories that didn't secede. The excerpt justifies the decision as a "fit and necessary war measure for suppressing said rebellion." Therefore, per the excerpt, emancipation was necessary to strengthen the war effort for the North. Choice *C* is the second-best answer, but the excerpt supports the contention that emancipation was part of an active war effort, rather than merely a punishment. Nothing in the excerpt describes the evil of slavery or the effect of emancipation on morale in the North.

Section 6: Reconstruction (1865–1889)

Westward Expansion: Economic Development

Mechanization Improvements

Technological innovations dramatically increased agricultural production, which resulted in steep reductions in food prices. Several American inventors, including the famed **Cyrus McCormick**, developed mechanized and steam-powered reaping, threshing, and winnowing equipment during the mid-nineteenth century. These inventions represented a seismic jump in terms of efficiency and agricultural production. During the latter half of the nineteenth century, northern factories began mass producing and marketing agricultural machines. Mechanization again increased at the end of the nineteenth century as tractors began to replace horses and mules in the operation of agricultural machines.

Mechanization caused an exponential increase in the size of harvests. Combine harvesters were especially efficient because they combined reaping, threshing, and winnowing operations for a number of essential food products, including corn, oats, soybeans, and wheat. As the supply of food rapidly expanded in the United States, food prices dropped to historical lows. This resolved some of the societal issues related to industrialization and urbanization; namely, that the working poor struggled to afford food, resulting in inferior nutritional consumption as compared to subsistence farmers. Overall, the agricultural boom strengthened food security for working-class households, and improved nutritional outcomes were evident based on the corresponding increase in Americans' average height.

Farmers' Cooperative Organizations

During the latter half of the nineteenth century, farmers sought to overcome challenges by entering cooperative organizations and organizing themselves politically.

Local collectives at the township and county level were commonplace, and these groups often entered into coalitions at the regional and national level. Most generally, cooperative organizations opposed the creeping power of the federal government and railroads. Farmers especially objected to the construction of transcontinental railroads and homestead acts due to the resulting reductions in land prices. Furthermore, cooperative organizations strengthened farmers' bargaining position vis-à-vis railroads and the powerful trusts spurring the consolidation of agricultural markets.

Cooperative agreements specialized in a variety of services, and examples include services related to the splitting of marketing and production costs, negotiating collective prices for transportation and market access, sharing expensive agricultural tools, and building political coalitions. One of the most important national cooperative organizations was the **Farmers Alliance**, an umbrella political advocacy group consisting of several high-profile cooperative organizations, including the National Farmers' Alliance and Industrial Union (Southern white farmers), Colored Farmers' National Alliance and Cooperative Union (Southern black farmers), and the National Farmers' Alliance (Midwestern farmers). The Farmers Alliance would later fuel the rise of the **Populist Party** (1892–1909).

New Markets in North America

After the end of the Civil War, America experienced a period of intense industrialization, immigration, and urbanization, and all three trends were interrelated. The process of industrialization had begun before the Civil War but expanded into more sectors of the economy in the later part of the century. This era is often called the **Second Industrial Revolution** and included growth in the chemical, petroleum, iron, steel, and telecommunications industries, which were fueled by government subsidies. For example, the Bessemer process made it much easier to produce high quality steel by removing impurities during the smelting process.

Causes of Economic Growth

Three large-scale trends contributed to an economic boom and development of new commercial centers during the late nineteenth century. First, the completion of the **First Transcontinental Railroad** (1869) and the further development of interconnected regional railway networks significantly reduced the costs of traveling west. Second, mineral resources triggered mass migrations to boomtowns. Gold generally attracted the largest crowds (in "gold rushes"), and industrial demands boosted the commercial value of other minerals, including copper, lead, silver, and zinc. Third, government policies facilitated and further incentivized westward expansion, such as homestead acts, commercial subsidies, and the unwavering support of the United States military in conflicts with American Indians over resources.

The wholesale acquisition of Western resources fueled an economic boom like few others in history. Midwestern cities experienced exponential population growth, rivaling and surpassing Northeastern metropolitan areas. By 1900, Chicago was the second most populous city in the United States, and more than half of America's top 25 largest cities were located in the Midwest and West. More localized centers of commerce also developed all throughout the continental United States. Sudden influxes of migrants turned rural areas into boomtowns, and skyrocketing economic growth incentivized the construction of large-scale housing, roadways, and local industries.

Westward Expansion: Social and Cultural Development

Migrating West for Opportunities

Floods of migrants traveled West to pursue greater independence, self-sufficiency, and economic opportunities after the American Civil War. Many migrants arrived seeking religious freedom, such as the Mormons who settled in Utah. Likewise, many Americans simply wanted to be landowners and establish livelihoods where they weren't entirely dependent on the whims of employers or markets to survive.

Many migrants sought fabulous riches working for the railroads and mines. The construction of railroads increased land values and provided a steady stream of employment opportunities. Migrant miners hoped to literally strike gold, but most eventually found work in the local economy as it developed in the surrounding area. Some boomtowns quickly went bust, while others continued to thrive even after the initial rush. For example, successive gold rushes led to San Francisco's becoming one of the top ten most populous American cities by the late 1890s.

Rural areas also experienced substantial population growth during the late nineteenth century. Family farms profited from their proximity to boomtowns and the railway networks that provided access to a national marketplace. Furthermore, ranching became a major industry as settlers seized control over sufficiently large areas of land where livestock could freely roam.

Competition for Land and Resources in the West

As waves of white settlers migrated westward in pursuit of economic prosperity, the region's long-established societies faced incredible cultural, economic, military, and political pressure. Mexican Americans were largely denied the right to consolidate control over valuable natural resources. Furthermore, when Mexican Americans attempted to assimilate, they suffered systematic discrimination. In effect, Western states' **Anti-Vagrancy laws** functioned as Jim Crow laws did in the New South.

American Indians similarly struggled to survive the onslaught of settlers, who were backed by a federal government that did everything in its power to deny American Indians' critical resources. For example, the United States military routinely ordered the slaughter of bison herds in order to drive American Indians away from valuable land. Unsurprisingly, military conflicts regularly erupted when white settlers seized indigenous lands.

The **Great Sioux War** of 1876–1877 was one of the last major armed conflicts in the West. A gold rush in the Dakota Black Hills triggered this conflict, and **Crazy Horse** initially led the Lakota and Sioux forces to a decisive victory over the infamous **Colonel Custer** at the **Battle of Little Big Horn**. However, like many of these conflicts, the Great Sioux War ended with enormous human suffering when federal troops massacred civilians at the Wounded Knee reservation.

Violated Treaties with American Indians

The United States repeatedly violated treaties with American Indians throughout the nineteenth century.

Prior to 1871, interactions between the federal government and American Indian tribes consistently followed the same pattern. First, white settlers would infringe on American Indians' historical territory. Second, a military conflict would ensue in which the federal government ultimately intervened on behalf of the settlers. Third, the federal government would sign a treaty with a specific American Indian tribe to acquire ownership of conquered territory and/or establish terms for peaceful relations. Fourth, white settlers would violate the terms of the agreement, triggering the beginning of another cycle.

The **Indian Appropriation Act** of 1871 went a step further than previous policies. According to this law, the United States unilaterally declared that tribes didn't qualify as foreign nations, meaning the federal government would no longer sign treaties of any kind with American Indian tribes. While the Indian Appropriation Act did have a provision to preserve preexisting treaties, meaningful enforcement was nonexistent. The United States then proceeded to pass a variety of laws to more fully deny tribal sovereignty. Most infamously, the **Dawes Act** (1887) seized approximately 93 million acres of American Indian land and then parceled it out to white settlers.

Assimilation v. Preservation of American Indians' Identity

The assimilation of American Indians was a longstanding policy ambition for the United States, dating back to the Washington administration. Federal policymakers believed American Indian culture would find its place in the American melting pot in the same way as immigrants' cultures had. During the late nineteenth century, the federal government took a variety of aggressive actions to Americanize and assimilate American Indians. Most infamously, the Department of the Interior enforced the **Code of**

Indian Offenses (1883) to prohibit any indigenous cultural practice that the federal government deemed an obstacle to assimilation.

Despite federal attempts at forced Americanization, indigenous populations resisted and actively sought to preserve their way of life. Many American Indians took up arms to defend their homeland from hordes of white settlers, and even when forced onto reservations, American Indians sought to become economically self-sufficient. Oftentimes, American Indians attempted to create a self-sufficient economy on the reservation to minimize their dependence on and interactions with the United States.

American Indian leaders also pressed legal challenges against the federal government, and when the Supreme Court rejected their claims, many tribes bypassed federal prohibitions on indigenous cultural practices with many historians drawing comparisons to how slaves resisted white supremacy and preserved traditions in private wherever possible.

The "New South"

The "New South" Economy

Following the Reconstruction era, the Southern economy underwent a modest industrialization period. The abolition of slavery threatened the Southern plantation-based economic system, and some Southern leaders believed the region needed to model itself after the North to sustain economic growth. As a result, some Southern politicians envisioned a **New South** based on urbanization and industrialization. The New South had some notable successes. For example, modernization programs in Atlanta featured investments in higher education and a railway transportation system, and by 1880, Atlanta overtook Savannah as Georgia's largest city by population. However, much remained the same in the New South.

Almost immediately after President Rutherford B. Hayes withdrew the remaining federal forces from the South in 1877, Southern states rushed to enact **Jim Crow laws**. These laws functioned as a racial caste system, denying African Americans' rights and lending support to white supremacy.

Faced with an oppressive political system and minimal economic opportunities, African Americans were forced into sharecropping and tenant farming. This exploitative system undercut the New South's progressive vision since sharecropping simply replaced slavery as the dominant labor system. While African Americans enjoyed more personal freedom as sharecroppers than they had as slaves, sharecropping sustained the hierarchical dominance of wealthy white landowners.

Plessy v. Ferguson

Although the Declaration of Independence declared "all men are created equal," blacks, women, and other minorities struggled for more than a century to make this dream a reality. The U.S. Constitution legalized slavery, and it was not abolished until the 13th Amendment was ratified in 1865. The 14th Amendment, ratified in 1868, granted African Americans citizenship, and the 15th Amendment, ratified in 1870, explicitly granted them the right to vote. However, white Southerners passed laws, known as the Jim Crow system, that prevented blacks from exercising their rights and, when that failed, they relied on violence and intimidation to oppress African Americans. For example, many Southern states required voters to pass literacy tests and used them to prevent blacks from casting a ballot. Whites were either exempt from the test or were held to much lower standards. Blacks who protested their oppression could be assaulted and even killed with impunity. In the 1896 decision **Plessy v. Ferguson**, the U.S. Supreme Court ruled that "separate but equal" schools for white and black students were permissible. In reality, black schools were almost always inferior to white schools. Thus, this ruling essentially marked the end of the Reconstruction Era political gains for African Americans.

Technological Innovation

Increasing the Production of Goods

Five factors contributed to the rapid acceleration of industrialization after the American Civil War.

First, technological innovation continued to progress throughout the latter half of the nineteenth century. Along with the further advancement of interchangeable parts and complex assembly lines, important innovations occurred in steam power, glass making chemical manufacturing, and transportation networks. Additionally, between 1865 and 1898, the Bessemer process fueled a 500% increase in American steel production.

Second, natural resources provided a major boost to industrialization. The discovery of precious metals functioned as an easily accessible source of capital for industrialists, and coal mining was invaluable due to industrialization's energy demands.

Third, new corporatized management structures increased efficiency in production, and the development of more advanced banking and credit systems helped business owners consolidate capital and invest in expansion.

Fourth, companies engaged in mass marketing for the first time in history due to the country's improved literacy rates, robust publishing industry, and strong class of consumers.

Fifth, the United States enjoyed an enormous labor force that rapidly outpaced its European rivals. In the aftermath of the American Civil War, African Americans living in the North secured employment at factories at high rates, and successive waves of immigration carried a steady supply of cheap labor to American businesses.

The Rise of Industrial Capitalism

Rapid Economic Development and Business Consolidation

During the **Second Industrial Revolution** (1870–1914), the American economy underwent a radical transformation due to the rise of large-scale industrial systems, technological advancements, and modern business organizations.

Innovations in assembly lines, the mass production of interchangeable parts, and electrification spurred rapid growth in American industrial production. As a result, the supply of consumer goods exponentially increased across nearly all economic sectors, which led to steep price reductions for consumer goods. Consumerism also increased due to the creation of new industrial employment opportunities, especially in terms of middle-class management positions, which boosted households' discretionary spending. In addition, businesses applied management principles known as **Taylorism** to reorganize departments, enhance supervision, and provide more detailed instructions to employees. Increased efficiency and profits led to more business consolidation, including the establishment of corporate trusts with widespread investments. For example, John D. Rockefeller's Standard Oil Company established a monopoly over the oil industry through the vertical integration of smaller companies it acquired.

Myriad technological breakthroughs drove this economic expansion, particularly in terms of advancements in steel, chemicals, fertilizers, electrical power, and mechanical engines. Several additional breakthroughs revolutionized international commercial networks. Intercontinental railways expedited the shipment of goods across North America, and modernized ships cut down travel times abroad. In addition, the invention of the telegraph facilitated communication with international business partners, which increased business investments and the dissemination of technical knowledge.

Democrats and Republicans both supported pro-growth economic policies, such as low taxes, limited regulations, and minimal oversight mechanisms. For much of this era, trade policy was the most divisive economic issue. Republicans favored maintaining high tariffs to protect domestic industries, and Democrats advocated for free trade to help businesses access foreign markets.

Corporate Consolidation

Business leaders maximized profits through corporate consolidation, particularly in terms of reorganizing commercial enterprises into large trusts and holding companies. Large trusts and holding companies led to vertical integration, meaning a large corporate entity controlled an entire supply chain and produced everything from individual parts to the finished product. For example, John D. Rockefeller's Standard Oil trust implemented **vertical integration** to streamline the construction of refineries and better coordinate logistics.

Vertical integration allowed large corporate enterprises to achieve economies of scale, meaning that economic costs declined as production increased. So vertical integration generally benefited consumers by reducing the price of goods and services. However, vertical integration also had critical drawbacks. Large corporate enterprises were able to wield their disproportionate economic power to undercut competitors and establish monopolies. Less competition resulted in a greater concentration of wealth amongst business elites who owned monopolies that systematically destroyed smaller enterprises. Likewise, the displacement of competition reduced employment opportunities in some sectors, and monopolies naturally held a coercive power to limit wages and benefits for employees. Lastly, since wealth so easily translated into political power, the rise of monopolies created critical issues related to political corruption.

Efforts to Control Markets in Asia and Latin America

The United States sought to expand American diplomatic influence and commercial networks across the world, especially in Latin America and Asia.

The United States historically viewed itself as the hegemonic power within the Western Hemisphere. During the early 1880s, President Benjamin Harrison's Secretary of State James G. Blaine pursued a strategy known as the **Big Brother policy** to revive the Monroe Doctrine and actively intervene in Latin American affairs. For example, the United States intervened in the Venezuelan crisis of 1895 to force the United Kingdom and Venezuela to settle its territorial dispute through arbitration.

The United States also leveraged its military prowess for commercial gain. Following the mysterious sinking of the **USS Maine**, the United States sparked the **Spanish-American War** (1898) to protect American plantations in Cuba and increase its presence in the Pacific Rim. The United States decisively defeated Spain, and gained control over Cuba, Puerto Rico, Guam, and the Philippines. Based on its improved geopolitical position in the Pacific Rim, the United States pushed for an **Open Door Policy** in China to undermine its European and Japanese competitors. While the Open Door Policy was ultimately unsuccessful, it cemented the United States as a global power.

Labor in the Gilded Age

Improvements in Americans' Standards of Living

Americans' standard of living changed dramatically over the latter half of the nineteenth century. Prior to the Industrial Revolution, the overwhelming majority of Americans were employed in the agricultural sector. As industrial production expanded throughout the nineteenth century, Americans became increasingly more likely to live in cities and work in factories. These changes had a mixed effect on Americans' standard of living.

On the one hand, industrialization triggered a steep decline in the price of goods, a greater diversification of goods and services, and the growth of a middle class. Consequently, a consumer culture swept across the United States as retail outlets attained the status of cultural centers. Cities also attracted diverse migrants from outlying rural areas as well as foreign countries, resulting in dynamic and syncretic cultural exchanges. Furthermore, literacy rates, life expectancy, and childhood survival rates generally increased, especially at the end of the nineteenth century.

Conversely, capital consolidation wildly outstripped real wage growth, which is why this period is known as the **Gilded Age** (1870–1900). As business elites achieved unprecedented levels of wealth, the working poor struggled to make ends meet. Conditions were the worst in working class neighborhoods due to the prevalence of overcrowding, dilapidated buildings, and untreated sewage.

Labor and Management Battles

The writer Mark Twain called the late 19th century the Gilded Age because the era was also one of extreme social inequality. Some corporations expanded and began to control entire industries. For example, by 1890, the Standard Oil Company produced 88 percent of all the refined oil in the nation. This made a few individuals, such as **John D. Rockefeller** who owned Standard Oil, extremely wealthy. On the other hand, many workers earned low wages and began to form labor unions, such as the American Federation of Labor in 1886, in order to demand better working conditions and higher pay. Strikes were one of the most common ways workers could express their dissatisfaction, and the **Pullman Strike** of 1894 was one of the largest such incidents in the 19th century. Workers went on strike after the Pullman Company, which manufactured railroad cars, cut wages by about 25 percent. More than 125,000 workers around the country walked off the job and attacked workers hired to replace them. Federal troops were sent in to end the strike, and more than eighty workers were killed or wounded during confrontations. The strike was unsuccessful, but Congress passed a law making Labor Day a federal holiday in order to placate union members.

Increases in Child Labor

Business magnates sought to enlist rural migrants, immigrants, children, and women into their workforces between 1865 and 1898. This trend had begun in northern cities in the run-up to the American Civil War, but the pace quickened afterward due to a massive spike in the demand for industrial labor.

Women and children joined the workforce in record numbers during this period. Both groups primarily worked for textile manufacturers, and they were often the least compensated. Some industries especially valued orphaned children because they were viewed as expendable assets capable of working in tight spaces such as coal shafts.

Immigration and Migration in the Gilded Age

Diversification of the Industrial Workforce

As the industrial workforce expanded, business owners had to diversify the employee pool. They enlisted rural migrants, immigrants, children, and women in increasing numbers in the second half of the nineteenth century.

Rural migrants generally moved to urban cities for economic opportunities, and since this group had previously worked in the agricultural sector, they were mostly placed in entry-level jobs on factory assembly lines. Likewise, immigrants frequently remained in port cities, working in factories to secure basic needs and potentially save enough to travel west. Consequently, factories became the most diverse workplaces in America. Along with immigration from Britain, Ireland, and Germany, immigration from Central and Eastern Europe increased markedly after 1880. In the West, railroads and factories hired Chinese immigrants, but a racist backlash led to the passage of the Chinese Exclusion Act (1882), which prohibited Chinese laborers from immigrating into the United States.

Immigrants Came Seeking Better Lives

Immigration also played an important part in the economic and social changes that occurred during the late nineteenth century. Immigration patterns changed during this time and immigrants from Southern and Eastern Europe, such as Italy and Poland, began to surpass the number of arrivals from Northern and Western Europe. An increasing number of immigrants also came from Asia. The immigrants sought economic opportunity in the United States because wages for unskilled workers were higher than in their home countries. Immigrants and internal migrants also moved to escape religious persecution and either poverty or the inability to readily improve their socioeconomic status. Some Americans resented the influx of immigrants because they spoke different languages and practiced Catholicism. In 1924, Congress passed a law that restricted immigration from Southern and Eastern Europe.

Urban Neighborhoods

Increased urbanization was the last factor that contributed to the rapid changes of the Gilded Age. Factories were located near cities in order to draw upon a large pool of potential employees. Immigrants flooded into cities in search of work, and new arrivals often settled in the same neighborhoods where their compatriots lived. Between 1860 and 1890, the urbanization rate increased from about 20 percent to 35 percent. Urban neighborhoods often formed from city dwellers with similar races, ethnicities, or socioeconomic classes. However, cities struggled to keep up with growing populations, and services such as sanitation and water often lagged behind demand. Immigrants often lived in crowded living conditions that facilitated the spread of diseases.

Responses to Immigration in the Gilded Age

Assimilation and Americanization

Americans continually and fiercely debated whether the government should implement assimilation and Americanization as immigration rates skyrocketed over the latter half of the nineteenth century.

The United States Census Bureau estimated that at least 20% of Americans were first- or second-generation immigrants. In addition to the sheer rise in total arrivals, immigrants' country of origin shifted dramatically in the 1880s. Prior to this, approximately 90% of immigrants to the US came from Northwestern Europe. In contrast, the vast majority of immigrants arriving at the end of the century were Southern and Eastern Europeans. Unlike earlier immigration waves, Southern and Eastern Europeans were less likely to speak English.

Societal elites feared the immigrants would struggle to be integrated, while the working classes generally feared immigrants would potentially drive down labor costs. As a result, public and voluntary organizations developed **assimilation** programs, such as English lessons and basic social services. Settlement houses were especially active in assimilating groups, particularly when located within ethnic urban neighborhoods. **Americanization** was also common, and it refers to a more forceful, if not mandated, mode of assimilation. Accordingly, immigrants were often forced to navigate how much American culture they would adopt, possibly at the expense of generational family traditions and values.

Social Darwinism

The last phase of American territorial expansion occurred as a result of the Spanish-American War in 1898. New ideas arose in the late nineteenth century that helped justify further expansion. Some intellectuals applied Charles Darwin's ideas of "survival of the fittest" to the human race and called this new concept **Social Darwinism**. They used this idea to justify why stronger groups of people colonized and exploited weaker groups. In addition, imperialists also used the idea of the **White Man's Burden** to justify further expansion. They claimed that Caucasians were obligated to civilize and govern groups thought to be less advanced.

These ideas were used to justify America's new status as a colonial power as a result of the **Spanish-American War**. Although Spain had once been a powerful empire, it had been in decline. The United States went to war against Spain in 1898 when the American battleship **USS Maine** exploded in Havana Harbor and killed more than 250 sailors. The U.S. Navy defeated the Spanish fleet in several engagements and then the Army followed up with a victory at San Juan Hill, which included the famous charge by Teddy Roosevelt and the Rough Riders.

The war lasted less than four months and made the United States a world power. The U.S. also acquired several Spanish colonies, including Puerto Rico, Guam, and the Philippines. Guam became an important refueling station for American naval forces in the Pacific and remains a U.S. territory today, along with Puerto Rico. When the United States occupied the Philippines, the Filipino people launched a rebellion in order to obtain their independence. The U.S. Army put down the insurrection, but in doing so, they committed many atrocities against the Filipino people. The Philippines would remain an American territory until 1946.

Jane Addams and Gender Equality Efforts

Women increasingly pursued educational and professional opportunities between 1865 and 1898. Industrialization generated a greater amount and broader range of employment opportunities, and women often entered the workforce to supplement the household income. Several universities were also founded in this period to empower women. For example, in 1871, Sophia Smith founded Smith College to provide women with the same educational opportunities as men.

As women seized upon educational and professional opportunities, they sought more active roles in voluntary organizations and progressive reform movements. The **Women's Christian Temperance Union**, which combatted the disruptive effect of alcoholism on American households, was the largest women-led voluntary organization in the United States. Aside from protecting families, women were incredibly active in combatting urban poverty, especially in connection with the settlement movement. Settlement houses offered free housing and social services to low-income and immigrant communities.

Voluntary organizations provided women with leadership experience that was vital to the women's suffrage movement. Jane Addams and Ellen Gates Starr co-founded Hull House, a legendary settlement house in Chicago, and they became leading activists for gender equality. Likewise, Elizabeth Cady Stanton and Susan B. Anthony were abolitionists and social activists who founded the National American Woman Suffrage Association.

Jane Addams is known as one of the most prominent reformers of the Progressive Era. She was a pioneer in Social Work and advocated for the health of mothers, the needs of children, world, peace, and public health. She was also an activist, author, and leader in the women's suffrage movement. She was the first American woman to be awarded the Nobel Peace Prize in 1931.

John Stuart Mills (1806-1873), an English philosopher and political economist, was considered the "most influential English-speaking philosopher of the nineteenth century" and was best known for being the first member of Parliament to advocate women's suffrage. His book *On Liberty* promoted utilitarianism, which advocates that people should always make decisions based on what would be the most net positive. In his work, Mills sought to limit the power exercised upon the individual by any ruling body and stated that moral actions are those that promote utility and increase individuals' and society's well-being. He called for limited constraints upon individual behavior that only restrict those actions that cause harm to others.

Development of the Middle Class

The Growth of the Middle Class

The American middle class developed in the late nineteenth century due to the diversification of jobs in the workforce. As corporations attempted to implement vertical integration and stimulate growth, there was more demand for managers, logistical specialists, clerical workers, and others in white-collar jobs. These jobs generally paid significantly more than working-class factory jobs, and higher wages led to the development of a distinctive middle class. The middle class enjoyed unprecedented amounts of leisure time, which fueled the development of entertainment industries.

Increased disposable income also strengthened American consumerism. Sears distributed millions of mail-order catalogs in the 1890s, and the resulting competition caused a steep decline in the price of consumer goods as local establishments sought to keep pace with national distributors. Lastly, mail-order businesses and large corporations began offering credit lines directly to consumers for the first time in history, which further enhanced Americans' buying power.

Although they were often paid significantly less than their male counterparts, women especially benefited from greater employment opportunities. At long last, unmarried women could achieve financial independence. In addition, dual sources of income lifted many working-class households into the middle class. Stronger employment prospects also led to the establishment of private women's colleges and more offerings for women at public institutions.

The Gospel of Wealth

Some elite business leaders practiced philanthropy to improve the living conditions for the working poor. The philanthropic movement gained some traction after business titan **Andrew Carnegie** published an article titled "**The Gospel of Wealth**" in 1889.

In "The Gospel of Wealth," Carnegie asserted that the wealthy had a moral obligation to reduce income inequality. Therefore, Carnegie implored his fellow captains of industry to spend their riches on improving the lives of the working poor. The "Gospel of Wealth" had a profound impact on elites' philanthropic contributions with the bulk of money being spent on public education, higher education, cultural centers, and the revitalization of urban centers.

At the same time, "The Gospel of Wealth" was inarguably a self-serving document that justified the accumulation of wealth. During the **Gilded Age** (1870–1900), wealth inequality had reached nearly unthinkable levels. For example, John D. Rockefeller and Andrew Carnegie, respectively, remain to this day the second and third richest men in modern history. Even with their magnanimous philanthropy, Gilded Age business leaders' consolidation of capital still generated tremendous family wealth, easily lasting for many generations to come. Therefore, many historians view "The Gospel of Wealth" as an attempt to undermine the passage of a federal income tax, which business elites staunchly opposed.

Reform in the Gilded Age

Critics Championed Alternative Visions for Society

A diverse array of critics challenged traditional economic and political power structures.

Artists played an essential role in popularizing progressive causes and spreading awareness about poverty. For example, cartoonist Thomas Nast frequently parodied corrupt public officials, racist organizations, and business elites in his popular political cartoons.

A late nineteenth-century religious movement known as the **Social Gospel** believed the Second Coming of Christ would only happen when humanity purified itself of its social ills. Social Gospel leaders participated in a variety of progressive causes, including public education, public housing, anti-corruption, and poverty reduction.

Socialists were another indispensable part of the progressive movement. In contrast to the established economic policy of the United States, socialists advocated for more labor protections, social programs to fight poverty, and limitations on capital consolidation. **Eugene V. Debs** was a prominent socialist leader, and he played an instrumental role in organizing strikes against railroads. Some socialists also formed utopian groups to establish independent communities, such as the Icarians' egalitarian communes. Like socialists, **agrarian reformers** pursued collective action to reduce the power of railroads and consolidated financial interests. During the 1890s, William Jennings Bryant led the left-wing, agrarian **Populist Party** to national prominence advocating for the gold standard and restrictions on financial speculation.

Controversies over the Role of Government in the Gilded Age

Arguments for Laissez-Faire Policies

Some Americans advocated for **laissez-faire** economic policies, particularly those Americans who already owned a wealth of resources. Generally speaking, laissez-faire economics is the most extreme form of a capitalist economic system. Supporters of this system oppose government intervention in the private sector based on a belief that the free market will most efficiently and effectively resolve economic crises. So, despite the undeniable existence of cyclical economic downturns, the laissez-faire economic approach asserts that free markets will generate the most economic growth over time.

During the late nineteenth century, some members of the Democratic Party, known as the **Bourbon Democrats**, explicitly adopted laissez-faire economics. The Bourbon Democrats believed limited government and free markets were the answer to the country's recurring economic crises, such as the Recession of 1882–1885 and Panic of 1893. Aside from opposing government regulation, the Bourbon Democrats supported the gold standard, anti-corruption legislation, reduced government spending, and lower tariffs. However, laissez-faire economics worked better in theory than in practice. For example, without the government actively engaging in trust busting, wealthy corporations inevitably consolidated power as they gained advantages related to economies of scale. Therefore, greater consolidation of wealth crushed competition, undermining the potential benefits of a free market.

Politics in the Gilded Age

Populism

Populism advocates for incorporating advances in technology, social organization, science, and economics into the government to benefit society. It is fueled by the idea that social goals should be achieved by the actions of the people, and not the dominant elites. It also advocates for more governmental control in regulating the economy. The term "populism" became popular in the 1890s by farmers and labor unions in reaction to the Gilded Age and economic instability, and returned in the 1950s. Some populist political parties in the U.S. include Greenback Party, Progressive Party of 1912, Progressive Party of 1924, and the Share Our Wealth movement by Huey Long.

Political Parties Remained Divided on Issues

Despite the relative peace that followed the American Civil War, partisan divisions remained alive and well in the American political party system.

In the aftermath of the American Civil War, the South seethed with resentment over federal military occupation, political restrictions, and legal interventions. Despite their lack of popular support, Republicans maintained control of the South until the presidential election of 1876. Republican Rutherford B. Hayes narrowly won the election, but only after agreeing to the **Compromise of 1877**, which returned the right to self-rule back to the Southern states. The federal government's withdrawal effectively killed the Republican Party in the South, triggering the return of sectionalism and partisanship.

Following the Compromise of 1877, Democrats dominated the South, and Republicans remained the most popular party in the North. Democrats primarily called for limited government, opposed tariffs, and supported racial segregation. During the 1890s, William Jennings Bryant's Populists took over the Democratic Party by condemning moneyed interests and political corruption. In contrast, the Republicans pursued a pro-business political agenda, including tariffs to protect domestic industry. Some Republican reformers adopted progressive and anti-corruption platform, but the party struggled to enact meaningful reforms due to its long-standing relationships with economic elites.

Political Machines

During the latter half of the nineteenth century, **political machines** rose to power and came to dominate American urban political institutions, especially in the North. Elite bosses led political machines, or political groups, and they exercised authority over socioeconomic systems through complex political patronage networks. Bosses provided "spoils" to loyal officials working with the political machine, such as the unlawful sharing of government revenue. For example, Tammany Hall's Boss Tweed paid twice as much to construct the New York County Courthouse as the United States paid for the Alaska Purchase. Overall, there can be no doubt political machines exacerbated existing issues with wealth inequality, power imbalances, and inefficiencies in government.

However, despite this overt corruption, political machines did serve an essential function in many Northern cities. The federal government didn't have the resources or power to adequately provide social services to the poor, and most local governments struggled to implement necessary reforms. Political machines somewhat successfully filled this void, though this admittedly came at a heavy cost. In addition, political machines seeking loyal voters often fought to assimilate immigrant groups and deliver essential services to them. For example, Irish Americans first obtained a meaningful voice in American politics through their rise in political machines.

Practice Quiz

Question 1 is based on the following passage:

> Those who are opposed to this proposition tell us that the issue of paper money is a function of the bank and that the government ought to go out of the banking business. I stand with Jefferson rather than with them, and tell them, as he did, that the issue of money is a function of the government and that the banks should go out of the governing business.
>
> If they dare to come out in the open field and defend the gold standard as a good thing, we shall fight them to the uttermost, having behind us the producing masses of the nation and the world. Having behind us the commercial interests and the laboring interests and all the toiling masses, we shall answer their demands for a gold standard by saying to them, you shall not press down upon the brow of labor this crown of thorns. You shall not crucify mankind upon a cross of gold.
>
> William Jennings Bryan, "Cross of Gold" speech, 1896

1. What is the main idea presented in the excerpt?
    a. Banks prefer the gold standard.
    b. Most Americans dislike the gold standard.
    c. Violence is justified when the government oppresses the masses.
    d. The government should set the monetary policy based on the will of the people.

2. Which of the following types of government intervention lowers prices, reassures the supply, and creates opportunity to compete with foreign vendors?
    a. Income redistribution
    b. Price controls
    c. Taxes
    d. Subsidies

3. What type of map would be the most useful for calculating data and differentiating between the characteristics of two places?
    a. Topographic maps
    b. Dot-density maps
    c. Isoline maps
    d. Flow-line maps

Question 4 is based on the following map:

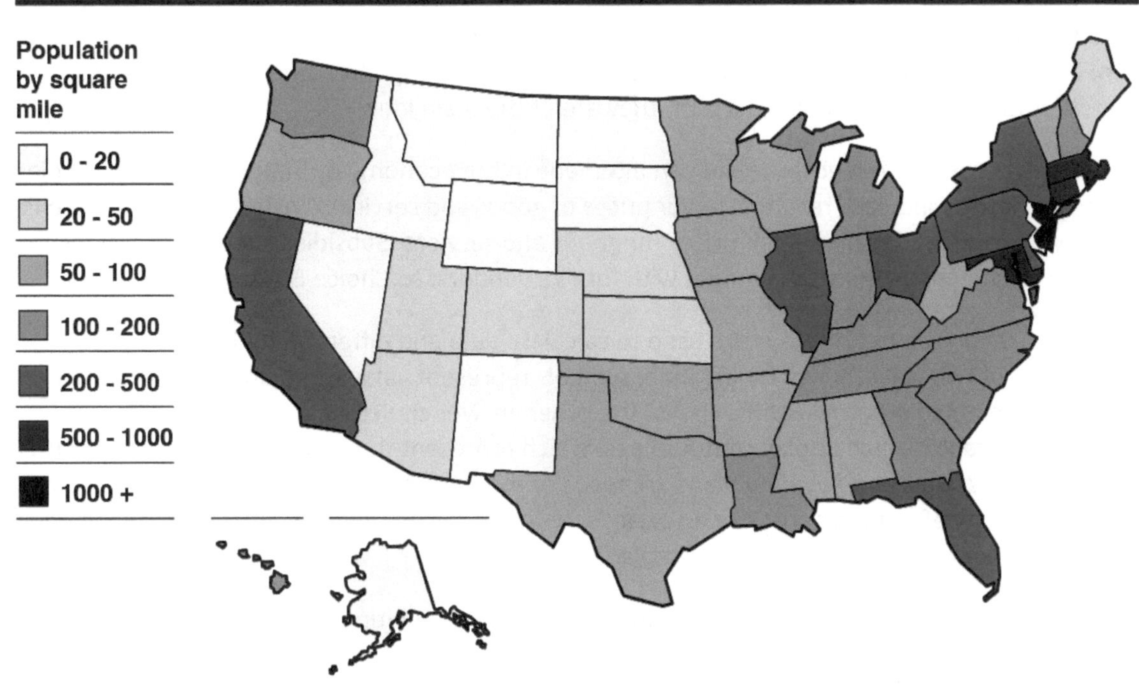

4. According to the map, what area of the United States has the highest population density?
   a. Northwest
   b. Northeast
   c. Southwest
   d. Southeast

5. What accounts for different parts of the Earth experiencing different seasons at the same time?
   a. Differences in the rate of Earth's rotation
   b. Ocean currents
   c. Tilt of the Earth's rotational axis
   d. Elevation

Answer Explanations

1. D: Choice *D* is correct. William Jennings Bryan's "Cross of Gold" is one of the most famous speeches in American history, launching his candidacy in the 1896 presidential election. The speech advocates for abolishing the gold standard and adopting a bimetallic system to provide more government control over monetary policy. The excerpt condemns the influence of banks in monetary policy, and without some reform, the masses should act to remove the gold standard. Although the other answer choices accurately state assertions from the excerpt, they aren't the main idea.

2. D: Choice *D* is correct. The government can intervene in the economy by imposing taxes, subsidies, and price controls to increase revenue, lower prices of goods and services, ensure product availability for the government, and maintain fair prices for goods and services. Subsidies lower prices, reassure the supply, and create opportunity to compete with foreign vendors, so Choice *D* is correct.

3. C: Choice *C* is correct. Isoline maps are used to calculate data and differentiate between the characteristics of two places. In an isoline map, symbols represent values, and lines can be drawn between two points to determine differences. The other answer choices are maps with different purposes. Topographic maps display contour lines, which represent the relative elevation of a particular place. Dot-density maps and flow-line maps are types of thematic maps. Dot-density maps illustrate the volume and density of a characteristic of an area. Flow-line maps use lines to illustrate the movement of goods, people, or even animals between two places.

4. B: Choice *B* is correct. The map is a density map illustrating population density by state in the United States. Accordingly, the darker areas have higher population density. The darkest area of the map is the Northeast, so Choice *B* is correct.

5. C: Choice *C* is correct. The tilt of the Earth's rotation causes the seasons due to the difference in direct exposure to the Sun. For example, the northern hemisphere is tilted directly toward the Sun from June 22 to September 23, which creates the summer in that part of the world. Conversely, the southern hemisphere is tilted away from the Sun and experiences winter during those months. Choice *A* is factually incorrect—the rate of Earth's rotation is constant. Choices *B* and *D* are factors in determining climate, but differences in climate don't cause the seasons.

Section 7: Imperialism and The World Wars (1890–1945)

Imperialism: Debates

Imperialists' Arguments

Imperialism gained traction in the United States at the tail end of the nineteenth century. Prior to this period, Americans generally opposed imperialism due to America's history with European colonization. However, American foreign policy preferences became more fluid as the country increasingly entered the world stage and competed with European powers.

American imperialists had several interrelated justifications, ranging from cultural to economic. Most imperialists argued that it was a necessity for the United States to acquire foreign territory and resources to sustain economic growth. Hardcore imperialists went even further, applying principles of evolution to geopolitics, arguing that strong states would dominate and annihilate weaker states. This motivation only increased as Americans settled the western frontier and grew desperate over the dwindling supply of undeveloped land.

Some imperialists combined pragmatic economic arguments with a narrative about how the United States was destined for greatness, essentially refashioning Manifest Destiny on a global scale. Similarly, feelings of cultural superiority led to moral arguments about how the United States had a moral obligation to spread democracy and commercial enterprise all over the world. This moral argument sometimes had a racial element, resembling how Spanish friars defended the conquest and enslavement of indigenous populations.

Anti-Imperialists' Arguments

Anti-imperialists denounced the growing popularity of ambitious and aggressive foreign policymaking as exploitative warmongering. In most cases, anti-imperialists criticized European powers for their oppressive colonial and imperial practices. Anti-imperialists commonly cited Enlightenment philosophers, America's Founding Fathers, and the Declaration of Independence (1776) to argue for the existence of an inalienable right to self-determination. Some radical anti-imperialists actually supported military interventions but only to support the local guerilla forces until they gained freedom from European powers. That being said, most imperialists were isolationists who adopted arguments from George Washington's Farewell Address (1796). They viewed European imperialism as inherently destabilizing despite its economic benefits.

In addition, some anti-imperialists were nativists, and they adopted racial theories to protest territorial expansionism. Nativists viewed imperialism as a threat because local populations might one day be granted citizenship, like what occurred after the Mexican-American War (1846–1848). For example, in the run-up to the Spanish-American War (1898), nativists railed against an intervention because they believed Cuba and Puerto Rico might eventually become American states, potentially resulting in a million people of color becoming American citizens. Because nativists mostly hoped to preserve America's connection to Northwestern Europe, they championed anti-imperialism and isolationism.

The Spanish–American War

American Victory in the Spanish-American War Effects

The United States' decisive victory in the **Spanish-American War** (April–August 1898) was a paradigm-shifting movement in American foreign policymaking, marking the beginning of the United States as an imperial force with a global reach. Spain was a crumbling empire prior to the conflict, and the United States landed the knockout blow, annexing Cuba, Puerto Rico, Guam, and the Philippines. This massive territorial acquisition reinforced American dominance over Latin America and served as a launching pad for American imperialists to challenge European control over the Southeast Pacific and Chinese mainland. However, great power presented its own challenges.

To gain Cuban support against Spain and guarantee Cuban independence, Congress passed the **Teller Amendment**. However, the United States immediately reneged on that promise after the fighting ended. American efforts to colonize the Philippines were similarly imperial in nature. Filipinos had been in the midst of revolting against Spain, and the nationalist movement felt no differently about the American imperialists. In response, American soldiers committed mass atrocities against Filipino nationalists, sympathizers, and civilians during the **Philippine-American War** (1899–1902). Approximately 18,000 Filipinos died in the fighting, and somewhere between 250,000 and 1 million civilians died of war-related famine and cholera outbreaks.

The Progressives

Goals of Progressives

The social inequalities and economic abuses of the Gilded Age did not go unnoticed, and in the 1890s, many reformers began to demand change. This period was called the **Progressive Era** and included activists in both the Democratic and Republican parties. The Progressives wanted to use scientific methods and government regulation to improve society. For example, they advocated the use of initiative, referendum, and recall to make government more responsive to its citizens. Progressives also argued that it was necessary to breakup large monopolies (known as **trust busting**) in order to promote equal economic competition. In 1911, Rockefeller's Standard Oil was split up into thirty-four different companies in order to promote competition, and the Federal Trade Commission was established in 1914 in order to prevent other monopolies from forming. Many Progressives also supported several constitutional amendments that were ratified in early twentieth century, including the 17th Amendment, which established the direct election of U.S. Senators in 1913 (previously state legislatures had elected senators). They also favored the Prohibition of alcohol that went into effect with the 18th Amendment in 1919. Progressives also advocated for women's rights and backed the 19th Amendment, which gave women the right to vote in 1920.

Disagreements Among Progressives

Progressives disagreed on a host of issues. Many Progressives emphasized democratizing the political system, addressing income inequality, and curing societal issues, especially in regard to working-class households in urban areas. These types of Progressives tended to be political activists, social workers, suffragettes, socialists, labor organizers, and/or agrarian populists.

Other Progressives pursued democratic reform and economic fairness through technocracy. Under a **technocratic government**, elite experts enjoy extraordinary power and control over the government to maximize efficiency. Although Progressive support for experts was considerable, technocrats didn't always make strong politicians, drawing heavy criticism for their relationships with powerful business leaders and politicians. In general, Progressive technocrats were most influential in urban areas, particularly when posing as an alternative to overtly corrupt party bosses.

Some Progressives hoped to maintain privileges and benefits they enjoyed under the status quo of traditional establishment. This type of contradictory Progressivism was commonplace throughout the country. Many Progressives sought to restrict immigration, believing the influx of cheap labor would further impoverish the urban working class. Likewise, Southern Progressives generally didn't challenge racial segregation or the denial of African Americans' political rights, although they often supported more democratization in areas where their interests were more aligned.

Progressive Amendments

The Progressive movement pushed for economic, political, and social reform to address issues related to industrialization and urbanization, expand democracy, and create moral reform.

Progressives' economic agenda mostly consisted of labor reform, social programs, and wealth redistribution through introducing taxation at the federal level. Additionally, Progressives pushed for more regulation to prevent financial speculators from causing market turmoil and contributing to recessions.

In terms of political policies, Progressives advocated primarily for more popular election of representatives and anticorruption legislation. A crowning political achievement for the Progressive movement was the **Seventeenth Amendment**, which required US senators to be directly elected. Prior to this constitutional amendment, state legislatures elected US senators, which resulted in significant corruption. More specific anticorruption legislation at the local level sought to break party bosses' and business elites' hold over the political system.

Pressing social issues included gender inequality, racial discrimination, and rampant alcoholism. Progressives were incredibly divided on social issues, and progress was slow. Little was accomplished in regard to repealing Jim Crow laws in the South or outlawing racial discrimination in the North. However, Progressives did manage to successively ratify the **Eighteenth Amendment** (1920) to criminalize the sale of alcohol as well as the **Nineteenth Amendment** (1920), which legalized women's suffrage.

Preservationists and Conservationists

Preservationists and **conservationists** advocated for the government to establish national parks and address the overuse and potential depletion of natural resources. Preservation aims are specifically geared toward protecting nature and natural resources from being used, whereas conservation focuses on using natural resources properly and in a sustainable way.

President **Theodore Roosevelt**, who led the nation between 1901 and 1909, is famous for bringing the United States of America into modernity through a series of modernization and conservation projects. Roosevelt is famous for enthusiastically offering the Panamanian governor $10 million per year to build and operate the Panama Canal. Operating under U.S. leadership between 1914 and 1999, the Panama Canal remained a last symbol of Roosevelt's diplomatic legacy in Latin America. The canal is a beacon of the United States' strong-armed diplomatic influence in Latin America during the years of the "Roosevelt

Corollary." The unilateral diplomatic tactics hashed out by the Roosevelt Corollary stated that the United States had the right, as military leader of the Western Hemisphere, to act as the "international police force" of the region. The Roosevelt Corollary, backed by an impressive U.S. Navy, allowed the United States to have unchecked power in Latin America for decades after the Roosevelt administration. During Roosevelt's presidency, the United States occupied many Latin American countries for self-serving reasons. Nevertheless, not all of Roosevelt's policies were as self-serving—the rough-and-tumble president is also responsible for establishing the National Park System in the United States and setting aside hundreds of thousands of acres of land for conservation.

World War I: Military and Diplomacy

The United States Enters WWI

World War I began in 1914 with the assassination of **Franz Ferdinand**, the apparent heir of the Austro-Hungarian Empire. A network of secret alliances meant that most European nations were quickly drawn into the conflict, although President **Woodrow Wilson** initially tried to keep the United States neutral, as this decision represented the United States' foreign policy tradition of staying out of European affairs. The majority of Americans agreed with this decision.

The war involved two major European alliances: the **Triple Entente** of Britain, France, and Russia, and the **Central Powers**, which included Germany and Austria-Hungary. The British implemented a naval blockade that was very successful, and the Germans retaliated by launching submarine attacks. German submarines attacked any ship carrying supplies to the Triple Entente, including the passenger ship **RMS Lusitania** in 1915. About 1,200 people died, including more than 100 Americans. The Germans temporarily halted their unrestricted submarine campaign, but eventually resumed the attacks in 1917. In addition, in 1917, Germany asked Mexico to attack the United States in a communiqué known as the **Zimmerman telegram**. These events led the United States to join the Triple Entente in April 1917, although significant numbers of American troops did not arrive in Europe until 1918. American reinforcement helped the British and French, who had been fighting continuously since 1914, launch a final offensive that defeated Germany in 1918. American forces suffered about 320,000 casualties. World War I also led to significant changes on the home front as women took on new responsibilities, and thousands of African Americans migrated north in search of work. World War I also led to a communist revolution that transformed Russia into the USSR in 1922.

The American Expeditionary Force

During the summer of 1917, the **American Expeditionary Force** (AEF) made their debut in Europe and changed the course of World War I. Although the United States had already been bankrolling and providing material assistance to the Allied powers for years, the establishment of the AEF laid bare the United States' commitment to defeating the Central powers. Backed with an enormous number of fresh troops and nearly unlimited supplies, the Allied powers surged to victory approximately sixteen months after the AEF first landed in France.

The AEF primarily fought under the command of US General **John J. Pershing**, and his forces were slowly acclimated to the battlefield, functioning as supplemental support for battle-hardened British and French divisions. However, by the fall of 1918, the AEF had garnered enough combat experience to begin operating independently. Pershing commanded the largest offensive force in the American military at the Battle of Saint-Mihiel (September 1918), heavily contributing to the Allied victory. Less than a month later, Pershing led more than one million AEF and French forces to victory during the

Meuse-Argonne offensive. Given the AEF's late arrival, American forces were spared from some of the carnage, although the 1918 influenza pandemic ravaged the AEF.

Refusal to Ratify the Treaty of Versailles

The United States' refusal to ratify the **Treaty of Versailles** (1920) was one of the most peculiar events in American history. President **Woodrow Wilson** held disproportionate influence over the negotiations, and he secured the inclusion of his most prized policies in the final draft. However, the US Senate refused to ratify the treaty, effectively submarining Wilson's plans. Few states have ever enjoyed the luxury of crafting a new world order for their benefit, and even fewer have proceeded to reject the ultimate agreement.

President Wilson had been a vocal supporter of self-determination to prevent imperial ambitions from triggering another devastating global conflict. In his **Fourteen Points** speech, Wilson laid out policies to restrict colonization, support independence movements, implement global disarmament, and promote free trade. Furthermore, President Wilson advocated for the establishment of an international organization tasked with promoting peaceful international relations, which led to the founding of the **League of Nations** (1920).

The US Senate was intensely skeptical of ceding any degree of sovereignty to an international organization. Given Americans' lukewarm and hostile support for World War I, American nationalists and isolationists had a relatively easy time rallying opposition to further enmeshing the United States in foreign affairs.

World War I: Home Front

Freedom of Speech Restrictions

Restrictions on Americans' **First Amendment** rights (the freedom of speech) increased during World War I. The conflict was deeply unpopular among the working classes; therefore, the federal government sought to suppress and strangle the antiwar movement in its infancy.

Congress passed the **Espionage Act** of 1917 and **Sedition Act** of 1918 to prevent free speech from undermining the war effort. The Supreme Court later affirmed the constitutionality of this extremely broad legislation, effectively allowing the federal government to suppress any speech proven to be even tangentially related to World War I. Unsurprisingly, the federal government and business leaders construed the acts to wage war on the organized labor movement, particularly after the beginning of the **Russian Revolution** (1917–1923).

Without any meaningful evidence, American leaders argued that American labor unions were part of a Bolshevik plot to overthrow the federal government, triggering a **Red Scare** (1917–1920). During the Red Scare, the federal government forcibly broke labor unions and arrested America's most famous socialist leader and labor organizer, **Eugene V. Debs**, over a speech expressing his opposition to draft and support for protests. After the Supreme Court upheld his conviction, Debs entered the presidential election of 1920 from prison, finishing in a distant third place.

Immigration Restrictions

The peak of European immigration occurred in 1907, just a few years before World War I. Nativist campaigns targeted at certain ethnic groups during and after World War I resulted in quotas being passed that placed restrictions on immigration for certain countries and regions or increased barriers to immigration.

However, these restrictions did not just crop up during the war; the late 1800s and early 1900s witnessed increased restrictions in immigration. Passed by President Chester A. Arthur, the **Chinese Exclusion Act** of 1882 inaugurated a decade-long moratorium on Chinese labor immigration.

Because xenophobia was so prevalent during World War I, the **Immigration Act of 1917** was enacted, establishing literacy requirements for immigrants and resultantly stopping immigration from most Asian nations. Likewise, the **Johnson-Reed Immigration Act of 1924** placed semi-permanent limitations on the number of immigrants who could enter the United States per year. The act established quotas based on national origin, limiting immigration from the Asia-Pacific Triangle. The act also placed quotas on European, African, and Middle Eastern immigration. Instead, it heavily favored immigrants from Northern and Western Europe, particularly Great Britain, Germany, and Ireland.

Some postwar reforms, however, have been more positively received by history. The **GI Bill**, for instance, provided returning World War II veterans with the money and support systems necessary to obtain work and/or a college education. The GI Bill has changed over the years based on unique postwar needs and contemporary sociohistorical contexts. Even the original GI Bill, however, has been criticized because of its marginalization of African Americans in a pre–civil rights movement world.

Economically-Motivated Migration to Urban Centers

Americans migrated from rural communities to urban centers during World War I (1914–1918), the Great Depression (1929–1941), and World War II (1939–1945) to pursue greater economic stability.

The American economy underwent a radical transformation during World War I. This conflict marked the first time the United States adopted a total war strategy, meaning every economic resource was directed toward the war effort. Cities were the centers of mass production, and the resulting increase in economic activity generated tremendous employment opportunities. Given the shortage of labor caused by men joining the armed services, women entered the workforce in large numbers for the first time. Likewise, African American sharecroppers migrated to cities and secured higher pay working on assembly lines.

The Great Depression decimated rural communities. Debt is an inherent part of farming, and millions of farmers defaulted during the Great Depression due to unstable food prices, insufficient labor, environmental issues, and/or the stress placed on supply chains. Non-agricultural rural employment also largely depended on agricultural production and/or farmers' discretionary spending. Lacking alternatives, millions of displaced families migrated to urban areas and sought entry-level work in manufacturing and construction.

Like in World War I, the United States adopted a total war strategy during World War II, and the urban manufacturing boom attracted rural migrants and opened new opportunities for historically oppressed groups. Many farmers and African Americans also migrated to rapidly industrializing West coast cities. Industrialization increased at such a torrid pace that urban areas experienced intense housing shortages due to the expansion of the urban workforce. As a result, many cities achieved all-time low levels of unemployment, which officially brought an end to the Great Depression.

The Great Migration

During the **Great Migration** (1916–1970), approximately six million African Americans left the South to pursue more lucrative economic opportunities and political rights in the Northeast, Midwest, and West.

Labor shortages during World War I triggered the Great Migration, as companies opened new jobs to meet industrial demands. More than 350,000 African Americans served in the **American Expeditionary Force** (AEF), and after fighting for their country, many joined the Great Migration to continue working as respected professionals. Several African American organizations, including the National Association for the Advancement of Colored People (NAACP) and the New Negro political movement, helped settle African Americans during the Great Migration.

Despite African Americans' improved economic mobility and political representation, the North was far from an idyllic paradise for people of color. Jobs on offer to African Americans were generally the most dangerous with the least compensation, and numerous private businesses openly refused to hire people of color. Housing was another major obstacle for African American migrants due to redlining, or the practice of barring African American families from certain communities. As a result, African Americans were routinely forced to settle in the most dilapidated housing units in neighborhoods with the least access to public services.

1920s: Innovations in Communication and Technology

Technological and Manufacturing Improvements

The American economy underwent dramatic changes between 1890 and 1945 due to a variety of modernizing factors. The creation of a complex credit system and increased white-collar employment increased Americans' disposable income, influenced the development of a consumer culture, and broadly raised the standard of living.

Americans' personal mobility increased through improvements in public transportation and mass production of automobiles. **Henry Ford** drove down the price of automobiles by using standardized parts and assembly lines. By 1918, Ford's innovative manufacturing techniques resulted in his Model T outnumbering the combined total of all other American cars. This success led to **Fordism**—the implementation of a system of mass production—gaining widespread acceptance in the manufacturing of consumer products.

New technological innovations and manufacturing procedures revolutionized the American economy by providing larger amounts of higher-quality products at lower prices. Some of the most important innovations, such as the combustion engine and petrochemicals, came from the discovery of new uses for petroleum. Other important innovations occurred in the construction of electric grids and skyscrapers, especially after the invention of reinforced concrete. Technology also strengthened communication systems and modernized entertainment. During the early twentieth century, telephones and radios became staples in American households. People were better able to stay connected and communicate with others. Additionally, movies gained steam in the 1930s when filmmakers incorporated sound.

Mass Media

A more unified national culture, as well as the awareness of the diversity and different regional cultures, rapidly spread as new forms of mass media, such as the radio and cinema, were developed and became more commonplace. **Mass media** refers to the various methods by which the majority of the general public receives news and information. Mass media includes television, newspapers, radio, magazines, online news outlets, and social media networks. The general public relies on mass media for political knowledge and cultural socialization, as well as the majority of their knowledge of current events, social issues, and political news. The following details the general evolution of mass media in the United States:

- Until the end of the nineteenth century, print media such as newspapers and magazines was the only form of mass communication.
- In the 1890s, after the invention of the radio, broadcast media become a popular form of communication, particularly among illiterate people.
- In the 1940s, television superseded both print and broadcast media as the most popular form of mass media.
- In 1947, President Harry Truman gave the first political speech on television.
- In 1952, Dwight Eisenhower was the first political candidate to air campaign ads on television.
- Today, the Internet is the most widespread mass media technology, and citizens have instant access to news and information, as well as interactive platforms on which they can communicate directly with political leaders or share their views through social media, blogs, and independent news sites.

The growth of mass media had a powerful effect on spreading culture and ideas, and shaping public opinion and politics.

1920s: Cultural and Political Controversies

Urban Growth

Population growth and modernization, sparked by the technological transformations of the Industrial Revolution, forever changed the physical environment of the planet, catalyzing the growth of urban centers. By 1920, urban centers were home to the majority of the population in the United States, as they afforded better economic opportunities, particularly for women and immigrants. Nearly 75% of the population in New York City, for example, was composed of new immigrants and first-generation Americans in 1910.

Migration Affected Art

Migration between 1890 and 1945 led to the development and/or evolution of stronger regional and ethnic identities. At the tail end of the nineteenth century, most American art and literature movements shared a deep commitment to realism; however, this largely gave way to more experimentation, which allowed artists to express more of their individual and collective lived experiences.

During the early twentieth century, American art movements developed with incredible regional and cultural diversity. The mass arrival of European immigrants in Northeastern urban areas energized the Ashcan, modernist, cubist, and abstract expressionist movements. Additionally, New York City birthed the **Harlem Renaissance** as African Americans left the South to pursue economic opportunities in the North during the **Great Migration** (1916–1970). The Harlem Renaissance reflected the experience of African Americans in a diverse array of artistic endeavors, including experimental jazz music and revolutionary literature. Other major early twentieth-century artistic movement developed as settlers moved into the American Southwest, resulting in artistic works based on iconographic desert landscape and wildlife.

Literature movements similarly reflected socioeconomic changes, ethnic experiences, and regional identities. The literature of William Faulkner and John Steinbeck reflected and shaped Southern and Western regional identities, respectively, during the Great Depression.

Cultural and Political Controversies

Cultural and political controversies roiled the United States during the **Roaring Twenties**, which matched this contradictory period's defining characteristics of economic prosperity and generational poverty. Progressives wielded scientific innovations and social reform to lift the United States into modernity. By the 1920s, most Americans enjoyed access to running water, electricity, radios, telephones, sanitation systems, automobiles, and cheap consumer and household products.

Many groups acted to protect traditional American society. Nativists secured the passage of the **Immigration Act of 1924** to restrict immigration for the alleged purpose of protecting American culture and jobs. Likewise, Southern states sought to reinforce Jim Crow laws to prevent the growing calls for racial equality after African Americans returned from fighting in World War I. Similar discrimination was also prevalent throughout the North, even in the most liberal states and communities. Conservative evangelicals successfully censored and criminalized certain scientific theories in many public school systems; however, the national conversation shifted toward secularism after **Clarence Darrow** defended a biology teacher's right to teach evolution in the infamous **Scopes Monkey Trial** (1925). Religious and women's rights groups were also at the forefront of passing **Prohibition**, which remains one of the most controversial and counterproductive policies in American history. Gender roles and women's rights issues were also debated.

The Great Depression

Economic Transitions

Millions of Americans began migrating from rural to urban areas during the run-up to World War I, and this migration continued during the Great Depression. Three factors heavily contributed to the continuation of this transition.

Between 1934 and 1940, a series of dust storms wracked the Great Plains in an event commonly referred to as the **Dust Bowl**. Insufficient knowledge of ecology and the proliferation of mechanized farming equipment triggered this man-made catastrophe. During the late 1920s and early 1930s, farmers plowed deep into virgin topsoil, displacing the native grass that provided structure and moisture. Consequently, droughts turned the soil into dust, and high winds blew it all away. Without access to arable land, farmers defaulted and abandoned rural communities en masse.

Although the Great Depression caused a massive downturn in urban areas, the sheer size of urban industries offered more economic opportunities than rural communities. In addition, New Deal programs more effectively provided social assistance and stimulated more economic growth in urban areas. For example, cities directly received money for social assistance through the **Federal Emergency Relief Administration** (FERA), and the **Public Works Administration** (PWA) provided funds to revive the construction industry. Large corporations also received substantial government funding to retain and hire more workers, and most of those corporations operated in American cities. As a result, unemployed rural migrants migrated to find work on assembly lines, which didn't typically require prior industrial experience.

Calls for a Stronger Financial Regulatory System

Although the United States produced dynamic levels of economic growth, the country's financial system was a near-perpetual disaster during the early twentieth century. Between 1890 and 1945, America's systematic lack of regulation and government oversight led to at least six distinct major recessions before culminating in the **Great Depression** (1929–1933).

The American banking system had been unstable since its founding in the early nineteenth century, and by the early twentieth century, the system lacked a central authority capable of injecting liquidity and enforcing a rules-based order. On **Black Tuesday**, October 29, 1929, unsustainable levels of American consumer debt combined with reckless financial speculation tanked the stock market. Although this was relatively common for the era, Black Tuesday occurred in the context of a global economic downturn, which soon turned into a global depression. The stock market collapse triggered cascading credit defaults, panic-based bank runs, and the collapse of consumer spending, as well as the call for a stronger national financial regulatory system to prevent similar events from occurring.

President Franklin D. Roosevelt made regulating the American financial system a major plank in his presidential platform and **New Deal** (1933–1939). Among other initiatives, New Deal policies strengthened the Federal Reserve central banking system, established the Federal Deposit Insurance Corporation (FDIC), and introduced regulations to increase transparency and thwart financial speculation.

A Limited Welfare State

The Great Depression upended liberalism in the United States. American liberalism had traditionally focused on maximizing individual liberties over addressing economic inequality, but the sudden influx of displaced, unemployed, and homeless Americans led to liberals establishing and defending a limited welfare state. President Franklin Delano Roosevelt explicitly campaigned against liberal beliefs regarding limited government, and the incredible popularity of his economic reforms tied American liberalism to poverty mitigation.

The **New Deal** represented the first large-scale effort to mitigate poverty through government spending. President Roosevelt created federal agencies and spearheaded legislation to reduce social upheaval by helping Americans meet their basic needs. The primary focus was on reducing unemployment. For example, the Civil Works Administration (1933–1934) and Works Progress Administration (1935–1943) combined to fund the creation of more than 10 million jobs. Other New Deal programs focused on housing and food subsidies, such as the Food Stamp Program (1939–1943) and Housing Act of 1937. One of the most effective and influential New Deal policies was the Social Security Act of 1935, which provided universal retirement pensions, unemployment insurance, and social assistance for poor children and disabled people. To fund these new agencies and policies, President Roosevelt introduced new taxes on wealthy Americans and corporations. The combination of limited social assistance and taxation on the wealthy has since remained the hallmark feature of American liberalism.

Despite conservative and business owners' hostility toward the new liberal conception of "big government," the New Deal was firmly committed to free market capitalism. For example, the United States handed over a significant amount of the funding for unemployment programs to private employers who promised to hire workers for specific projects. This reflects elite liberal policymakers' unbroken faith in the efficiency of free markets as well as their desire to undercut Socialist and Communist movements.

The New Deal

Franklin Roosevelt's New Deal

In 1932, in response to the looming global Great Depression of the 1930s, U.S. voters elected President Franklin Delano Roosevelt (FDR) to office because his presidential campaign promised to pull the United States out of economic despair. Unlike his predecessor—President Herbert Hoover—FDR eventually accepted the fact that the federal government would have to play a role in reviving the tattered U.S. economy. On March 4, 1933, FDR pledged a "**New Deal**" to the American people, one that would regain the trust of down-and-out American workers. This promise of a New Deal was followed by a deluge of socialist-democratic legislation. The New Deal attempted to revive the American economy and end the Great Depression through public works projects carried out by organizations such as the U.S. Civilian Conservation Corps. These public works projects and government-backed organizations provided jobs to unemployed men and women across the country, and helped stimulate economic recovery for the country.

Reception of the New Deal

By the end of the 1930s, the FDR administration had spent nearly $10 billion on the construction of hundreds of thousands of public buildings, roads, bridges, and airports. The New Deal also created new government agencies that could help struggling businesses and farms; it dispersed billions of dollars to welfare and relief programs for the poor. The New Deal, however, was just the beginning of socialist-democratic policies being infused into the economic fiber of the United States. Populist and radical movements pushed FDR toward expanding the New Deal and working to further the efforts to change the national economy. At the same time, conservative opponents in Congress and the Supreme Court fought to limit the scope of the New Deal.

Although the New Deal economy only improved slowly prior to the advent of World War II, the changes brought about by FDR's administration transformed the entire essence of the U.S. government's beliefs regarding the role of government in business and the economy. Some describe FDR's policies as the beginning of a **New Deal Order** that continued well into the Obama administration of the early 2000s. Others pejoratively call his policies the beginning of the U.S. "welfare state." Regardless of the terminology used to describe the New Deal programs, one cannot deny that the New Deal inevitably revolutionized the relationship between the federal government and the economy. The New Deal extended the reach of federal government, paving the way to expanded executive powers.

The New Deal's Legacy

The New Deal (1933–1939) is largely responsible for shaping the modern American regulatory system. Along with constructing the regulatory system that survived for decades after the end of the Roosevelt administration, the New Deal established numerous critical federal agencies, commonly referred to as the **alphabet agencies** due to the popularity of their acronyms. Examples of present-day alphabet agencies with roots in the New Deal include the Social Security Administration (SSA), National Labor Review Board (NLRB), and Securities and Exchange Commission (SEC).

President Roosevelt's political coalition also lasted for decades, ensuring the Democratic Party's intractable national relevance. This New Deal coalition is commonly described as a "big tent" political coalition because it consisted of working-class whites, African Americans, immigrants, environmentalists, socialists, technocrats, and elite liberals. Never before in American history had the working classes been politically united, and the Democratic party alignment of many of those in these groups has remained.

Historians and economists continue to debate the New Deal's impact on the Great Depression. Although it's unlikely the New Deal was solely responsible for ending the Great Depression, it certainly laid the foundation for a stable American government. Additionally, the New Deal's expansion of the federal government's economic role was invaluable in World War II, facilitating and centralizing processes for wartime production.

Interwar Foreign Policy

Unilateral Foreign Policy

Although isolationists effectively prevented Congress from signing the Treaty of Versailles or joining the League of Nations, the United States did anything but retreat from the international world order.

The United States held the diplomatic influence and military power to unilaterally intervene in a variety of conflicts in pursuit of its national interests. During the 1920s and 1930s, the United States organized several disarmament treaties, such as the London Naval Treaty (1930). The United States also worked to protect its financial investment in a recovered Europe, particularly in acting as the mediator in disputes over German debts owed to France under the Treaty of Versailles. For example, the United States played a key role in negotiating the Dawes Plan (1924) to create a more feasible debt-servicing plan.

Aside from diplomacy and investments, the United States also frequently leaned on its immense military power. The most brutal interventions occurred during the **Banana Wars** (1898–1934). Between 1915 and 1934, the United States successfully occupied and/or coerced more than a half dozen Latin American countries to protect American corporate interests. Likewise, immediately after the end of World War I, the United States sent AEF divisions to support capitalist factions fighting Communists in the Russian Revolution (1917–1923).

Fascism and the Attack on Pearl Harbor

In the period between the world wars, **fascism** became popular in many European countries that were ravaged by the Great Depression. Fascism is a political ideology that advocates for a dictatorship in order to provide stability and unity. Adolf Hitler emerged as a prominent fascist leader in Germany and eventually brought the Nazi party to power in 1933. Germany aligned with Italy and Japan in 1940 to form the **Axis Alliance**. Their goal was to establish a German empire in Europe and place Japan in control over Asia. The League of Nations could not diffuse the conflict. World War II broke out when Germany invaded Poland in 1939 and many countries declared war on Germany. When Germany invaded the Soviet Union in June 1941, the Soviets immediately allied with Britain.

Hitler quickly conquered most of Europe, except for Britain, and attacked the USSR in 1941. The United States sent military equipment and weapons to Britain and the USSR, but did not formally join the war until the Japanese attacked Pearl Harbor on December 7, 1941.

World War II: Mobilization

Economic Factors Helped End the Great Depression and World War II

Like nearly all of the other combatants, the United States adopted a total war strategy during World War II. Total war strategies involve mass mobilization of all resources and the entire workforce. For example, the United States rationed consumer goods and seized control over private industries to better reallocate resources for the war effort. In effect, the free market gave way to a command-based economic system, meaning the government unilaterally directed everything from production to consumption in a similar way as Communist regimes. Wartime demand for industrial production triggered an unprecedented economic boom, and as a result, the number of unemployed Americans decreased from 7.7 million to 1.5 million between 1940 and 1942, effectively ending the Great Depression.

American industrial production was crucial for the Allied victory. When presented with projections on the United States' industrial capacity, Nazi leaders mocked it as propaganda. By the time American troops arrived in Europe, the United States had wildly exceeded the most optimistic projections. In addition to outfitting 16 million American soldiers with the latest weapons and equipment, the United States' Lend-Lease Program allowed Great Britain and the Soviet Union to withstand Nazi invasions and eventually launch crucial offensive campaigns. Overall, the United States provided the present-day equivalent of $560 billion worth of food, oil, steel, warships, warplanes, and weaponry to the Allied powers.

Wartime Opportunities for Women and Minorities

As during World War I, women played an important role on the home front by working in factories to build guns, tanks, planes, and ships. African Americans, Native Americans, and Japanese Americans also contributed by fighting on the front lines.

With 16 million Americans serving overseas and demands on industrial production reaching historic levels, factories loosened the restrictions on the employment of women and people of color during World War II. Many of these jobs disappeared after the soldiers returned from overseas; however, it had a lasting impact. Posters like "Rosie the Riveter" broke traditional gender norms, laying the foundation for more women to find work outside of the household. Similarly, African Americans who served in the US Armed Forces or worked in factories learned valuable professional skills, which lifted many families into the middle class for the first time in generational history.

Despite this significant economic improvement, the United States still reinforced existing and introduced new oppressive policies as wartime measures. Even after 1.2 million African Americans fought for their country, the federal government still refused to intervene in the South to remove Jim Crow laws.

Japanese Americans also suffered great hardships. Without any supporting evidence, President Roosevelt issued an executive order to round up approximately 110,000 Japanese Americans and forcibly placed them in internment camps. Federal legislation intended to reimburse Japanese Americans was wildly insufficient, and many families permanently lost their homes and businesses to internment.

Immigration from the Western Hemisphere

Migration from the Western Hemisphere rapidly increased in the early twentieth century, particularly in comparison to immigrants coming from the Eastern Hemisphere. The Immigration Act of 1924 outright banned all immigration from Asia, established the US Border Control, and created a legal mechanism for deportation. Additionally, the **Immigration Act of 1924** implemented restrictive quotas for Eastern and Southeastern Europeans. These immigration restrictions underscored the growing tide of nativism in the United States.

Along with restricting the arrival of new immigrants, nativists enacted and revamped anti-immigration legislation. For example, many Western states began enforcing anti-vagrancy legislation that was first passed to deny political and property rights to Mexicans. However, nativist groups failed to prevent Congress from carving out exceptions explicitly for Mexicans in the Immigration Act of 1917. Likewise, the Immigration Act of 1924 didn't institute the same quota system for the Western Hemisphere, resulting in more immigration from the Caribbean and South America.

Congressional leniency toward Hispanic immigrants was the direct product of America's dependence on cheap labor. Once the Great Depression forced desperate white Americans to accept low-paying and dangerous work, the federal government immediately forcibly repatriated between 400,000 and two million people of Mexican descent, including American citizens.

World War II: Military

Fighting Against Fascism

The American foreign policy establishment characterized World War II as a global fight for the future of democracy. This wasn't anything new. Ever since the Revolutionary War (1775–1783), American politicians, journalists, and citizens had portrayed nearly every military conflict as an absolutely necessary measure for defending American freedom. World War II was different because the existential threat to democracy and freedom became increasingly self-evident as time progressed.

Nazi Germany and Japan were fascist powers willing to pursue global domination by any means necessary. Nearly every war involves some war crimes; however, the Axis powers differed in the strategic orchestration of mass killings. Nazi concentration and death camps systematically murdered an estimated two-thirds of European Jews during the Holocaust. On top of this, Nazi Germany oversaw the killing of approximately five million Slavs, Romani, and Soviet prisoners of war.

Although Americans didn't learn the full scope of the Holocaust for years after it commenced, Japanese war crimes in China and Korea were common knowledge. Overall, Japanese imperial forces killed between three million and fourteen million civilians in large-scale massacres and forced labor camps. As such, it wasn't hyperbolic or hysterical to describe the Axis powers as a genuine existential threat to democracy and freedom, a feeling that resonated with most Americans at the time.

The United States' Military Victory

The U.S. entered the war when Japan bombed Pearl Harbor in Hawaii on December 7, 1941. Battles raged in Europe and the Pacific, and the Allied forces won an important victory in June 1942 at the **Battle of Midway**. At this battle, the U.S. stopped the Japanese from advancing and prevented the invasion of Australia. In 1943, Axis troops in North Africa surrendered to the Allies, who then began to invade Italy, and finally France on June 6, 1944 (known as **D-Day**), which resulted in severe losses on both sides. In early 1945, President Roosevelt met with British Prime Minister **Winston Churchill** and Soviet director Joseph Stalin in Yalta, Crimea to plan their final assault on Germany and discuss postwar strategies. The Allies continued their attack, liberating Nazi death camps. This forced Hitler to commit suicide, and Germany surrendered in May. However, Japan did not yield, even after the capture of Okinawa in June. As a result, the U.S. dropped an atomic bomb on the Japanese cities of Hiroshima and then Nagasaki, forcing Japan to surrender in early September.

Many factors contributed to the United States' success in World War II.

The United States was an economic powerhouse, providing a consistent supply of money, steel, weapons, and food to the Allied powers. Even with 16 million American soldiers fighting overseas, the production continually increased as a stream of women and people of color entered the industrial workforce. The Allied powers also made use of groundbreaking technological innovations, such as anti-aircraft radar and code-breaking computers.

The Allied powers jointly and cooperatively waged a multi-theater war. After the Americans' daring D-Day amphibious invasion of Nazi-held beaches in Normandy, American and British forces drove the Nazis out of Western Europe and North Africa. At the same time, the Soviet Union resiliently held the line against a Nazi onslaught and eventually turned the tides.

The United States took the lead in the Pacific theater in an "island-hopping" strategy to create space for an aggressive air bombing campaign and clear a path to Japan. President Harry S. Truman authorized the first-ever use of atomic weapons on the Japanese cities of Nagasaki and Hiroshima in August 1945, effectively ending the war. Although many activists have criticized the use of nuclear weapons, and the decision remains controversial to this day, an invasion would have left many millions more people dead.

Postwar Diplomacy

Postwar Conditions for Various Nations

World War II had a devastating impact on Europe and Asia. Nearly all Asian and European states had death tolls in the millions, and entire urban centers lay in ruins. For example, an American firebombing campaign incinerated nearly 16 square miles of Tokyo. As a result, European and Asian countries struggled to find a footing in the conflict's immediate aftermath, relying heavily on American financial and military assistance to rebuild critical industries.

In contrast, the United States had escaped the conflict with minimal damage to domestic industries and exponentially fewer civilian casualties compared to all of the other major combatants. Furthermore, American economic production also dwarfed all of its competitors, and Western Europe functioned as an ideal export market for American goods. America's wartime loans and continued financial assistance also translated into durable political influence in Western Europe.

The United States' position in the global hierarchy was strong even compared to the Soviet Union, the only other remaining superpower. Somewhere between 13 million and 27 million Soviet citizens died in the fighting, which led all combatants by a wide margin. As such, the United States emerged from World War II as one of the most powerful states in modern history.

Toward the end of World War II, a group of fifty nations (including the U.S. and the Soviet Union) formed the **United Nations** as a peacekeeping group. However, Communism still continued to spread throughout the world, including to Latin America, Africa, and Asia. When Communist North Korea invaded South Korea in June 1950, the U.N. sent a group of troops led by the U.S. to help South Korea. This action led to a three-year conflict that ended in a cease-fire in 1953. Although war was never officially declared and neither side won, the fighting showcased President Truman's hard stance against Communism.

Practice Quiz

Questions 1–5 are based on the following poem. Read it carefully then answer the questions.

I sit and sew—a useless task it seems,
My hands grown tired, my head weighed down with dreams—
The panoply of war, the martial tred of men,
Grim-faced, stern-eyed, gazing beyond the ken
Of lesser souls, whose eyes have not seen Death,
Nor learned to hold their lives but as a breath—
But—I must sit and sew.

I sit and sew—my heart aches with desire—
That pageant terrible, that fiercely pouring fire
On wasted fields, and writhing grotesque things
Once men. My soul in pity flings
Appealing cries, yearning only to go
There in that holocaust of hell, those fields of woe—
But—I must sit and sew.

The little useless seam, the idle patch;
Why dream I here beneath my homely thatch,
When there they lie in sodden mud and rain,
Pitifully calling me, the quick ones and the slain?
You need me, Christ! It is no roseate dream
That beckons me—this pretty futile seam,
It stifles me—God, must I sit and sew?

Poem "I Sit and Sew" by Alice Moore Dunbar-Nelson, 1918

1. In line 9, the speaker mentions a "pageant." What is she referring to?
   a. A beauty pageant
   b. The current war
   c. A popular play
   d. A wedding celebration

2. In the first stanza, who are the "martial tred of men, / Grim-faced, stern-eyed" that the speaker mentions in lines 3 and 4?
   a. Children
   b. Enemies
   c. Soldiers
   d. Neighbors

3. What idea does the speaker effectively contrast in this poem?
   a. The idea between the usefulness of sewing and the uselessness of war, namely that men's bodies are literally being wasted on the battlefield while sewing gives the opportunity of creating clothes for those same bodies.
   b. The idea between right and wrong, specifically that the war and everything relating to it is immoral, and the domestic side of life, including sewing, can be seen as doing good.
   c. The idea between sacrifice and selfishness; the speaker is admitting that she is being selfish for wanting to pursue her passion of sewing rather than helping out with the war.
   d. The idea between activeness and passiveness in the sense that the speaker views sewing as passiveness and longs to do something active in order to help out in the war.

4. What type of poetic lines are included in this poem?
   a. English sonnets
   b. Alternating tercets
   c. Rhyming couplets
   d. Syllabic haikus

5. How many stanzas does this poem have?
   a. 1
   b. 2
   c. 3
   d. 4

Answer Explanations

1. B: The speaker is referring to the current war, Choice *B*. The lines say: "I set and sew—my heart aches with desire— / That pageant terrible, that fiercely pouring fire / On wasted fields, and writhing grotesque things / Once men" (lines 8–11). Pageant is a metaphor for the battlefield in this poem. After she mentions the word "pageant," the speaker then goes on to describe the "pageant," or war, by describing the fire, fields, and dying men.

2. C: The speaker is referring to soldiers in these lines, so Choice *C* is correct. If we look at the surrounding context clues, the word "war" is mentioned before the description of these men. The word "tred" refers to a sort of weary marching.

3. D: The speaker effectively contrasts the idea between activeness and passiveness in the sense that the speaker views sewing as something passive and longs to do something active in order to help out in the war. Let's look at the poem for proof of this contrast. In the first stanza, the dull act of sewing is set in contrast with the horror that happens in her dreams. In the second stanza, the massacre in the war is contrasted by her, again "sitting and sewing" and yearning to help. Finally, in the third stanza, her "useless seam" is contrasted with the soldiers dying in the mud. The stark contrast of the comforts and ease of sewing to the pain and suffering of soldiers in active duty is a central theme in this poem.

4. C: Poetic lines that can be seen in this poem are rhyming couplets. Rhyming couplets are two pairs of lines that end with rhyming words. We see this all the way through, except for the last line in each stanza, which ends with the word "sew." Here are some examples of the end rhymes of the rhyming couplets: "seems" and "dreams," "things" and "flings," "rain" and "slain."

5. C: A stanza is a group of lines that make up a repeating metrical unit of a poem. We see that there are three stanzas, and each stanza consists of seven lines each. The seven lines have three rhyming couplets (six lines) and end with a seventh line that has no end rhyme. However, the last word in every unit is "sew," which makes a cohesive repetition in the poem.

Section 8: The Cold War Era (1945–1980)

The Cold War from 1945 to 1980

War Against Communism

Within two years of World War II, the world was involved in a different kind of war—a **Cold War**—that pitted capitalism and Communism against each other. World War II left Europe on the brink of collapse, leaving the United States and Soviet Union as the world's undisputed remaining superpowers. The United States and its Allies embarked on a campaign of containment in an attempt to keep Communism from spreading to other countries, and to create a global free-market economy instead.

Postwar U.S. Foreign Policy

The United States developed a foreign policy after the war that was based on international security and aid, and economic institutions and infrastructures that supported the free-market economy. In the 1940s, U.S. president Harry S. Truman, in an effort to contain Communism, offered U.S. military and economic protection to any nation threatened by Communist takeover. By 1949, the United States, Canada, and ten European nations agreed to the same idea in an alliance known as the **North Atlantic Treaty Organization (NATO)**. When West Germany was invited into NATO in 1955, the Soviet Union responded with a similar alliance known as the **Warsaw Pact**. The Warsaw Pact and NATO were vehicles for the United States and Soviet Union to flex their military might. In addition to conventional arms, the two superpowers competed in a nuclear arms race throughout the Cold War. The nuclear arms race created a situation where each country could destroy the world many times over at the push of a button. There were several close calls during the conflict due to mixed signals, misunderstandings, or provocation—the most notorious being the **Cuban Missile Crisis** when the Soviet Union placed nuclear missiles in Cuba, ninety miles away from Florida.

Containing Communism

The United States fought a series of proxy wars against the Soviet Union to prevent the spread of Communism. The **Korean War**, 1950-1953, was an attempt to keep Communism from spreading into Korea. China and the Soviet Union joined together to fight the United States and Allies until an armistice was signed that divided Korea into a Communist North and a democratic South along the thirty-eighth parallel. The thirty-eighth parallel was an important demarcation during the war itself, as America was cautious to pursue the North Koreans back across the parallel or else risk escalating the proxy war into a conventional one against the Soviets.

The **Vietnam Conflict**, 1955-1975, was another proxy war pitting the United States against Communism. China and the Soviet Union provided extensive aid to the Communist **Viet Cong** guerilla fighters and the more conventional North Vietnamese army. Although the United States was the superior conventional military force, the American military struggled mightily against the guerillas using the dense jungle as cover. As intense opposition to the war mounted in the United States, the United States withdrew after the North Vietnamese captured Saigon in April 1975. The Soviet Union similarly struggled against guerilla forces backed by the United States during the **Soviet-Afghan War**, which lasted between 1979 and 1989. The United States provided military and financial support to the Afghans during the conflict, many of who would later found al-Qaeda or join the Taliban to fight the United States, including Osama bin Laden.

Conflict and Détente

Tensions fluctuated between the United States and the Soviet Union during the Cold War (1947–1991), ranging from large-scale indirect hot wars to periods of easing hostilities (**détente**). The major hot wars, or conflicts in which the Americans and/or Soviets overtly committed substantial personnel and supplies to the fighting, were the Korean War (1950–1953), Vietnam War (1955–1975), and Soviet-Afghan War (1979–1989). Additionally, throughout the Cold War, the Soviets and Americans both covertly funded and supplied many dozens of proxy forces in armed conflicts.

Periods of détente typically featured more dialogue and less indirect fighting compared to overt hot wars. The longest period of détente occurred in the 1970s as American president Richard Nixon and Soviet general secretary Leonid Brezhnev sought to avert further nuclear escalation by establishing stronger working dialogue. Several major treaties, including the **Anti-Ballistic Missile Treaty** (1972) and the nonbinding **Helsinki Accords** (1975), were signed in the 1970s in an attempt to improve relations and encourage disarmament. However, even in the best of times, both superpowers never fully stopped arming proxies and conducting a variety of disinformation campaigns and election interference in foreign countries. Détente officially ended when the Soviet Union invaded Afghanistan in 1979.

The Red Scare

Exposing Communists and Containing Communism

The **Red Scare** referred to the propagation of the fear of Communism and of the spread of Communism throughout the United States. While there was a Red Scare after World War I, there was a second Red Scare after World War II that was also called **McCarthyism**. McCarthyism which is a term in history and political science used to describe a period in American history that witnessed Wisconsin senator Joseph McCarthy lead the charge in a series of accusatory investigations and trials that sought to uncover and criminalize communist sympathies in U.S. society. Throughout the 1950s, McCarthy, who was elected to the Senate in 1946, rose to prominence in the 1950s when he made unsubstantiated claims about over 205 communists infiltrating the State Department. These claims led to a series of investigations and public hearings, which reached their peak in 1954 with thirty-six days of televised hearings. These hearings also symbolized the beginning of the end for McCarthyism. McCarthy's claims remained unsubstantiated despite their publicity, and by 1957 he had been censored by the Senate. McCarthyism is now a term that has become synonymous with Cold War fears and any type of public defamation or indiscriminate allegations.

Karl Marx (1818–1883), a philosopher, social scientist, historian, and revolutionary, is considered one of the most influential Socialist thinkers of the nineteenth century. His ideas became known as **Marxism**, and Marx heavily influenced powerful Socialist and Communist leaders, such as **Vladimir Lenin**, with his 1848 pamphlet *The Communist Manifesto.* In this pamphlet, he explained that, in a capitalist society, perpetual "class struggle" exists in which a ruling class (**bourgeois**) controls the means of production and exploits the working class (**proletariat**), who are forced to sell labor for wages. He advocated for the working class to rebel against the ruling class and establish a classless society with collective ownership of the means of production. He envisioned world history as a series of stages in which capitalism eventually collapses into Communism.

Economy After 1945

Economic Growth

The United States' annual **gross domestic product** (GDP) continually grew between 1950 and 1970 and, in some years, increased by as much as eight percent. Economists believe four factors played an outsized role in America's rapid economic expansion.

First, technological innovations increased the efficiency and profitability of commercial enterprises. The development of commercial airlines expedited long-distance travel times, and the invention of color television provided a new way for businesses to reach customers. In addition, some innovations created new economic sectors, especially in relation to computers.

Second, post–World War II euphoria and economic prosperity produced a baby boom. The resulting population increase drove up consumer spending and industrial productivity rates. The baby boomer generation was also incredibly productive due to the low costs of higher education and housing.

Third, heavy taxes on economic elites boosted government spending, which translated to more government services and infrastructure investments. For example, Congress passed the Federal Aid Highway Assistance Act (1956) to fund the construction of more than 40,000 miles of interconnected federal highways,

Fourth, the private sector experienced significant gains based on a virtuous cycle of increased consumer spending, mass manufacturing innovations, and strong demand for American products abroad.

Suburbs and a Migration to the Sun Belt

During the 1950s and 1960s, Americans enjoyed more social mobility than any other national population. The United States led the world in industrial production, manufacturing exports, and consumer spending. Telephones and televisions further broadened economic opportunities and tightened community bonds. Additionally, many American families were lifted into the middle class with assistance from the **GI Bill** (1944), which provided veterans with subsidized loans, unemployment benefits, and tuition assistance. Between 1944 and 1956, nearly eight million American veterans claimed tuition assistance under the GI Bill, which improved household incomes and expanded America's supply of skilled labor.

The explosive growth of the American middle class led to rapid suburbanization, particularly after the integration of public schools triggered a phenomenon referred to as "**white flight**." Some American families moved farther away than the nearby suburbs and relocated to the **Sun Bel**t region, which refers to the Southeastern and Southwestern regions of the United States. The Sun Belt offered a more appealing climate and lower tax rates than the Northeast and Midwest. In addition, the Sun Belt was also home to several economic sectors, such as the aerospace, defense, and oil industries, that experienced rapid growth in the 1960s and 1970s.

Culture after 1945

Mass Culture and the Counter-Culture Movement

In the postwar years, mass culture was more homogenized than it typically had been. This homogeny inspired many artists, intellectuals, and young people to be somewhat rebellious and challenge conformity. The **counter-culture movement** became more popular during the 1960s as millions of children from the Baby Boomers generation entered into adulthood. Veterans came home after World War II and started families, and, by the 1960s, many of these young adults also felt disaffected and rebellious. Their parents criticized them because they began to wear colorful clothing and the boys let their hair grow out. Many members of the counter-culture movement, now called hippies, inherited the beatnik's interest in African and Asian cultures. Writer Ken Kesey traveled around the country on a bus encouraging people to experiment with psychedelic drugs, such as LSD. The counter-culture movement influenced musicians and avant-garde artists.

The counter-culture movement was also closely connected to other protest movements during the 1960s, including the Civil Rights movement. Many members of the counter-culture movement during the 1960s also opposed the war in Vietnam. The Baby Boomers could be conscripted to fight in Vietnam whether they wanted to or not. In 1965, young men began burning their draft cards, which was a criminal offense, in protest. Massive demonstrations against the war occurred around the country, especially on college campuses, but many other people also refused to support the war effort, including clergymen and even some veterans who had fought in Vietnam. The counter-culture movement disappeared during the 1970s but had a lasting impact on the social and cultural history of the United States.

Early Steps in the Civil Rights Movement (1940s and 1950s)

Legal and Political Successes in Ending Segregation

Activists began organizing the civil rights movement in the 1940s to achieve racial equality by ending segregation and enfranchising African Americans. The general strategy was to build public support and pressure the federal government to enforce the Fourteenth and Fifteenth amendments.

Many historians consider A. Philip Randolph and Bayard Rustin's **March on Washington Movement** (1941–1946) to be the beginning of the civil rights movement. Randolph and Rustin's nonviolent tactics heavily contributed to the desegregation of the military (1948) and inspired a new generation of civil rights activists, including Martin Luther King Jr. The civil rights movement then gained steam in the late 1940s and 1950s as activists developed new legal strategies, such as boycotts, sit-ins, and litigation. Activists enjoyed considerable success in targeting specific businesses with boycotts. After Claudette Colvin and Rosa Parks courageously refused to give up their seats on Montgomery, Ala., buses in 1955, King led a successful bus boycott. Similarly, in 1958, the **National Association for the Advancement of Colored People** (NAACP) Youth Council conducted sit-ins at a lunch counter in Kansas, and their victory sparked a nationwide movement.

Targeted litigation also propelled the civil rights movement, and the NAACP led several efforts to bring legal challenges against discriminatory laws. Five of these test cases were combined in the famous **Brown v. Board of Education** (1954), and the Supreme Court ultimately ruled that the segregation of public schools was unconstitutional. Three years later, President Dwight D. Eisenhower enforced the

Supreme Court's decision by ordering the 101st Airborne Division to escort nine African American schoolchildren ("**Little Rock Nine**") into an illegally segregated school.

Despite these notable achievements, progress was a gradual process. An overwhelming majority of white Americans characterized the civil rights movement as the work of outside agitators and denounced King as a race baiter. Jim Crow laws remained in effect, and the grotesque lynching of **Emmett Till**—a 14 year-old boy wrongly accused of whistling at a white woman—was more of a rule than an exception. Still, early civil rights activists' dedication and sacrifices paved the way for landmark victories in the 1960s.

Governmental Efforts to Promote Racial Equality

All three branches of the United States government implemented measures to desegregate the nation and promote racial equality. The armed services became desegregated in 1948 with Executive Order 9981 by President Harry S. Truman. When the Supreme Court ruled that school segregation was illegal in 1954 in the revolutionary case **Brown v. the Board of Education**, the **Civil Rights Movement** was set in motion. This movement continued throughout the 1950s and 1960s and included dozens of nonviolent protests, such as the Montgomery bus boycott in Alabama. The boycott was organized after **Rosa Parks** was arrested because she refused to give up her seat on the bus to a white man. The Southern Christian Leadership Conference (SCLC) was soon formed as a way to bring African Americans together to help fight segregation in a peaceful way. The Reverend **Dr. Martin Luther King, Jr.** was its first president. Dr. King and his supporters kept up the fight throughout the 1960s, staging sit-ins at segregated lunch counters, **Freedom Rides** on segregated buses, and marches and protests in segregated cities, such as Birmingham, Alabama. The demonstrations often ended in violence and police brutality, which served to aid the cause and led to the passage of the **Civil Rights Act** in 1964. As the broadest and arguably impactful civil rights legislature since Reconstruction, the Civil Rights Act called for the desegregation of schools and public facilities, and made it illegal for employers to discriminate based on race or ethnicity.

America as a World Power

Cold War Conflict in Latin America

The United States practiced a supercharged version of the Monroe Doctrine as it endeavored to keep Communism out of its proverbial backyard. Although the United States publicly championed democracy and freedom, such things were only ever considered when they conveniently coincided with American commercial and geopolitical interests.

The United States backed proxy wars and coup attempts in more than a dozen Latin American countries between 1945 and 1980. Material support was most often provided to groups aligned against left-wing governments. Most infamously, in 1973, the United States backed the overthrow of the democratically elected Chilean president **Salvador Allende**. With help from his American allies, General **Augusto Pinochet** then instituted and seized control over a military dictatorship. Pinochet is most remembered for zealously supporting free markets and brazenly ordering secret police to kidnap, imprison, and/or assassinate thousands of dissidents. The Chilean coup d'état was far more the rule than the exception.

Long-standing American proxy forces, such as the Guatemalan White Hand and Nicaraguan Contras, also regularly deployed death squads to terrorize indigenous populations, socialist communes, and left-wing governments. Overall, American foreign policy was always ready and willing to take whatever means necessary to protect its geopolitical interests and international capitalism.

Debates Over Military Activity

Although the American public generally supported massive military spending during the Cold War, some aspects of the United States military were incredibly controversial.

During his famous farewell address in 1961, President **Dwight D. Eisenhower** delivered a warning about how the growing military-industrial complex threatened American democracy by consolidating unwarranted power. Although antiwar activists continually condemned the military-industrial complex as it expanded throughout the Cold War, reform was never attempted due to strong anti-Communist sentiments, bureaucratic inertia, and the effect of arms manufacturers on domestic employment.

Antiwar activists also frequently protested against nuclear proliferation, arguing it was immoral to build weapons of mass destruction; however, nuclear stockpile reductions didn't occur until the end of the Cold War.

Americans debated the power of the executive branch, which has grown continuously since the 1930s. Additionally, antiwar activists accused the US government of using its extensive enforcement powers to infiltrate, harass, and squash left-wing political movements in the United States. Those accusations turned out to be true. Under the leadership of **Edgar Hoover**, the Federal Bureau of Investigation (FBI) conducted a covert program known as the COunter INTELligence PROgram (COINTELPRO) (1956–1971) to infiltrate, harass, discredit, and annihilate left-wing groups, including the Black Panthers, Chicano Movement, and American Indian Movement (AIM).

New International Allies

Following the end of World War II, decolonization and nationalist movements resulted in the formation of more than a hundred newly independent states in Africa, Asia, and the Middle East. An overwhelming number of these states attempted to remain as neutral as possible during the Cold War because stability is the lifeblood of economic and political development. In addition, most new states were reluctant to cede authority to global superpowers given what they had suffered in the past.

During the 1960s, states joined the **Non-Aligned Movement** to collectively announce their neutrality and avoid being collateral damage in a foreign ideological conflict. According to Cuban leader Fidel Castro's **Havana Declaration** (1979), the Non-Alignment stood in solidarity with all countries that experienced colonialism, imperialism, racism, and foreign intervention of any kind. Some of the member states also had powerful incentives to seek collective security and publicly declare neutrality, particularly those states with left-wing governments, such as Cuba and Yugoslavia. Despite the Non-Aligned Movement's efforts, American and Soviet policymakers gave little credence to foreign countries' proclamations of neutrality, especially if a country occupied valuable geopolitical space or possessed strategic assets. The superpowers were also effective at enlisting the help of client states through coercion, financial incentives, and military assistance.

The Vietnam War

During World War II, Vietnamese rebels worked with the Allied powers to overthrow Japanese Imperial Forces, and upon their victory, the rebels expected to receive independence from France, which had colonized Vietnam in the late nineteenth century as part of its French Indochina colony. France refused to free Vietnam, and the United States provided France with an overwhelming amount of financial and material support to prevent the spread of Communism across Southeast Asia. In turn, the Soviet Union and China backed the Communist rebel faction, which sought independence for Vietnam.

Following the **Geneva Accords** of 1954, Vietnam split into Communist North Vietnam and capitalist South Vietnam, which resulted in the region becoming one of the active fronts in the Cold War. To deter the Soviet-backed North Vietnamese forces from invading, in 1955 the United States began providing more financial and military assistance to South Vietnam. Following a series of naval skirmishes known as the **Gulf of Tonkin** (1964), President Lyndon B. Johnson distorted and exploited the chaos to justify a full-scale American military intervention. Much of the fighting occurred in Vietnam's dense jungles, and both sides committed atrocities at an alarming rate. One of those atrocities, the **My Lai massacre** (1968), involved American forces murdering hundreds of Vietnamese villagers in cold blood.

The United States held a decisive advantage throughout the conflict due to its air superiority and massive bombing campaigns of North Vietnam and Laos. For example, the United States dropped more bombs on Laos alone than it did in the entirety of World War II. In addition, the United States conducted a secret bombing campaign against Cambodia to destroy Communist supply lines.

Despite its military victories, many Americans opposed the war, which caused anti-war protests and unrest. Anti-war opposition reached a fever pitch in the aftermath of North Vietnam's **Tet Offensive** (1968). Although the Tet Offensive was a military disaster, it was a public relations coup for North Vietnam because it thoroughly disproved President Johnson's claims that the conflict was nearly over. As a result, the United States dramatically reduced its combat forces, and a cease-fire was signed in 1973. North Vietnamese forces then steamrolled through South Vietnam, and the last US forces pulled out in 1975 shortly before the fall of Saigon, which officially ended the Vietnam War.

The Great Society

Concern for Poverty

As Europe sifted through the ashes in the aftermath of World War II, the United States occupied a dominant economic position. A large supply of blue-collar manufacturing jobs lifted millions of Americans into the middle class, and the United States invested significant amounts of its newfound wealth on major infrastructure projects to support the surging birth rate. At the same time, tens of millions were locked out of this idyllic society.

The federal government provided minimal assistance to alleviate poverty. Slum-like housing was pervasive in urban areas. Additionally, many rural communities and urban neighborhoods lacked access to essential services. African Americans and people of color especially suffered in the postwar socioeconomic system due to the prevalence of segregation, racial discrimination, voting restrictions, and artificial limitations placed on economic pursuits.

President Lyndon B. Johnson took action to eliminate poverty through his **War on Poverty**—a set of policy initiatives. The War on Poverty was the second-largest expansion of America's social safety after the New Deal, and many of its programs, including Medicaid, Medicare, and subsidies for food, have survived through the present day. Additionally, the War on Poverty dramatically increased federal funding for public education, job training, and community services.

Liberalism

Liberalism arguably peaked in the 1960s in terms of its control over the White House and both houses of Congress. A major part of liberals' emergence as the clear-cut electoral favorite was based on a combination of hawkish foreign policy and progressive domestic reform.

Liberal politicians supported a variety of military interventions to contain Communism. **President John F. Kennedy**, a New England liberal Democrat, authorized the failed **Bay of Pigs** invasion (1961) to covertly overthrow Cuba's Communist regime and took America further down the road to a full-fledged armed conflict in Vietnam. His successor, liberal Democrat Lyndon B. Johnson, exaggerated and exploited the **Gulf of Tonkin incident** (1964)—an alleged Vietnamese attack on American warships—to justify a proper full-scale invasion of Vietnam.

Anti-Communism insulated liberals from conservative attacks, many of which characterized ending segregation and enfranchising people of color as a Soviet plot to destroy America to push through sweeping domestic reform.

Combined with his expertise in congressional procedures and penchant for coercion, President Johnson masterfully leveraged this liberal groundswell to pass a series of landmark legislation, including the Civil Rights Act (1964), Food Stamp Act (1964), Voting Rights Act (1965), and Social Security Act (1965).

The Great Society

The **Great Society** was another major government program that the Democratic Party supported. President Lyndon B. Johnson sought to end poverty and improve education. For example, he raised the minimum wage and created programs to provide poor Americans with job training. The Great Society also implemented a number of Civil Rights laws to address racial discrimination.

The Immigration and Nationality Act of 1965

Immigrants flocked to the United States in the mid-twentieth century to gain political freedoms, pursue opportunities in the booming economy, and protect their families from social unrest.

During the early 1960s, the United States was still using the **National Origins Formula** to restrict immigration from outside Northwestern Europe and Latin America. The **Immigration and Nationality Act of 1965** abolished and repealed the restrictive quota system and established a foundation for contemporary immigration policy. However, Congress did include a provision to limit immigration from the Western Hemisphere for the first time in American history.

The Immigration and Nationality Act of 1965 ushered in many demographic changes. The lifting of restrictions on Asian immigrants led to sharp increases in Chinese, Japanese, Korean, and Vietnamese immigration. Likewise, immigration from most African countries reached record highs after 1965. At the same time, Hispanic immigration officially declined, although estimates of illegal border crossing steadily increased as the Cold War destabilized Latin America and forced families to flee for safety. Aside from changing immigrants' demographic composition, the removal of the National Origins Formula led to a steep rise in total immigration. For example, foreign-born people accounted for five percent of the United States' population in 1965, and by 2016, it had increased to 14 percent.

The African American Civil Rights Movement (1960s)

Civil Rights Activists

Martin Luther King Jr. was a Civil Rights leader and activist as well as a Baptist minister. Dr. King argued for nonviolent resistance during the Civil Rights movement, for which he won the Nobel Peace Prize in 1964. Dr. King was assassinated on April 4, 1968, in Memphis, Tennessee.

Dr. Martin Luther King Jr. gave his speech "I Have a Dream" as part of the 1963 March on Washington. Drawing on Lincoln's past speech at Gettysburg, Dr. King argued that America's journey to true equality was not over yet. His references to biblical passages gave the speech a spiritual tone, but he also mentioned specific locations across the nation to signify how local struggles were tied with national consequences. By emphasizing his optimism, Dr. King's speech reflects not only civil rights activism but also the American dream of freedom and progress.

Cesar Chavez was a labor union activist who organized transient Hispanic agricultural workers in an effort to obtain better working conditions in the 1960s and 1970s. He co-founded the National Farm Workers Association. Chavez became a historical icon after his death and is famous for popularizing the slogan "Sí, se puede," or "Yes, it can be done."

Betty Friedan was an American feminist and writer in the second wave of feminism in the 1960s who was elected the first president of the **Nation Organization for Women** (NOW). Her book, *The Feminine Mystique,* is often credited with beginning this second wave. Friedan aimed to empower women to be in an equal partnership with men. She also led the **Women's Strike for Equality** in 1970, which advocated for equal opportunities for women in jobs and education.

Debates Over Nonviolence

Much of America was still resistant toward desegregating the country and promoting racial equality. Racial tensions were at an all-time high in the early to mid-1960s. This led to social and political unrest both within the country as a whole, and slowed the progress of civil rights activists. Not all civil rights activists were united in their ideas and actions to advocate for change. Particularly after 1965, there was a marked rise in the debates between civil rights activists over violent versus nonviolent approaches toward the movement. An African American human rights activist and Muslim minister, **Malcolm X** advocated for the rights of African Americans. He became a member of the Nation of Islam, and through that platform promoted the separation of black and white Americans and black supremacy. Malcolm X rejected the Civil Rights movement for its emphasis on integration as well as passive resistance. Malcolm X is known to his admirers as a courageous and important figure in African American history.

Supreme Court Decisions Expanded Civil Rights

During the 1960s, the Supreme Court handed down a series of landmark decisions that greatly expanded civil rights and protected civil liberties.

The Supreme Court expanded civil rights through its prohibitions on racial discrimination. In **Bailey v. Patterson** (1962), the Supreme Court prohibited the segregation of interstate and intrastate transportation systems. Combined with the court's decision in **Brown v. Board of Education** (1954), this decision effectively ended the racial segregation of public places. In **Loving v. Virginia** (1967), the Supreme Court found Virginia's Racial Integrity Act (1924) to be unconstitutional and prohibited race-based restrictions on marriage. In **Jones v. Alfred H. Mayer Co.** (1968), the court reversed prior precedents and relied on the Civil Rights Act of 1886 to prohibit racial discrimination in both public and private commercial transactions.

Numerous landmark Supreme Court decisions strengthened civil liberties during the 1960s. In **Mapp v. Ohio** (1961), the Supreme Court ruled that the Fourth Amendment also protected people from unreasonable searches and seizures conducted by state law enforcement as well as federal law enforcement. In **Engel v. Vitale** (1962), the court reaffirmed the separation of church and state by invalidating a New York statute that forced schoolchildren to recite a prayer. In **Gideon v. Wainwright** (1963), the Supreme Court found that the government must provide criminal defendants with an attorney if they otherwise cannot afford legal representation. In **Griswold v. Connecticut** (1965), the court laid the foundation for a constitutional right to privacy in its finding that married people had the right to obtain and use contraception. In **Miranda v. Arizona** (1966), the Supreme Court threw out a defendant's confession because the police violated his Fifth Amendment protection from self-incrimination by failing to inform him of his right to remain silent. In **Tinker v. Des Moines** (1969), the court found the wearing of an anti-war armband in school to be permissible free speech under the First Amendment.

The Civil Rights Movement Expands

Latino, American Indian, and Asian American Civil Rights Movements

Asian Americans, American Indians, and Latinos had mixed results in advocating for greater equality and reparations for past abuses.

Asian American political movements lobbied Congress to outlaw racial discrimination in employment and public settings. Additionally, Asian Americans pushed for the overturn of disproportionately restrictive immigration laws that targeted Asian migrants, such as the **Asian Exclusion Act of 1924**. They achieved a notable success through the passage of the significantly more liberal **Immigration and Nationality Act of 1965**, which removed significant obstacles for millions of Asian immigrants.

During the 1960s and 1970s, numerous American Indian and Latino activists founded political movements modeled after the civil rights and Black Power movements. The **Chicano Movement** formed around the desire to empower Mexican Americans to fight back against systematic racial discrimination and seek justice for the generation of Mexican Americans who were collectively deported during the Great Depression. Likewise, the **American Indian Movement** (AIM) and **Red Power Movement** encouraged American Indians to be proud of their heritage and collectively defend their historic homeland from the federal government. Both of these movements adopted many of the civil rights movement's use of civil disobedience; however, they also had more confrontational elements, particularly when organizing against antiwar actions.

Feminist and LGBT Activists

The women's rights and lesbian, gay, bisexual, and transgender (LGBT) movements gained steam in the mid-twentieth century, achieving some groundbreaking victories in the fight for legal and socioeconomic equality.

After World War II, although many women lost their factory jobs to soldiers returning home, the conflict marked a major turning point for women. As women continued to seek more advanced levels of educational and professional opportunities, feminists mobilized the women's rights movement to push for more societal equality, equal compensation, birth control access, and legal protection against sexual violence. The Supreme Court's decision to uphold the constitutionality of abortion in ***Roe v. Wade*** (1973) was a major victory for the budding feminist movement; however, they faced a fierce backlash from social conservatives and Christian evangelicals who condemned abortion and pushed back against gender equality.

After a group of LGBT people bravely resisted a police raid at the **Stonewall Riots** (1969), several LGBT activists formed the **Gay Liberation Movement** to forcibly resist police harassment and raise awareness of LGBT issues. During the 1970s and early 1980s, the LGBT Rights Movement formed to advocate for legal equality and support LGBT politicians, such as the legendary **Harvey Milk**, the first openly gay person to serve in the US government.

Feminists in the Counterculture Movement

Although women had achieved political equality, they continued to demand reform throughout the 20th century. In the early 1900s, **Margaret Sanger** provided women with information about birth control, which was illegal at the time. Women entered the industrial workforce in large numbers during World War II, but when the war ended, they were fired so that veterans would have jobs when they came home. Many women were frustrated when told they had to return to their domestic lives. **Simone de Beauvoir**, a French writer, published her book *The Second Sex* after World War II, and an English translation was published in 1953. It highlighted the unequal treatment of women throughout history and sparked a feminist movement in the United States. In 1963, **Betty Friedan** published a book called *The Feminine Mystique*, which revealed how frustrated many suburban wives were with the social norms that kept them at home. During the 1960s, women participated in the sexual revolution and exerted more control over their own sexuality. In 1972, Congress passed **Title IX**, which prohibited sexual discrimination in education and expanded women's sports programs. In the 1970s, women's rights activists also pushed for greater access to birth control, and in 1973 the Supreme Court issued the controversial decision **Roe v. Wade**, which removed many barriers to abortion services. Women also demanded greater protection from domestic abuse and greater access to divorce.

During the twentieth century, many American women made notable achievements, including Amelia Earhart, who was the first woman to cross the Atlantic in an airplane in 1928. In 1981, Sandra Day O'Connor became the first woman to serve on the Supreme Court. In 1983, Sally Ride became the first female astronaut. In 1984, Geraldine Ferraro became the first woman to run for vice-president, although she was unsuccessful. However, many activists continue to demand reform in the 21st century. For example, women only account for 20 percent of the U.S. Senate and House of Representatives. Furthermore, women only earn 79 percent of what men in similar jobs are paid. In 1980, President Jimmy Carter declared March to be women's history month.

Youth Culture of the 1960s

Anti-War Protests

Following the end of World War II, Americans broadly supported anti-Communist policies and believed they were necessary to win the Cold War. The United States' intervention in the Korean War caused minimal backlash among the public. In addition, the vast majority of Americans acquiesced to political purges against alleged Communists, and nearly all Americans either supported or ignored their countries' perpetual involvement in regime change all over the world. This passivity ended in 1964 when the United States escalated its involvement in the Vietnam War. Various factors contributed to the public's antagonism toward the war, including the unprecedented coverage of a military conflict on color television and the organizational experience many protest leaders gained in the civil rights movement.

Anti-war demonstrations were overwhelmingly peaceful and incredibly diverse in terms of race, ethnicity, gender, age, religion, educational attainment, and profession. However, protestors increasingly took more radical action after reporters uncovered covert bombing campaigns and mass atrocities during the late 1960s. As a result, protests occasionally erupted in violence. For example, National Guardsmen killed four protestors at Kent State University in 1970, which led to renewed calls for more aggressive protest tactics. Fearing further escalation and radicalization, the United States opted to pull out combat forces in 1973 and fully withdraw in 1975.

Some groups on the Left also rejected liberal policies, arguing that political leaders did too little to transform the racial and economic status quo at home and pursued immoral policies abroad.

Some left-wing Americans went further than liberal Democrats in demanding more racial, economic, and gender equality. During the 1960s and 1970s, activists founded thousands of influential grassroots political institutions and movements. Although these groups never formed a cohesive movement, they're commonly classified as the "**New Left**" based on their shared criticism of capitalism, imperialism, and other hierarchical power structures. Most New Left groups called for the merging of labor organizations and social activism to oppose America's authoritarian and antidemocratic elements. Rather than participating in liberal efforts to reform economic and political systems, the New Left favored more radical direct action to eradicate poverty and achieve justice.

New Left groups differed wildly in their chosen causes and approaches. The **Students for a Democratic Society** (SDS) was one of the largest New Left groups, and its student leadership cadre organized a number of actions to support the antiwar movement before it splintered in the late 1960s. The **Youth International Party** was most well known for its anarchist political leanings and satirical street theater protests. The **Weather Underground** led the militant and hyper-revolutionary wing of the New Left, and its members engaged in a variety of unlawful acts, ranging from jailbreaks to bombing campaigns.

The Environment and Natural Resources from 1968 to 1980

US Involvement in the Middle East and a National Energy Policy

The United States vigorously sought to maximize its commercial interests in the Middle East as the region decolonized during the aftermath of World War II. The region was especially critical because it contained an overwhelming majority of the world's proven oil deposits. In addition to functioning as a vehicular and industrial power source, petroleum was a necessary component of several emergent economic sectors, including plastic and agricultural petrochemicals. Furthermore, the Middle East held immense geopolitical value because it functioned as a land bridge between the communist East and capitalist West.

The United States worked closely with its chief ally, the United Kingdom, to protect their mutual corporate interests in the Middle East, including oil-rich Bahrain, Iraq, Iran, Kuwait, and Qatar, as British colonies gained independence. When independence movements threatened to nationalize their country's oil supply, the United States and United Kingdom responded with extreme measures. For example, in 1953, American and British foreign policymakers backed a successful coup d'état in Iran.

During the 1970s, oil crises racked the global market, particularly after the **Iranian Revolution** (1979) ousted the American-backed Shah from power. In response, the United States invested in alternative sources of foreign oil production as well as its own domestic capabilities.

Environmental Legislature

America's manufacturing boom unleashed a host of environmental problems. During the postwar era, nearly all American cities suffered from chronic smog, and many communities completely lost access to locally sourced clean drinking water due to agricultural and industrial chemical runoff. Furthermore, commercial developers bulldozed vast stretches of American wilderness, and industrialists exploited natural resources at unsustainable rates. As environmental issues mounted in the 1960s, environmental activism surged, especially after the publication of Rachel Carson's *Silent Spring* (1962).

The environmental movement's first major achievement was securing the passage of the **Clean Air Act** (1963). The Clean Air Act was the first environmental law in American history with a national scope, and its air quality regulations were some of the strongest in the world. Growing support for environmentalism later motivated President Nixon to establish the **Environmental Protection Agency** (EPA) in 1970. The EPA enjoys the power to promulgate regulations, and it can also conduct enforcement operations when Congress provides specific statutory authorizations. The Clean Water Act (1972) was another landmark piece of environmental legislation. Among other initiatives, the Clean Water Act provided funding for wastewater treatment, created a framework to help states regulate pollution, and protected wetland ecosystems.

Society in Transition

Conservatives Challenged Liberal Laws

Conservatives did their best to thwart the rising tide of liberalism in the 1960s.

During the 1960s, conservatives called for tax cuts, federal budget cuts, and more emphasis on states' rights. Like during the Civil War, states' rights energized southern conservatives who wanted to obstruct integration at all costs. For example, during the early 1960s, several southern states refused to fully comply with the Supreme Court's landmark decision in *Brown v. Board of Education* (1954), which found segregated public schools to be unconstitutional. Likewise, conservatives consistently worked to undermine the civil rights movement and the War on Poverty. In addition to limited government and segregation, conservatives supported more radical action to contain Communism. For example, the 1964 Republican presidential candidate, Barry Goldwater, openly discussed the possibility of limited nuclear strikes in Vietnam.

Conservatives regularly condemned many liberal policies in stark moral terms. Under this view, conservatives portrayed integration and gender equality as evidence of moral decay. The nexus between Christian morality and conservative policies merged during the 1960s as states attempted to outlaw abortion and diminish birth control access, culminating with conservatives' outrage over the Supreme Court's decision to uphold women's right to abortion as constitutional in *Roe v. Wade* (1973).

Waning Trust in the Government

The US government struggled to maintain its legitimacy and project its authority during the 1970s.

The **Watergate scandal** (1972–1974) infamously eroded American confidence and trust in government. Although **Richard Nixon** went on to win the presidential election of 1972 in a historic landslide victory, he ordered staffers to burglarize the democratic national election during the summer before the election. President Nixon initially attempted to cover up his involvement but, faced with a likely conviction in the Senate, resigned in 1974. President **Gerald Ford** pardoned Nixon to help the country heal; however, it only served to ignite a storm of protests and disillusionment.

The anti–Vietnam War movement reached a fever pitch in the 1970s and heavily influenced President Nixon's decision to withdraw American forces. Furthermore, several Middle Eastern crises challenged the United States. Arab states responded to American support for Israel in the **Yom Kippur War** (1973) with an oil embargo, which intensified a global economic downturn. From 1973 to 1980, the United States struggled to break out of a deep recession that featured both high unemployment and high inflation. The **Iranian Revolution** (1979) added to the turmoil as the victorious nationalists held Americans hostage and threatened the global oil supply.

Clashes Between Conservatives and Liberals

Conservatives and liberals spent the 1970s locked in a culture war over numerous political, cultural, and social issues.

The **Sexual Revolution** (1960–1980) horrified social conservatives, particularly the Christian fundamentalist wing of the rising conservative movement. Conservatives denounced everything from unmarried cohabitation to family planning. The debate over abortion was perhaps the most controversial because it amounted to a zero-sum game, arguing between women's rights to have control over their own bodies and Christian beliefs of life beginning at conception.

Race was another divisive topic. Conservatives generally believed that federal intervention interfered with their individual rights. On the other side, many African American political groups condemned budget cuts as thinly veiled class warfare, and there were frequent protests over racial injustices in urban areas.

Given the popularity of liberal landmark legislation passed in the 1960s, conservatives generally pursued a strategy known as "starving the beast." Rather than attempting to overturn the legislation, Republicans advocated for shrinking the federal budgets and slashing taxes to decrease government revenue. Although liberal Democrats generally succeeded in protecting national social programs, they were less successful at the local level. For example, California conservatives successfully enacted **Proposition 13** (1978)—a state constitutional amendment that capped property taxes, resulting in massive state budget cuts.

Evangelicals and Religious Conservatives

The Christian evangelical movement experienced a major revival after World War II. During the 1950s, American evangelical leaders deemphasized strict biblical interpretations and prioritized personal spiritual connections. In addition, many evangelicals attempted to develop more interfaith dialogue and promote more tolerance. However, evangelicalism made a sharp turn toward fundamentalism in the late 1960s and 1970s as church leaders increasingly demanded followers to abide by the leaders' strict gospel interpretations. Evangelicals also frequently adopted television as an effective method of proselytizing. Many Christian theologians have criticized Christian fundamentalists and televangelists for espousing prosperity gospel, which ties divine blessings to wealth accumulation.

Evangelicals regularly engaged in social activism to protest acts they found immoral, such as premarital sex and abortion, and they became more politically conscious during the Goldwater and Nixon presidential campaigns. During the late 1970s, **Jerry Falwell, Sr.**, organized a powerful evangelical-led political advocacy group known as the **Moral Majority** (1979). The Moral Majority worked closely with both of Ronald Reagan's presidential campaigns as he crafted a coalition based on elite business interests, foreign policy hawks, social conservatives, and evangelicals. Ever since the Moral Majority group formed, evangelicals have remained a permanent fixture in the modern-day Republican party.

Practice Quiz

Questions 1–3 are based on the following passage:

> When researchers and engineers undertake a large-scale scientific project, they may end up making discoveries and developing technologies that have far wider uses than originally intended. This is especially true in NASA, one of the most influential and innovative scientific organizations in America. NASA spinoff technology refers to innovations originally developed for NASA space projects that are now used in a wide range of different commercial fields. Many consumers are unaware that products they are buying are based on NASA research! Spinoff technology proves that it is worthwhile to invest in science research because it could enrich people's lives in unexpected ways.
>
> The first spinoff technology worth mentioning is baby food. In space, where astronauts have limited access to fresh food and fewer options with their daily meals, malnutrition is a serious concern. Consequently, NASA researchers were looking for ways to enhance the nutritional value of astronauts' food. Scientists found that a certain type of algae could be added to food, improving the food's neurological benefits. When experts in the commercial food industry learned of this algae's potential to boost brain health, they were quick to begin their own research. The nutritional substance from algae then developed into a product called life's DHA, which can be found in over 90 percent of infant food sold in America.
>
> Another intriguing example of a spinoff technology can be found in fashion. People who are always dropping their sunglasses may have invested in a pair of sunglasses with scratch resistant lenses—that is, it's impossible to scratch the glass, even if the glasses are dropped on an abrasive surface. This innovation is incredibly advantageous for people who are clumsy, but most shoppers don't know that this technology was originally developed by NASA. Scientists first created scratch resistant glass to help protect costly and crucial equipment from getting scratched in space, especially the helmet visors in space suits. However, sunglass companies later realized that this technology could be profitable for their products, and they licensed the technology from NASA.

1. What is the main purpose of this article?
    a. To advise consumers to do more research before making a purchase
    b. To persuade readers to support NASA research
    c. To tell a narrative about the history of space technology
    d. To define and describe instances of spinoff technology

2. What is the organizational structure of this article?
    a. A general definition followed by more specific examples
    b. A general opinion followed by supporting arguments
    c. An important moment in history followed by chronological details
    d. A popular misconception followed by counterevidence

3. Why did NASA scientists research algae?
    a. They already knew algae was healthy for babies.
    b. They were interested in how to grow food in space.
    c. They were looking for ways to add health benefits to food.
    d. They hoped to use it to protect expensive research equipment.

4. Which of the following was NOT a movement that was going on in the 1960s?
    a. Civil Rights Movement
    b. End the War Movement
    c. Women's Rights Movement
    d. LGBTQ Rights Movement

5. The case of Brown v. Board of Education reversed what landmark Supreme Court doctrine?
    a. Judicial review doctrine
    b. Public safety exception
    c. Due process doctrine
    d. Separate but equal doctrine

Answer Explanations

1. D: To define and describe instances of spinoff technology. This is an example of a purpose question—*why* did the author write this? The article contains facts, definitions, and other objective information without telling a story or arguing an opinion. In this case, the purpose of the article is to inform the reader. The only answer choice that is related to giving information is Choice *D*: to define and describe.

2. A: A general definition followed by more specific examples. This organization question asks readers to analyze the structure of the essay. The topic of the essay is about spinoff technology; the first paragraph gives a general definition of the concept, while the following two paragraphs offer more detailed examples to help illustrate this idea.

3. C: They were looking for ways to add health benefits to food. This reading comprehension question can be answered based on the second paragraph—scientists were concerned about astronauts' nutrition and began researching useful nutritional supplements. Choice *A* in particular is not true because it reverses the order of discovery (first NASA identified algae for astronaut use, and then it was further developed for use in baby food).

4. B: The 1960s were a time of growth for the United States. Everyone was pushing for rights and for changes to the system, and people were beginning to challenge the government. The Civil Rights Movement, led by leaders like Martin Luther King Jr., dominated the 1960s leading up to the Civil Rights Act. Women's rights were also key throughout the decade, as well as the movement for LGBTQ rights. End the War was still a decade off, however, with Vietnam still around the corner.

5. D: Brown v. Board of Education set the stage for the fight for civil rights throughout the United States and was the first true rebuff to segregation. Judicial review was one hundred years earlier. The public safety exception has to do with Miranda Rights. The due process doctrine doesn't apply here, either. That leaves separate but equal, the Plessy v. Ferguson case that the Court overruled, setting the stage for change.

Section 9: Modern Times (1980–Present)

Reagan and Conservatism

Ronald Reagan's Presidential Victory

In the presidential election of 1980, Republican nominee **Ronald Reagan** carried forty-three states, and the Republicans won a majority in the U.S. Senate after twenty-eight years of Democratic control. Reagan presented an optimistic message and broadcasted a television advertisement that proclaimed "It's morning again in America." He promised to restore America's military power, cut government regulations for many industries, and reduce taxes. Reagan enjoyed the support of resurgent conservative Christian evangelicals, who wanted to restore morality to American society. They were particularly concerned about issues such as abortion. The **Moral Majority**, founded by Baptist minister Jerry Falwell in 1979, was one key group that helped Reagan win the election. This coalition helped realign party loyalties, as more liberal Republicans and conservative Democrats shifted their allegiance.

Conservative Efforts to Counteract Liberal Programs

Conservatives' demands to shrink the size and scope of the government reached new heights with Ronald Reagan's election in 1980. They argued that programs championed by liberal administrations were counterproductive in stimulated economic growth and reducing poverty. In general, conservatives believe the free market fights poverty more efficiently and effectively than government programs; therefore, they often singularly focus on ways to spur economic growth. According to free-market theories, a rising tide of economic prosperity would lift American households into the middle class and beyond. However, this has not worked in practice. Despite the unprecedented generation of wealth during the late twentieth and early twenty-first centuries, Americans' real wages did not meaningfully increase, and the United States has plummeted down global ranks of economic mobility.

From 1980 through the present, Republican politicians have been more successful at cutting taxes and gutting government revenue than drastically cutting the largest social programs, such as Social Security and Medicare. Entitlement programs are extremely popular among constituents, including those who might otherwise oppose government spending, and the law of inertia weighs against making massive structural changes to long-running programs. Although liberal voters have consistently rejected spending cuts, the Democratic establishment is far more flexible. For example, the Democratic Clinton administration supported and secured more aggressive social safety net cuts than most of his Republican counterparts.

Policy Debates

American policymakers have continuously debated free-trade agreements, social programs, and financial regulation since 1980.

Free-trade agreements, such as the **North American Free Trade Agreement** (1994), have come under heavy scrutiny as more corporations outsource positions to reduce labor costs. Despite devastating job losses, there's elite bipartisan agreement that free trade reduces consumer costs and generates economic growth. However, the Trump administration has placed unprecedented scrutiny on free trade as it seeks to revive American manufacturing.

The scope of America's social safety net has faced existential challenges since the early 1980s. Both political establishments categorically reject European-style cradle-to-grave social service systems; however, there's fierce debate over whether programs should exist at all. Some liberals have fought to expand existing programs, whereas Democrats have mostly acquiesced to Republican demands for privatization and balanced budgets.

Nearly every presidential administration has loosened regulations and/or failed to reform the American financial system. Deregulation has worsened the severity of bust cycles, which routinely impoverish American households and enrich financial elites. Additionally, the system is highly unstable and would have entirely collapsed during the **Great Recession** (2007–2009) without government intervention. Although there is broad public support for reform, only nominal and piecemeal legislation has ever been implemented.

Conservative Beliefs Advanced After 1980

Ronald Reagan's landslide victories in the 1980 and 1984 presidential elections birthed the modern Republican Party. President Reagan crafted a coalition consisting of elite business interests, middle-class households, social conservatives, and Christian evangelicals. The combination of pro-growth economic policies and social conservatism is still the driving force behind American conservatism today.

Pro-growth policies seek to limit the government's role in the economy. President Reagan pursued a distinct economic agenda that's commonly referred to as **Reaganomics**, which included slashing taxes, eliminating social programs, repealing business regulations, removing government oversight, and undermining labor unions. Modern conservatives have adopted Reaganomics with few exceptions. When out of power, Republican politicians vehemently resist the expansion of social services based on arguments about national debt.

Similarly, social conservatism seeks to protect the private sphere from government intrusion and defend traditional values, such as two-parent households and abstinence before marriage. Ronald Reagan fostered a tight relationship with evangelical leaders, which led to the Republican Party elevating its rejection of abortion and same-sex marriage to high-profile policy positions. Modern-day conservatives have continued to fiercely oppose abortion, but after **Obergefell v. Hodges** (2015) legalized same-sex marriage, conservatives have shifted toward upholding the concept of two genders to limit the rights of transgender people. In addition, present-day conservative values have conflicted with modern conceptions of multiculturalism and political correctness.

Debates Over Social Issues

Heated debates have erupted throughout the United States over a wide range of social issues, including immigration, diversity, and gender.

In relatively recent history, immigration has become the single most divisive political issue since slavery. Conservatives have become so radicalized on immigration that amnesty for undocumented immigrants, which Ronald Reagan granted and George W. Bush supported, is a total nonstarter. For example, the Republican base's anger over moderate immigration reform forced out Republican House majority leader Eric Cantor and House speaker John Boehner.

Diversity, gender, and family issues have similarly fueled long-term culture wars in recent times. Conservatives have consistently and systematically opposed the continued application of civil rights–era legislation. Although liberals generally champion diversity, conservatives present themselves as the protectors of what they deem to be traditional American cultural aspects, such as Christianity and European heritage. Similar sides exist in the debate over sexuality, with liberals defending tolerance and conservatives holding to traditional interpretations of sex. Likewise, gender issues have escalated as more women entered the workforce in the 1980s and then climbed the corporate ladder. Enduring controversies related to gender include the gender wage gap, sexual harassment, sexual violence, and the transition away from traditional family roles.

The End of the Cold War

Reagan's Anti-Communist Efforts

President Ronald Reagan pursued an aggressive anti-Communist policy program, and conveyed his anti-Communist objectives through speeches, diplomatic efforts, and military decisions.

First, the Reagan administration demanded and secured the largest peacetime buildup of conventional and nuclear weapons in American history. During the first term alone, American military spending doubled, and that only accounts for officially declared spending.

Second, the Reagan administration was more covert in its application of raw American military power, particularly in avoiding large-scale confrontations with the Soviet Union. However, that's not to say President Reagan was a peacenik. One of the Reagan administration's more successful proxy wars was the financing and arming of the ***mujahideen*** in the **Afghan-Soviet War** (1979–1989). On the other end of the spectrum, the **Iran-Contra Affair** (1985–1987) involved serial violations of a federal embargo on weapon sales to Iran and Reagan officials using the cash payments to illegally arm right-wing Nicaraguan death squads (***Contras***).

Third, President Reagan artfully delivered high-profile speeches to strengthen diplomatic initiatives. Most famously, Reagan's "Evil Empire" speech (1983) framed the Cold War as an existential struggle between good and evil that solidified America's capitalist coalition. Likewise, President Reagan famously implored Soviet leaders to tear down the **Berlin Wall** in 1987, which occurred two years later.

Ending the Cold War

The Reagan administration placed maximum pressure on the Soviet Union in the hopes of further destabilizing the Soviet system as it teetered toward an outright collapse. Most broadly, President Reagan pursued a policy of peace through strength. In practice, this involved an aggressive expansion of America's nuclear stockpile and massive public investments in military preparedness.

President Reagan understood that the Soviet Union couldn't afford to keep pace with American defense spending due to its many financial and political issues. Combined with a decade of stagnant economic growth, the political situation was in turmoil as Eastern European nationalist movements began to increasingly seek independence. As a result, Soviet leaders were forced to decide between falling behind in the arms race or suffering a deadly blow to its economic system.

With military pressure serving as the proverbial stick, President Reagan treated diplomacy as the carrot to entice Soviet leaders into negotiating nuclear weapon reductions, reducing tensions with the West, and implementing liberal economic and political reforms. Between 1985 and 1988, President Reagan held four diplomatic summits with Soviet leader **Mikhail Gorbachev**, and they formed an unlikely but fruitful working relationship that produced several important treaties, including the Intermediate-Range Nuclear Forces (INF) Treaty (1987).

Post-War Position

The end of the Cold War left the United States in a delicate but powerful position as the sole remaining global superpower. In the absence of Soviet pushback, the United States rushed to open diplomatic channels and integrate former Soviet states in Eastern Europe into the global capitalist system. Along with free-trade agreements, the United States was eager to expand the membership of international organizations it largely controlled, including the North Atlantic Treaty Organization (NATO), International Monetary Fund (IMF), and the World Trade Organization (WTO).

Unlike other historical imperial projects, American hegemony is unique in its reliance on soft power, particularly consumer culture and entertainment, to popularize its free-trade and corporate agenda. Still, the American imperial regime has faced a barrage of geopolitical challenges in defending the international system it largely dominates. This has forced American policymakers to decide whether and how the United States should function as a world police, either by authorizing UN peacekeeping missions or conducting military interventions. Some of these interventions have been disastrous for the United States' reputation. More specifically, the **War on Terror** has dealt a serious blow to America's standing within the global community as a good faith actor and worthy leader.

A Changing Economy

Digital Communication Advancements Increase Economic Productivity

Despite the recurring cycles of financial busts and soaring wealth inequality, digital communication innovations have spurred unbelievable gains in productivity since 1980. In fact, even when controlling for inflation, American productivity nearly tripled between 1980 and 2019, as measured by the difference in real gross domestic product (GDP). Digital communications first elevated production in the 1980s when television established itself as an essential platform for mass marketing. The internet and mobile phones have since further expedited commercial interactions and accelerated industrial automation. Finally, some digital communication companies, such as Google and Facebook, now rank among the most profitable corporations in the world.

Unlike previous communication innovations, the internet allows users to exchange libraries of information and audiovisual content with lightning speed. As such, digital communications increased the efficiency of global economic relationships like never before, and Americans were in the strongest position to consolidate market control given the United States' disproportionate influence within the global capitalist system it crafted after the end of the Cold War. From the comfort of their homes, enterprising Americans could source and manufacture products overseas, create global marketing campaigns, provide technological assistance, and pursue a host of other economic opportunities in the newly integrated global market.

Technological Innovations and Social Networks

Technological innovations have totally transformed American daily life and culture. Computing power has produced exponential increases in production efficiencies, fueling the economic sprint toward mechanical automation. For example, the iPhone from Apple® has approximately 100,000 times the computing power than the computer that was used to send the Apollo 11 mission to the moon in 1969.

Enhanced computing power has been a continual driver of growth and opened myriad employment opportunities in digital-based economic sectors. In addition, the internet constructed and organized a network of shocking complexity and scope. Social networks have created digital platforms with billions of members.

Mobile phones possibly had the most dynamic and transformative impact on daily life by bringing the power of a laptop computer in the pocket of nearly every American citizen, streamlining communication on all fronts. With mobile phones, Americans could reliably and immediately communicate with their contacts in endless ways, ranging from phone calls to social media platforms. This was a major breakthrough for businesses looking to directly engage with customers, and the development of location services (geographic information system [GPS]) resulted in mobile phones functioning like an interactive map. Along with processing power, mobile phones are equipped with high-end cameras, adding an audiovisual component to social and commercial interactions.

Employment Changes

The American economy has radically shifted from industrial- to service-oriented sectors over the last several decades. As free trade expanded after the Cold War, American manufacturing declined so rapidly that the industrial Midwest became commonly known as the **Rust Belt**. With steady blue-collar employment increasingly difficult to find, many former factory workers were forced to make do in the hospitality sector and gig economy, or short-term contractual work. Many economists and politicians have pushed for funding to provide for a smooth transition; however, companies in the emergent technological sector have led the transition toward a workforce full of independent contractors instead of employees to save money and boost profits.

President Reagan's privatization blitz pushed American unions to the edge of a cliff, and globalization has threatened to deliver a death strike. Union membership consistently declined for decades as American companies continue to scramble for cheaper sources of labor. Free market enthusiasts contend that American unions aren't viable under the prevailing market conditions because businesses cannot compete in the hypercompetitive global marketplace without remaining flexible. Regardless of whether this is true, the decline of union membership has coincided with the stagnation of working and middle-class wages.

Stagnation of Real Wages

Ever since the country's founding, the **American Dream** has served as a beacon of hope for people aspiring to reach the middle class as embodied by home ownership, self-sufficiency, and disposable income. Given the vast amounts of undeveloped land within its territories, the American Dream remained a more achievable reality than the socioeconomic mobility on offer anywhere else in the world for centuries. Automation, globalization, and privatization have taken a hatchet to working and middle-class families' **real wages**, or wages after adjustments for inflation. At the same time, most white-collar positions have experienced significant real wage growth, particularly at the executive level. The resulting record-breaking economic inequality has since threatened to unravel American economic, political, and social systems.

The **millennial generation**, consisting of those born between 1980 and 1995, has been hit the hardest by wage stagnation and economic inequality. For example, millennials account for approximately 25 percent of the population while holding an estimated three percent of the country's wealth. They earn less in real wages than their grandparents' generations because the real costs for housing, education, and health care have all skyrocketed. On top of their middling economic prospects, young generations of Americans will be forced to assume and manage the mountain of debt amassed by earlier generations.

Migration and Immigration in the 1990s and 2000s

Southern and Western Influences

Although all of American society has rapidly evolved since 1980, nowhere is the transformation more self-evident than in the American South and West.

Like the rest of the United States, the economy in the American South has become more service oriented and urbanized. For the first time in history, several southern states have grown to become some of the wealthiest in the United States. Texas boasts the second-highest GDP, and Florida ranks fourth. In terms of politics and culture, the ascendance of African American communities has challenged traditional southern conservatism. Many southern states have majority African American populations, and those communities have gained more independence and cultural influence in relatively recent history.

The American West has experienced a staggering amount of development since 1980. California is the center of American entertainment as well as a cradle of technological innovation. Economic prosperity has led to California becoming the most populous state by a wide margin, and its GDP is the fifth highest in the entire world. Compared with most other regions in the country, the politics in the West feature features a broader ideological range, and Western culture tends to place more emphasis on tolerance and acceptance than anywhere else in the country.

Latin American and Asian Immigration

Immigrants' country of origin has shifted toward Asia, the Caribbean, Central America, and South America since 1980. As executive-level and academic interactions have increased throughout the global economy, American-based multinational corporations have helped skilled workers obtain visas to work in sensitive and critical industries, such as technology and energy. On average, such workers have been arriving from China, India, Japan, South Korea, and South America since 1980. In addition, many immigrants continue to embark for the traditional purpose of pursuing the American Dream. Asian immigrants often seek to establish small businesses in the United States, enter the middle class, and help their children obtain a quality education. Most Asian and South American immigrants settle in metropolitan areas where there's a sizable immigrant population, such as Chinatowns and Korea towns.

Central American and Caribbean immigrant groups differ markedly from their contemporaries. Compared to Asian and South American immigrants, they are significantly more likely to resemble refugees fleeing from abject poverty, societal chaos, and perpetual violence. Although many of these immigrants find safe havens in large cities, they also commonly work as migrant laborers in rural area, serving as a critical source of cheap agricultural labor.

Challenges of the 21st Century

In the wake of attacks on the World Trade Center and the Pentagon, the United States launched military efforts against terrorism and lengthy, controversial conflicts in Afghanistan and Iraq.

On September 11, 2001, Al-Qaeda members hijacked American airliners and successfully bombed the World Trade Center and the Pentagon. In response, President **George W. Bush** leveraged public anger to launch large-scale invasions of Afghanistan and Iraq.

The **War in Afghanistan** (2001–present) is the longest war in American history. Although the Taliban sheltered and provided material aid to Al-Qaeda's leader, **Osama bin Laden**, the state and broader public had almost no connection to terrorism. The American invasion forced the Taliban into a strategic retreat; however, as time passed, the United States began prioritizing other conflicts. Both the Obama and Trump administrations have toyed with the idea of a full withdrawal; however, they fear the consequences of abandoning Afghanistan's new and relatively democratic government.

The **Iraq War** began with Bush officials knowingly presenting disinformation to Congress, the United Nations, and the mainstream media, largely to falsely tie Iraqi dictator **Saddam Hussein** to weapons of mass destruction. Although the American military quickly annihilated the Iraqi state, Iraqis' resistance to the occupation led to a sectarian insurrection that undermined all hopes of building a stable and self-sufficient government. The conflict is widely considered to be the greatest strategic foreign blunder in American history.

The War on Terrorism

Activists challenged whether the **War on Terror** was worth its costs to human rights and civil liberties. In the immediate aftermath of the 9/11 terrorist attacks, Congress rushed to pass the **Authorization for Use of Military Force** (AUMF) of 2001, and only Barbara Lee (D-CA) voted against the bill that became law on September 18, 2001. Human rights activists feared this broad delegation of executive power essentially gave the White House blanket permission to wage a global war. The AUMF remains law in 2020, and annual authorizations rarely face meaningful challenges despite their global application.

Shortly after AUMF, conservative Congress led the charge to introduce legislation known as the **Patriot Act** to expand the War on Terror into digital spaces. Congress believed monitoring the conversations of suspected terrorists was critical for protecting the homeland. During the Bush and Obama administrations, cabinet-level public officials repeatedly and adamantly denied under oath that all American citizens were subject to widespread surveillance. **Edward Snowden**, a National Security Agency (NSA) contractor, proved these denials to be categorically false when he leaked evidence of domestic surveillance networks to the press in 2013. No government official was ever charged with perjury, and little has been done to reform the system.

Climate Change and the Dependence on Fossil Fuels

American policymakers and activists have raised concerns over the United States' dependence on fossil fuels and the resulting damage inflicted on the environment. Although the primary proximate cause of the War on Terror was inarguably the 9/11 terrorist attacks, American interests in the Middle East date back to at least World War II.

The United States and its Western European allies have long sought to maximize their influence and control over the region's oil production. Saddam Hussein had previously challenged American oil interests in Kuwait, and American policymakers were eager to prevent any future meddling. Overall, the United States' dependence on the global oil trade was a major contributing factor behind American invasions and occupations in the Middle East.

Aside from seeking to reduce American military commitments, the realities of climate change have raised hard questions about oil and resource consumption in the United States. Global temperatures have markedly increased for decades, and scientific experts have concluded that economic activity is driving this trend. In fact, oil companies have known about fossil fuels' profound impact on climate change since at least 1977. Although most scientific recommendations have been ignored, green energy has gained significant popular support in recent years.

The United States as a Superpower

Nearly sixteen years after the terrorist attacks on the World Trade Center in New York City, the United States is still entangled in the politics of the Middle East and still finding ways to cope with the ongoing threat of global terrorism. The events of September 11, 2011—often referred to simply as "9/11"—galvanized the United States of America into a self-declared war on terrorism. These events have, presumably, challenged and changed many relationships between the United States and the world while simultaneously extending the post-9/11 paradigm. Some scholars, for instance, saw the war on terrorism as the final blow to old Cold War politics. However, recent military events in Eastern Europe, Syria, and the broader Middle East indicate that the Cold War may be "heating up" again on the geopolitical stage.

The United States' economy remains the largest in the world, making it a strong contender to continue its role as "Leader of the Free World." Although U.S. economic hegemony has declined, relatively, in an era of globalization and **North American Free Trade Agreement** (NAFTA), the United States is poised to be an economic player in the coming decades.

Practice Quiz

Questions 1–3 refer to the map below.

Map Depicting Population of the United States of America (2011)

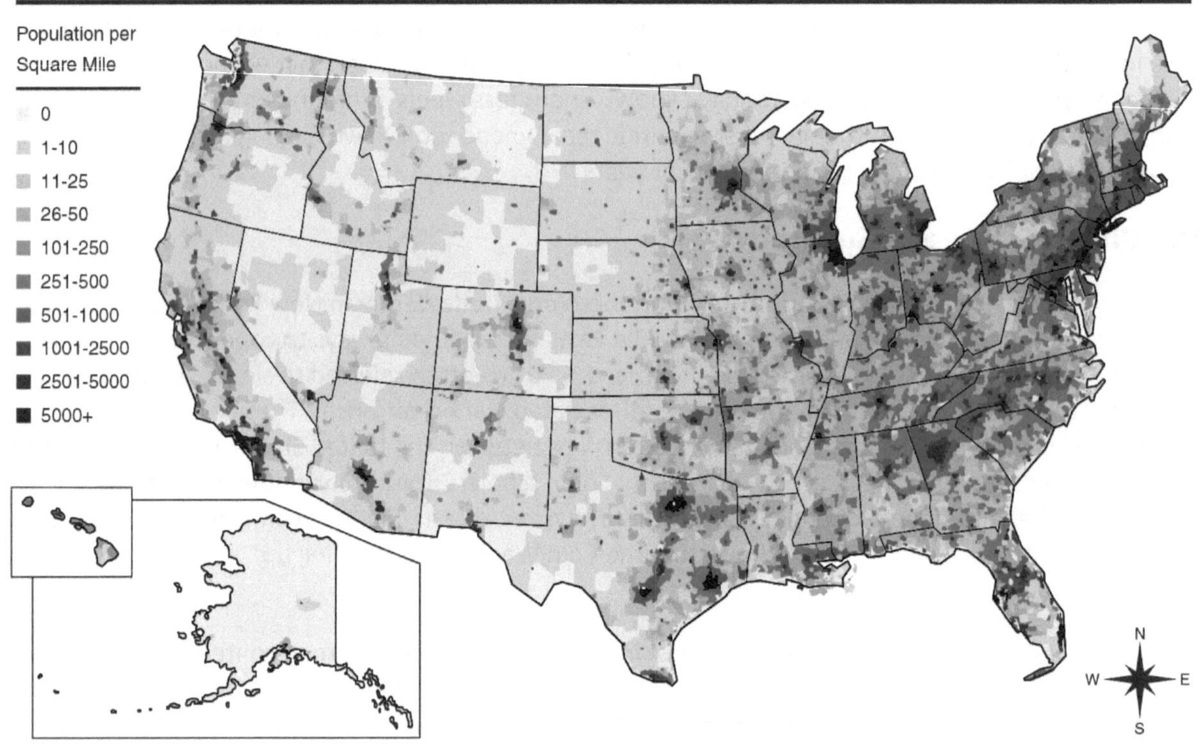

1. Which measurement does the data on the map primarily illustrate?
    a. Agricultural density
    b. Arithmetic density
    c. Physiological density
    d. Population distribution

2. Which technique does the map use to plot the relevant information?
    a. Area patterns
    b. Clustering
    c. Dispersal
    d. Line patterns

3. Based on the map, which region is most likely to have the highest population density?
   a. Northeast
   b. Northwest
   c. Central
   d. Southeast

Please use the map below to answer Questions 4 and 5:

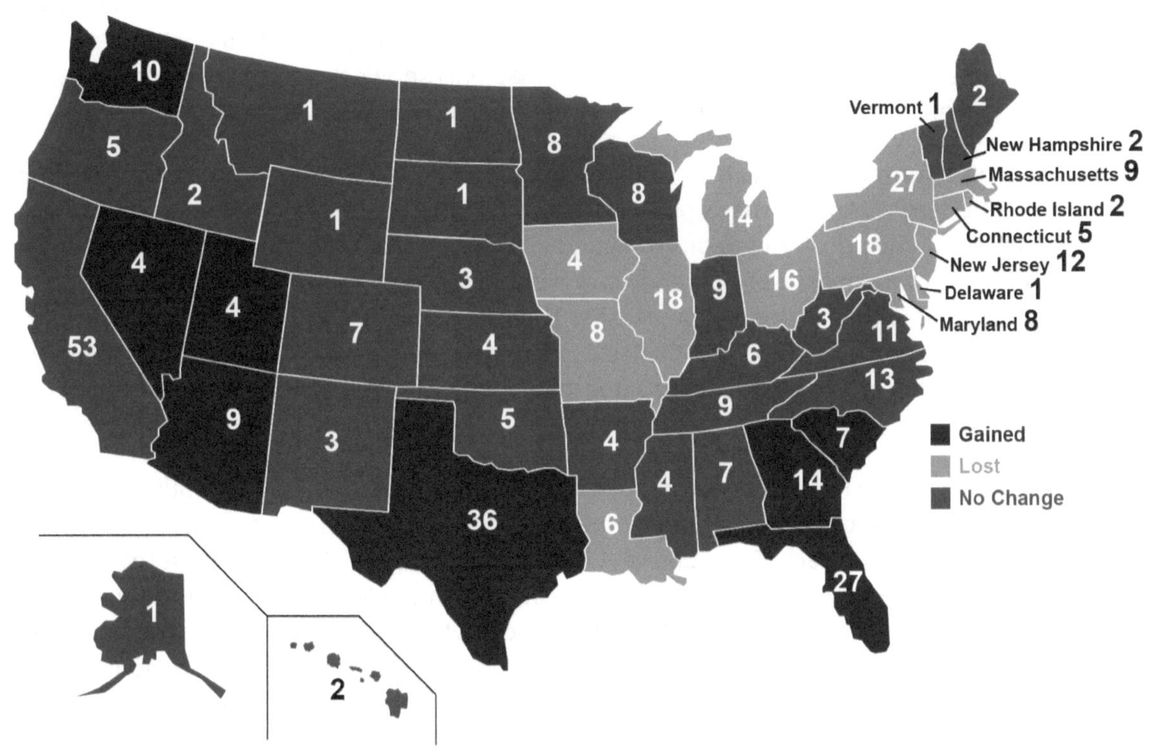

4. How many total electoral votes are accounted for by the states that gained representatives as a result of the 2010 U.S. census?
   a. 123
   b. 111
   c. 97
   d. 88

5. Which of the following statements is reflected in the map?
   a. More states gained or lost representatives than experienced no change at all.
   b. Most states that gained representatives were concentrated in the Pacific Northwest and Great Plains regions.
   c. Most states that lost representatives were concentrated in the Midwest and Northeast.
   d. More least-populous states lost representatives than more-populous states.

Answer Explanations

1. B: The map depicts "Population per Square Mile," and this data is represented in the shading pattern. Arithmetic density is calculated by dividing a population by some unit of measure. Given the information contained in the title and legend, the map is depicting the arithmetic density of the United States. Thus, Choice *B* is the correct answer. Agricultural density is calculated by dividing the number of farmers by the amount of arable land. Nothing in this map suggests it relates to agriculture, so Choice *A* is incorrect. Physiological density is calculated by dividing the total population by the amount of arable land. The legend doesn't refer to arable land, so Choice *C* is incorrect. Population distribution relates to the patterns of movement and settlement for a group. The map only shows the current population per square mile, not where the population has previously been, so Choice *D* is incorrect.

2. A: The map plots information through slight differences in shading patterns, which symbolize various levels of arithmetic density. Area patterns plot data based on differences in the pattern. Thus, Choice *A* is the correct answer. While clustering is often used to analyze population density, the map is using shading. The defining characteristic of clustering patterns is a series of points with tight clusters of points illustrating areas with high population density. Therefore, Choice *B* is incorrect. Dispersal patterns are used to plot population distribution, so Choice *C* is incorrect. Line patterns illustrate relationships based on the space between lines, and the map doesn't contain this type of line. Therefore, Choice *D* is incorrect.

3. A: The legend indicates that the areas with the darkest shading have the highest population density. Compared to the rest of the country, the entire Northeast region is a much darker shade of gray, with some areas appearing almost black. Thus, Choice *A* is the correct answer. The Northwest region has an area of high population density on the coast, but it doesn't match the Northeast region. Therefore, Choice *B* is incorrect. The Central region has a fairly high population density compared to the Northwest region and the Southwest region, but the shading isn't as dark as it is in the Northeast region. Therefore, Choice *C* is incorrect. The Southeast region has the second highest population density on the map. Although the Florida coasts have incredibly dark shading, the rest of the Southeast region doesn't match the Northeast region, so Choice *D* is incorrect.

4. B: If you add up the representatives in states that gained representation, the total is 111. All other answer choices are incorrect.

5. C: Most states that lost representatives are located in the Rust Belt—the Midwest and Northeast—as illustrated by the light grey states on the map. Choice *B* is incorrect because most states that gained representation were scattered in the South and the West, not the Pacific Northwest and Great Plains. Choice *A* is incorrect because more states remained unchanged than lost or grained representation.

Section 10: Historical Analyzation

Reading for Meaning in Social Studies

Main Ideas and Details in Social Studies Readings

Determining the Main Ideas

As mentioned, the **main idea** is more detailed than the topic of a piece of writing and it provides the author's central point of the text. It can be expressed through a complete sentence and is often found in the beginning, middle, or end of a paragraph. In most nonfiction books, the first sentence of the passage usually (but not always) states the main idea.

Using Details to Make Inferences or Claims

Once a reader has determined an author's thesis or main idea, he or she will need to understand how textual evidence supports interpretation of that thesis or main idea. Test takers will be asked direct questions regarding an author's main idea and may be asked to identify evidence that would support those ideas. This will require test takers to comprehend literal and figurative meanings within the text passage, be able to draw inferences from provided information, and be able to separate important evidence from minor supporting detail. It's often helpful to skim test questions and answer options prior to critically reading informational text; however, test takers should avoid the temptation to solely look for the correct answers. Just trying to find the "right answer" may cause test takers to miss important supporting textual evidence. Making mental note of test questions is only helpful as a guide when reading.

After identifying an author's thesis or main idea, a test taker should look at the supporting details that the author provides to back up their assertions, identifying those additional pieces of information that help expand the thesis. From there, test takers should examine the additional information and related details for credibility, the author's use of outside sources, and be able to point to direct evidence that supports the author's claims. It's also imperative that test takers be able to identify what is strong support and what is merely additional information that is nice to know but not necessary. Being able to make this differentiation will help test takers effectively answer questions regarding an author's use of supporting evidence within informational text.

Social Studies Vocabulary

Although general literacy is usually enough to understand social studies texts, some authors use specialized vocabulary for the field of social studies. Traditionally, these specialized vocabulary terms can be separated into eight major categories: people, places, events, groups, movements, eras, documents, and analytical trends. The field of social studies centers on those who have shaped history on both the microcosmic and macrocosmic levels. Much of the social studies vocabulary terms test takers encounter is focused on famous leaders or historical agents. An **agent** is someone who does something; historical agents do something historically significant.

Social studies concepts also include geography and are linked with geography in general, so it is important that test takers have a good understanding of place and its influences on history. Additionally, it is important for test takers to understand historical events: wars, assassinations, political victories, resignations, marches, parades, and celebrations. Groups are also important to understanding social studies. In particular, some groups form social movements, factions of people devoted to some larger changes. At times, these movements succeed in changing history; at other times, they fail. Historians tend to also categorize history in segments of time known as eras. Eras can be as strict as decades (for example, the Roaring Twenties) or as fluid as ideas (for example, the Progressive Era).

Sometimes social studies texts also refer to the titles of primary and secondary texts, which have their own unique vocabulary terms. An example of an important primary text is the Declaration of Independence, while a secondary text might be a textbook discussing the Declaration of Independence. All these concepts—from people to documents—influence historical analyses, which are usually secondary texts. Historians and scholars may create their own analytical paradigms, which carry their own specialized vocabulary. For instance, some historians refer to themselves as quantitative historians because their analytical lenses are influenced heavily by quantitative data. Quantitative historians have their own specialized vocabulary for analytical trends.

Below are examples of the eight major categories of social studies vocabulary: people, places, events, groups, movements, eras, documents, and analytical trends.

People
King James I of England: The King of England who granted the charter that would help found the Jamestown Colony; the Jamestown colony is named after him. **John Smith:** A famous English explorer who played an important role in the survival of the Jamestown colony. **Powhatan:** A well-known Native American leader who led a tribe known as the Powhatans; he was the father of a famous Native American woman known as Pocahontas. **Pocahontas:** A well-known Native American woman who served as a mediator between the Powhatans and the Jamestown colony; she was the daughter of a respected Native American chief known as Powhatan. **William Bradford**: A famous Puritan settler who signed the Mayflower Compact, served as governor for nearly 30 years, and wrote *Of Plymouth Plantation*. **Bartolome de las Casas:** Known as the "Protector of the Indians," he was a priest who wrote a treatise that shed light on the mistreatment of Native Americans in the New World. **Charles Townshend:** British chancellor of the exchequer and responsible for the passage of the highly controversial Townshend Acts in 1767. **Crispus Attucks:** Murdered by British soldiers in reaction to colonial protests, Crispus Attucks, a black colonist, became the first casualty of the so-called Boston Massacre. Some people even memorialize him as a martyr of the American Revolution, claiming that his bloodshed marked the beginning of the struggle for independence. **Thomas Paine:** Thomas Paine was an English-born American political activist, philosopher, political theorist and revolutionary. He was the author of *Common Sense*, a foundational document that helped stir the American Revolution.

James Madison: Known as both a Founding Father and the Father of the Constitution, he served as the fourth president of the United States, preceded by Thomas Jefferson and succeeded by James Monroe.

Thomas Jefferson: A Founding Father who became the third president of the United States, Jefferson was famous for his involvement in the Declaration of Independence, the Louisiana Purchase, and the creation of the Jeffersonian Republican platform.

General Andrew Jackson: A famous general during the War of 1812, who led the United States to an impressive victory at the Battle of New Orleans. He later became a controversial US president known for expanding democracy while simultaneously perpetuating white supremacy.

James K. Polk: Known for his expansionist policies in an era that witnessed rapid westward annexation, occupation, and settlement, he is forever known as the president who led the United States in a (successful) border war with Mexico, the Mexican-American War.

Dred Scott: An escaped slave who catapulted the United States in a US Supreme Court case known as *Dred Scott v. Sanford* (1857). The Dred Scott decision, which reinforced the rights of slave owners and slave states, helped pave the way to the ideological battles over slavery that culminated in the Civil War.

Abraham Lincoln: Known for entering office when the nation was divided over slavery between the North and South, he is one of the most recognized presidents because of his involvement in the Civil War, his approval of the Emancipation Proclamation, and his untimely assassination by John Wilkes Booth.

Ulysses S. Grant: A famous Civil War general whose presidency was marred by corruptions such as the Whiskey Ring during the Gilded Age.

General Robert E. Lee: The most skilled Confederate military leader during the Civil War, Lee ended up surrendering at the Appomattox Courthouse in Virginia, which marked the end of the conflict between North and South.

Places

Mesoamerica: A historical region that includes modern-day Mexico and Central America.

Mississippi River: The longest river on the North American continent, the Mississippi is known for its vast estuaries and its cultural contributions to American history.

Great Lakes Region: A geographic region in North America that surrounds the large lakes that separate the modern-day United States and Canada

Reservations: Federal land, often of poor quality, set aside for Native Americans to live on in the United States.

Jamestown: Located on the coast of modern-day Virginia and founded in 1607, it became the first successful English colony in North America. Previous colonization attempts by the English (for example, Roanoke Island) were failures.

Plymouth: A religiously based English colony founded by Puritan Separatists in 1620.

Roanoke Island: A colony off the coast of Virginia that the English tried to settle in the 16th century.

James River: A river near coastal Virginia that served as a source of water for the Jamestown colony.

Chesapeake Bay: A large coastal estuary that served as a harbor for the early Jamestown colony.

Plymouth Harbor: The anchorage site of the ***Mayflower***; it is located in modern-day Massachusetts.

Massachusetts Bay Colony: An English colony composed of modern-day Maine, New Hampshire, Vermont, Massachusetts, and Connecticut; it was created through a joint-stock charter and eventually subsumed the old Plymouth Colony.

New England Colonies: The English colonies of the Northeast; this region included the Massachusetts Bay Colony (which acquired the Plymouth Colony), Rhode Island, Connecticut, and New Hampshire.

Middle Colonies: The English colonies located between the New England colonies and the Southern Colonies; this region included New York, New Jersey, Pennsylvania, and Delaware.

Southern Colonies: The English colonies located between Florida and the Middle Colonies; this region included Maryland, Virginia, North Carolina, South Carolina, and Georgia.

Mystic River Valley: A region in southeastern Connecticut that witnessed the massacre of the Pequot Native Americans by the English colonists.

Atlantic World: A word historians use to describe interactions that took place on either side of and on the Atlantic Ocean, particularly during the Age of Exploration and Colonization.

Appalachian Mountains: A well-known North American mountain range that extends from Georgia to Maine.

Louisiana Territory: A large tract of land west of the Mississippi River in North America. This land exchanged hands from one empire to the next throughout the 16th, 17th, and 18th centuries; the United States eventually purchased the land from the French in 1803.

Rio Grande River: The body of water that serves as a natural boundary between the United States and Mexico, flowing around the border of Texas and into the Gulf of Mexico.

Republic of Texas: Prior to American annexation, the name given to the independent state that emerged out of the Texas Revolution against Mexico; this republic lasted roughly ten years before statehood.

Trans-Appalachia: The region west of the Appalachian Mountains.

Confederate States of America: The name given to states that seceded from the United States Union during the Civil War. The Confederate States, also known as the Confederacy, formed a short-lived independent nation that lost to the Union during the Civil War.

Events

French and Indian War: English colonists in the New World fought against the French and their Native American allies. This conflict was an extension of a larger conflict between England and France called the Seven Years' War. The French and Indian War caused the Thirteen Colonies to accumulate a lot of debt, paving the way to the American Revolution.

American Revolution: A colonial revolt and war for independence that pitted American colonists against the British Crown.

Starving Time: Refers to a harsh period of struggle and starvation in the Jamestown colony in the winter of 1609–1610.

Pequot War: An armed conflict that pitted the English colonists and their Native American allies against the Pequot Indians of New England; this conflict lasted from 1636 to 1638.

King Philip's War: A bloody war pitting the English colonists and their allies against the Wampanoag indigenous tribe of New England and their chief, Metacom. The war resulted in over 5,000 deaths.

Boston Massacre: A conflict that stemmed from American protests over British quartering and taxation policies in the Thirteen Colonies. It led to the death of several American colonists and was sensationalized by Patriots as a strategic massacre.

Boston Tea Party: A famous protest that witnessed English colonists dumping dozens of tea crates into Boston harbor. It is known as one of the events that helped ignite the American Revolution.

Lexington and Concord: Often categorized as the locations of the first shots fired in the American War for Independence. These battles were fought in 1775, before the Declaration of Independence was even signed or even created.

Stamp Act Controversy: The controversy and protests in the American colonies surrounding the passage of the Stamp Act of 1765.

Constitutional Convention: A historical event, hosted in Philadelphia, Pennsylvania, that witnessed the end of the Articles of Confederation (and its coinciding Critical Period) and the adoption of a new national Constitution with a Bill of Rights.

Shays' Rebellion: Typically seen as a symbol of the weakness of the United States under the Articles of Confederation, it was a lengthy uprising by disaffected farmers in western Massachusetts under the leadership of Daniel Shays.

Great Compromise: A famous agreement during the Constitutional Convention that helped establish Congress into a two-part (or "bicameral") legislature with a House and Senate.

Three-Fifths Compromise: A controversial constitutional compromise that designated a slave as three fifths of a person when it came to census data, for electoral and legislative reasons.

Louisiana Purchase: This transaction, carried out by Thomas Jefferson, saw the United States expand by one third and the French lose most of its territory in the New World.

War of 1812: A three-year war between the United States and Great Britain that witnessed the burning of the original White House and an eventual American victory in 1815.

Battle at Baltimore: The famous battle in the War of 1812 that inspired Francis Scott Key to write the "Star-Spangled Banner," a poem that later became the United States' national anthem.

Battle of New Orleans: A battle made famous by the leadership and victory of Andrew Jackson; it is considered part of the War of 1812, but it actually occurred after the war ended via official treaty between the United States and Great Britain.

Mexican-American War: An armed conflict that lasted between 1846 to 1848 that began as a skirmish over borders and territories, but ended with the official cession of one third of the Mexican nation to the United States.

American Civil War: A deadly civil conflict between the North and South—the Union and Confederacy—that helped end slavery and eventually reunified a nation that had long been divided over the institution of slavery.

Battle of Gettysburg: A Civil War victory by the Union at Gettysburg, Pennsylvania in 1863 that helped turn the tide against the Confederates.

Groups

Olmec: The earliest Native American civilization in Mexico.

Maya: An early Mesoamerican civilization that began building its great pyramids around 250 CE and then disappeared around 900 CE.

Aztec: A Mesoamerican civilization that flourished in Mexico from about 1300 CE to 1521 CE but was eventually conquered by Spanish conquistadors under leadership of Hernán Cortés.

Inca: The largest civilization in the pre-Columbian Americas, it emerged in the highlands of Peru in the 13th century and was eventually conquered by Spanish conquistadors in 1572.

Iroquois: A political confederation of five northeastern Native American tribes that rose to prominence during colonial times.

Five Civilized Tribes: A group of prominent tribes in the Southeast region of North American continent that collaborated and traded with the colonists; the tribes included the Cherokee, Chickasaw, Choctaw, Creek, and Seminole tribes.

Separatists: Radical English Protestants who wanted to separate from the Church of England, this group founded Plymouth Colony.

Church of England: The official Protestant church of England; it separated from the Catholic Church in the 16th century under the leadership of King Henry VIII.

Pequot Indians: A group of Native Americans who originally resided in a territory that is now the modern-day state of Connecticut; this group fought against the English settlers in the Pequot War (1636–1638).

Mohegan: A Native American tribe that unified with the Pequot in present-day Connecticut during the era of European colonization.

Narragansett: An Algonquin Native American tribe that allied with the New England colonists during the Pequot War (1636–1638).

Parliament: The name given to the British legislature, which created taxes and acts that displeased the colonists in the years leading up to the American Revolution.

Patriots: The name given to the network of leaders, organizers, and militiamen who led a revolution against the British government in the Thirteen Colonies.

First Continental Congress: One of the first examples of colonial unity, it witnessed several colonies, represented by delegates, coming together to petition the alleged wrongdoings and overstepped boundaries of King George III and the British Crown in America.

Second Continental Congress: The second famous convening of the colonists during the revolutionary era in American history, which helped birth the Declaration of Independence on July 4, 1776.

Minutemen: A fast-acting group of civilian militiamen who were ready to form a standing army within a minute's time during the years of the American Revolution.

Tories: A group of American colonists who chose not to side with the revolutionists during the American War for Independence; they chose instead to stay loyal to the British.

Liberty Boys: A secret network of discontented colonists who strategically participated in both acts of protest and espionage against the British Crown in the Revolutionary Era.

Federalists: A group that emerged in the years leading up to the Constitutional Convention; they preferred federal rights over states' rights.

Anti-Federalists: A group that emerged in the years leading up to the Constitutional Convention; they preferred states' rights over federal rights.

Democratic-Republican Party: Also known as the Democratic Republicans and formed by Thomas Jefferson and James Madison around 1792, this American political party opposed the new Federalist Party's centralizing policies.

Jeffersonian Republicans: Named after Thomas Jefferson, the third president of the United States, this group trusted agrarian (farming) values.

Republican Party: Still in existence today as one of the main two political parties in the U.S., it was organized in the years prior to the Civil War. The first Republican President was Abraham Lincoln.

Democratic Party: Still in existence today as one of the main two political parties in the U.S., this political party emerged during the 1820s and 1830s with the democratic fervor surrounding the rise of President Andrew Jackson.

Movements

Women's Suffrage: The name given to the movement that secured women's right to vote in the United States in the early 20th century; women were the last group to gain this right in America.

Jacksonian Democracy: A phrase used to describe the rapid expansion of suffrage to include working class white men during Andrew Jackson's ascendancy to the presidency.

Eras

Industrial Revolution: The term used to refer to an era in global history that witnessed a paradigm shift in culture and economics; an 18th, 19th, and early 20th century global transformation that emphasized mechanized manufacturing processes over agrarian production.

Market Revolution: America's transition from an agrarian economy to a full-blown market economy, which eventually paved the way to the Industrial Revolution.

Critical Period: A phrase sometimes used to refer to the instability of the nation under the Articles of Confederation.

Age of Expansion: Refers to an era in US history following the Louisiana Purchase and extending all the way to the early 20th century, characterized by expansion of territories and borders.

Sectional Crisis: An era of political crisis in the United States in the antebellum period that created a division between North and South, free states and slave states.

Antebellum: Literally means "before the war"; it refers to the time period leading up to the American Civil War.

Populism: Support for the concerns of ordinary people.

Reconstruction: Deemed a failure by some historians because it perpetuated the oppression of African-Americans and resolved little tension between North and South, the era of Reconstruction directly followed the Civil War and tried to rebuild a devastated nation.

Documents

Mayflower Compact: The first governing document of the Plymouth Colony, which was signed by William Bradford and his fellow Puritan Separatists.

Declaration of Independence: A document adopted by the American colonies in 1776 to declare the colonies free from British rule.

Treaty of Paris: A treaty between the Spanish, British, and French Empires following the Seven Years' War; as a result of the treaty, the French relinquished a significant amount of land in North America.

Townshend Acts: These acts, created and implemented by Charles Townshend, a British Parliamentary leader, offended the American colonists because they enforced more taxes (on things such as tea) and greater British control over the colonies.

Tea Act of 1773: This law led to the Boston Tea Party because American colonists were enraged that the British would tax one of their favorite commodities, tea.

Proclamation of 1763: This royal directive angered American colonists because it stated that they were not allowed to transverse or settle territory west of the Appalachian Mountains.

Stamp Act of 1765: This act allowed the British to tax all stamps, which were needed on official documents in the colonies such as marriage licenses.

The Quartering Act: The colonists were angered by this act because it mandated that all colonists must house, or quarter, British soldiers without any royal compensation.

Treaty of Paris (1783): The documents, signed by the United States and Great Britain, that officially ended the American War for Independence in 1783.

Common Sense: A pamphlet written by Thomas Paine in 1775–76 advocating independence from Great Britain to people in the Thirteen Colonies.

Coercive Acts: Also known as the Intolerable Acts, a series of aggressive British statutes that were passed in 1774. They were designed to punish the Massachusetts colonists for their participation in the protests of Boston Tea Party; the colonists claimed the acts were "coercive" or "intolerable" in their revolutionary propaganda.

Quebec Act: A controversial act that instigated the Protestant sensitivities of the American colonists by making it legal for Roman Catholics to practice in Quebec.

Articles of Confederation: Created in 1777, this document established the first central government for the United States; it was replaced by the US Constitution in 1789.

US Constitution: The governing document of the United States that replaced the Articles of Confederation in 1789 and strengthened the federal government.

Bill of Rights: The first ten proposed and ratified amendments to the US Constitution, which spelled out specific personal rights such as the right to free speech.

Star-Spangled Banner: Written by Francis Scott Key at the Battle of Baltimore during the War of 1812, this poem became the national anthem of the United States 100 years after its creation.

Treaty of Ghent: The official end of the War of 1812 came about as a result of the signing of this treaty. However, some skirmishes between the United States and Great Britain continued for months after its signing, due to delays in communication.

Indian Removal Act: A controversial act signed by President Andrew Jackson in 1830 that removed Native Americans to federal territory in the West, which resulted in the Trail of Tears.

Treaty of Guadalupe Hidalgo: Bringing about the end of the Mexican-American War, this 1848 treaty transitioned about one third of Mexican territory into the hands of the United States.

Gadsden Purchase: Following the Mexican Cession after the Mexican-American War, this 1853 purchase from Mexico transferred a small sliver of northern Mexico (modern-day Arizona and New Mexico) into the possession of the United States.

Fugitive Slave Act: A divisive law created during the antebellum period in American history that made it illegal to house or assist runaway slaves in any capacity.

Emancipation Proclamation: The document that freed slaves in the United States; it was created by President Lincoln during the Civil War in 1863.

Gettysburg Address: A famous Abraham Lincoln speech, delivered in 1863 on the site of the Battle of Gettysburg, that is iconic for its passion and brevity

Jim Crow laws: Laws that reinforced the institutionalized segregation of the South from Reconstruction until the Civil Rights Movement of the 1960s.

Analytical Trends

Consensus History: A style of American historiography that downplays conflict and complexity, focusing on unity and nationalism.

Modernism: A philosophy that took hold in the late 19th and early 20th century that gave rise to histories and literature that emphasized the beauties and the pangs of modernity.

New Left: A 1960s political movement that championed such causes as anti-war activism, women's rights, and other issues.

Postmodernism: A departure from modernism, this literary, artistic, and architectural movement also affected history and philosophy. It focuses on the tenuousness of authority and truth and interpretation of texts.

Progressivism: A view of history and philosophy categorized by a larger search for order and a belief in human progress.

General Social Studies Terms

American Exceptionalism: A worldview that claims the United States is historically unique and more powerful than other nations.

Reductive: Oversimplifying a subject, debate, or narrative.

Nuanced: A subtly different view or varying argument that promotes a unique perspective.

Historically Accurate: Authentic or true, in terms of historical validity or honesty.

Indigenous People: A way of referring to any group who originated in a particular place, in contrast to people who arrived later, as conquerors, immigrants, or slaves.

Historical Narrative: A spoken or written account of history, as told from a specific viewpoint or perspective.

Eurocentrism: A worldview that favors a European narrative of progress.

Colonial Economy: A phrase used to describe the system of production, consumption, and trade that emerged during the period of European colonization.

Joint-Stock Company: A business entity in which shareholders own a share of the company's profit; many joint-stock companies are responsible for founding colonies in the New World.

Mayflower: The English ship that famously transported the Separatist Puritans to their new settlement at Plymouth.

Archive: To place or organize documents or materials in storage for future use.

Savage: A pejorative term the English used to describe the Native Americans as barbarous or uncivilized.

Bolster: A verb that means to support or reinforce.

Proselytizing: Trying to convert someone to a particular faith or religion.

Exploitation: Taking advantage of someone or something for selfish reasons, such as profit.

Genocidal: An adjective used to describe the systematic attempt to kill off an entire group of people, whether defined by religion, ethnicity, or race.

Paradigm Shifting: A phrase coined by Thomas Kuhn to describe large waves of historical and scientific change that fundamentally change the ways people understand the world around them.

Capitalism: The dominant political and economic philosophy of the United States, which focuses on creating a free market in which there is competition between businesses.

Slavery: An institution built upon the bondage and forced labor of human beings. Slavery preceded the foundation of the United States and continued until the Civil War era and the Emancipation Proclamation.

Protesting: When a person or group makes a public statement of disagreement; it can take the form of marches, gatherings, silences, and even boycotts.

Boycotting: A specific type of protest that focuses on finances and economics; it is the refusal to purchase or use a particular service or product, in an effort to force political or social change.

Electoral College: In the United States, it is a voting system that allows selected representatives to vote on behalf of the people. It is an example of limited democracy.

Industrialization: The widespread development of manufacturing industries in a region, country, or culture.

Agrarian: A term used to describe a society or culture that relies heavily on farming for trade and subsistence.

Republic: A classical form of government adopted by the United States (and the Republic of Texas) because it placed the power of the people in the hands of elected officials who are supposed to stand for public opinion.

Self-Sufficiency: Needing no outside help to sustain one's own life, especially when it comes to food production.

Virtue: Behavior showing high moral standards.

Yeoman: A term for a farmer who works a small, individually owned plot of land. Thomas Jefferson believed democracy could be sustained through the independence of yeoman farmers.

Discontent: A feeling of dissatisfaction, typically with the prevailing social or political situation.

Revisionism: The re-interpretation of the historical record, usually in a way that distorts or alters the prevailing understanding.

Sanitize: Literally, to clean; in social sciences it means to alter something regarded as less acceptable so as to make it more palatable.

Subjugation: The action of bringing someone or something under domination or control.

Terminological: Connected with the meanings of words, especially the technical words and expressions used in a particular subject.

Egalitarian: A term that is synonymous with ultimate equality or when people or society share material or immaterial power equally.

Anti-Egalitarian: Contrary to principles of social equality and fairness.

Cultural Milieu: The cultural and social environment that surrounds a person. It comes from a French term meaning "middle place."

Working Class: A term used as label for a laboring class that gained momentum during the Industrial Revolution.

White Supremacy: A system of beliefs that upholds white people as the supreme race while discriminating against other races.

Duel: An archaic way of resolving disputes that involved a highly structured form of violence; it was often performed with guns and involved a series of sport-like rules and procedures.

Immigration: The action of coming to live permanently in a foreign country.

Urbanization: The process of making an area more urban or populated.

Industrialization: The widespread development of manufacturing industries in a region, country, or culture.

Artisan: A worker who is highly skilled in a trade, especially one involving handicrafts.

Cash-Crop Agriculture: The growing of agricultural crops for money, in contrast to crops grown for subsistence. Before to the Civil War, cotton was an American cash crop.

Manufacturing: Using mechanized instruments or technology to make a particular good or product (for example, automobile manufacturing).

Suffrage: A term used to describe the right to vote; historically, it originally belonged to men or land-owners. It was extended gradually to other groups, with women being the last to earn the right.

Aristocratic: Having to do with a form of government that places strength in the hands of a small, privileged ruling class.

Insurgency: An act of rebellion or revolt against a government or ruler.

Elitism: A tendency to promote the wealthier portions of the population.

Hierarchical: Organized in order of rank.

Deference: Humble submission and respect.

Angst: Intense feelings of distress or anxiety that can be felt either personally or collectively.

Tyranny: Cruel and oppressive government or rule.

Spurious: Not what it purports to be; false or fake.

Rhetoric: The name given to any form of communication, written or oral, that carries power as an art and discourse; a personalized and recognizable style of personal or collective communication.

Plebeian: A commoner; a common person.

Racist: An individual who takes seriously the strict parameters of racial constructs and discriminates against other races as a result.

Racial Exclusivity: Excluding a person or group of persons because of their race.

Cotton Gin: A cotton-separating invention created by Eli Whitney in 1793 that was supposed to ease the burden of slavery through mechanized means but actually increased the demand for slave labor on cotton plantations.

Plantations: A large estate farmed by slaves or tenant farmers who live there but do not own the land. During the antebellum period in American history, plantations served as the epicenter of slave labor; these plantations capitalized on the institution of slavery to produce large cash crops such as tobacco and cotton.

How Authors Use Language in Social Studies

Often history is interpreted or taught as a mere timeline or a series of bland facts about the past, but history should also be understood as a "lived experience." All humans are *a part of* history—they are the historical actors and personas who make positive (or negative) changes in the world. Human beings are constantly interacting with the super-structural forces of history. History occurs in interlocking webs of mutual reciprocity.

History happens in a context of local and global events. The people recording that history (in whatever format) are part of that context and therefore shaped by it. No one merely records statistics, facts, and figures. Each thing recorded is done so because it is important for some reason to the one recording it.

Those who study history must do their best to understand the people and places they study as well as understand themselves in their own historical context.

Good historians ask questions prior to reading or studying what has been left for them by prior generations. What was important to the person who left this record? Were they rich or poor? Were they weak or powerful? What was their particular view of the world? What was their view of themselves and the group(s) they belonged to and their perceived place in history? These and other questions are critical to better understanding what was recorded and why it was considered important. It also helps provide a context for understanding the record left for posterity.

The historian must also understand their own biases, worldview, preconceptions, and context so that they can be aware of who they are and what they believe, because it influences the way they read, interpret, and understand the historical record.

Social studies deal with many different documents and recordings, all using written or spoken language. Language can be found in diaries, journals, political cartoons, old maps, treatises, constitutions, treaties, laws, advertisements, deeds, archives, inventory reports, and financial receipts. These are all examples of **primary sources**. Social studies also uses language in textbooks, monographs, academic journals, encyclopedias, online blogs, contemporary maps, charts, tables, and graphs. These are all examples of **secondary sources**. Language can even be found on old artifacts, archeological discoveries, monuments, and museum exhibits. These are all examples of historical objects that can fall into the categories of either primary or secondary sources. Language is the primary method of capturing history and documenting its meaning. Although social studies can examine artifacts without language (for example, the artifacts used in anthropology and archeology), most social studies documents use language. The languages may change from culture to culture, but language use is itself a unifying component of all major cultural histories.

Thus, it is important for test takers to become detectives of social studies language. Every student must be prepared to understand the purpose and biases embedded in language. For instance, if a document repeatedly uses words such as *liberty*, *freedom*, and *inalienable rights*, it is likely that the authors of these documents believe in these concepts so much that they wanted to disseminate these words to a broader audience. Additionally, if advertisements consistently use the word "cool," then the creators of these advertisements are likely using this word for a specific purpose, such as to appeal to teenagers concerned with their image. Every language-based source carries its own perspective and biases. Thus, students must be prepared to link language to not only the historical context (for example, the era of the Early Republic), but also to the beliefs of the author(s).

Fact Versus Opinion

A fact is information that can be proven true. If information can be disproved, it is not a fact. For example, water freezes at or below thirty-two degrees Fahrenheit. An argument stating that water freezes at seventy degrees Fahrenheit cannot be supported by data and is therefore not a fact. Facts tend to be associated with science, mathematics, and statistics.

Opinions are information open to debate. Opinions are often tied to subjective concepts like equality, morals, and rights. They can also be controversial. An affirmative argument for a position—such as gun control—can be just as effective as an opposing argument against it.

Biases and stereotypes are viewpoints based in opinion and held despite evidence that they are incorrect. A bias is an individual prejudice. Biased people ignore evidence that contradicts their position while offering as proof any evidence that supports it. A stereotype is a widely held belief projected onto a group. Those who stereotype tend to make assumptions based on what others have told them and usually have little firsthand experience with the group or item in question.

Readers must read critically to discern between fact and opinion and to notice bias and stereotypes.

Claims and Evidence in Social Studies

Determining Whether a Claim Is or Is Not Supported by Evidence

Valid claims must have sufficient evidence that fully support the claims and conclusions. Critical readers examine the facts and evidence used to support an author's claim. They check the facts against other sources to be sure those facts are correct. They also check the validity of the sources used to be sure those sources are credible, academic, and/or peer-reviewed. Consider that when an author uses another person's opinion to support their argument, even if it is an expert's opinion, it is still only an opinion and should not be taken as fact. A strong argument uses valid, measurable facts to support ideas. Even then, the reader may disagree with the argument as it may be rooted in their personal beliefs.

An authoritative argument may use the facts to sway the reader. For example, in a paper on global warming, many experts differ in their opinions of what alternative fuels can be used to aid in offsetting it. Because of this, a writer may choose to only use the information and expert opinion that supports their viewpoint.

Students must be able to distinguish between reliable and unreliable sources in order to develop a well-written research report. When choosing print sources, typically published works that have been edited and clearly identify the author or authors are considered credible sources. Peer-reviewed journals and research conducted by scholars are likewise considered to be credible sources of information.

When deciding on what Internet sources to use, it is also a sound practice for researchers to look closely at each website's universal resource locator, the *URL*. Generally speaking, websites with .edu, .gov, or .org as the Top Level Domain are considered reliable, but the researcher must still question any possible political or social bias. Personal blogs, tweets, personal websites, online forums, and any site that clearly demonstrates bias, strong opinions, or persuasive language are considered unreliable sources.

Comparing Information that Differs Between Sources

If one were to analyze current events, they will get a clearer view of how this works. The same event can be recorded by two different people and sound like two different events because of the way the information is reported. For example, two people might report on an event during a time of war. The first might be a pacifist and therefore would be opposed to the war and that bias would be seen in how they reported on the conflict. Someone else might speak of the same events and make them seem heroic because they are very much in favor of their country's involvement in the conflict. The same historical event is being recorded but with two very different intents, understandings, and interpretations.

The historian who comes to this information (or the modern reader in the current events case) needs to also be aware of their personal views and how that affects their understanding of what they are reading. They may read sympathetically if they share the bias of the original author. They may also react in great opposition to what was recorded if their own view varies sharply from that of the original recorder.

Awareness of the times, backgrounds, purposes, and influences on both the original recorder and the one examining the record must be taken into account when analyzing historical sources.

Analyzing Historical Events and Arguments

Making Inferences

Inference refers to the reader's ability to understand the unwritten text, i.e., "read between the lines" in terms of an author's intent or message. The strategy asks that a reader not take everything he or she reads at face value but instead, add their own interpretation of what the author seems to be trying to convey. A reader's ability to make inferences relies on their ability to think clearly and logically about the text. It does not ask that the reader make wild speculation or guess about the material but demands that he or she be able to come to a sound conclusion about the material.

An author's use of less literal words and phrases requires readers to make more inference when they read. Since inference involves **deduction**—deriving conclusions from ideas assumed to be true—there's more room for interpretation. Still, critical readers who employ inference, if careful in their thinking, can still arrive at the logical, sound conclusions the author intends.

Connections Between Different Social Studies Elements (People, Events, Places, Processes)

Analyzing Cause-and-Effect Relationships

Every time someone studies history, it is very much a collision of past, present, and future. Historians are concerned for the past, rooted in the present, and thinking about the future. Historical analysis is, therefore, a process infusing the present in the past in hopes of predicting (or deterring) certain social interactions in the future.

When examining the historical narratives of events, it is important to understand the relationship between causes and effects. A cause can be defined as something, whether an event, social change, or other factor, that contributes to the occurrence of certain events; the results of causes are called effects. Those terms may seem simple enough, but they have drastic implications on how one explores history. Events such as the American Revolution or the Civil Rights Movement may appear to occur spontaneously, but a closer examination will reveal that these events depended on earlier phenomena and patterns that influenced the course of history.

There can be multiple causes and effects for any situation. The existence of multiple causes can be seen through the settling of the American West. Many historians have emphasized the role of manifest destiny—the national vision of expanding across the continent—as a driving force behind the growth of the United States. Yet there were many different influences behind the expansion westward. Northern abolitionists and southern planters saw the frontier as a way to either extend or limit slavery. Economic opportunities in the West also encouraged travel westward, as did the gradual pacification, relocation, or eradication of Native American tribes. In fact, manifest destiny as well as economic and political reasons played significant roles in justifying the pacification, relocation, or eradication of the Native American tribal nations.

Even an individual cause can be subdivided into smaller factors or stretched out in a gradual process. Although there were numerous issues that led to the Civil War, slavery was the primary cause. However, that topic stretched back to the very founding of the nation, and the existence of slavery was a controversial topic during the creation of the Declaration of Independence and the Constitution. The abolition movement as a whole did not start until the 1830s, but nevertheless, slavery is a cause that gradually grew more important over the following decades. In addition, opponents of slavery were divided by different motivations—some believed that it stifled the economy, while others focused on moral issues.

On the other end of the spectrum, a single event can have numerous results. The rise of the telegraph, for example, had several effects on American history. The telegraph allowed news to travel much quicker and turned events into immediate national news, such as the sinking of the USS Maine, which sparked the Spanish-American War. In addition, the telegraph helped make railroads run more efficiently by improving the links between stations. The faster speed of both travel and communications led to a shift in time itself, and localized times were replaced by standardized time zones across the nation.

By looking at different examples of cause and effect closely, it becomes clear that no event occurs without one—if not multiple—causes behind it, and that each historical event can have a variety of direct and indirect consequences.

One of the most critical elements of cause-and-effect relationships is how they are relevant not only in studying history but also in contemporary events. People must realize that events and developments today will likely have a number of consequences later on. Therefore, the study of cause and effect remains vital in understanding the past, the present, and the future.

Describing the Connections Between People, Places, Environments, Processes, and Events

The primary role of social studies is to illuminate connections between people, places, environments, processes, and events. Therefore, test takers must be prepared to examine correlations and causations in social studies. Correlations are connections that do not necessarily show any signs of causation. Two things are correlated when they happen to the same people, or in the same circumstances, or at the same time. For example, the increased popularity of apocalyptic literature in 2008 and 2009 can be **correlated** with the Great Recession that occurred around that time. However, these two events might not be **causally related**. A relationship is causal when one thing causes another to happen. In other words, the rise in apocalyptic literature may be caused by other cultural changes, such as an increasing disenchantment with humanity, a disenchantment caused by an increase in global wars and genocide.

Other connections can be discovered by analyzing causation. For instance, the mass immigration of Irish workers to the United States in the 19th century can likely be understood as a cause and effect scenario spawned by the great potato famine of that era—immigrants had to flee Ireland because their families were going to starve to death. In this instance, one thing caused another. Students of social studies must constantly be on the search for these connections. They must study the ways in which geography (for example, the Rio Grande River) affects immigration patterns (for example, undocumented immigration from Mexico to America in the 20th and 21st centuries). They must even be aware of the ways in which people (for example, Adolf Hitler) influence events (the rise of Nazi Germany in the 1930s and 1940s).

Connections are discussed in passages, political cartoons, and test questions. Test takers must be able to contextualize, historicize, and analyze connections. Too often the field of social studies is taught as a linear timeline. But, in reality, the field of social studies is more like a complex web of ideas, characters, events, eras, movements, counter-movements, and belief systems. Additionally, views of historical events change throughout history. Today we may analyze slavery differently than the era in which slavery was legal in the United States. Therefore, students of social studies must also be aware of their own connections to history and all the variables that form its foundations. Below is one example of a cognitive map showing the connections between people, places, environments, processes, and events in social studies.

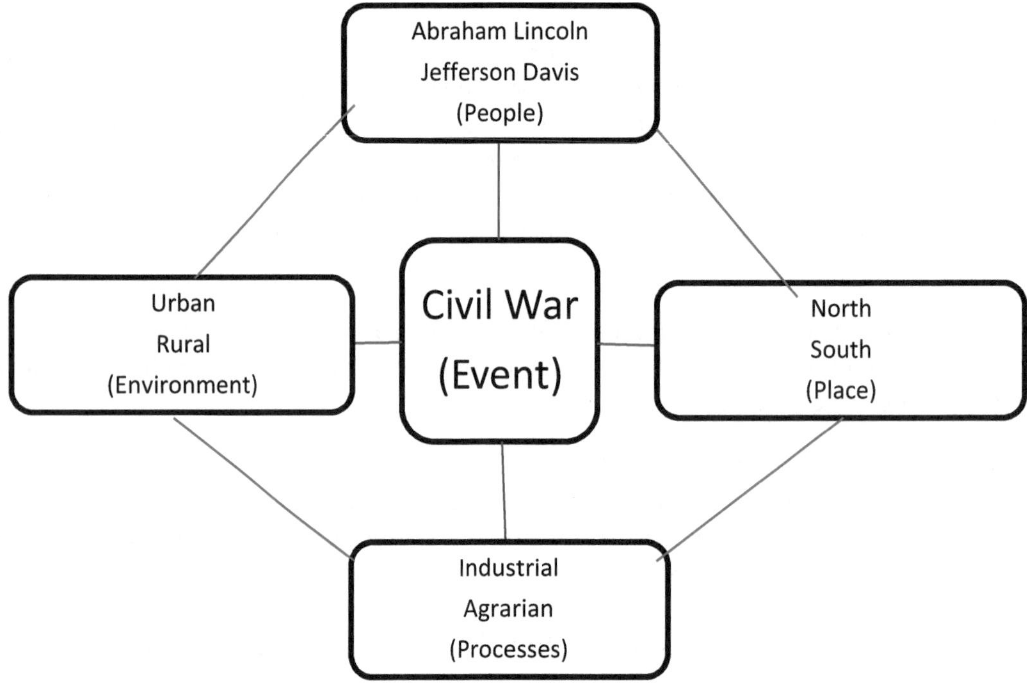

Putting Events in Order and Understanding the Steps in a Process

Social studies students must understand how to determine the timeline/chronology of events through a process called sequencing. Sequencing allows students to gain a better understanding of change over time in history. Social studies classrooms often employ test questions that force students to recall the correct chronology, or time order, of important historical events.

Along with sequencing, social studies students should be able to carry out a process known as categorizing. Categorizing is the process by which historical themes, events, agents, persons, movements, or ideas are placed in designated categories that help students understand their historical significance. Categorization is usually most effective when certain words or phrases are organized by themes or concepts. For instance, the categorical concept of "economic depression" could help students better understand such historical events as the Panic of 1819, the Great Depression, and the Great Recession. Categorization allows students to link unrelated events in history.

Identifying associations and cause-and-effect relationships strengthens a student's ability to sequence events in history. All U.S. history is a series of associated events leading to still other events. A cause is what made something happen. An effect is what happens because of something. Understanding cause-and-effect helps students to understand the proverbial *why* of history; it helps them breathe more meaning into history.

Comparing and contrasting is another strategy that will make students more historically informed. In history, we often compare two or more things to understand their similarities and differences better. Part of the historical process is understanding what historical characteristics are unique or utterly common. Students might, for instance, compare and contrast the American Revolution to the Texas

Revolution to gain a better understanding of the ways in which such variables as time, geographic location, and contributing persons affect history.

Summarizing is a strategy that is also used often throughout the historical process in a social studies classroom. Students will not only have to summarize the meaning of historical events or eras, but they will also need to know how to summarize the important points of primary and secondary sources. Summaries allow students to convey their knowledge in a short, concise, digestible fashion. Part of summarizing requires that students find the main idea of a particular article, source, or paragraph. Main ideas help students make their summaries even more concise and effective. Summarizing sometimes requires students to make generalizations or draw inferences/conclusions. Often there are "gaps of information" in the sources provided to students. Students will have to use background knowledge and critical-thinking skills to fill in these gaps with generalizations (broad, sweeping statements) or inferences/conclusions (educated guesses, predictions, or assumptions).

Analyzing the Relationship of Events, Processes, and/or Ideas

Events, processes, and ideas can be related in different ways. Earlier events don't necessarily *cause* later ones; in many cases, they simply occurred prior to the later event. For example, although the battles at Concord and Lexington may seem to be instantaneous eruptions of violence during the American Revolution, they stemmed from a variety of factors. The most obvious influences behind those two battles were the assortment of taxes and policies imposed on the Thirteen Colonies following the French and Indian War from 1754 to 1763. Taxation without direct representation, combined with the deployment of British soldiers to enforce these policies, greatly increased American resistance. Earlier events, such as the Boston Massacre and the Boston Tea Party, similarly stemmed from conflicts between British soldiers and local colonists over perceived tyranny and rebelliousness. Therefore, the start of the American Revolution progressed from earlier developments.

The Effect of Different Social Studies Concepts on an Argument or Point Of View

Analyzing How Events and Situations Shape the Author's Point of View

Many people want to rise above their historical contexts, but it is an impossibility. Whether one likes it or not, the ideas of humanity are always influenced by the forces of history. The individual and collective consciousness of humanity is often dictated by historical events and situations. A Jew writing in Germany during World War II would inevitably be affected in some capacity by the anti-Semitic tendencies of Nazism. A Texas-based Mexican national writing during the Mexican-American War of the 1840s would inevitably be influenced by American expansionism. A college student writing and liking posts on Facebook during the Great Recession of 2008 would inevitably be exposed to the effects of the stock market's decline. Even if the author does not comment on these events, they still shape the author's point of view. When analyzing a history text or a historical cartoon, test takers should first ask key questions: "When, where, and why was this documented created?" Often the answers to these questions provide test takers with the evidence they need to properly analyze the documents and answer multiple choice questions.

In some cases, the author of a document explicitly comments on history. The author may refer to historical persons, events, or dates. Test takers should take note of these persons, events, and dates because they offer evidence for answering questions or prompts. For instance, a primary source such as Anne Frank's diary directly refers to the events of World War II and the aggressions of Germans. In other cases, it is up to the test taker to decode the implicit messages embedded in a text in order to gain a better understanding of historical influences. A good place to start with this decoding process is the date the document was created. If test takers know the date of a document, they can begin to illuminate historical correlations. For instance, a historian writing in the 1960s might not explicitly discuss the historical opinions of the New Left (a political movement of the 1960s), but a test taker may be able to decode the implicit messages embedded in the text and infer that the historian may have been influenced by that era of political thought.

Evaluating Whether the Author's Evidence is Factual, Relevant, and Sufficient

It's important to read any piece of writing critically. The goal is to discover the point and purpose of what the author is writing about through analysis. It's also crucial to establish the point or stance the author has taken on the topic of the piece. After determining the author's perspective, readers can then more effectively develop their own viewpoints on the subject.

If the argument is that wind energy is the best solution, the author will use facts that support this idea. That same author may leave out relevant facts on solar energy. The way the author uses facts can influence the reader, so it's important to consider the facts being used, how those facts are being presented, and what information might be left out.

Making Judgments About How Different Ideas Impact the Author's Argument

To reach supportable judgments and conclusions in social studies, teachers and students must be prepared to categorize and synthesize a variety of primary and secondary sources, paying close attention to which sources are legitimate sources of fact or opinion. Students must also be able to justifiably quote information from these sources to establish historical generalizations, or "general statements that identify themes that unite or separate source materials." Often, a generalization identifies key features, relationships, or differences found throughout multiple sources.

Identifying Bias

Bias exists in all forms of written and visual documentation. In social studies, it is especially important to look out for bias, in both primary and secondary sources. Bias can stem from various sources, including: historical context, cultural background, personal beliefs, political affiliation, and religious values. All these things shape the way an individual sees and writes about history and society. For example, a conservative author writing in the late 1980s may have been likely to support the political initiative known as the War on Drugs.

This likelihood is due to political affiliation and historical context. The 1980s was a conservative era in American politics, thanks to the rise of President Ronald Reagan. It was also a historical era that responded accordingly to the crack epidemic and gained conservative support for expanded police enforcement. Additionally, a communist political cartoonist in the Soviet Union during the Cold War may be likely to paint a picture of the United States as an aggressor. That era of history pitted the Soviet Union against the United States on a global level. Biases even emerge in secondary sources; people analyzing history are influenced by their own cultural-historical contexts.

Propaganda in Social Studies Readings

There are times in which biases are so extreme that they take the form of propaganda. Propaganda means written, spoken, or visual texts that try to influence or control the opinions of audiences. Two examples of propaganda are the texts and political cartoons published by Nazi Germany during Adolf Hitler's era of leadership. These materials tried to influence or control the beliefs of Germany by exposing them to extreme biases. GED test takers often have to decode texts and political cartoons by exposing biases or propagandistic tendencies.

Using Numbers and Graphics in Social Studies

Using Data Presented in Visual Form, Including Maps, Charts, Graphs, and Tables

Making Sense of Information that is Presented in Different Ways

Primary sources contain firsthand documentation of a historical event or era. Primary sources are provided by people who have experienced an historical era or event. Primary sources capture a specific moment, context, or era in history. They are valued as eyewitness accounts and personal perspectives. Examples include diaries, memoirs, journals, letters, interviews, photographs, context-specific artwork, government documents, constitutions, newspapers, personal items, libraries, and archives. Another example of a primary source is the Declaration of Independence. This historical document captures the revolutionary sentiment of an era in American history.

Authors of secondary sources write about events, contexts, and eras in history with a relative amount of experiential, geographic, or temporal distance. Normally, secondary source authors aren't firsthand witnesses. In some cases, they may have experienced an event, but they are offering secondhand, retrospective accounts of their experience. All scholars and historians produce secondary sources—they gather primary source information and synthesize it for a new generation of students. Monographs, biographies, magazine articles, scholarly journals, theses, dissertations, textbooks, and encyclopedias are all secondary sources. In some rare instances, secondary sources become so enmeshed in their era of inquiry that they later become primary sources for future scholars and analysts.

Both primary and secondary sources of information are useful. They both offer invaluable insight that helps the writer learn more about the subject matter. However, researchers are cautioned to examine the information closely and to consider the time period as well as the cultural, political, and social climate in which accounts were given. Learning to distinguish between reliable sources of information and questionable accounts is paramount to a quality research report.

Representing Textual Data into Visual Form

Students should not only be able to analyze maps and other infographics, but they should also be able to create graphs, charts, tables, documents, maps, timelines, and other visual materials to represent geographic, political, historical, economic, and cultural features. Students should be made aware of the different options they have to present data. They should understand that maps visually display geographic features, and they can be used to illustrate key relationships in human geography and natural geography. Maps can indicate themes in history, politics, economics, culture, social relationships, and demographic distributions.

Students can also choose to display data or information in a variety of graphs: Bar graphs compare two or more things with parallel bars; line graphs show change over time with strategic points placed carefully between vertical and horizontal axes; and pie graphs divide wholes into percentages or parts. Likewise, students can choose to use timelines or tables to present data/information. Timelines arrange events or ideas into chronological order, and tables arrange words or numbers into columns or rows. These are just some of the visual tools teachers and students can use to help visually convey their historical questions or ideas.

Using Graphs with Appropriate Labeling, and Using the Data to Predict Trends

Being "literate" in social studies means that teachers and students must be ready to interpret a variety of forms of data. In social studies, data is usually numerical or statistical information offered in the form of a graph, chart, table, document, map, or timeline.

Sometimes valuable data can also be embedded in documents, maps, or timelines. Thus, it is important that every student is also exposed to these data-based tools in a social studies classroom. Much like all sources, students should be challenged to determine the validity of the data presented in graphs, charts, tables, documents, maps, and timelines.

Dependent and Independent Variables

As mentioned, the independent variable in an experiment or process is the one that is manipulated, while the dependent one experiences change because of the manipulations to the independent variable.

Correlation Versus Causation

In social studies, much like in basic statistics, correlation does not always imply causation. Correlation means events occur together, in a relation of more than just random chance. Causation means one thing causes other another. In social studies, one event can be shown to lead to another. For example, the bombing of Pearl Harbor by the Japanese led to the entrance of the United States in the Second World War. The bombing of Pearl Harbor encouraged President Franklin Delano Roosevelt and the United States Congress to declare war on Japan. This example shows a clear line of cause and effect, one that is indisputable in terms of historical evidence.

However, when discussing the Great Depression in America, historians are far less likely to come to a consensus about the cause. Since there are a multitude of variables contributing to the Great Depression, delineating a clear line of causation is more difficult. Instead, historians can discuss the correlation of factors that led to the Depression, which include: increased inflation, increased debt, various taxes and policies, fear, isolationism, corruption, and the excesses of the Roaring Twenties. It is hard to come up with a clear formula of "this equaled that" when it comes to the Great Depression. Thus, it is more applicable to discuss the historical correlations between people, trends, and events.

Using Statistics in Social Studies

Mean, Median, Mode, and Range of a Data Set

Recall that the center of a set of data (statistical values) can be represented by its mean, median, or mode. These are sometimes referred to as measures of central tendency. Measures of central tendency can also be used to analyze and understand data related to history and social studies.

The mean is the average of the data set. The mean can be calculated by adding the data values and dividing by the sample size (the number of data points). Suppose a student has test scores of 93, 84, 88, 72, 91, and 77. To find the mean, or average, the scores are added and the sum is divided by 6 because there are 6 test scores:

$$\frac{93 + 84 + 88 + 72 + 91 + 77}{6} = \frac{505}{6} = 84.17$$

Given the mean of a data set and the sum of the data points, the sample size can be determined by dividing the sum by the mean. Suppose you are told that Kate averaged 12 points per game and scored a total of 156 points for the season. The number of games that she played (the sample size or the number of data points) can be determined by dividing the total points (sum of data points) by her average (mean of data points): $\frac{156}{12} = 13$. Therefore, Kate played in 13 games this season.

If given the mean of a data set and the sample size, the sum of the data points can be determined by multiplying the mean and sample size. Suppose you are told that Tom worked 6 days last week for an average of 5.5 hours per day. The total number of hours worked for the week (sum of data points) can be determined by multiplying his daily average (mean of data points) by the number of days worked (sample size):

$$5.5 \times 6 = 33$$

Therefore, Tom worked a total of 33 hours last week.

The median of a data set is the value of the data point in the middle when the sample is arranged in numerical order. To find the median of a data set, the values are written in order from least to greatest. The lowest and highest values are simultaneously eliminated, repeating until the value in the middle remains. Suppose the salaries of math teachers are: $35,000; $38,500; $41,000; $42,000; $42,000; $44,500; $49,000. The values are listed from least to greatest to find the median. The lowest and highest values are eliminated until only the middle value remains. Repeating this step three times reveals a median salary of $42,000. If the sample set has an even number of data points, two values will remain after all others are eliminated. In this case, the mean of the two middle values is the median. Consider the following data set: 7, 9, 10, 13, 14, 14. Eliminating the lowest and highest values twice leaves two values, 10 and 13, in the middle. The mean of these values $\left(\frac{10+13}{2}\right)$ is the median. Therefore, the set has a median of 11.5.

The mode of a data set is the value that appears most often. A data set may have a single mode, multiple modes, or no mode. If different values repeat equally as often, multiple modes exist. If no value repeats, no mode exists. Consider the following data sets:

- A: 7, 9, 10, 13, 14, 14
- B: 37, 44, 33, 37, 49, 44, 51, 34, 37, 33, 44
- C: 173, 154, 151, 168, 155

Set A has a mode of 14. Set B has modes of 37 and 44. Set C has no mode.

The range of a data set is the difference between the highest and the lowest values in the set. The range can be considered the span of the data set. To determine the range, the smallest value in the set is subtracted from the largest value. The ranges for the data sets A, B, and C above are calculated as follows:

A: $14 - 7 = 7$

B: $51 - 33 = 18$

C: $173 - 151 = 22$

Practice Quiz

Questions 1–3 refer to the passage below:

> It hath been shewn to have been the constant Opinion of there being a North-west Passage, from the Time soon after which the South Sea was discovered near the Western Part of America, and that this Opinion was adopted by the greatest Men not only in the Time they lived, but whose Eminence and great Abilities are revered by the present Age. That there is a Sea to Westward of Hudson's Bay, there hath been given the concurrent Testimony of Indians; and of Navigators and Indians that there is a Streight which unites such Sea with the Western Ocean. The Voyage which lead us into these Considerations, hath so many Circumstances relating to it, which, now they have been considered, shew the greatest Probability of its being authentick; which carry with them as much the Evidence of a Fact, afford as great a Degree of Credibility as we have for any Transaction done a long Time since, which hath not been of a publick Nature and transacted in the Face of the World, so as to fall under the Notice of every one, though under the Disadvantage that the Intent on one Part must have been to have it concealed and buried in Oblivion.

Excerpt from *The Great Probability of a Northwest Passage* by Thomas Jefferys, 1768

1. Which of the following events most directly triggered increased interest in the maritime route described in the passage?
    a. Vasco da Gama sailing around the Cape of Good Hope in 1488.
    b. Christopher Columbus reaching the Caribbean in 1492.
    c. Ferdinand Magellan's expedition circumnavigating the world in 1522.
    d. Henry Hudson exploring the Hudson Bay in 1611.

2. Which of the following was a long-term consequence of explorers looking for a "North-west passage"?
    a. European powers gained a faster route to the Pacific Ocean.
    b. European powers abandoned international trade networks.
    c. European powers forged alliances with Amerindian empires.
    d. European powers colonized the Americas.

3. Which of the following people most likely funded the expeditions alluded to in the passage?
    a. Monarch
    b. Feudal lord
    c. Leader of a merchant trade guild
    d. Military general

Questions 4–5 refer to the passage below:

> What is dangerous for Japan is, not the imitation of the outer features of the West, but the acceptance of the motive force of the Western nationalism as her own. Her social ideals are already showing signs of defeat at the hands of politics. I can see her motto, taken from science, "Survival of the Fittest," writ large at the entrance of her present-day history—the motto whose meaning is, "Help yourself, and never heed what it costs to others"; the motto of the blind man who only believes in what he can touch, because he cannot see. But those who can see know that men are so closely knit that when you strike others the blow comes back to yourself. The moral law, which is the greatest discovery of man, is the discovery of this wonderful truth, that man becomes all the truer the more he realizes himself in others. This truth has not only a subjective value but is manifested in every department of our life. And nations who sedulously cultivate moral blindness as the cult of patriotism will end their existence in a sudden and violent death.

Excerpt from the essay "Nationalism in Japan" by Rabindranath Tagore, 1917

4. Which of the following BEST summarizes the "outer features of the West" that Japan adopted in the nineteenth century?
    a. Japan enacted a written constitution and modernized its military in the nineteenth century.
    b. Japan outlawed Shintoism and orchestrated mass conversions to Christianity.
    c. Japan encouraged nationalism to strengthen the Shogun.
    d. Japan adopted European moral laws and other positive social ideals.

5. Nationalism had the LEAST influence on which one of the following world events?
    a. German unification
    b. Latin American wars of independence
    c. Russo-Turkish War
    d. War of the Spanish Succession

Answer Explanations

1. B: Jefferys is referencing the Northwest Passage. There were rumors about a Northwest Passage to Asia prior to Columbus reaching the Caribbean, and his voyage ignited a firestorm of interest. From 1492 to 1800, European powers sponsored many hundreds of expeditions to locate the route. Thus, Choice *B* is the correct answer. Vasco da Gama sailing around the Cape of Good Hope led to increased European trade with East Africa, India, and China, but his journey around Africa was unrelated to the Northwest Passage. So, Choice *A* is incorrect. Ferdinand Magellan's circumnavigation of the world didn't increase interest in a Northwest Passage because his expedition traveled to Asia across the southern portion of the Atlantic Ocean. So, Choice *C* is incorrect. Choice *D* is the second best answer. European explorers believed the Northwest Passage was located to the west of Hudson Bay, and the passage mentions Hudson Bay. However, the voyage of Christopher Columbus was the inciting incident for the entire Age of Discovery, so Choice *D* is incorrect.

2. D: European explorers never found the Northwest Passage, but the search uncovered the Americas' economic potential. European colonization started almost immediately after Columbus reached the Caribbean, and it spread across both continents as explorers continued to search for the elusive route to Asia. Thus, Choice *D* is the correct answer. Although Ferdinand Magellan found a passage to Asia through the southern Atlantic, it was much slower than sailing around the Cape of Good Hope. So, Choice *A* is incorrect. The search for a Northwest Passage exponentially increased international trade, so Choice *B* is incorrect. European powers occasionally made strategic short-term alliances with individual Amerindian tribes, but alliances weren't a long-term consequence of European exploration in the Americas. As such, Choice *C* is incorrect.

3. A: European monarchies were the primary sponsors of maritime expeditions that searched for an alternative route to Asia via a Northwest Passage in the Atlantic Ocean. Thus, Choice *A* is the correct answer. Feudal political systems collapsed in the fifteenth century, and the passage was published in 1768. So, Choice *B* is incorrect. Choice *C* is the second best answer. Some wealthy merchants invested in joint-stock companies that sponsored expeditions, but maritime expeditions typically required a royal charter. As such, the monarchy was still always involved in maritime expeditions during the eighteenth century. In addition, joint-stock companies were independent legal entities, so they were rarely connected to trade guilds. Therefore, Choice *C* is incorrect. Although maritime expeditions usually included a militarized component, military generals were not a primary source of funding. So, Choice *D* is incorrect.

4. A: The passage mentions that Japan has already imitated the "outer features of the West" before issuing a warning against nationalism. During the late nineteenth century, Japan followed the example of great European powers by modernizing its navy and adopting the Meiji Constitution in writing. Both of these reforms fall under the category of "outer features of the West" as the phrase is used in the passage. Nationalism is defined in spiritual terms throughout the passage, so it would be an "inner feature of the West." Thus, Choice *A* is the correct answer. Shintoism is a traditional Japanese religion, and it's not mentioned in the passage. Japan also didn't orchestrate mass conversions to Christianity, so Choice *B* is incorrect. The Shogun was a Japanese military dictatorship that held power between 1185 and 1868. Japanese modernization efforts dissolved the Shogun, and nationalism was adopted under the new imperial Japanese regime. So, Choice *C* is incorrect. Choice *D* is incorrect because Japan didn't adopt European moral laws or social ideals; rather, Japan embraced nationalism in the late-eighteenth and early-nineteenth centuries.

5. D: The Prussian political leader Otto von Bismarck leveraged nationalism to rally support for German unification, which occurred in 1871. So, Choice *A* is incorrect. Mexican nationalists defeated Spanish colonizers in the Mexican Revolution, and Simon Bolivar led nationalist revolts across South America during the early nineteenth century. So, Choice *B* is incorrect. The Russo-Turkish War was largely caused by nationalist revolts in Bulgaria, Montenegro, and Romania against the Ottoman Empire, so Choice *C* is incorrect. The War of the Spanish Succession was fought in the early eighteenth century, which predates the rise of nationalism in continental Europe. Thus, Choice *D* is the correct answer.

Section 11: U.S. Government

The Role of the Citizen in a Democratic Society

Citizens express their political beliefs and public opinion through participation in politics. The conventional ways citizens can participate in politics in a democratic state include:

- Obeying laws
- Voting in elections
- Running for public office
- Staying interested in and informed of current events
- Learning U.S. history
- Attending public hearings to be informed and to express opinions on issues, especially on the local level
- Forming interest groups to promote common goals
- Forming political action committees (PACs) that raise money to influence policy decisions
- Petitioning government to create awareness of issues
- Campaigning for a candidate
- Contributing to campaigns
- Using mass media to express political ideas, opinions, and grievances

Obeying Laws

Citizens living in a democracy have several rights and responsibilities to uphold. The first duty is that they uphold the established laws of the government. In a democracy, a system of nationwide laws is necessary to ensure that there is some degree of order. Therefore, citizens must obey the laws and also help enforce them because a law that is inadequately enforced is almost useless. Optimally, a democratic society's laws will be accepted and followed by the community as a whole.

However, conflict can occur when an unjust law is passed. For example, much of the civil rights movement centered around Jim Crow laws in the South that supported segregation between black and whites. Yet these practices were encoded in state laws, which created a dilemma for African Americans who wanted equality but also wanted to respect the law. Fortunately, a democracy offers a system in which government leaders and policies are constantly open to change in accordance with the will of citizens. Citizens can influence the laws that are passed by voting for and electing members of the legislative and executive branches to represent them at the local, state, and national levels.

Voting

In a democratic state, the most common way to participate in politics is by voting for candidates in an election. Voting allows the citizens of a state to influence policy by selecting the candidates who share their views and make policy decisions that best suit their interests, or candidates who they believe are most capable of leading the country. In Canada, all citizens over 18—regardless of gender, race, or religion—are allowed to vote.

Since the Progressive movement and the increased social activism of the 1890s to the 1920s that sought to eliminate corruption in government, direct participation in politics through voting has increased. Citizens can participate by voting in the following types of elections:

- Direct primaries: Citizens can nominate candidates for public office.
- National, state, and municipal elections: Citizens elect their representatives in government.
- Recall elections: Citizens can petition the government to vote an official out of office before their term ends.
- Referendums: Citizens can vote directly on proposed laws or amendments to the state constitution.
- Voter initiatives: Citizens can petition their local or state government to propose laws that will be approved or rejected by voters.

Running for Public Office

Citizens also have the ability to run for elected office. By becoming leaders in the government, citizens can demonstrate their engagement and help determine government policy. Citizen involvement in the selection of leaders is vital in a democracy because it helps to prevent the formation of an elite group that does not answer to the public. Without the engagement of citizens who run for office, voters are limited in their ability to select candidates that appeal to them. In this case, voting options would become stagnant, inhibiting the nation's ability to grow and change over time. As long as citizens are willing to take a stand for their vision of Canada, the government will remain dynamic and diverse.

Citizen Interest

These features of a democracy give it the potential to reshape itself continually in response to new developments in society. In order for a democracy to function, it is of the utmost importance that citizens care about the course of politics and be aware of current issues. Apathy among citizens is a constant problem that threatens the endurance of democracies. Citizens should have a desire to take part in the political process, lest they simply accept the status quo and fail to fulfill their civic role. Moreover, they must have acute knowledge of the political processes and the issues that they can address as citizens. A fear among the Founding Fathers was the prevalence of mob rule, in which the common people did not take interest in politics except to vote for their patrons; this was the usual course of politics in the colonial era, as the common people left the decisions to the established elites. Without understanding the world around them, citizens may not fully grasp the significance of political actions and thereby fail to make wise decisions in that regard. Therefore, citizens must stay informed about current affairs, ranging from local to global matters, so that they can properly address them as voters or elected leaders.

Historical Knowledge

Furthermore, knowledge of the nation's history is essential for healthy citizenship. History continues to have an influence on present political decisions. For example, Supreme Court rulings often take into account previous legal precedents and verdicts, so it is important to know about those past events and how they affect the current processes. It is especially critical that citizens are aware of the context in which laws were established because it helps clarify the purpose of those laws. For example, an understanding of the problems with the Articles of Confederation allows people to comprehend some of the reasons behind the framework of the Constitution. In addition, history as a whole shapes the course of societies and the world; therefore, citizens should draw on this knowledge of the past to realize the full consequences of current actions. Issues such as climate change, conflict in the Middle East, and civil rights struggles are rooted in events and cultural developments that reach back centuries and should be addressed.

Therefore, education is a high priority in democracies because it has the potential to instill younger generations of citizens with the right mindset and knowledge required to do their part in shaping the nation. Optimally, education should cover a variety of different subjects, ranging from mathematics to biology, so that individuals can explore whatever paths they wish to take in life. Even so, social studies are especially important because students should understand how democracies function and understand the history of the nation and world. Historical studies should cover national and local events as well because they help provide the basis for the understanding of contemporary politics. Social studies courses should also address the histories of foreign nations because contemporary politics has global consequences. In addition, history lessons should remain open to multiple perspectives, even those that might criticize a nation's past actions, because citizens should be exposed to diverse perspectives that they can apply as voters and leaders.

The Structure and Functions of Different Levels of the U.S. Government

A **political institution** is an organization created by the government to enact and enforce laws, act as a mediator during conflict, create economic policy, establish social systems, and carry out some power. These institutions maintain a rigid structure of internal rules and oversight, especially if the power is delegated, like agencies under the executive branch.

The Constitution established a federal government divided into three branches: legislative, executive, and judicial.

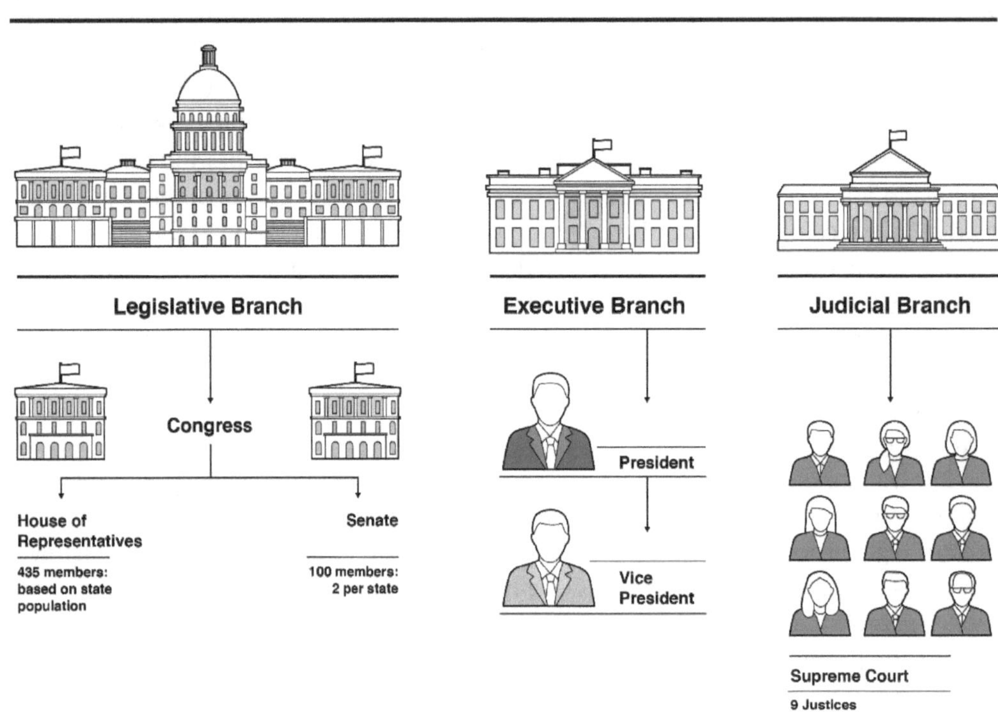

Executive Branch

The **executive branch** is responsible for enforcing the laws. The executive branch consists of the president, the vice president, the president's cabinet, and federal agencies created by Congress to execute some delegated.

The president of the United States:

- Serves a four-year term and is limited to two terms in office
- Is the chief executive officer of the United States and commander-in-chief of the armed forces
- Is elected by the Electoral College
- Appoints cabinet members, federal judges, and the heads of federal agencies
- Vetoes or signs bills into law
- Handles foreign affairs, including appointing diplomats and negotiating treaties
- Must be thirty-five years old, a natural-born U.S. citizen, and have lived in the United States for at least fourteen years

The vice president:

- Serves four-year terms alongside and at the will of the president
- Acts as president of the Senate
- Assumes the presidency if the president is incapacitated
- Assumes any additional duties assigned by the president

The cabinet members:

- Are appointed by the president
- Act as heads for the fifteen executive departments
- Advise the president in matters relating to their departments and carry out delegated power

Note that the president can only sign and veto laws and cannot initiate them himself. As head of the executive branch, it is the responsibility of the president to execute and enforce the laws passed by the legislative branch.

Although Congress delegates their legislative authority to agencies in an enabling statute, they are located in the executive branch because they are tasked with executing their delegating authority. The president enjoys the power of appointment and removal over all federal agency workers, except those tasked with quasi-legislative or quasi-judicial powers.

Legislative Branch

The **legislative branch** is responsible for enacting federal laws. This branch possesses the power to declare war, regulate interstate commerce, approve or reject presidential appointments, and investigate the other branches. The legislative branch is *bicameral*, meaning it consists of two houses: the lower house, called the House of Representatives, and the upper house, known as the Senate. Both houses are elected by popular vote.

Members of both houses are intended to represent the interests of the constituents in their home states and to bring their concerns to a national level. Ideas for laws, called bills, are proposed in one chamber and then are voted upon according to the body's rules; should the bill pass the first round of voting, the other legislative chamber must approve it before it can be sent to the president.

The two houses (or chambers) are similar though they differ on some procedures such as how debates on bills take place.

House of Representatives

The **House of Representatives** is responsible for enacting bills relating to revenue, impeaching federal officers including the president and Supreme Court justices, and electing the president in the case of no candidate reaching a majority in the Electoral College.

In the House of Representatives:

- Each state's representation in the House of Representatives is determined proportionally by population, with the total number of voting seats limited to 435.
- There are six nonvoting members from Washington, D.C., Puerto Rico, American Samoa, Guam, Northern Mariana Islands, and the U.S. Virgin Islands.
- The Speaker of the House is elected by the other representatives and is responsible for presiding over the House. In the event that the president and vice president are unable to fulfill their duties, the Speaker of the House will succeed to the presidency.
- The representatives of the House serve two-year terms.
- The requirements for eligibility in the House include:
    - Must be twenty-five years of age
    - Must have been a U.S. citizen for at least seven years
    - Must be a resident of the state they are representing by the time of the election

Senate

The Senate has the exclusive powers to confirm or reject all presidential appointments, ratify treaties, and try impeachment cases initiated by the House of Representatives.

In the Senate:

- The number of representatives is one hundred, with two representatives from each state.
- The vice president presides over the Senate and breaks the tie, if necessary.
- The representatives serve six-year terms.
- The requirements for eligibility in the Senate include:
    - Must be thirty years of age
    - Must have been a U.S. citizen for the past nine years
    - Must be a resident of the state they are representing at the time of their election

Legislative Process

Although all members of the houses make the final voting, the senators and representatives serve on committees and subcommittees dedicated to specific areas of policy. These committees are responsible for debating the merit of bills, revising bills, and passing or killing bills that are assigned to their committee. If it passes, they then present the bill to the entire Senate or House of Representatives (depending on which they are a part of). In most cases, a bill can be introduced in either the Senate or the House, but a majority vote of both houses is required to approve a new bill before the president may sign the bill into law.

Judicial Branch

The *judicial branch*, though it cannot pass laws itself, is tasked with interpreting the law and ensuring citizens receive due process under the law. The judicial branch consists of the Supreme Court, the highest court in the country, overseeing all federal and state courts. Lower federal courts are the district courts and court of appeals.

The Supreme Court:

- Judges are appointed by the president and confirmed by the Senate.
- Judges serve until retirement, death, or impeachment.
- Judges possess sole power to judge the constitutionality of a law.
- Judges set precedents for lower courts based on their decisions.
- Judges try appeals that have proceeded from the lower district courts.

Checks and Balances

Notice that a system of checks and balances between the branches exists. This is to ensure that no branch oversteps its authority. They include:

- Checks on the Legislative Branch:
    - The president can veto bills passed by Congress.
    - The president can call special sessions of Congress.
    - The judicial branch can rule legislation unconstitutional.
- Checks on the Executive Branch:
    - Congress has the power to override presidential vetoes by a two-thirds majority vote.
    - Congress can impeach or remove a president, and the chief justice of the Supreme Court presides over impeachment proceedings.
    - Congress can refuse to approve presidential appointments or ratify treaties.
- Checks on the Judicial Branch:
    - The president appoints justices to the Supreme Court, as well as district court and court of appeals judges.
    - The president can pardon federal prisoners.
    - The executive branch can refuse to enforce court decisions.
    - Congress can create federal courts below the Supreme Court.
    - Congress can determine the number of Supreme Court justices.
    - Congress can set the salaries of federal judges.
    - Congress can refuse to approve presidential appointments of judges.
    - Congress can impeach and convict federal judges.

The three branches of government operate separately, but they must rely on each other to create, enforce, and interpret the laws of the United States.

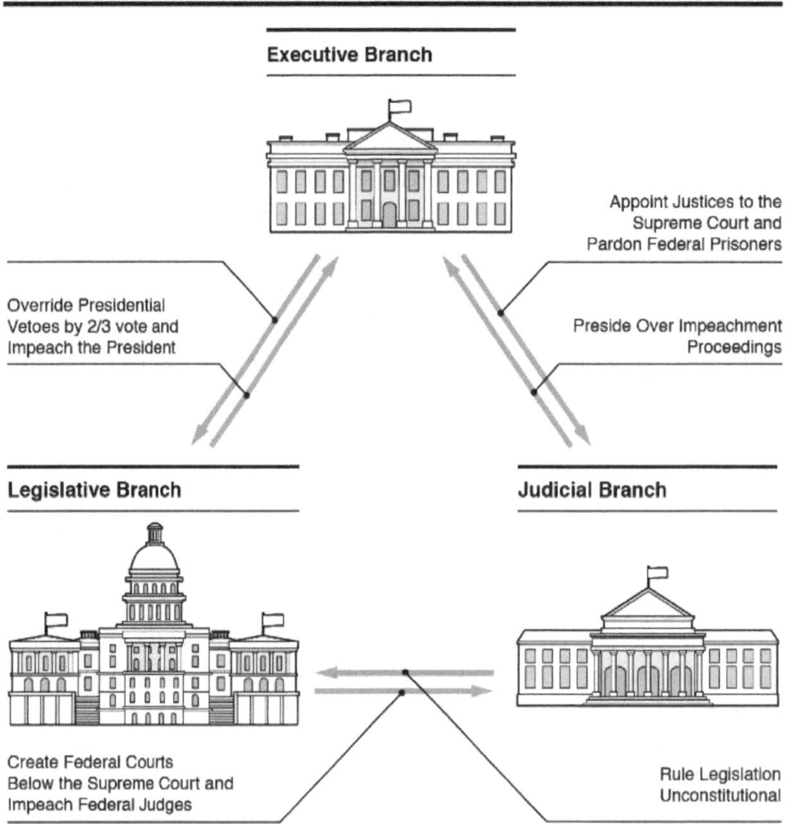

How Laws are Enacted and Enforced

To enact a new law:

- The bill is introduced to Congress.
- The bill is sent to the appropriate committee for review and revision.
- The approved bill is sent to the Speaker of the House and the majority party leader of the Senate, who places the bill on the calendar for review.
- The houses debate the merits of the bill and recommend amendments.
    - In the House of Representatives, those who wish to debate about a bill are allowed only a few minutes to speak, and amendments to the bill are limited.
    - In the Senate, debates and amendments are unlimited, and those who wish to postpone a vote may do so by filibuster, refusing to stop speaking.
- The approved bill is revised in both houses to ensure identical wording in both bills.
- The revised bill is returned to both houses for final approval.
- The bill is sent to the president, who may

- Sign the bill into law
- Veto the bill
- Take no action, resulting in the bill becoming law if Congress remains in session for ten days or dying if Congress adjourns before ten days have passed

The Role of State Government

While the federal government manages the nation as a whole, state governments address issues pertaining to their specific territory. In the past, states claimed the right, known as nullification, to refuse to enforce federal laws that they considered unconstitutional. However, conflicts between state and federal authority, particularly in the South in regard to first, slavery, and later, discrimination, have led to increased federal power, and states cannot defy federal laws. Even so, the Tenth Amendment limits federal power to those powers specifically granted in the Constitution, and the rest of the powers are retained by the states and citizens. Therefore, individual state governments are left in charge of decisions with immediate effects on their citizens, such as state laws and taxes.

In this way, the powers of government are separated both horizontally between the three branches of government (executive, legislative, and judicial) and vertically between the levels of government (federal, state, and local).

Like the federal government, state governments consist of executive, judicial, and legislative branches, but the exact configuration of those branches varies between states. For example, while most states follow the bicameral structure of Congress, Nebraska has only a single legislative chamber. Additionally, requirements to run for office, length of terms, and other details vary from state to state. State governments have considerable authority within their states, but they cannot impose their power on other states.

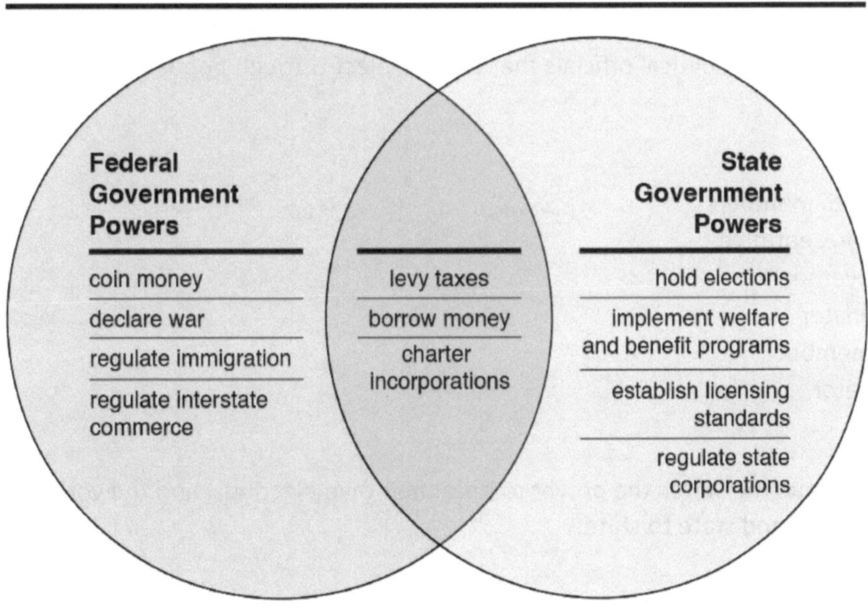

The Role of Local Government

Local governments, which include town governments, county boards, library districts, and other agencies, are especially variable in their composition. They often reflect the overall views of their state governments but also have their own values, rules, and structures. Generally, local governments function in a democratic fashion, although the exact form of government depends on its role. Depending on the location within the state, local government may have considerable or minimal authority based on the population and prosperity of the area; some counties may have strong influence in the state, while others may have a limited impact.

Native American Tribes

Native American tribes are treated as dependent nations that answer to the federal government but may be immune to state jurisdiction. As with local governments, the exact form of governance is left up to the tribes, which ranges from small councils to complex systems of government. Other U.S. territories, including the District of Columbia (site of Washington, D.C.) and acquired islands, such as Guam and Puerto Rico, have representation within Congress, but their legislators cannot vote on bills.

Election System

As members of a Constitutional Republic with certain aspects of a *democracy*, U.S. citizens are empowered to elect most government leaders, but the process varies between branch and level of government. Presidential elections at the national level use the *Electoral College* system. Rather than electing the president directly, citizens cast their ballots to select *electors* that represent each state in the college.

Legislative branches at the federal and state level are also determined by elections. In some areas, judges are elected, but in other states judges are appointed by elected officials. The U.S. has a *two-party system*, meaning that most government control is under two major parties: the Republican Party and the Democratic Party. It should be noted that the two-party system was not designed by the Constitution but gradually emerged over time.

Electoral Process

During the *electoral process*, the citizens of a state decide who will represent them at the local, state, and federal level. Different political officials that citizens elect through popular vote include but are not limited to:

- City mayor
- City council members
- State representative
- State governor
- State senator
- House member
- U.S. Senator
- President

The Constitution grants the states the power to hold their own elections, and the voting process often varies from city to city and state to state.

While a popular vote decides nearly all local and state elections, the president of the United States is elected by the *Electoral College*, rather than by popular vote. Presidential elections occur every four years on the first Tuesday after the first Monday in November.

The electoral process for the president of the United States includes:

Primary Elections and Caucuses

In a presidential election, *nominees* from the two major parties, as well as some third parties, run against each other. To determine who will win the nomination from each party, the states hold *primary elections* or *caucuses*.

During the primary elections, the states vote for who they want to win their party's nomination. In some states, primary elections are closed, meaning voters may only vote for candidates from their registered party, but other states hold *open primaries* in which voters may vote in either party's primary.

Some states hold *caucuses* in which the members of a political party meet in small groups, and the decisions of those groups determine the party's candidate.

Each state holds a number of delegates proportional to its population, and the candidate with the most delegate votes receives the domination. Some states give all of their delegates (*winner-take-all*) to the primary or caucus winner, while some others split the votes more proportionally.

Conventions

The two major parties hold national conventions to determine who will be the nominee to run for president from each party. The *delegates* each candidate won in the primary elections or caucuses are the voters who represent their states at the national conventions. The candidate who wins the most delegate votes is given the nomination. Political parties establish their own internal requirements and procedures for how a nominee is nominated.

Conventions are typically spread across several days, and leaders of the party give speeches, culminating with the candidate accepting the nomination at the end.

Campaigning

Once the nominees are selected from each party, they continue campaigning into the national election. Prior to the mid-1800s, candidates did not actively campaign for themselves, considering it dishonorable to the office, but campaigning is now rampant. Modern campaigning includes, but is not limited to:

- Raising money
- Meeting with citizens and public officials around the country
- Giving speeches
- Issuing policy proposals
- Running internal polls to determine strategy
- Organizing strategic voter outreach in important districts
- Participating in debates organized by a third-party private debate commission
- Advertising on television, through mail, or on the Internet

General Election

On the first Tuesday after the first Monday in November of an election year, every four years, the people cast their votes by secret ballot for president in a *general election*. Voters may vote for any candidate, regardless of their party affiliation. The outcome of the popular vote does not decide the election; instead, the winner is determined by the Electoral College.

Electoral College

When the people cast their votes for president in the general election, they are casting their votes for the *electors* from the *Electoral College* who will elect the president. In order to win the presidential election, a nominee must win 270 of the 538 electoral votes. The number of electors is equal to the total number of senators and representatives from each state plus three electoral votes for Washington D.C. which does not have any voting members in the legislative branch.

The electors typically vote based on the popular vote from their states. Although the Constitution does not require electors to vote for the popular vote winner of their state, no elector voting against the popular vote of their state has ever changed the outcome of an election. Due to the Electoral College, a nominee may win the popular vote and still lose the election.

For example, let's imagine that there are only two states — Wyoming and New Mexico — in a presidential election. Wyoming has three electoral votes and awards them all to the winner of the election by majority vote. New Mexico has five electoral votes and also awards them all to the winner of the election by majority vote. If 500,000 people in Wyoming vote and the Republican candidate wins by a vote of 300,000 to 200,000, the Republican candidate will win the three electoral votes for the state. If the same number of people vote in New Mexico, but the Republican candidate loses the state by a vote of 249,000 to 251,000, the Democratic candidate wins the five electoral votes from that state. This means the Republican candidate will have received 549,000 popular votes but only three electoral votes, while the Democratic candidate will have received 451,000 popular votes but will have won five electoral votes. Thus, the Republican won the popular vote by a considerable margin, but the Democratic candidate will have been awarded more electoral votes, which are the only ones that matter.

	Wyoming	**New Mexico**	**Total # of Votes**
Republican Votes	300,000	249,000	**549,000**
Democratic Votes	200,000	251,000	**451,000**
Republican Electoral Votes	3	0	**3**
Democratic Electoral Votes	0	5	**5**

If no one wins the majority of electoral votes in the presidential election, the House of Representatives decides the presidency, as required by the Twelfth Amendment. They may only vote for the top three candidates, and each state delegation votes as a single bloc. Twenty-six votes, a simple majority, are required to elect the president. The House has only elected the president twice, in 1801 and 1825.

Here how many electoral votes each state and the District of Columbia have:

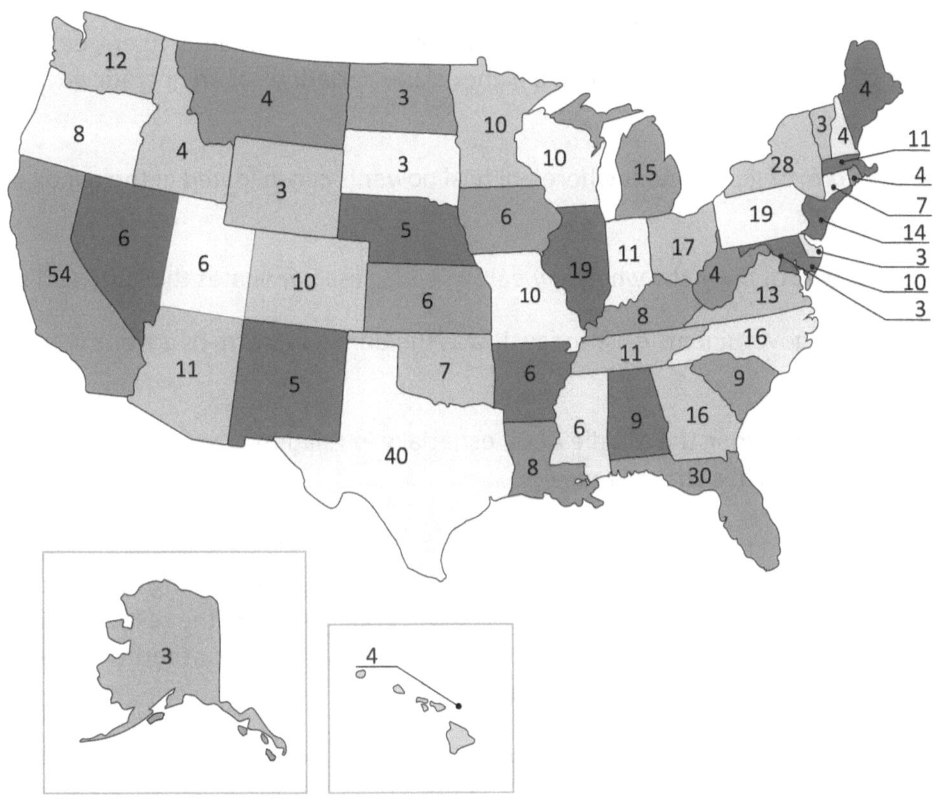

Purposes and Characteristics of Various Governance Systems

Government is the physical manifestation of the political entity or ruling body of a state. It includes the formal institutions that manage and maintain a society. The form of government does not determine the state's *economic system*, though these concepts are often closely tied. Many forms of government are based on a society's economic system. However, while the form of government refers to the methods by which a society is managed, the term *economy* refers to the management of resources in a society. Many forms of government exist, often as hybrids of two or more forms of government or economic systems. Forms of government can be distinguished based on protection of civil liberties, protection of rights, distribution of power, power of government, and principles of Federalism.

Regime is the term used to describe the ruling body and corresponding political conditions under which citizens live. A regime is defined by the amount of power the government possesses and the number of people who comprise the ruling body. It is closely related to the form of government because the form of government largely creates the political conditions. Regimes are governmental bodies that control both the form and the limit of term of their office. For example, authoritarianism is an example of a form of government and type of regime. A regime is considered to be ongoing until the culture, priorities, and values of the government are altered, either through a peaceful transition of power or a violent overthrow of the current regime.

The forms of government operated by regimes include:

Aristocracy

An *aristocracy* is a form of government composed of a small group of wealthy rulers, either holding hereditary titles of nobility or membership in a higher class. Variations of aristocratic governments include:

- Oligarchy: form of government where political power is consolidated in the hands of a small group of people
- Plutocracy: type of oligarchy where a wealthy, elite class dominates the state and society

Though no aristocratic governments exist today, it was the dominant form of government during ancient times, including the:

- Vassals and lords during the Middle Ages, especially in relation to feudalism
- City-state of Sparta in ancient Greece

Authoritarian

An authoritarian state is one in which a single party rules indefinitely. The ruling body operates with unrivaled control and complete power to make policy decisions, including the restriction of denying civil liberties such as freedom of speech, press, religion, and protest. Forms of authoritarian governments include autocracy, dictatorship, and totalitarianism.

- The Soviet Union, Nazi Germany, and modern-day North Korea are all examples of states with authoritarian governments.

Democracy

Democracy is a form of government in which the people act as the ruling body by electing representatives to voice their views. Forms of democratic governments include:

- Direct democracy: democratic government in which the people make direct decisions on specific policies by majority vote of all eligible voters, like in ancient Athens
- Representative democracy: democratic government in which the people elect representatives to vote in a legislative body. This form of government is also known as a representative republic or indirect democracy. Representative democracy is currently the most popular form of government in the world.

The presidential and parliamentary systems are the most common forms of representative democracy. In the presidential system, the executive operates in its own branch distinct from the legislature. In addition, the president is typically both the head of state and head of government. Examples of presidential systems include Brazil, Nigeria, and the United States.

In the parliamentary system, the prime minister serves as the head of government. The legislative branch, typically a parliament, elects the prime minister and also has the authority to replace the prime minister with a vote of no confidence. This practically means that the parliament has considerable influence over the office of prime minister. Parliamentary systems often include a president as the head of state, but the office is mostly ceremonial, functioning like a figurehead. Examples of parliamentary systems include Germany, Australia, and Pakistan.

The presidential system is better designed to distribute power between separate branches of government, which theoretically provides more stability. Presidents serve for a limited number of years, while prime ministers serve until death, resignation, or dismissal.

In the parliamentary system, the interconnectedness between parliament and the prime minister facilitates efficient governance, capable of adjusting to developing situations. In contrast, the presidential system is more prone to political gridlock because there is no direct connection between the legislative and executive branches. The legislature in a presidential system cannot replace the executive, like in the parliamentary system. The separation of powers in a presidential system can lead to disagreement between the executive and legislature, causing gridlock and other delays in governance.

Federalism is a set of principles that divides power between a central government and regional governments. Sovereign states often combine into a federation, and in doing so, they cede some degree of sovereignty to a functional central government that handles broad national policies. The United States and Canada are examples of governments with a Federalist structure.

Monarchy

Monarchy is a form of government in which the state is ruled by a sovereign leader. This leader is called a monarch and is typically a hereditary ruler. Monarchs have often justified their power due to some divine right to rule. Types of monarchies include:

- Absolute monarchy: a monarchy in which the monarch has complete power over the people and the state
- Constitutional monarchy: a type of monarchy in which the citizens of the state are protected by a constitution. A separate branch, typically a parliament, makes legislative decisions, and the monarch and legislature share power.
- Crowned republic: a type of monarchy in which the monarch holds only a ceremonial position and the people hold sovereignty over the state. It is defined by the monarch's lack of executive power.

Examples of monarchies:

- Kingdom of Saudi Arabia is an absolute monarchy.
- Australia is a crowned republic.

Practice Quiz

1. Which part of the legislative process differs in the House and the Senate?
    a. Who may introduce the bill
    b. How debates about a bill are conducted
    c. Who may veto the bill
    d. What wording the bill contains

2. The presidential and parliamentary systems differ in which of the following ways?
    a. The presidential system establishes a separation of powers.
    b. The legislature elects the chief executive in a presidential system.
    c. Voters directly elect the prime minister in a parliamentary system.
    d. The parliamentary system never includes a president.

3. Under Federalism, which is considered a concurrent power held by both the states and the federal government?
    a. Hold elections
    b. Regulate immigration
    c. Expand the territories of a state
    d. Pass and enforce laws

4. The United States elects the president by which of the following ways?
    a. Popular majority vote
    b. Plurality vote
    c. Electoral College
    d. Party list system

5. Which check does the legislative branch possess over the judicial branch?
    a. Appoint judges
    b. Call special sessions of Congress
    c. Rule legislation unconstitutional
    d. Determine the number of Supreme Court judges

Answer Explanations

1. B: The process by which the House and Senate may debate a bill differs. In the House, how long a speaker may debate a bill is limited, while in the Senate, speakers may debate the bill indefinitely and delay voting on the bill by filibuster—a practice in which a speaker refuses to stop speaking until a majority vote stops the filibuster or the time for the vote passes. In both the House and the Senate, anyone may introduce a bill. Only the president of the United States may veto the bill, so neither the House nor Senate holds that power. Before the bill may be presented to the president to be signed, the wording of the bill must be identical in both houses. Another procedural difference is that the number of amendments is limited in the House but not the Senate; however, this does not appear as an answer choice.

2. A: The presidential system establishes a separation of powers. In the presidential system, voters directly elect the chief executive, and the presidential system establishes a separation of powers between different branches of government. In contrast, the parliament elects the chief executive, and the increased collaboration and dependency creates a more responsive government. Choices *B* and *C* confuse how the executive is elected in each system. Choice *D* is incorrect because many parliamentary systems include a president, though the status of head of state is often purely ceremonial.

3. D: Both the states and the federal government may propose, enact, and enforce laws. States pass legislation that concerns the states in their state legislative houses, while the federal government passes federal laws in Congress. Only states may hold elections and determine voting procedures, even for federal offices such as the president of the United States, and only the federal government may expand any state territory, change state lines, admit new states into the nation, or regulate immigration and pass laws regarding naturalization of citizens.

4. C: The president of the United States is elected by the Electoral College. The number of electors for each state depends on the state's total number of senators and representatives. The president must receive a majority (270) of the electoral votes (538), and if this doesn't occur, the Twelfth Amendment empowers the House of Representatives to elect the president. Choices *A, B,* and *C* are different methods for electing candidates.

5. D: The Constitution granted Congress the power to decide how many justices should be on the court, and Congress first decided on six judges in the Judiciary Act of 1789. The Constitution granted the power to appoint judges and to call special sessions of Congress to the president. Only the Supreme Court may interpret the laws enacted by Congress and rule a law unconstitutional and subsequently overturn the law.

Section 12: Economics

Fundamental Economic Concepts

Economics is the study of human behavior in response to the production, consumption, and distribution of assets or wealth. Economics can help individuals or societies make decisions for themselves dependent upon their needs, wants, and resources. Economics is divided into two subgroups: microeconomics and macroeconomics.

Microeconomics is the study of individual or small group behaviors and patterns related to markets of goods and services. It specifically looks at single factors that could affect these behaviors and decisions. For example, the use of coupons in a grocery store could affect an individual's product choice, quantity purchased, and overall savings that could be directed to a different purchase. **Microeconomics** encompasses the study of many things, including scarcity, choice, opportunity costs, economics systems, factors of production, supply and demand, market efficiency, the role of government, distribution of income, and product markets.

Macroeconomics examines a much larger scale of the economy. It focuses on how aggregate factors such as demand, output, and spending habits affect the people in a society or nation. For example, if a national company moves its production overseas to save on costs, how will production, labor, and capital be affected? Macroeconomics analyzes all aggregate indicators and the microeconomic factors that influence the economy. Governments and corporations use macroeconomic models to help formulate economic policies and strategies.

Microeconomics

Scarcity

People have different needs and wants, and the question arises, are the resources available to supply those needs and wants? Limited resources and high demand create scarcity. When a product is scarce, there is a short supply of it. For example, when the newest version of a cellphone is released, people line up to buy the phone or put their name on a wait list if the phone is not immediately available. The new cellphone may become a scarce commodity. In turn, the phone company may raise their prices, knowing that people may be willing to pay more for an item in such high demand. If a competing company lowers the cost of the phone but has contingencies, such as extended contracts or hidden fees, the buyer will still have the opportunity to purchase the scarce product. Limited resources and extremely high demand create scarcity and, in turn, cause companies to acquire opportunity costs.

Factors of Production

There are four factors of production:

- Land: both renewable and nonrenewable resources
- Labor: effort put forth by people to produce goods and services
- Capital: the tools used to create goods and services
- Entrepreneurs: persons who combine land, labor, and capital to create new goods and services

The four factors of production are used to create goods and services to make economic profit. All four factors strongly impact one another.

Supply and Demand

Supply and demand are the most important concepts of economics in a market economy. Supply is the amount of a product that a market can offer. Demand is the quantity of a product needed or desired by buyers. The price of a product is directly related to supply and demand. The price of a product and the demand for that product go hand in hand in a market economy. For example, when there are a variety of treats at a bakery, certain treats are in higher demand than others. The bakery can raise the cost of the more demanded items as supplies get limited. Conversely, the bakery can sell the less desirable treats by lowering the cost of those items as an incentive for buyers to purchase them.

Product Markets

Product markets are where goods and services are bought and sold. Product markets provide a place for sellers to offer goods and services and for consumers to purchase them. The annual value of goods and services exchanged throughout the year is measured by the Gross Domestic Product (GDP), a monetary measure of goods and services made either quarterly or annually. Department stores, gas stations, grocery stores, and other retail stores are all examples of product markets. However, product markets do not include any raw or unfinished materials.

Theory of the Firm

The behavior of firms is composed of several theories varying between short- and long-term goals. There are four basic firm behaviors: perfect competition, profit maximization, short run, and long run. Each firm follows a pattern, depending on its desired outcome. Theory of the Firm posits that firms, after conducting market research, make decisions that will maximize their profits.

- Perfect competition:
- In perfect competition, several businesses are selling the same product simultaneously.
- There are so many businesses and consumers that none will directly impact the market.
- Each business and consumer is aware of the competing businesses and markets.
- Profit maximization:
- Firms decide the quantity of a product that needs to be produced in order to receive maximum profit gains. Profit is the total amount of revenue made after subtracting costs.
- Short run:
- A short amount of time where fixed prices cannot be adjusted
- The quantity of the product depends on the varying amount of labor. Less labor means less product.
- Long run:
- An amount of time where fixed prices can be adjusted
- Firms try to maximize production while minimizing labor costs.

Overall, microeconomics operates on a small scale, focusing on how individuals or small groups use and assign resources.

Macroeconomics

Macroeconomics analyzes the economy as a whole. It studies unemployment, interest rates, price levels, and national income, which are all factors that can affect the nation as a whole, and not just individual households. Macroeconomics studies all large factors to determine how, or if, they will affect future trend patterns of production, consumption, and economic growth.

Measures of Economic Performance

Measurements of economic performance determine if an economy is growing, stagnant, or deteriorating. To measure the growth and sustainability of an economy, several indicators can be used. Economic indicators provide data that economists can use to determine if there are faulty processes or if some form of intervention is needed.

One of the main indicators of a country's economic performance is the Gross Domestic Product (GDP). GDP growth provides important information that can be used to determine fiscal or financial policies. The GDP does not measure income distribution, quality of life, or losses due to natural disasters. For example, if a community lost everything to a hurricane, it would take a long time to rebuild the community and stabilize its economy. That is why there is a need to take into account more balanced performance measures when factoring overall economic performance.

Other indicators used to measure economic performance are unemployment or employment rates, inflation, savings, investments, surpluses and deficits, debt, labor, trade terms, the HDI (Human Development Index), and the HPI (Human Poverty Index).

Unemployment

Unemployment occurs when an individual does not have a job, is actively trying to find employment, and is not getting paid. Official unemployment rates do not factor in the number of people who have stopped looking for work, but true unemployment rates do.

There are three types of unemployment: cyclical, frictional, and structural.

Cyclical
Comes as a result of the regular economic cycle and variations in supply and demand. This usually occurs during a recession.
Frictional
When workers voluntarily leave their jobs. An example would be a person changing careers.
Structural
When companies' needs change and a person no longer possesses the skills needed.

Given the nature of a market economy and the fluctuations of the labor market, a 100 percent employment rate is impossible to reach.

Inflation

Inflation is when the value of money decreases and the cost of goods and services increases over time. Supply, demand, and money reserves all affect inflation. Generally, inflation is measured by the **Consumer Price Index (CPI)**, a tool that tracks price changes of goods and services. The CPI measures goods and services such as gasoline, cars, clothing, and food. When the cost of goods and services increase, manufacturers may reduce the quantity they produce due to lower demand. This decreases the purchasing power of the consumer. Basically, as more money is printed, it holds less and less value in purchasing power. When inflation occurs, consumers spend and save less because their currency is worth less. However, if inflation occurs steadily over time, the people can better plan and prepare for future necessities.

Inflation can vary from year to year, usually never fluctuating more than 2 percent. Central banks try to prevent drastic increases or decreases of inflation to prohibit prices from rising or falling too far. Inflation can also vary based on different monetary currencies. Although rare, any country's economy may experience hyperinflation (when inflation rates increase to over 50 percent), while other economies may experience deflation (when the cost of goods and services decrease over time). Deflation occurs when the inflation rate drops below zero percent.

Business Cycle

A business cycle is when the Gross Domestic Product (GDP) moves downward and upward over a long-term growth trend. These cycles help determine where the economy currently stands, as well as where it could be heading. Business cycles usually occur almost every six years and have four phases: expansion, peak, contraction, and trough. Here are some characteristics of each phase:

- Expansion:
- Increased employment rates and economic growth
- Production and sales increase
- On a graph, expansion is where the lines climb.
- Peak:
- Employment rates are at or above full employment and the economy is at maximum productivity.
- On a graph, the peak is the top of the hill, where expansion has reached its maximum.
- Contraction:
- When growth starts slowing
- Unemployment is on the rise.
- On a graph, contraction is where the graph begins to slide back down or contract.
- Trough:
- The cycle has hit bottom and is waiting for the next cycle to start again.
- On a graph, the trough is the bottom of the contraction prior to when it starts to climb back up.

When the economy is expanding or "booming," the business cycle is going from a trough to a peak. When the economy is headed down and toward a recession, the business cycle is going from a peak to a trough.

Four phases of a business cycle:

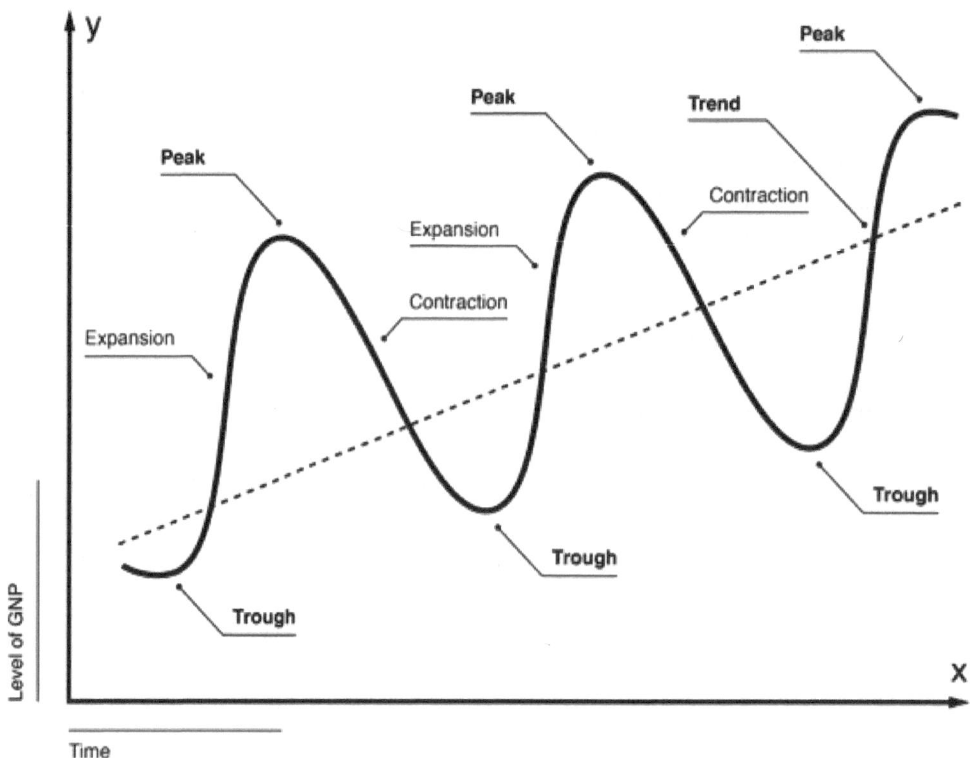

Economic Growth

The most common tool for measuring economic growth is the **Gross Domestic Product (GDP)**. The increase of goods and services over time indicates positive movement in economic growth. The quantity of goods and services produced is not always an indicator of economic growth, however; the value of the goods and services produced matters more than the quantity.

There are many causes of economic growth, which can be short- or long-term. In the short term, if aggregate demand (the total demand for goods and services produced at a given time) increases, then the overall GDP increases as well. As the GDP increases, interest rates may decrease, which may encourage greater spending and investing. Real estate prices may also rise, and there may be lower income taxes. All of these short-term factors can stimulate economic growth.

In the long term, if aggregate supply (the total supply of goods or services in a given time period) increases, then there is potential for an increase in capital as well. With more working capital, more infrastructure and jobs can be created. With more jobs, there is an increased employment rate, and education and training for jobs will improve. New technologies will be developed, and new raw materials may be discovered. All of these long-term factors can also stimulate economic growth.

Other causes of economic growth include low inflation and stability. Lower inflation rates encourage more investing as opposed to higher inflation rates that cause market instability. Stability encourages businesses to continue investing. If the market is unstable, investors may question the volatility of the market.

Potential Costs of Economic Growth:

- Inflation: When economic growth occurs, inflation tends to be high. If supply cannot keep up with demand, then the inflation rate may be unmanageable.

- Economic booms and recessions: The economy goes through cycles of booms and recessions. This causes inflation to fluctuate over time, which puts the economy into a continuous cycle of rising and falling.
- Account inefficiencies: When the economy grows, consumers and businesses increase their import spending. The increase of import spending affects the current account and causes a shortage.
- Environmental costs: When the economy is growing, there is an abundance of output, which may result in more pollutants and a reduction in quality of life.
- Inequalities: Growth occurs differently among members of society. While the wealthy may be getting richer, those living in poverty may just be getting on their feet. So, while economic growth is happening, it may happen at very different rates.

While these potential costs could affect economic growth, if the growth is consistent and stable, then it can occur without severe inflation swings. As technology improves, new ways of production can reduce negative environmental factors as well.

Government Involvement in the Economy

Governments have considerable influence over the flow of economies. When a government has full control over the economic decisions of a nation, it is called a command system. This was the case in many absolute monarchies such as eighteenth-century France; King Louis XIV built his economy on the concept of mercantilism, which believed that the state should manage all resources, particularly by accumulating gold and silver. This system of economics discouraged exports and thereby limited trade.

In contrast, the market system is guided by the concept of capitalism, in which individuals and businesses have the freedom to manage their own economic decisions. This allows for private property and increases the opportunities for entrepreneurship and trade. Early proponents of capitalism emphasized *laissez-faire* policies, which means "let it be," and argued that the government should not be involved with the economy at all. They believed that the market is guided by self-interest and that individuals will optimally work for their personal success. However, individuals' interests do not necessarily correlate with the needs of the overall economy. For example, during a financial recession, consumers may decide to save up their money rather than make purchases; doing so helps them in the short run but further reduces demand in a slumping economy. Therefore, most capitalist governments still assert a degree of control over their economies while still allowing for private business.

Likewise, many command system economies have relied heavily on private businesses. With the end of most absolute monarchies, communism has been the primary form of command system economies in the modern era. Communism is a form of socialism that emphasizes communal ownership of property and government control over production. The high degree of government control gives more stability to the economy, but it also creates considerable flaws. The monopolization of the economy by the government limits its ability to respond to local economic conditions because certain regions often have unique resources and needs. With the collapse of the Soviet Union and other communist states, command systems have been largely replaced with market systems.

The U.S. government helps to manage the nation's economy through a market system in several ways. First and foremost, the federal government is responsible for the production of money for use within the economy; depending on how the government manages the monetary flow, it may lead to a stable economy, deflation, or inflation. Second, state and federal governments impose taxes on individuals, corporations, and goods. For example, a tariff might be imposed on imports in order to stimulate demand for local goods in the economy. Third, the government can pass laws that require additional regulation or inspections. In addition, the government has passed antitrust laws to inhibit the growth of private monopolies, which could limit free growth in the market system. Debates continue over whether the government should take further action to manage private industries or reduce its control over the private sector.

Just as governments can affect the direction of the economy, so can the economy can have significant implications on government policies. Financial stability is critical in maintaining a prosperous state. A healthy economy will allow for new developments that contribute to the nation's growth and create jobs. On the other hand, an economic crisis, such as a recession or depression, can gravely damage a government's stability. Without a stable economy, business opportunities plummet, and people begin to lose income and employment. This, in turn, leads to frustration and discontent in the population, which can lead to criticism of the government. This could very well lead to demands for new leadership to resolve the economic crisis.

The dangers of a destabilized economy can be seen with the downfall of the French monarchy. The mercantilist approach to economics stifled French trade. Furthermore, regional aristocracies remained exempt from government taxes, which limited the government's revenues. This was compounded by expensive wars and poor harvests that led to criticism of King Louis XIV's government. The problems persisted for decades, and Louis XIV was forced to convene the Estates-General, a legislative body of representatives from across France, to address the crisis. The economic crises at the end of the eighteenth century were critical in the beginning of the French Revolution. Those financial issues, in turn, at least partially stemmed from both the government's control of the economy through mercantilism and its inability to impose economic authority over local regions.

Economic Systems

Economic systems determine what is being produced, who is producing it, who receives the product, and the money generated by the sale of the product. There are two basic types of economic systems: market economies (including free and competitive markets), and planned or command economies.

- Market Economies are characterized by:
- Privately owned businesses, groups, or individuals providing goods or services based on demand.
- Demand determines the types of goods and services produced (supply).
- Two types: competitive market and free market.

Competitive Market	Free Market
Due to the large number of both buyers and sellers, there is no way any one seller or buyer can control the market or price.	Voluntary private trades between buyers and sellers determine markets and prices without government intervention or monopolies.

- Planned or Command Economies:
- Government or central authority determines market prices of goods and services.
- Government or central authority determines what is being produced and the quantity of production.
- Advantage: large number of shared goods such as public services (transportation, schools, or hospitals).
- Disadvantages of command economies include wastefulness of resources.

Market Efficiency and the Role of Government (Taxes, Subsidies, and Price Controls)

Market efficiency is directly affected by supply and demand. The government can help the market stay efficient by either stepping in when the market is inefficient and/or providing the means necessary for markets to run properly. For example, society needs two types of infrastructure: physical (bridges, roads, etc.) and institutional (courts, laws, etc.). The government may impose taxes, subsidies, and price controls to increase revenue, lower prices of goods and services, ensure product availability for the government, and maintain fair prices for goods and services.

The Purpose of Taxes, Subsidies, and Price Controls

Taxes	Subsidies	Price Controls
-Generate government revenue -Discourage purchase or use of "bad" products such as alcohol or cigarettes	-Lower the price of goods and services -Reassure the supply of goods and services -Allow opportunities to compete with overseas vendors	-Act as emergency measures when government intervention is necessary -Set a minimum or maximum price for goods and services

Money and Banking

Money is a means of exchange that provides a convenient way for sellers and consumers to understand the value of their goods and services. As opposed to bartering (when sellers and consumers exchange goods or services as equal trades), money is convenient for both buyers and sellers.

There are three main forms of money: commodity, fiat, and bank. Here are characteristics of each form:

- Commodity money: a valuable good, such as precious metals or tobacco, used as money
- Fiat money: currency that has no intrinsic value but is recognized by the government as valuable for trade, such as paper money
- Bank money: Money that is credited by a bank to those who deposit it into bank accounts, such as checking and savings accounts or credit

While price levels within the economy set the demand for money, most countries have central banks that supply the actual money. Essentially, banks buy and sell money. Borrowers can take loans and pay back the bank, with interest, providing the bank with extra capital.

A central bank has control over the printing and distribution of money. Central banks serve three main purposes: manage monetary growth to help steer the direction of the economy, be a backup to commercial banks that are suffering, and provide options and alternatives to government taxation.

The Federal Reserve is the central bank of the United States. The Federal Reserve controls banking systems and determines the value of money in the United States. Basically, the Federal Reserve is the bank for banks.

All Western economies have to keep a minimum amount of protected cash called *required reserve*. Once banks meet those minimums, they can then lend or loan the excess to consumers. The required reserves are used within a fractional reserve banking system (fractional because a small portion is kept separate and safe). Not only do banks reserve, manage, and loan money, but they also help form monetary policies.

Monetary Policy

The central bank and other government committees control the amount of money that is made and distributed. The money supply determines monetary policy. Three main features sustain monetary policy:

- Assuring the minimum amount held within banks (bank reserves): when banks are required to hold more money in reserve funds, they are less willing to lend money to help control inflation.
- Adjusting interest rates: raising interest rates makes borrowing more costly, which can slow down unsustainable growth and lower inflation. Lowering interest rates encourages borrowing and can stimulate struggling economies.
- Purchasing and selling bonds (open market operations): Controlling the money supply by buying bonds to increase it and selling bonds to reduce it.

In the United States, the Federal Reserve maintains monetary policy. There are two main types of monetary policy: expansionary and contractionary.

- Expansionary monetary policy:
- Increases the money supply
- Lowers unemployment
- Increases consumer spending
- Increases private sector borrowing
- Possibly decreases interest rates to very low levels, even near zero
- Decreases reserve requirements and federal funds
- Contractionary monetary policy:
- Decreases the money supply
- Helps control inflation
- Possibly increases unemployment due to slowdowns in economic growth
- Decreases consumer spending
- Decreases loans and/or borrowing

The Federal Reserve uses monetary policy to try to achieve maximum employment and secure inflation rates. Because the Federal Reserve is the "bank of banks," it truly strives to be the last-resort option for distressed banks. This is because once these kinds of institutions begin to rely on the Federal Reserve for help, all parts of the banking industry—such as those dealing with loans, bonds, interest rates, and mortgages—are affected.

International Trade and Exchange Rates

International trade is when countries import and export goods and services. Countries often want to deal in terms of their own currency. Therefore, when importing or exporting goods or services, consumers and businesses need to enter the market using the same form of currency. For example, if the United States would like to trade with China, the U.S. may have to trade in China's form of currency, the *Yuan*, versus the dollar, depending on the business.

The exchange rate is what one country's currency will exchange for another. The government and the market (supply and demand) determine the exchange rate. There are two forms of exchange rates: fixed and floating. Fixed exchange rates involve government interventions (like central banks) to help keep the exchange rates stable. Floating, or "flexible," exchange rates constantly change because they rely on supply and demand needs. While each type of exchange rate has advantages and disadvantages, the rate truly depends on the current state of each country's economy. Therefore, each exchange rate may differ from country to country.

Advantages and Disadvantages of Fixed Versus Floating Exchange Rates			
Fixed Exchange Rate: government intervention to help keep exchange rates stable		Floating or "Flexible" Exchange Rate: Supply and demand determines the exchange rate	
Advantages -Stable prices -Stable foreign exchange rates -Exports are more competitive and in turn more profitable	*Disadvantages* -Requires a large amount of reserve funds -Possibly mispricing currency values -Inflation increases	*Advantages* -Central bank involvement is not needed. -Facilitates free trade	*Disadvantages* -Currency speculation -Exchange rate risks -Inflation increases

Countries may have differing economic statuses and exchange rates, but they rely on one another for goods and services. Prices of imports and exports are affected by the strength of another country's currency. For example, if the United States dollar is at a higher value than another country's currency, imports will be less expensive because the dollar will have more value than that of the country selling its good or service. On the other hand, if the dollar is at a low value compared to the currency of another country, importers will tend to avoid buying international items from that country. However, U.S. exporters to that country could benefit from the low value of the dollar.

Fiscal Policy

Fiscal policy refers to how the government adjusts spending and tax rates to influence the functions of the economy. Fiscal policies can either increase or decrease tax rates and spending. These policies represent a tricky balancing act, because if the government increases taxes too much, consumer spending and monetary value will decrease. Conversely, if the government lowers taxes, consumers will have more money in their pockets to buy more goods and services, which increases demand and the need for companies to supply those goods and services. Due to the higher demand, suppliers can add jobs to fulfill that demand. While increases in supply, demand, and jobs are positive for the overall economy, they may result in a devaluation of the dollar and less purchasing power.

Consumer Economics

Economics is closely linked with the flow of resources, technology, and population in societies. The use of natural resources, such as water and fossil fuels, has always depended in part on the pressures of the economy. A supply of a specific good may be limited in the market, but with sufficient demand, sellers are incentivized to increase the available quantity. Unfortunately, the demand for certain objects can often be unlimited, and a high price or limited supply may prevent consumers from obtaining the product or service. If the sellers succumb to the consumers' demand and continue to exploit a scarce resource, supply could potentially be exhausted.

The resources for most products, both renewable and nonrenewable, are finite. This is a particularly difficult issue with nonrenewable resources, but even renewable resources often have limits: organic products such as trees and animals require stable populations and sufficient habitats to support those populations. Furthermore, the costs of certain decisions can have detrimental effects on other resources. For example, industrialization provides economic benefits in many countries but also has had the negative effect of polluting surrounding environments; the pollution, in turn, often eliminates or harms fish, plants, and other potential resources.

The control of resources within an economy is particularly important in determining how resources are used. While demand may change with the consumers' choices and preferences, supply depends on the objectives of the producers. They determine how much of their supply they allot for sale, and in the case of monopolies, they might have sole access to the resource. They might limit their use of resources or gather more to meet the demand. Consumers can choose which sellers they rely on for their supply, except in the case of a monopoly because there is no alternative supplier. Therefore, the function of supply within an economy can drastically influence how the resources are exploited.

The availability of resources, in turn, affects the human population. Humans require basic resources such as food and water for survival, as well as additional resources for healthy lifestyles. Therefore, access to these resources helps determine the survival rate of humans. For much of human existence, economies have had limited ability to extract resources from the natural world, which restricted the growth rate of populations. However, the development of new technologies, combined with increasing demand for certain products, has pushed resource use to a new level. On one hand, this led to higher living standards and lower death rates. On the other hand, the increasing exploitation of resources has increased the world's population as a whole to unsustainable levels. The rising population leads to higher demand for resources that cannot be met. This creates poverty, reduced living conditions, and higher death rates. As a result, economics can significantly influence local and world population levels.

Technology is also intricately related to population, resources, and economics. The role of demand within economies has incentivized people to innovate new technologies that enable societies to have a higher quality of life and greater access to resources. Entrepreneurs expand technologies by finding ways to create new products for the market. The Industrial Revolution, in particular, illustrates the relationship between economics and technology because the ambitions of businessmen led to new infrastructure that enabled more efficient and sophisticated use of resources. Many of these inventions reduced the amount of work necessary for individuals and allowed the development of leisure activities, which in turn created new economic markets. However, economic systems can also limit the growth of technology. In the case of monopolies, the lack of alternative suppliers reduces the incentive to meet and exceed consumer expectations. Moreover, as demonstrated by the effects of economics on resources, technology's increasing ability to extract resources can lead to their depletion and create significant issues that need to be addressed.

Distribution of Income

Distribution of income refers to how wages are spread across a society or segments of a society. If everyone made the same amount of money, the distribution of income would be equal. That is not the case in most societies. Wealth varies among people and companies. Income inequality gaps are present in America and many other nations. Taxes provide an option to redistribute income or wealth because they provide revenue to build new infrastructure and provide cash benefits to some of the poorest members in society.

Choice and Opportunity Costs

When an individual decides between possibilities, that individual is making a choice. Choices allow people to compare opportunity costs. Opportunity costs are benefits that a person could have received, but gave up, in choosing another course of action. What is an individual willing to trade or give up for a different choice? For example, if an individual pays someone to mow the lawn because he or she would rather spend that time doing something else, then the opportunity cost of paying someone to mow the lawn is worth the time gained from not doing the job himself or herself.

On a larger scale, governments and communities have to assess different opportunity costs when it comes to using taxpayers' money. Should the government build a new school, repair roads, or allocate funds to local hospitals? Each choice has a tradeoff, and decision makers must choose which option they think is best.

Practice Quiz

1. Which of the following is the subgroup of economics that studies large-scale economic issues such as unemployment, interest rates, price levels, and national income?
   a. Microeconomics
   b. Macroeconomics
   c. Scarcity
   d. Supply and demand

2. Which is NOT an indicator of economic growth?
   a. GDP (Gross Domestic Product)
   b. Unemployment
   c. Inflation
   d. Theory of the Firm

3. In a business cycle, a recession occurs between which cycles?
   a. Expansion, peak
   b. Peak, contraction
   c. Contraction, trough
   d. Trough, expansion

4. What determines the exchange rate in a “floating” or “flexible” exchange?
   a. The government
   b. Taxes
   c. The Federal Reserve
   d. The market

5. Which statement is true about inflation and purchasing power?
   a. As inflation decreases, purchasing power increases.
   b. As inflation increases, purchasing power decreases.
   c. As inflation increases, purchasing power increases.
   d. As inflation decreases, purchasing power decreases.

Answer Explanations

1. B: Macroeconomics. Macroeconomics studies the economy on a large scale and focuses on issues such as unemployment, interest rates, price levels, and national income. Microeconomics studies more individual or small group behaviors such as scarcity or supply and demand. Scarcity is incorrect because it refers to the availability of goods and services. Supply and demand is also incorrect because it refers to the quantity of goods and services that is produced and/or needed.

2. D: Theory of The Firm. Behaviors of firms is not an indicator of economic growth because it refers to the behavior that firms follow to reach their desired outcome. GDP, unemployment, and inflation are all indicators that help determine economic growth.

3. C: Contraction and trough. A recession occurs between the contraction and trough phases of the business cycle. Between expansion and peak phases, employment and productivity are on the rise, causing a "boom." Between the peak and contraction, unemployment rates are starting to fall, but have not yet hit an all-time low. Between trough and expansion phases, the economy is getting back on its feet and starting to increase employment again.

4. D: The market. The market, through supply and demand, determines the exchange rate with a "flexible" or "floating" exchange rate. The government is not a correct answer because it is involved in "fixed" exchange rates to help keep exchange rates stable. Taxes is also incorrect because they create government revenue. The Federal Reserve is the bank of banks.

5. B: As inflation increases, purchasing power decreases. As more money is printed, the monetary value of the dollar drops and, in turn, decreases the purchasing power of goods and services. So, as inflation increases, consumers are not spending as much and the value of the dollar is low.

Section 13: Geography

Concepts and Terminology of Physical and Human Geography

Geographers utilize a variety of maps in their study of the spatial world. Projections are maps that represent the spherical globe on a flat surface. Conformal projections attempt to preserve shape but distort size and area. For example, the most well-known projection, the *Mercator projection*, drastically distorts the size of land areas at the poles. In this particular map, Antarctica, one of the smallest continents, appears massive, while the areas closer to the equator are depicted more accurately. Other projections attempt to lessen the amount of distortion; the equal-area projection, for example, attempts to accurately represent the size of landforms. However, equal-area projections alter the shapes and angles of landforms regardless of their positioning on the map. Other projections are hybrids of the two primary models. For example, the Robinson projection tries to balance form and area in order to create a more visually accurate representation of the spatial world. Despite the efforts to maintain consistency with shapes, projections cannot provide accurate representations of the Earth's surface due to their flat, two-dimensional nature. In this sense, projections are useful symbols of space, but they do not always provide the most accurate portrayal of reality.

Unlike projections, topographic maps display contour lines, which represent the relative elevation of a particular place and are very useful for surveyors, engineers, and/or travelers. For example, hikers may refer to topographic maps to calculate their daily climbs.

Similar to topographic maps, **isoline maps** are also useful for calculating data and differentiating between the characteristics of two places. These maps use symbols to represent values and lines to connect points with the same value. For example, an isoline map could display average temperatures of a given area. The sections which share the same average temperature would be grouped together by lines. Additionally, isoline maps can help geographers study the world by generating questions. For example, is elevation the only reason for differences in temperature? If not, what other factors could cause the disparity between the values?

Thematic maps are also quite useful because they display the geographical distribution of complex political, physical, social, cultural, economic, or historical themes. For example, a thematic map could indicate an area's election results using a different color for each candidate. There are several different kinds of thematic maps, including dot-density maps and flow-line maps. A *dot-density map* uses dots to illustrate volume and density; these dots could represent a certain population, or the number of specific events that have taken place in an area. Flow-line maps utilize lines of varying thicknesses to illustrate the movement of goods, people, or even animals between two places. Thicker lines represent a greater number of moving elements, and thinner lines represent a smaller number.

Using Geographic Concepts to Analyze Spatial Phenomena

Using Mental Maps to Organize Spatial Information

Mental maps are exactly what they sound like: maps that exist within someone's mind. The cognitive image of a particular place may differ from person to person, however. Furthermore, mental maps can enable people to travel from point A to point B efficiently. Someone may utilize their mental map to determine the best route on public transit, the least hilly bike path, or the roadways that have the least amount of traffic. Mental maps tend to be more informative when a person has had more experiences in that particular place.

Maps and Scale

Since maps represent a large area on a much smaller two-dimensional space, they must utilize a scale. Scale is simply the ratio of a distance on the ground to the corresponding distance on paper. Geographers and cartographers attempt to make the image on paper representative of the actual place. The United States Geological Survey (USGS) utilizes the mathematical ratio of 1/24,000 in all of its topographical maps. This scale means that one inch on the map is equivalent to 24,000 inches—or nearly two-thirds of a mile—on the ground. Large-scale maps represent a smaller area with greater detail, while small-scale maps are representative of much larger areas with less detail.

Recognizing and Interpreting Spatial Patterns

Two primary realms exist within the study of geography. The first, **physical geography**, essentially correlates with the land, water, and foliage of the Earth. The second, **human geography**, is the study of the Earth's people and how they interact with their environment. Several geographical factors impact the human condition, such as access to natural resources. For example, human populations tend to be higher around more reliable sources of fresh water. The metropolitan area of New York City, which has abundant freshwater resources, is home to over 18 million people. Australia, on the other hand, an entire country and continent, has much less accessibility to fresh water and houses only 7 million more people. Although water is not the only factor in this disparity, it certainly plays a role in population density—the total number of people in a particular place divided by the total land area, usually in square miles or square kilometers. Australia's population density is about 7 people per square mile, while the most densely populated nation on Earth, Bangladesh, is home to 2,889 people per square mile.

Population density can have a devastating impact on both the physical environment/ecosystem and the humans who live within the environment/ecosystem of a particular place. For example, Delhi, one of India's most populated cities, is home to nearly five million gasoline-powered vehicles. Each day, those vehicles emit an enormous amount of carbon monoxide into the atmosphere, which directly affects the Delhi citizens' quality of life. In fact, the smog and pollution problems have gotten so severe that many drivers cannot see fifty feet in front of them. Additionally, densely populated areas within third-world nations, or developing nations, struggle significantly in their quest to balance the demands of the modern economy with their nation's lack of infrastructure. For example, nearly as many automobiles operate every day in major American cities like New York and Los Angeles as they do in Delhi, but they create significantly less pollution due to cleaner burning engines, better fuels, and governmental emission regulations.

Although it is a significant factor, population density is not the only source of strain on a place's resources. Historical forces such as civil war, religious conflict, genocide, and government corruption can also profoundly alter the lives of a nation's citizens. For example, the war-torn nation of Somalia has not had a functioning government for nearly three decades. As a result, the nation's citizens have virtually no access to hospital care, vaccinations, or proper facilities for childbirth. Due to these and other factors, the nation's *infant mortality rate*, or the total number of child deaths per 1,000 live births, stands at a whopping 98.39/1000. When compared to Iceland's 1.82/1000, it's quite evident that Somalia struggles to provide basic services in the realm of childbirth and there is a dire need for humanitarian assistance.

Literacy rates, like infant mortality rates, are also excellent indicators of the relative level of development in a particular place. Many developing nations have both economic and social factors that hinder their ability to educate their own citizens. Due to radical religious factions within some nations like Afghanistan and Pakistan, girls are often denied the ability to attend school, which further reduces the nation's overall literacy rate. For example, girls in Afghanistan have a 24.2 percent literacy rate, one of the lowest rates of any record-keeping nation on Earth.

Although literacy rates are useful in determining a nation's development level, high literacy rates do exist within developing nations. For example, Suriname, which has a significantly lower GDP than Afghanistan, enjoys a 94 percent literacy rate among both sexes. Utilizing this and other data, geographers can create questions regarding how such phenomena occur. How is Suriname able to educate its population more effectively with fewer financial resources? Is it something inherent within their culture? Demographic data, such as population density, the infant mortality rate, and the literacy rate all provide insight into the characteristics of a particular place and help geographers better understand the spatial world.

Locating and Using Sources of Geographic Data

In order to fully understand both geographic realms, geographers must utilize various sources of data. For instance, geographers can use data and comparative analysis to determine the different factors that affect quality of life, such as population density, infant mortality rates, and literacy rates. In addition, organizations such as the **Population Reference Bureau** and the **Central Intelligence Agency** provide incredible amounts of demographic data that are readily accessible for anyone.

The **CIA World Factbook** is an indispensable resource for anyone interested in geography. Providing information about land area, literacy rates, birth rates, and economics, this resource is one of the most comprehensive on the Internet. In addition, the **Population Reference Bureau (PRB)** provides students of geography with an abundant supply of information. The PRB provides a treasure trove of analyses related to human populations including HIV rates, immigration rates, poverty rates, and more.

Furthermore, the United States Census Bureau provides similar information about the dynamics of the American population. Not only does this source focus on the data geographers need to understand the world, but it also provides information about upcoming classes, online workshops, and even includes an online library of resources for both students and teachers.

Websites for each source can be found below:

- Population Reference Bureau: www.prb.org
- United States Census Bureau: www.census.gov
- CIA World Factbook: https://www.cia.gov/library/publications/the-world-factbook/

Spatial Concepts

Location is the central theme in understanding spatial concepts. In geography, there are two primary types of location: relative and absolute. Relative location involves locating objects by their proximity to another object. For example, a person giving directions may refer to well-known landmarks, highways, or intersections along the route to provide a better frame of reference. Absolute location is the exact latitudinal and longitudinal position on the globe. A common way of identifying **absolute location** is through the use of digital, satellite-based technologies such as **GPS (Global Positioning System),** which uses sensors that interact with satellites orbiting the Earth. Coordinates correspond with positions on a manmade grid system using imaginary lines known as latitude (also known as parallels) and longitude (also known as meridians).

Lines of latitude run parallel to the *Equator* and measure distance from north to south. Lines of longitude run parallel to the *Prime Meridian* and measure distance from east to west.

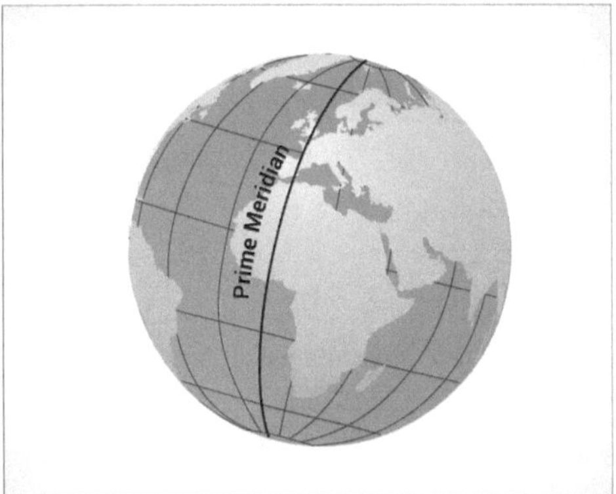

The Equator and the Prime Meridian serve as anchors of the grid system and create the basis for absolute location. They also divide the Earth into **hemispheres**. The Equator divides the Earth into the northern and southern hemispheres, while the Prime Meridian establishes the eastern and western hemispheres. Lines of latitude are measured by degrees from 0 at the Equator to 90 at the North and South Poles. Lines of longitude are measured by degrees from 0 at the Prime Meridian to 180 at the International Date Line. Coordinates are used to express a specific location using its latitude and longitude and are always expressed in the following format: degree north or south followed by degree east or west (for example, 40°N, 50°E). Since there is great distance between lines of latitude and longitude, absolute locations are often found in between two lines. In those cases, degrees are broken down into *minutes* and *seconds*, which are expressed in this manner: (40° 53′ 44″ N, 50° 22′ 65″ E).

Other major lines of latitude include the Tropics of Cancer (23.5 degrees north) and Capricorn (23.5 degrees south). These lines correspond with the **Earth's tilt** and mark the positions on the Earth where the sun is directly overhead on the solstices. The tilt and rotation of the earth determine the seasons (or lack thereof) in a given location. For example, the northern hemisphere is tilted directly toward the sun from June 21 to September 21, which creates the summer season in that part of the world. Conversely, the southern hemisphere is tilted away from the direct rays of the sun and experiences winter during those same months.

The area between the **Tropic of Cancer** and the **Tropic of Capricorn** (called the tropics) has more direct exposure to the sun, tends to be warmer year-round, and experiences fewer variations in seasonal temperatures.

Most of the Earth's population lives in the area between the Tropic of Cancer and the Arctic Circle (66.5 degrees north), which is one of the middle latitudes. In the Southern Hemisphere, the middle latitudes exist between the Tropic of Capricorn and the Antarctic Circle (66.5 degrees south). In both of these places, indirect rays of the sun strike the Earth. Therefore, seasons are more pronounced, and milder temperatures generally prevail. The final region, known as the *high latitudes*, is found north of the Arctic Circle and south of the Antarctic Circle. These regions generally tend to be cold all year, and experience nearly twenty-four hours of sunlight during their respective *summer solstice* and twenty-four hours of darkness during the *winter solstice*.

Seasons in the Southern Hemispheres are opposite of those in the Northern Hemisphere due to the position of the Earth as it rotates around the sun. An **equinox** occurs when the sun's rays are directly over the Equator, and day and night are of almost equal length throughout the world. Equinoxes occur twice a year; the autumnal equinox occurs around September 22nd, while the spring equinox occurs around March 20th. Since the Northern and Southern hemispheres experience opposite seasons, the season names vary based on location (i.e. when the Northern Hemisphere is experiencing summer, the Southern Hemisphere is in winter).

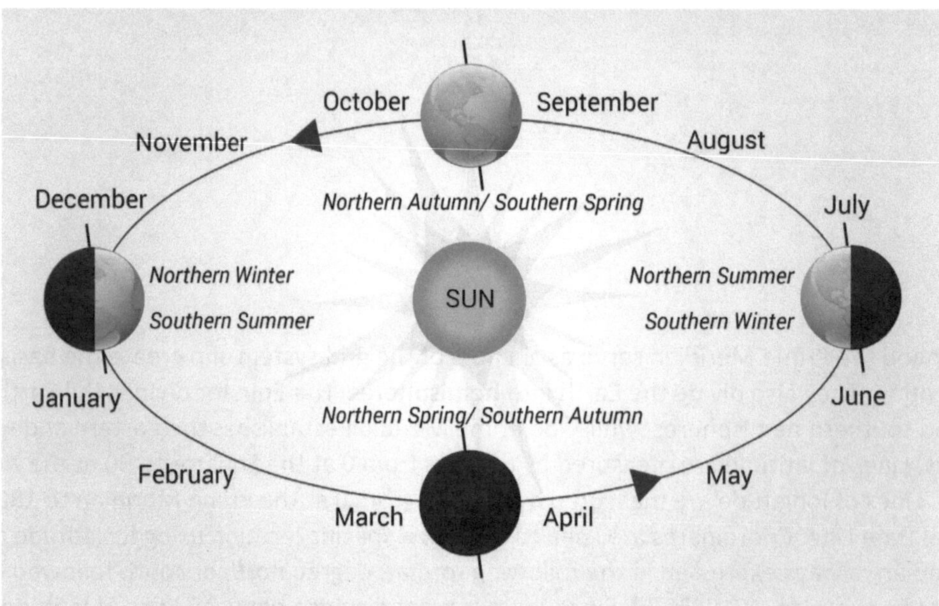

Place

While absolute and relative location identify where something is, the concept of place identifies the distinguishing physical and human characteristics of specific locations. People use **toponyms**, names of locations, to define and further orient themselves with their sense of place. Toponyms may be derived from geographical features, important historical figures in the area, or even wildlife commonly found there. For example, many cities in the state of Texas are named in honor of military leaders who fought in the Texas Revolution (such as Houston and Austin), while Mississippi and Alabama got their toponyms from Native American words.

Regions

Geographers divide the world into regions to help them understand differences inherent within the world, its people, and its environment. As mentioned previously, lines of latitude and longitude divide the Earth into solar regions relative to the amount of sunlight they receive. Additionally, geographers identify formal and functional regions.

Formal regions are spatially defined areas that have overarching similarities or some level of *homogeneity* or *uniformity*. Although not exactly alike, a formal region generally has at least one characteristic that is consistent throughout the entire area. For example, the United States could be classified as one massive formal region because English is the primary language spoken in all fifty states. Even more specifically, the United States is a linguistic region—a place where everyone generally speaks the same language.

Functional regions are areas that also have similar characteristics but do not have clear boundaries. Large cities and their metropolitan areas form functional regions, as people from outside the official city limit must travel into the city regularly for work, entertainment, restaurants, etc. Other determining factors of a functional region could be a sports team, a school district, or a shopping center. For example, New York City has two professional baseball, basketball, and football teams. As a result, its citizens may have affinities for different teams even though they live in the same city. Conversely, a citizen in rural Idaho may cheer for the Seattle Seahawks, even though they live over 500 miles from Seattle.

Economic, Political, and Social Factors

Effects of Physical Processes, Climate Patterns, and Natural Hazards on Human Societies

The Earth's surface, like many other things in the broader universe, does not remain the same for long; in fact, it changes daily. The Earth's surface is subject to a variety of physical processes that continue to shape its appearance. Water, wind, temperature, or sunlight play a role in continually altering the Earth's surface.

Erosion involves the movement of soil from one place to another and can be caused by a variety of stimuli including ice, snow, water, wind, and ocean waves. Wind erosion occurs in generally flat, dry areas with loose topsoil. Over time, the persistent winds can dislodge significant amounts of soil into the air, reshaping the land and wreaking havoc on those who depend on agriculture for their livelihoods. Water can also cause erosion. For example, erosion caused by the Colorado River helped to form the Grand Canyon. Over time, the river moved millions of tons of soil, cutting a huge gorge in the Earth along the way.

In water erosion, material carried by the water is referred to as *sediment*. With time, some sediment can collect at the mouths of rivers, forming *deltas*, which become small islands of fertile soil. This process of detaching loose soils and transporting them to a different location where they remain for an extended period of time is referred to as **deposition**, which is the end result of the erosion process.

In contrast to erosion, *weathering* does not involve the movement of any outside stimuli. Instead, the surface of the Earth is broken down physically or chemically. *Physical weathering* involves the effects of atmospheric conditions such as water, ice, heat, or pressure. For example, when ice forms in the cracks of large rocks or pavement, it can break down or split open the material. *Chemical weathering* generally occurs in warmer climates and involves organic material that breaks down rocks, minerals, or soil. Scientists believe this process led to the creation of fossil fuels such as oil, coal, and natural gas.

Climate Patterns

Weather is the condition of the Earth's atmosphere at a particular time. *Climate* is different; instead of focusing on one particular day, climate is the relative pattern of weather in a place for an extended period of time. For example, the city of Atlanta, Georgia generally has a humid subtropical climate; however, it also occasionally experiences snowstorms in the winter months. Over time, geographers, meteorologists, and other Earth scientists have determined these patterns that are indicative to north Georgia. Almost all parts of the world have predictable climate patterns, which are influenced by the surrounding geography.

The Central Coast of California is an example of a place with a predictable climate pattern. Santa Barbara, California, one of the region's larger cities, has almost the same temperature for most of the year, with only minimal fluctuation during the winter months. The temperatures there, which average between 75° and 65° Fahrenheit regardless of the time of year, are influenced by a variety of different climatological factors including elevation, location relative to the mountains and ocean, and ocean currents.

Other factors affecting climate include elevation, prevailing winds, vegetation, and latitudinal position on the globe.

Natural hazards also affect human societies. In tropical and subtropical climates, hurricanes and typhoons that form over warm water can have devastating effects. Additionally, tornadoes, which are powerful cyclonic windstorms, are responsible for widespread destruction in many parts of the world. Earthquakes, caused by shifting plates along faults deep below the Earth's surface, also bring widespread devastation, particularly in nations with poor infrastructure. For example, San Francisco, which experiences earthquakes regularly due to its position near the San Andreas Fault, saw relatively little destruction and death as a result of a major earthquake in 1989. However, in 2010, an earthquake of similar magnitude reportedly killed over 200,000 people in the Western Hemisphere's poorest nation, Haiti.

Although a variety of factors may be responsible for the disparity, modern engineering methods and better building materials most likely helped to minimize destruction in San Francisco. Other natural hazards, such as tsunamis, mudslides, avalanches, forest fires, dust storms, flooding, volcanic eruptions, and blizzards, also affect human societies throughout the world.

Characteristics and Spatial Distribution of Earth's Ecosystems

Earth is an incredibly large place filled with a variety of land and water ecosystems. *Marine ecosystems* cover over 75 percent of the Earth's surface and contain over 95 percent of the Earth's water. Marine ecosystems can be broken down into two primary subgroups: *freshwater ecosystems*, which only encompass around 2 percent of the earth's surface; and *ocean ecosystems*, which make up over 70 percent. Terrestrial ecosystems vary based on latitudinal distance from the equator, elevation, and proximity to mountains or bodies of water. For example, in the high latitudinal regions north of the Arctic Circle and south of the Antarctic Circle, frozen *tundra* dominates. Tundra, which is characterized by low temperatures, short growing seasons, and minimal vegetation, is only found in regions that are far away from the direct rays of the sun.

In contrast, *deserts* can be found throughout the globe and are created by different ecological factors. For example, the world's largest desert, the Sahara, is almost entirely within the tropics; however, other deserts like the Gobi in China, the Mojave in the United States, and the Atacama in Chile, are close to mountain ranges such as the Himalayas, the Sierra Nevada, and the Andes, respectively.

In the United States, temperate deciduous forests dominate the southeastern region. The midwestern states such as Nebraska, Kansas, and the Dakotas, are primarily grasslands. The states of the Rocky Mountains can have decidedly different climates relative to elevation. Denver, Colorado, will often see snowfalls well into April or May due to colder temperatures, whereas cities in the eastern part of the state, with much lower elevations, may see their last significant snowfall in March.

The tropics generally experience warmer temperatures due to their position on the Earth in relation to the sun. However, like most of the world, the tropics also experience a variety of climatological regions. In Brazil, Southeast Asia, Central America, and even Northern Australia, tropical rainforests are common. These forests, which are known for abundant vegetation, daily rainfall, and a wide variety of animal life, are essential to the health of the world's ecosystems. For example, the Amazon Rain Forest's billions of trees produce substantial amounts of oxygen and absorb an equivalent amount of carbon dioxide—the substance that many climatologists assert is causing climate change or global warming.

Unlike temperate deciduous forests whose trees lose their leaves during the fall and winter months, *tropical rain forests* are always lush, green, and warm. In fact, some rainforests are so dense with vegetation that a few indigenous tribes have managed to exist within them without being influenced by any sort of modern technology, virtually maintaining their ancient way of life in the modern era.

The world's largest land ecosystem, the taiga, is found primarily in high latitudinal areas, which receive very little direct sunlight. These forests are generally made up of *coniferous* trees, which do not lose their leaves at any point during the year as *deciduous* trees do. Taigas are cold-climate regions that make up almost 30 percent of the world's land area. These forests dominate the northern regions of Canada, Scandinavia, and Russia, and provide the vast majority of the world's lumber.

Climates are influenced by five major factors: elevation, latitude, proximity to mountains, ocean currents, and wind patterns. For example, the cold currents off the coast of California provide the West Coast of the United States with pleasant year-round temperatures. Conversely, Western Europe, which is at the nearly the same latitude as most of Canada, is influenced by the warm waters of the *Gulf Stream*, an ocean current that acts as a conveyor belt, moving warm tropical waters to the icy north. In fact, the Gulf Stream's influence is so profound that it even keeps Iceland—an island nation in the far North Atlantic—relatively warm.

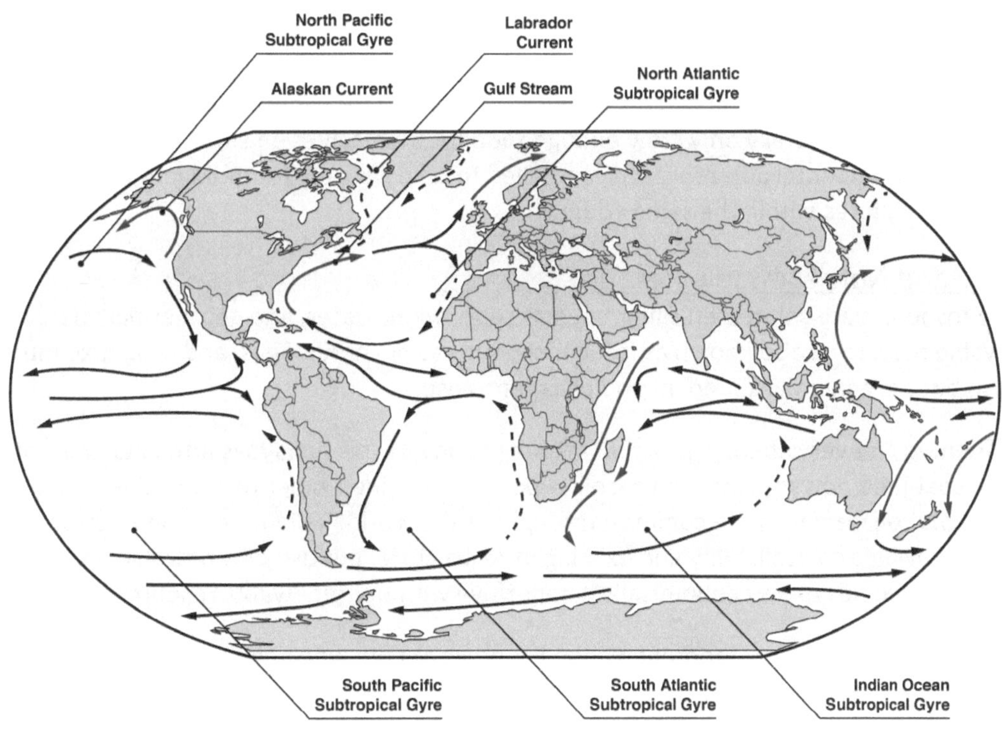

Interrelationships Between Humans and Their Environment

Humans both adapt themselves to their environment and adapt their environment to suit their needs. Humans create social systems with the goal of providing people with access to what they need to live more productive, fulfilling, and meaningful lives. Sometimes, humans create destructive systems, but generally speaking, humans tend to leverage their environments to make their lives easier. For example, in warmer climates, people tend to wear lighter clothing such as shorts, linen shirts, and hats. In the excessively sun-drenched nations of the Middle East, both men and women wear flowing white clothing complete with both a head and neck covering in order to prevent the blistering effects of exposure to the sun. Likewise, the native Inuit peoples of northern Canada and Alaska use the thick furs from the animals they kill to insulate their bodies against the bitter cold.

Humans must also manipulate their environments to ensure that they have sufficient access to food and water. In locations where water is not readily available, humans have had to invent ways to redirect water for drinking or agriculture. For example, the city of Los Angeles, America's second most populous city, did not have adequate freshwater resources to sustain its population. However, city and state officials realized that abundant water resources existed approximately three hundred miles to the east. Rather than relocating some of its population to areas with more abundant water resources, the State of California undertook one of the largest construction projects in the history of the world, the Los Angeles Aqueduct, which is a massive water transportation system that connects water-rich areas with the thirsty citizens of Los Angeles.

Farming is another way in which humans use the environment for their advantage. The very first permanent British Colony in North America, Jamestown, VA, was characterized by a hot and humid climate with fertile soil. Consequently, its inhabitants engaged in agriculture for both food and profit. Twelve years after Jamestown's founding in 1607, it was producing millions of dollars of tobacco each year. In order to sustain this booming industry, millions of African slaves and indentured servants from Europe were imported to provide labor.

Conversely, poor soil in the New England colonies did not allow for widespread cash crop production, and the settlers there generally only grew enough food for themselves on small subsistence farms. Due in part to this environmental difference, slavery failed to take a strong foothold in these states, thus creating distinct cultures within the same country.

Renewable and Nonrenewable Resources

Renewable resources are self-replenishing, such as solar, wind, water, and geothermal energy. Nonrenewable resources, also known as fossil fuels, such as oil, natural gas, and coal, take much longer to replenish but are generally abundant and cheaper to use.

While solar energy is everywhere, the actual means to convert the sun's rays into energy is not. Conversely, coal-fired power plants and gasoline-powered engines, older technologies used during the industrial revolution, remain quite common throughout the world. Reliance on nonrenewable resources continues to grow due to availability and existing infrastructure, but use of renewable energy is also increasing as it becomes more economically competitive with nonrenewable resources.

In addition to sources of energy, nonrenewable resources also include any materials that can be exhausted, such as precious metals, precious stones, and freshwater underground aquifers. Although abundant, most nonrenewable sources of energy are not sustainable because their replenishment takes so long. While renewable resources are sustainable, their use must be properly overseen so that they remain renewable. For example, the beautiful African island of Madagascar is home to some of the most amazing rainforest trees in the world. Logging companies cut, milled, and sold thousands of them in order to make quick profits without planning how to ensure the continued health of the forests. In this way, renewable resources were mismanaged and thus essentially became nonrenewable due to the length of time it takes for replacement trees to grow. In contrast, many United States paper companies that harvest pine trees must utilize planning techniques to ensure that mature pine trees will always be available. In this manner, these resources remain renewable for human use in a sustainable fashion.

Renewable sources of energy are relatively new in the modern economy. Even though electric cars, wind turbines, and solar panels are becoming more common, they still do not provide enough energy to power the world's economy. As a result, reliance on older forms of energy continues, which can have a devastating effect on the environment. Beijing, China, which has seen a massive boom in industrial jobs, is also one of the most polluted places on Earth. Furthermore, developing nations with very little modern infrastructure also rely heavily on fossil fuels due to the ease in which they are converted into usable energy. Even the United States, which has one of the most developed infrastructures in the world, still relies almost exclusively on fossil fuels, with only ten percent of the required energy coming from renewable sources.

Spatial Patterns of Cultural and Economic Activities

Spatial patterns refer to where things are in the world. Elements of both physical and human geography have spatial patterns regarding where they appear on Earth.

Ethnicity

An ethnic group, or ethnicity, is essentially a group of people with a common language, society, culture, or ancestral heritage. Different ethnicities developed over centuries through historical forces, the impact of religious traditions, and other factors. Thousands of years ago, it was more common for ethnic groups to remain in one area with only occasional interaction with outside groups.

In the modern world, different ethnicities interact on a regular basis due to better transportation resources and the processes of globalization. For example, in countries like the United States and Canada, it is not uncommon for schools, workplaces, or communities to have people of Asian, African, Caucasian, European, Indian, or Native descent.

In less developed parts of the world, travel is limited due to the lack of infrastructure. Consequently, ethnic groups develop in small areas that can differ greatly from other people just a few miles away. For example, on the Balkan Peninsula in southeastern Europe, a variety of different ethnic groups live in close proximity to one another. Croats, Albanians, Serbs, Bosnians, and others all share the same land but have very different worldviews, traditions, and religious influences. Unfortunately, this diversity has not always been a positive characteristic, such as when Bosnia was the scene of a horrible genocide against Albanians in an "ethnic cleansing" effort that continued throughout the late 20th century.

Linguistics

Linguistics, or the study of language, groups certain languages together according to their commonalities. For example, the Romance languages—French, Spanish, Italian, Romanian, and Portuguese—all share language traits from Latin. These languages, also known as *vernaculars*, or more commonly spoken *dialects*, evolved over centuries of physical isolation on the European continent. The Spanish form of Latin emerged into today's Spanish language.

Similarly, the Bantu people of Africa travelled extensively and spread their language, now called Swahili, which became the first Pan-African language. Since thousands of languages exist, it is important to have a widespread means of communication that can interconnect people from different parts of the world. One way to do this is through a lingua franca, or a common language used for business, diplomacy, and other cross-national relationships. English is a primary lingua franca around the world, but there are many others in use as well.

Religion
Religion has played a tremendous role in creating the world's cultures. Devout Christians crossed the Atlantic in hopes of finding religious freedom in New England, Muslim missionaries and traders travelled to the Spice Islands of the East Indies to teach about the Koran, and Buddhist monks traversed the Himalayan Mountains into Tibet to spread their faith.

In some countries, religion helps to shape legal systems. These nations, termed *theocracies*, have no separation of church and state and are more common in Islamic nations such as Saudi Arabia, Iran, and Qatar. In contrast, even though religion has played a tremendous role in the history of the United States, its government remains *secular*, or nonreligious, due to the influence of European Enlightenment philosophy at the time of its inception.

Like ethnicity and language, religion is a primary way that individuals and people groups self-identify. As a result, religious influences can shape a region's laws, architecture, literature, and music. For example, when the Ottoman Turks, who are Muslim, conquered Constantinople, which was once the home of the Eastern Orthodox Christian Church, they replaced Christian places of worship with mosques. Additionally, they replaced different forms of Roman architecture with those influenced by Arabic traditions.

Economics
Economic activity also has a spatial component. Nations with few natural resources generally tend to import what they need from nations willing to export raw materials to them. Furthermore, areas that are home to certain raw materials generally tend to alter their environment in order to maintain production of those materials. In the San Joaquin Valley of California, an area known for extreme heat and desert-like conditions, local residents have engineered elaborate drip irrigation systems to adequately water lemon, lime, olive, and orange trees, utilizing the warm temperatures to constantly produce citrus fruits. Additionally, other nations with abundant petroleum reserves build elaborate infrastructures in order to pump, house, refine, and transport their materials to nations who require gasoline, diesel, or natural gas.

Essentially, inhabitants of different spatial regions on Earth create jobs, infrastructure, and transportation systems to ensure the continued flow of goods, raw materials, and resources out of their location so long as financial resources keep flowing into the area.

Patterns of Migration and Settlement
Migration is governed by two primary causes: push factors that cause someone to leave an area, and pull factors that lure someone to a particular place. These two factors often work in concert with one another. For example, the United States of America has experienced significant *internal migration* from the industrial states in the Northeast (such as New York, New Jersey, Connecticut) to the Southern and Western states. This massive migration, which continues into the present-day, is due to high rents in the northeast, dreadfully cold winters, and lack of adequate retirement housing, all of which are push factors. These push factors lead to migration to the *Sunbelt*, a term geographers use to describe states with warm climates and less intense winters.

International migration also takes place between countries, continents, and other regions. The United States has long been the world's leading nation in regard to *immigration*, the process by which people permanently relocate to a new nation. Conversely, developing nations that suffer from high levels of poverty, pollution, warfare, and other violence all have significant push factors, which cause people to leave and move elsewhere. This process, known as *emigration*, is when people in a particular area leave in order to seek a better life in a different—usually better—location.

The Development and Changing Nature of Agriculture

Since the genesis of farming as a means of food production, agriculture has been essential to human existence. Humans no longer had to forage and hunt for food, and more consistent food supplies allowed societies to stabilize and grow. In modern times, farming has changed drastically in order to keep up with the increasing world population.

Until the twentieth century, the vast majority of people on Earth engaged in *subsistence farming*, the practice of growing only enough food to feed oneself and one's family. Inventions such as the steel plow, the mechanical reaper, and the seed drill allowed farmers to produce more crops on the same amount of land. As food became cheaper and easier to obtain, populations grew, but fewer people farmed. After the advent of mechanized farming in developed nations, small farms became less common, and many were either abandoned or absorbed by massive commercial farms producing staple crops and cash crops.

In recent years, agricultural practices have undergone further changes in order to keep up with the rapidly growing population. Due in part to the *Green Revolution*, which introduced the widespread use of fertilizers to produce massive amounts of crops, farming techniques and practices continue to evolve. For example, *genetically modified organisms*, or *GMOs*, are plants or animals whose genetic makeup has been modified using different strands of DNA in hopes of producing more resilient strains of staple crops, livestock, and other foodstuffs. This process, which is a form of *biotechnology*, attempts to solve the world's food production problems through the use of genetic engineering. Although these crops are abundant and resistant to pests, drought, or frost, they are also the subject of intense scrutiny.

For example, the international food company, Monsanto, has faced an incredible amount of criticism regarding its use of GMOs. Many activists assert that such artificial food production processes are inherently problematic and that the resulting food products are dangerous to human health. Despite the controversy, GMOs and biotechnologies continue to change the agricultural landscape and the world's food supply.

Agribusinesses exist throughout the world and produce food for human consumption as well as farming equipment, fertilizers, agrichemicals, and breeding and slaughtering services for livestock. These companies are generally headquartered near the product they produce, like the cereal manufacturer General Mills in the Midwestern United States located near its supply of wheat and corn—the primary ingredients in its cereals.

Contemporary Patterns and Impacts of Development, Industrialization, and Globalization

As mentioned previously, developing nations are those that are struggling to modernize their economy, infrastructure, and government systems. Many of these nations may have difficulty providing basic services to their citizens like clean water, adequate roads, or even police protection. Furthermore, government corruption makes life even more difficult for these countries' citizens.

In contrast, developed nations are those that have relatively high *Gross Domestic Products (GDP)*, or the total value of all goods and services produced in the nation in a given year. The United States, one of the wealthiest nations on Earth, has a GDP of over twenty-one trillion dollars, while Haiti, one of the poorest nations in the Western Hemisphere, has a GDP of over fourteen billion dollars. This comparison is not intended to disparage Haiti or other developing nations, but rather to show that extreme inequities exist in very close proximity to one another, and it may be difficult for developing nations to meet the needs of their citizens and move their economic infrastructure forward toward modernization.

In the modern world, industrialization is the initial key to modernization and development. For developed nations, the process of industrialization took place centuries ago. England, where the Industrial Revolution began, actually began to utilize factories in the early 1700s. Later, the United States and some Western European nations followed suit, using raw materials brought in from their colonies abroad to make finished products. For example, elaborate weaving machines spun cotton into fabric, allowing for the mass production of textiles. As a result, nations that perfected the textile process were able to sell their products around the world, which produced enormous profits. Over time, those nations were able to accumulate wealth, improve their nation's infrastructure, and provide more services for their citizens.

Nations throughout the world are undergoing a similar process in modern times. China exemplifies this concept. While agriculture is still a dominant sector of the Chinese economy, millions of citizens are flocking to major cities like Beijing, Shanghai, and Hangzhou due to the availability of factory jobs that allow workers a certain element of social mobility, or the ability to rise up to a better socioeconomic situation.

Due to improvements in transportation and communication, the world has become figuratively smaller. For example, university students now compete directly with others all over the world to obtain the skills that employers desire. Additionally, many corporations in developed nations have begun to *outsource* labor to nations with high levels of educational achievement but lower wage expectations. **Globalization**, the process of opening the marketplace to all nations throughout the world, has only just started to take hold in the modern economy. As industrial sites shift to the developing world, more opportunities become available for those nation's citizens as well.

However, due to the massive amounts of pollution produced by factories, the process of globalization also has had significant ecological impacts. The most widely known impact, *climate change*, which most climatologists assert is caused by an increase of carbon dioxide in the atmosphere, remains a serious problem that has posed challenges for developing nations, who need industries in order to raise their standard of living, and developed nations, whose citizens use a tremendous amount of fossil fuels to run their cars, heat their homes, and maintain their ways of life.

Demographic Patterns and Demographic Change

Demography, the study of human populations, investigates a variety of factors related to the human experience. For instance, several variables impact the geographical movement of people, such as economics, climate, natural disasters, or internal unrest. A recent example of this phenomenon is found in the millions of Syrian immigrants who have moved as far away as possible from the danger in their war-torn homeland.

As previously mentioned, people tend to live near reliable sources of food and water and away from extreme temperatures. Furthermore, the vast majority of people live in the Northern Hemisphere because more land lies in that part of the Earth.

In keeping with these factors, human populations tend to be greater where human necessities are easily accessible, or at least more readily available. In other words, such areas have a greater chance of having a higher population density than places without such characteristics.

As push and pull factors fluctuate over time, demographic patterns on Earth will also change. While thousands of Europeans fled their homelands in the 1940s due to the impact of the Second World War, the opposite is true today as thousands of migrants arrive on European shores each month due to conflicts in the Levant and difficult economic conditions in Northern Africa. Furthermore, people tend to migrate to places with a greater economic potential for themselves and their families. As a result, developed nations such as the United States, Germany, Canada, and Australia have a net gain of migrants, while developing nations such as Somalia, Zambia, and Cambodia generally tend to see thousands of their citizens seek better lives elsewhere.

Religion and religious conflict also play a role in determining the composition and location of human populations. For example, the Nation of Israel won its independence in 1948 and has since attracted thousands of Jewish people from all over the world. Additionally, the United States has long been a popular destination due to its promise of religious freedom inherent within its own Constitution. In contrast, nations like Saudi Arabia and Iran do not typically tolerate different religions, resulting in a decidedly uniform religious—and oftentimes ethnic—composition. Other factors such as economic opportunity, social unrest, and cost of living also play a vital role in demographic composition.

Basic Concepts of Political Geography

Nation, state, and nation-state are terms with very similar meanings, but knowing the differences aids in a better understanding of geography. A nation is a group of people who share the same cultural, linguistic, and historical heritage. A **state** is a political unit with sovereignty, or the ability to make its own decisions within defined borders. A **nation-state** is both a nation and a sovereignly governed state. For example, the province of Quebec is considered its own nation, distinct from the rest of Canada in language and culture, but is subject to the sovereign state of Canada's governance.

The United Kingdom encompasses four member states: England, Wales, Northern Ireland, and Scotland. Although citizens of those countries may consider themselves to be sovereign, or self-governing, the reality is that they cannot make decisions regarding international trade, declarations of war, or other important decisions regarding the rest of the world. Instead, they are *semi-autonomous*, meaning that they can make some decisions regarding how their own state is run but must yield more major powers to a centralized authority. In the United States, this sort of system is called *Federalism*, or the sharing of power among Local, State, and Federal entities, each of whom is assigned different roles in the overall system of government.

Nation-states and their boundaries are not always permanent. For example, after the fall of the Soviet Union in 1991, new nations emerged that had once been a part of the larger entity called the Union of Soviet Socialists Republics. These formerly sovereign nations were no longer forced to be a part of a unifying communist government, and as a result, they regained their autonomy and became newly independent nations that were no longer *satellite nations* of the Soviet Union.

In a historical sense, the United States can be seen as a prime example of how national boundaries change. After the conclusion of the American Revolution in 1781, the Treaty of Paris defined the United States' western boundary as the Mississippi River; today, after a series of conflicts with Native American groups, the Mexican government, Hawaiian leadership, the Spanish, and the purchase of Alaska from the Russians, the boundaries of the United States have changed drastically. In a similar fashion, nations in Europe, Africa, and Asia have all shifted their boundaries due to warfare, cultural movements, and language barriers.

In the modern world, boundaries continue to change. For example, the Kurds, an ethnic minority and an excellent example of a nation, are still fighting for control of their right to self-determination, but have been unsuccessful in establishing a state for themselves. In contrast, the oil-rich region of South Sudan, which has significant cultural, ethnic, and religious differences from Northern Sudan, successfully won its independence in a bloody civil war, which established the nation's newest independent state.

In recent years, Russia has made the world nervous by aggressively annexing the Crimean Peninsula, which has been part of Ukraine since the end of the Cold War. Even the United Kingdom and Canada have seen their own people nearly vote for their own rights to self-determination. In 1995, Quebec narrowly voted against becoming a sovereign state through a tightly contested referendum. Similarly, Scotland voted to remain part of the Crown even though many Scots see themselves as inherently different from other regions within the UK.

Decolonization, or the removal of dependency on colonizers, has altered the political landscape of Africa, allowed more autonomy for the African people, and redefined the boundaries of the entire continent. Essentially, political geography across the globe is constantly changing.

Interpreting Maps

Geographical concepts are visually conveyed through maps. The map below illustrates some key points about geography.

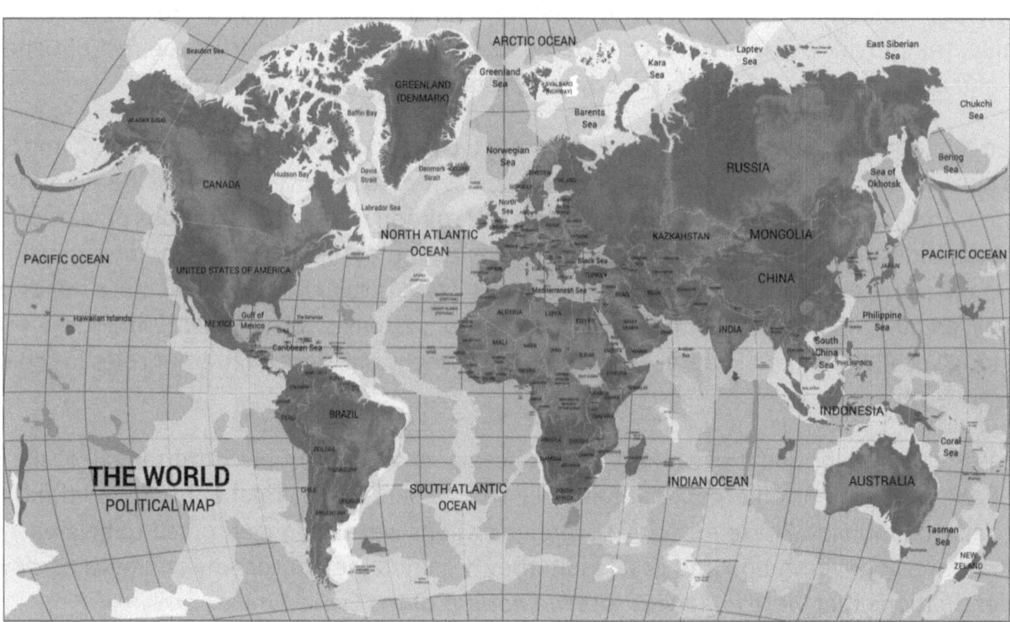

This is a traditional map of the world that displays all countries and six of the seven continents. Countries are the most common regional identifiers, and they can be identified on this map by their labels. The continents are not identified on this map, with the exception of Australia, but they are larger landmasses that encompass most of the countries in their respective areas; the other five visible continents are North America, South America, Europe, Africa, and Asia. The seventh continent, Antarctica, is found at the South Pole and has been omitted from the map.

The absence of Antarctica leads into the issues of distortion, in which geographical features are altered on a map. Some degree of distortion is to be expected with a two-dimensional flat map of the world because the earth is a sphere. A map projection transforms a spherical map of the world into a flattened perspective, but the process generally alters the spatial appearance of landmasses. For instance, Greenland often appears, such as in the map above, larger than it really is.

Furthermore, Antarctica's exclusion from the map is, in fact, a different sort of distortion—that of the mapmakers' biases. Mapmakers determine which features are included on the map and which ones are not. Antarctica, for example, is often missing from maps because, unlike the other continents, it has a limited human population. Moreover, a study of the world reveals that many of the distinctions on maps are human constructions.

Maps reveal key features about the world. Some maps display variations in topography, or the differences in elevation of the terrain. A section of a topographical map can be viewed below. Where the lines are closer together, the terrain is steeper, and when the lines are more spread out, the terrain is flatter.

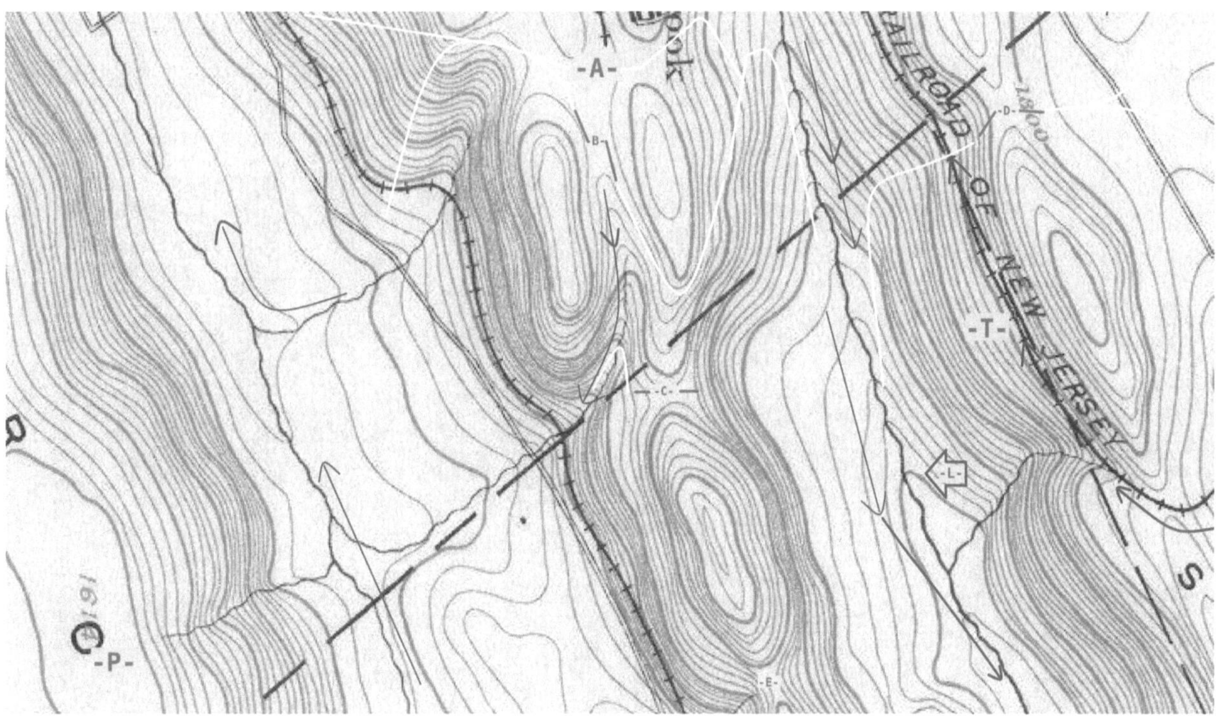

On some colored maps, the oceans, represented in blue between the continents, vary in coloration depending on depth. The differences demonstrate *bathymetry*, which is the study of the ocean floor's depth. Paler areas represent less depth, while darker spots reflect greater depth.

Maps may also display horizonal and vertical lines representing latitude and longitude. The horizontal lines, known as parallels, mark the calculated latitude of those locations and reveal how far north or south these areas are from the equator, which bisects the map horizontally.

Longitude, as signified by the vertical lines, determines how far east or west different regions are from each other. The lines of longitude, known as meridians, are also the basis for time zones, which determine the time for different regions. As one travels west between time zones, the given time moves backward accordingly. Conversely, if one travels east, the time moves forward.

There are two particularly significant longitudinal lines. First, the Prime [Greenwich] Meridian marks zero degrees in longitude, and thus determines the other lines. The line circles the globe and divides it into the Eastern and Western hemispheres. Second, the International Date Line represents the change between calendar days. By traveling westward across the International Date Line, a traveler would essentially leap forward a day. For example, a person departing from the United States on Sunday would arrive in Japan on Monday. By traveling eastward across the line, a traveler would go backward a day. For example, a person departing from China on Monday would arrive in Canada on Sunday.

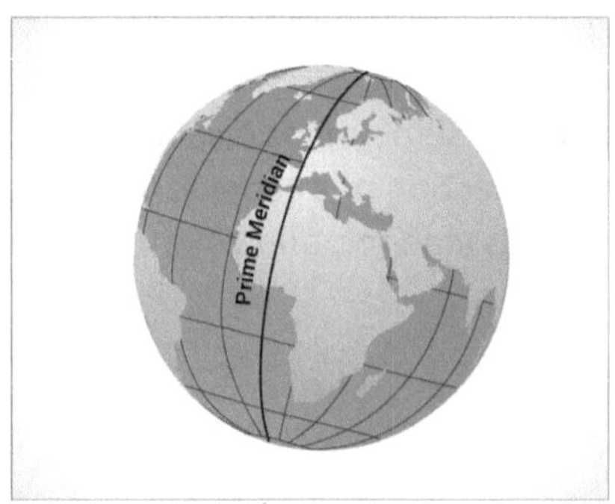

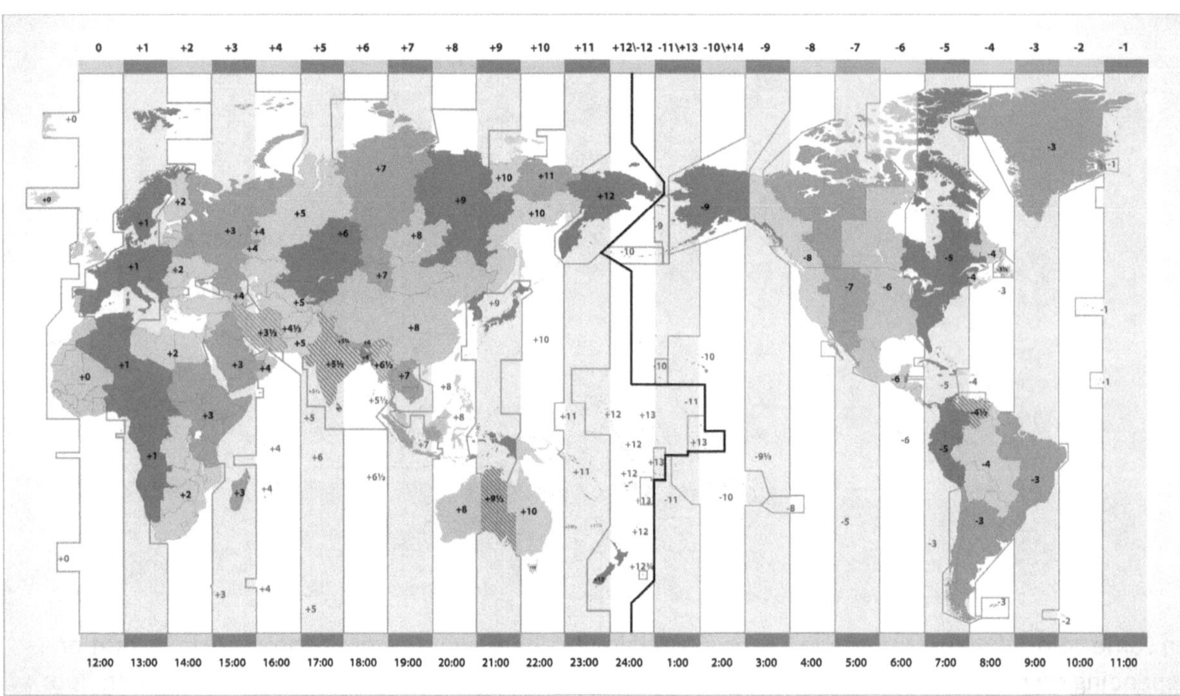

Although world maps are useful in showing the overall arrangement of continents and nations, it is also important at times to look more closely at individual countries because they have unique features that are only visible on more detailed maps.

For example, take the following map of the United States of America. The country is split into multiple states that have their own cultures and localized governments. Other countries are often split into various divisions, such as provinces, and while these features are ignored for the sake of clarity on larger maps, they are important when studying specific nations. Individual states can be further subdivided into counties and townships, and they may have their own maps that can be examined for closer analysis.

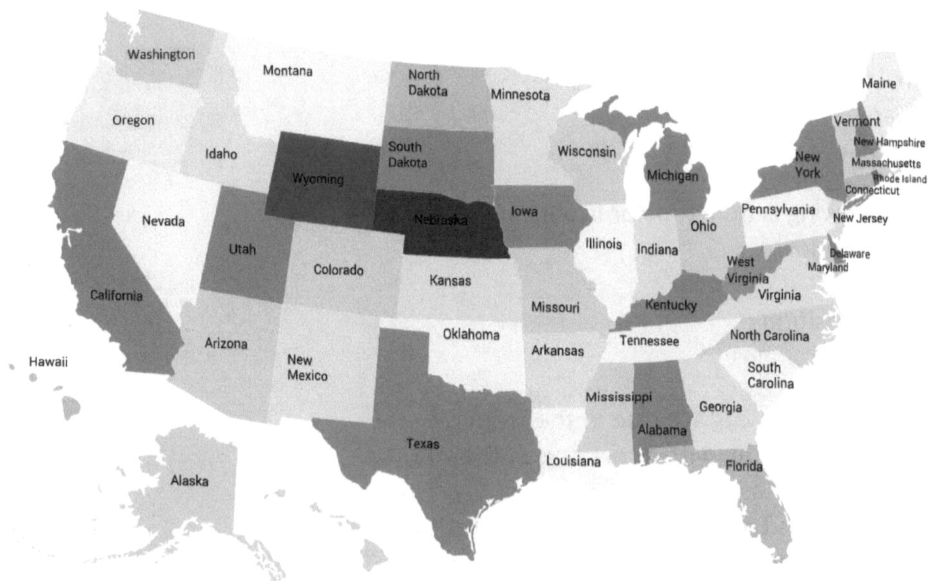

Finally, one of the first steps in examining any map should be to locate its key or legend, which will explain what different symbols represent on the map. As these symbols can be arbitrary depending on the maker, a key will help to clarify the different meanings.

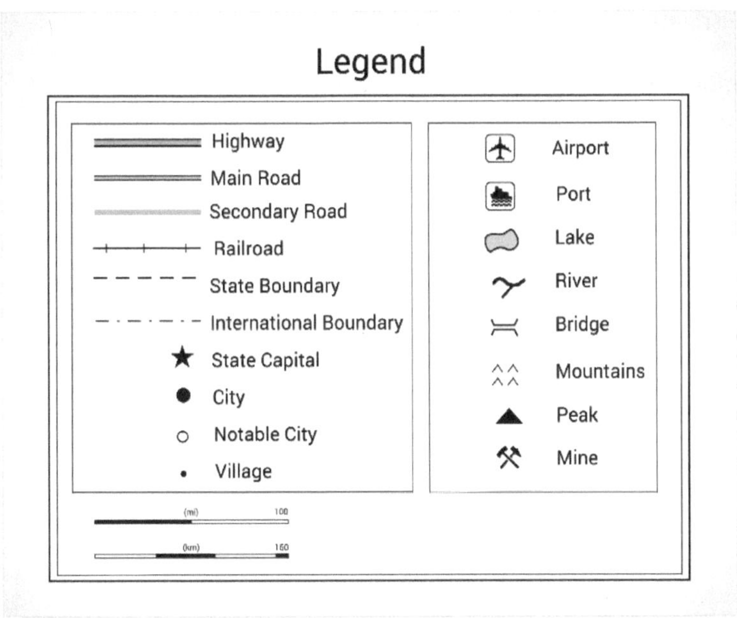

Practice Quiz

1. Which type of map illustrates the world's climatological regions?
   a. Topographic Map
   b. Conformal Projection
   c. Isoline Map
   d. Thematic Map

2. Which of the following is NOT a factor in a location's climate?
   a. Latitudinal position
   b. Elevation
   c. Longitudinal position
   d. Proximity to mountains

3. All but which of the following are true of the Tropics?
   a. They are consistently hit with direct rays of the sun.
   b. They fall between the Tropics of Cancer and Capricorn.
   c. They are nearer the Equator than the Middle Latitudes.
   d. They are always warmer than other parts of the Globe.

4. In recent years, agricultural production has been affected by which of the following?
   a. The prevalence of biotechnology and GMOs
   b. Weaker crop yields due to poor soil
   c. Plagues of pests, which have limited food production
   d. Revolutions in irrigation, which utilize salinated water

5. Literacy rates are more likely to be higher in which area?
   a. Developing nations
   b. Northern Hemispherical Nations
   c. Developed Nations
   d. Near centers of trade

Answer Explanations

1. D: Thematic maps create certain themes in which they attempt to illustrate a certain phenomenon or pattern. The obvious theme of a climate map is the climates in the represented areas. Thematic maps are very extensive and can include thousands of different themes, which makes them quite useful for students of geography. Topographic maps are utilized to show physical features, conformal projections attempt to illustrate the globe in an undistorted fashion, and isoline maps illustrate differences in variables between two points on a map.

2. C: Longitudinal position, or a place's location either east or west, has no bearing on the place's climate. In contrast, a place's latitudinal position, or its distance away from the direct rays of the sun in the Tropics, greatly affects its climate. Additionally, proximity to mountains, which can block wind patterns, and elevation, which generally lowers temperature by three degrees for every one thousand feet gained, also impacts climate.

3. D: Although nearest the direct rays of the sun, the Tropics are not always warm. In fact, the nations of Ecuador and Peru, which are entirely within the Tropics, are home to the Andes Mountains, which remain snowcapped the entire year. This climatological anomaly is also due to cooler ocean currents and the orographic effect. Choices *A, B,* and *C* are all true of the tropics.

4. A: The use of biotechnology and GMOs has increased the total amount of food on Earth. Additionally, it has helped to sustain the Earth's growing population; however, many activists assert that scientists are creating crops that, in the long run, will be destructive to human health, even though not enough evidence exists to prove such an allegation. Agricultural production has not been affected by poorer soil, plagues of pests, or the use of saline for irrigation purposes.

5. C: Developed Nations have better infrastructural systems, which can include government, transportation, financial, and educational institutions. Consequently, its citizens tend to have higher rates of literacy, due to the sheer availability of educational resources and government sanctioned educational systems. In contrast, developing nations struggle to provide educational resources to their citizens. Nations in the Northern Hemisphere have no greater availability to educational resources than those in the Southern Hemisphere, and centers of trade don't necessarily equate to higher levels of education as many may exist in poorer nations with fewer resources.

Practice Test

Multiple-Choice Questions

1. Which of the following statements best describes the relationship, if any, between the revolutions in America and France?
   a. The French Revolution inspired the American Revolution.
   b. The American Revolution inspired the French Revolution.
   c. They both occurred simultaneously.
   d. There was no connection between the French and American revolutions.

2. All of the following are negative demographic indicators EXCEPT which of the following?
   a. High Infant Mortality Rates
   b. Low Literacy Rates
   c. High Population Density
   d. Low Life Expectancy

3. A homeowner hires a landscape company to mow the grass because he or she would like to use that time to do something else. The trade-off of paying someone to do a job to make more valuable use of time is an example of what?
   a. Economic systems
   b. Supply and demand
   c. Opportunity cost
   d. Inflation

4. Which of the following military technologies did NOT play a role in World War I from 1914 to 1918?
   a. The atomic bomb
   b. Poison gas
   c. Armored tanks
   d. Aircraft

5. Which of the following correctly lists the Thirteen Colonies?
   a. Connecticut, Delaware, Georgia, Maryland, Massachusetts, New Hampshire, New Jersey, New York, North Carolina, Pennsylvania, Rhode Island, South Carolina, Virginia
   b. Carolina, Connecticut, Delaware, Maryland, Massachusetts, New Hampshire, New Jersey, New York, Ohio, Pennsylvania, Rhode Island, Virginia, West Virginia
   c. Connecticut, Delaware, Georgia, Maine, Massachusetts, New Hampshire, New Jersey, New York, North Carolina, South Carolina, Pennsylvania, Vermont, Virginia
   d. Canada, Connecticut, Delaware, Georgia, Florida, Maryland, Massachusetts, New Hampshire, New York, North Carolina, Rhode Island, South Carolina, Virginia

6. Which of the following consequences did NOT result from the discovery of the New World in 1492 CE?
   a. Proof that the world was round instead of flat
   b. The deaths of millions of Native Americans
   c. Biological exchange between Europe and the New World
   d. The creation of new syncretic religions

7. Which of the following was an important development in the twentieth century?
   a. The United States and the Soviet Union officially declared war on each other in the Cold War.
   b. The League of Nations signed the Kyoto Protocol.
   c. World War I ended when the United States defeated Japan.
   d. India violently partitioned into India and Pakistan after the end of colonialism.

Questions 8–12 are based upon the following passage:

> Four score and seven years ago our fathers brought forth on this continent, a new nation, conceived in liberty, and dedicated to the proposition that all men are created equal.
>
> Now we are engaged in a great civil war, testing whether that nation, or any nation so conceived and so dedicated, can long endure. We are met on a great battlefield of that war. We have come to dedicate a portion of that field, as a final resting place for those who here gave their lives that this nation might live. It is altogether fitting and proper that we should do this.
>
> But, in a larger sense, we cannot dedicate, we cannot consecrate, we cannot hallow this ground.. The brave men, living and dead, who struggled here, have consecrated it, far above our poor power to add or detract. The world will little note, nor long remember what we say here, but it can never forget what they did here. It is for us the living, rather, to be dedicated here to the unfinished work which they who fought here have thus far so nobly advanced. It is rather for us to be here and dedicated to the great task remaining before us—that from these honored dead we take increased devotion to that cause for which they gave the last full measure of devotion—that we here highly resolve that these dead shall not have died in vain—that this nation, under God, shall have a new birth of freedom—and that government of people, by the people, for the people, shall not perish from the earth.

Excerpt from Abraham Lincoln's Address Delivered at the Dedication of the Cemetery at Gettysburg, 1863.

8. Which of the following is the best description for the phrase *four score and seven years ago*?
   a. A unit of measurement
   b. A period of time
   c. A literary movement
   d. A statement of political reform

9. What is the setting of this text?
   a. A battleship off of the coast of France
   b. A desert plain on the Sahara Desert
   c. A battlefield in North America
   d. The residence of Abraham Lincoln

10. What message is the author trying to convey through this address?
    a. The audience should perpetuate the ideals of freedom that the soldiers died fighting for.
    b. The audience should honor the dead by establishing an annual memorial service.
    c. The audience should form a militia that would overturn the current political structure.
    d. The audience should forget the lives that were lost and discredit the soldiers.

11. In the following selection, what does the word *resolve* mean?

    . . . we here highly resolve that these dead shall not have died in vain—that this nation, under God, shall have a new birth of freedom—and that government of people, by the people, for the people, shall not perish from the earth.

    a. Foresee
    b. Request
    c. Prescribe
    d. Decide

12. What is the effect of Lincoln's statement in the following excerpt from the passage?

    But, in a larger sense, we cannot dedicate, we cannot consecrate, we cannot hallow this ground.. The brave men, living and dead, who struggled here, have consecrated it, far above our poor power to add or detract.

    a. His comparison emphasizes the great sacrifice of the soldiers who fought in the war.
    b. His comparison serves as a reminder of the inadequacies of his audience.
    c. His comparison serves as a catalyst for guilt and shame among audience members.
    d. His comparison attempts to illuminate the great differences between soldiers and civilians.

Questions 13–14 are based on the following passage:

> In general, the orientations on the left emphasize social and economic equality and advocate for government intervention to achieve it. Orientations on the right of the spectrum generally value the existing and historical political institutions and oppose government intervention, especially in regard to the economy.
>
> **Communism** is a radical political ideology that seeks to establish common ownership over production and abolish social status and money. Communists believe that the world is split between two social classes—capitalists and the working class (often referred to as the proletariat). Communist politics assert that conflict arises from the inequality between the ruling class and the working class; thus, Communism favors a classless society.
>
> **Conservatism** is a political ideology that prioritizes traditional institutions within a culture and civilization. Conservatives, in general, oppose modern developments and value stability. Since Conservatism depends on the traditional institution, this ideology differs greatly from country to country. Conservatives often emphasize the traditional family structure and the importance of individual self-reliance. Fiscal Conservatism is one of the most common variants, and in general, the proponents of fiscal Conservatism oppose government spending and public debt.
>
> **Progressivism** maintains that progress in the form of scientific and technological advancement, social change, and economic development improve the quality of human life. Progressive ideals

include the view that the political and economic interests of the ruling class suppress progress, which results in perpetual social and economic inequality.

Libertarianism opposes state intervention on society and the economy. Libertarians advocate for a weak central government, favoring more local rule, and seek to maximize personal autonomy and protect personal freedom. Libertarians often follow a conservative approach to government, especially in the context of power and intervention, but favor a progressive approach to rights and freedom, especially those tied to personal liberty, like freedom of speech.

Liberalism developed during the Age of Enlightenment in opposition to absolute monarchy, royal privilege, and state religion. In general, Liberalism emphasizes liberty and equality, and liberals support freedom of speech, freedom of religion, free markets, civil rights, gender equality, and secular governance. Liberals support government intervention into private matters to further social justice and fight inequality; thus, liberals often favor social welfare organizations and economic safety nets to combat income inequality.

Fascism is a form of totalitarianism that became popular in Europe after World War I. Fascists advocate for a centralized government led by an all-powerful dictator, tasked with preparing for total war and mobilizing all resources to benefit the state. This orientation's distinguishing features include a consolidated and centralized government.

Socialism is closely tied to an economic system. Socialists prioritize the health of the community over the rights of individuals, seeking collective and equitable ownership over the means of production. Socialists tend to be willing to work to elect Socialist policies, like social security, universal health care, unemployment benefits, and other programs related to building a societal safety net.

13. Using the information from the passages above and the introduction about left-axis and right-axis political orientations, which of the following correctly categorizes the orientations mentioned in the passage?

a. Left-axis ideologies: Socialism, Progressivism, Liberalism; Right-axis ideologies: Fascism, Libertarianism, Communism, Conservatism
b. Left-axis ideologies: Socialism, Progressivism, Liberalism, Communism; Right-axis ideologies: Fascism, Libertarianism, Conservatism
c. Left-axis ideologies: Socialism, Progressivism, Libertarianism, Liberalism; Right-axis ideologies: Fascism, Communism, Conservatism
d. Left-axis ideologies: Socialism, Progressivism, Libertarianism, Communism; Right-axis ideologies: Fascism, Liberalism, Conservatism

14. Which of the following correctly states one of the biggest differences between Fascism and Libertarianism?

a. Fascists favor a powerful, centralized government, whereas Libertarians favor powerful local rule.
b. Fascists prioritize governmental spending on strengthening the military, whereas Libertarians believe governmental involvement in terms of power and intervention should be minimal.
c. Fascists favor a powerful localized government, whereas Libertarians favor a powerful, centralized government.
d. Fascists believe governmental involvement in terms of power and intervention should be minimal, whereas Libertarians prioritize governmental spending on strengthening the military.

Questions 15–18 are based on the following passage:

> Immigrants and emigrants move for physical, cultural, economic, and political reasons. An immigrant is a person who comes from another country to the one currently being discussed, While an emigrant is a person who leaves their home country to settle elsewhere. Geographers traditionally separate reasons for migration into push and pull factors. Political push factors include war, government-induced violence and intimidation, genocide, or oppression. Economic push factors include economic depressions or panics, among other factors. Political pull factors include things like the lure of democracy, safety, and liberty. Economic pull factors include job creation, higher wages, and low unemployment rates. Environmental push factors include flooding, natural disasters, droughts, nuclear contamination, and water contamination. Environmental pull factors include more hospitable climates, low chances of natural disasters, and outdoor aesthetics.

15. Using the information from the passage, as well as your knowledge of social studies concepts, which of the following statements is correct?
    a. Refugees may immigrate from their country because of political push factors.
    b. Refugees may emigrate from their country because of political push factors.
    c. Refugees may immigrate from their country because of political pull factors.
    d. Refugees may emigrate from their country because of political pull factors.

16. During the 1960s–1980s, deindustrialization in cities in the Industrial North (now called the "Rust Belt"), including hubs like Buffalo, Cleveland, Chicago, and Milwaukee, would be considered an example of which of the following?
    a. Political push factor
    b. Political pull factor
    c. Economic push factor
    d. Economic pull factor

17. In the late 19th and early 20th centuries, millions of people immigrated to the United States from Europe because they were enamored by the purported freedoms in the United States. This would be an example of which of the following?
    a. Political push factor
    b. Political pull factor
    c. Economic push factor
    d. Economic pull factor

18. The relocation of many people from the Sahel region of North Africa to other areas because of intense droughts is an example of which of the following?
    a. Political push factor
    b. Political pull factor
    c. Environmental push factor
    d. Environmental pull factor

Question 19 is based on the following map:

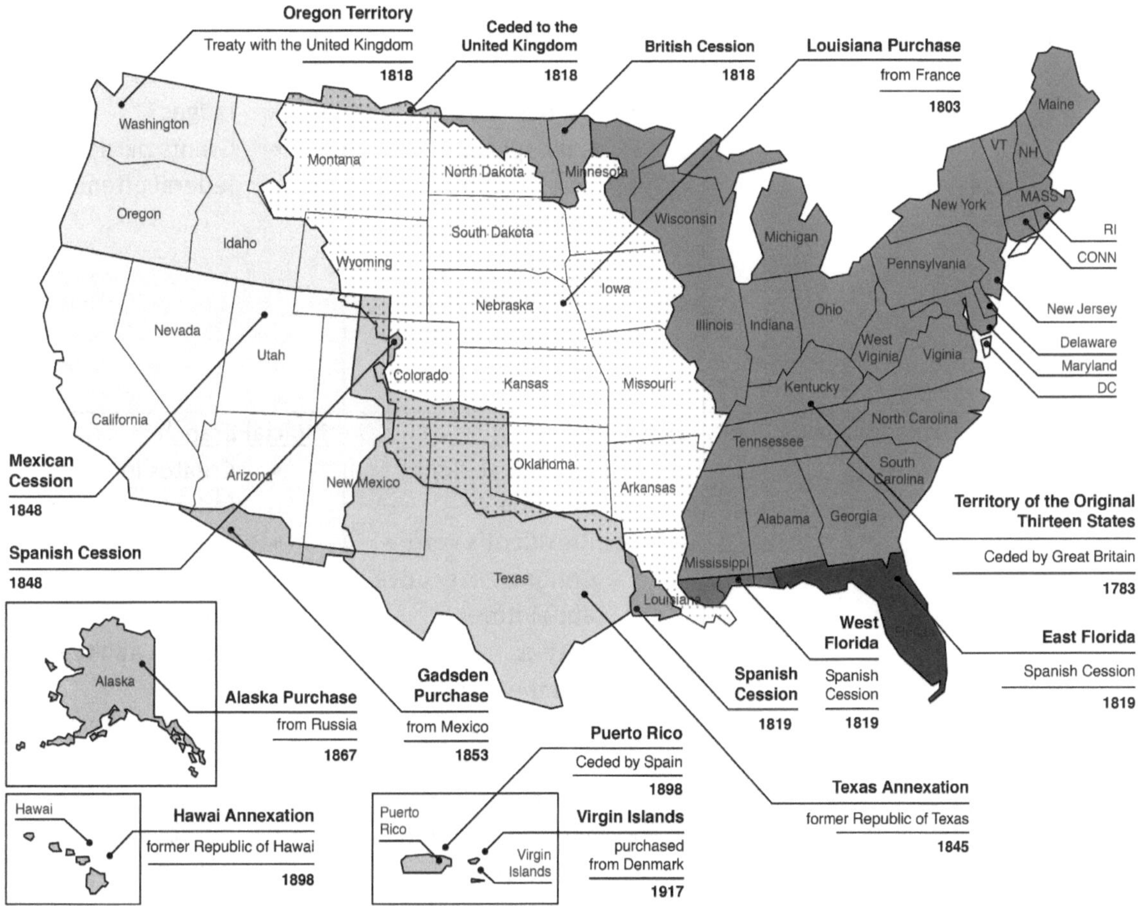

19. What current state did the United States gain through military force with a non-native nation-state?
    a. Nebraska
    b. Missouri
    c. Alaska
    d. Nevada

20. Which of these choices BEST describes a participatory democracy?
    a. A system in which only the educated and wealthy members of society vote and decide upon the leaders of the country
    b. A system in which groups come together to advance certain select interests
    c. A system that emphasizes everyone contributing to the political system
    d. A system in which one group makes decisions for the population at large

Questions 21 and 22 are based on the following table:

Branch	Role	Checks & Balances on Other Branches	
Executive	Carries out the laws	<u>Legislative Branch</u> • Proposes laws • Vetoes laws • Calls special sessions of Congress • Makes appointments • Negotiates foreign treaties	<u>Judicial Branch</u> • Appoints federal judges • Grants pardons to federal offenders
Legislative	Makes the laws	<u>Executive Branch</u> • Has the ability to override a President's veto • Confirms executive appointments • Ratifies treaties • Has the ability to declare war • Appropriates money • Has the ability to impeach and remove President	<u>Judicial Branch</u> • Creates lower federal courts • Has the ability to impeach and remove judges • Has the ability to propose amendments to overrule judicial decisions • Approves appointments of federal judges
Judicial	Interprets the laws	<u>Executive Branch</u> • Has the ability to declare executive actions unconstitutional	<u>Legislative Branch</u> • Has the ability to declare acts of Congress unconstitutional

21. Using the table provided and your understanding of checks and balances, which of the following is true regarding legislation?

a. Members of Congress debate and vote on legislation, although the president may request that legislators consider a certain proposal. The legislation will pass through Congress if it receives a three-quarters majority in both chambers, but the president can veto legislation that he or she disagrees with. The Supreme Court may review legislation and declare it unconstitutional.
b. Members of Congress debate and vote on legislation, although the president may request that legislators consider a certain proposal. The legislation will pass through Congress if it receives a two-thirds majority in both chambers, but the president can veto legislation that he or she disagrees with. The Supreme Court may review legislation and declare it unconstitutional.
c. Members of Congress debate and vote on legislation, although the president may request that legislators consider a certain proposal. The president may veto legislation that he or she disagrees with, but Congress can override the veto with a three-quarters majority in both chambers. The Supreme Court may review legislation and declare it unconstitutional.
d. Members of Congress debate and vote on legislation, although the president may request that legislators consider a certain proposal. The president may veto legislation that he or she disagrees with, but Congress can override the veto with a two-thirds majority in both chambers. The Supreme Court may review legislation and declare it unconstitutional.

22. Using the table provided and your understanding of checks and balances, which of the following is true regarding federal judges?

a. The Legislative branch appoints federal judges, but the Executive branch can impeach and remove judges.
b. The Executive branch appoints federal judges, but the Legislative branch can impeach and remove judges.
c. The Judicial branch appoints federal judges, but the Executive branch can impeach and remove judges.
d. The Judicial branch appoints federal judges, but the Legislative branch can impeach and remove judges.

Questions 23 and 24 are based on the following passage:

> The creed which accepts as the foundation of morals, Utility, or the Greatest-Happiness Principle, holds that actions are right in proportion as they tend to promote happiness, wrong as they tend to produce the reverse of happiness. By happiness is intended pleasure, and the absence of pain; by unhappiness, pain, and the privation of pleasure.
>
> The utilitarian morality does recognise in human beings the power of sacrificing their own greatest good for the good of others. It only refuses to admit that the sacrifice is itself a good. A sacrifice which does not increase, or tend to increase, the sum total of happiness, it considers as wasted.

Excerpt from John Stuart Mills' <u>Utilitarianism</u>, 1861

23. What is the meaning of the "Utility"?
    a. Actions should be judged based on the net total of pleasure.
    b. Actions requiring sacrifice can never be valuable.
    c. Actions promoting sacrifice that increase happiness are more valuable than actions that only increase happiness.
    d. Actions can be valuable even if the pain outweighs the pleasure.

24. What is John Stuart Mills best known for?
    a. For being a social justice advocate during the Civil Rights Movement.
    b. For being the fifth Vice President of the United States.
    c. For being the first member of Parliament to advocate for women's right to vote.
    d. For making the call to counterattack after Pearl Harbor.

Questions 25 and 26 are based on the following passage:

> The history of all hitherto existing society is the history of class struggles.
>
> Freeman and slave, patrician and plebeian, lord and serf, guildmaster and journeyman, in a word, oppressor and oppressed, stood in constant opposition to one another, carried on an uninterrupted, now hidden, now open fight, that each time ended, either in the revolutionary reconstitution of society at large, or in the common ruin of the contending classes.
>
> Let the ruling classes tremble at a Communistic revolution. The proletarians have nothing to lose but their chains. They have a world to win.
>
> Workingmen of all countries unite!

Karl Marx and Friedrich Engels, The Communist Manifesto, 1848

25. What's the main idea presented in the passage?
    a. Working men are morally superior to the ruling class.
    b. Every society will come to an end at some point.
    c. History is defined by class struggle, and working men must now unite and fight the ruling class to gain freedom.
    d. Working men are in the same position as the slave, plebeian, serf, and journeyman.

26. Which of the following identities did Karl Marx NOT adhere to?
    a. Revolutionary
    b. Fascist
    c. Social scientist
    d. Historian

Questions 27 and 28 are based on the following image:

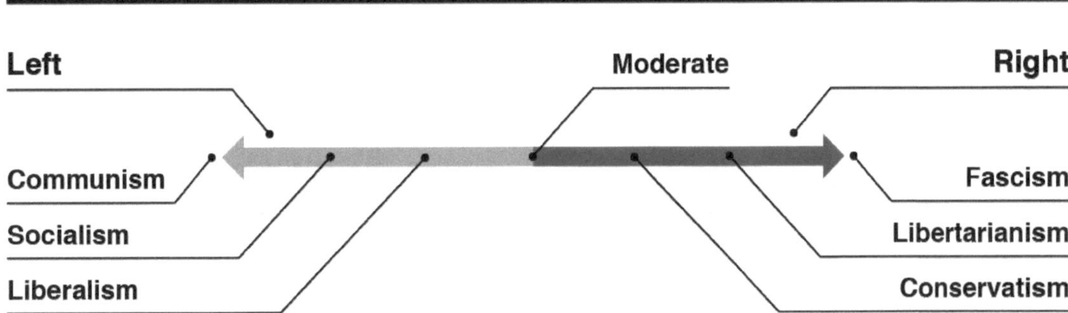

27. Of the following ideologies, which one advocates for the most radical government intervention to achieve social and economic equality?
    a. Socialism
    b. Liberalism
    c. Libertarianism
    d. Fascism

28. Of the following ideologies, which one prioritizes stability and traditional institutions within a culture?
    a. Socialism
    b. Liberalism
    c. Conservatism
    d. Libertarianism

Questions 29 and 30 are based on the following diagram:

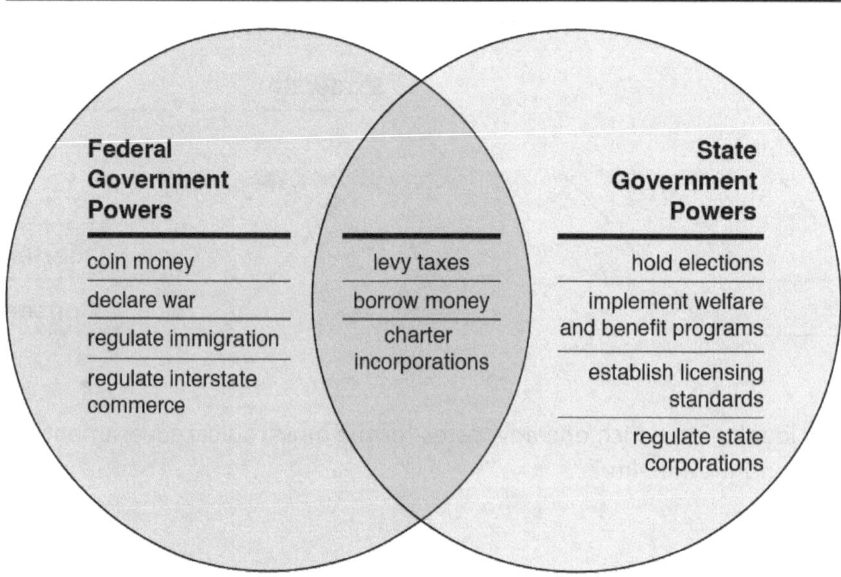

29. Which of the following terms best describes the missing title in the circles?
   a. Reserved powers
   b. Implied powers
   c. Delegated powers
   d. Concurrent powers

30. Although not listed on the diagram as depicted, implied powers do what?
   a. Implied powers are the specific powers granted to the federal government by the Constitution.
   b. Implied powers are the unwritten powers that can be reasonably inferred from the Constitution.
   c. Implied powers are the reasonable powers required by the government to manage the nation's affairs and maintain sovereignty.
   d. Implied powers are the unspecified powers belonging to the state that are not expressly granted to the federal government or denied to the state by the Constitution .

Questions 31 and 32 are based on the following passage:

> Ambition must be made to counteract ambition. The interest of the man must be connected with the constitutional rights of the place. It may be a reflection on human nature, that such devices should be necessary to control the abuses of government. But what is government itself, but the greatest of all reflections on human nature?
>
> If men were angels, no government would be necessary. If angels were to govern men, neither external nor internal controls on government would be necessary. In framing a government which is to be administered by men over men, the great difficulty lies in this: you must first enable the government to control the governed; and in the next place oblige it to control itself.

Alexander Hamilton or James Madison, aka *Publius*, "Federalist No. 50," 1788

31. What is the main idea presented in the excerpt?
    a. Men are inherently immoral and abusive.
    b. The best form of government is the type that angels would construct.
    c. Government reflects human nature.
    d. An effective government requires a separation of powers to regulate itself.

32. What were the "Federalist Papers"?
    a. Debates anonymously between the Federalists and the Anti-Federalists.
    b. A document identifying basic liberties.
    c. A document which articulated America's system of government.
    d. A document that required the colonists to pay a tax on legal documents, newspapers, magazines and other printed materials.

Questions 33 and 34 are based on the following diagram:

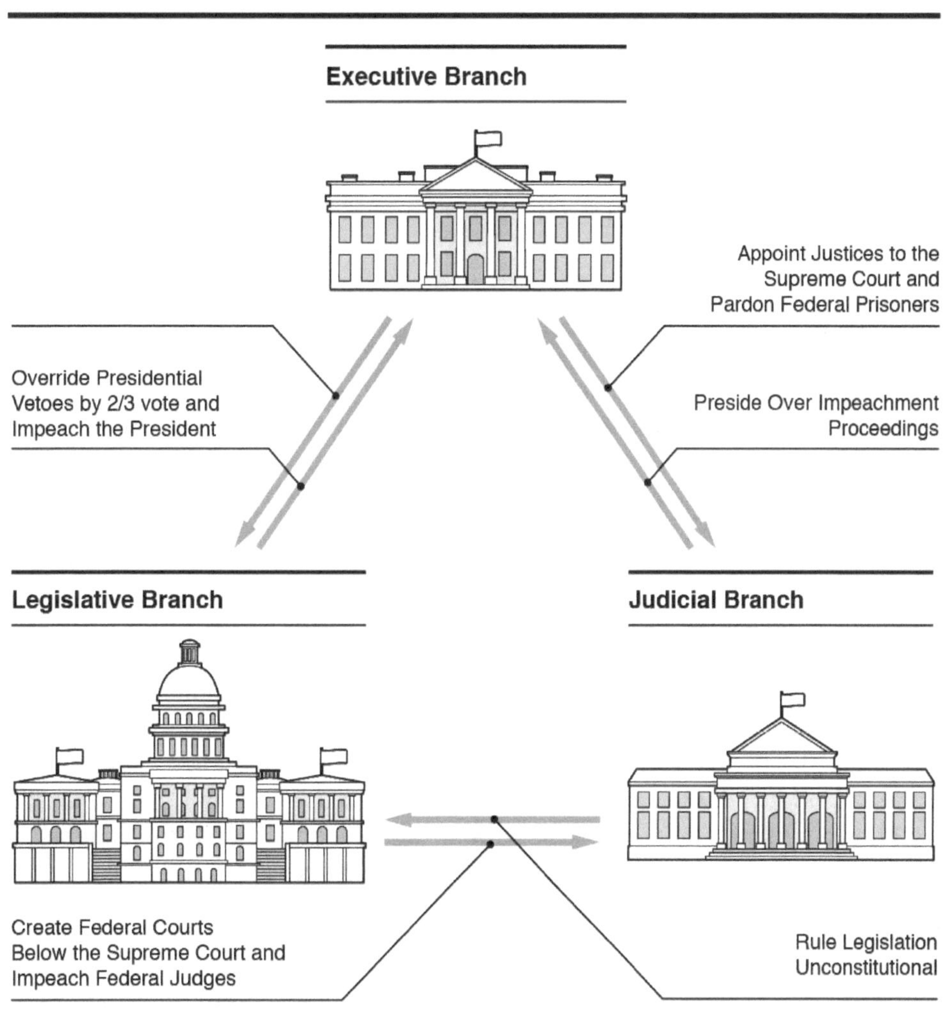

33. Which of the following answer choices best completes the diagram?
    a. Impeach congressmen and veto legislation
    b. Call special sessions of Congress and refuse to enforce laws
    c. Call special sessions of Congress and veto legislation
    d. Impeach congressmen and refuse to enforce laws

34. What amendment guarantees American citizens the right to keep and bear arms?
    a. First Amendment
    b. Second Amendment
    c. Third Amendment
    d. Fourth Amendment

Questions 35 and 36 are based on the following table:

Presidential Election of 1824			
Candidate	**Electoral Votes**	**Popular Votes**	**State Votes in the House of Representatives**
Andrew Jackson	99	153,544	7
John Quincy Adams	84	108,740	13
William H. Crawford	41	46,618	4
Henry Clay	37	47,136	0

35. Who won the presidential election of 1824?
    a. Andrew Jackson
    b. John Quincy Adams
    c. William H. Crawford
    d. Henry Clay

36. What electoral system can result in a second round of voting commonly referred to as a runoff?
    a. Majority systems
    b. Plurality systems
    c. Single transferable systems
    d. Party list systems

Questions 37–42 are based upon the following passage:

> Fellow citizens—Pardon me, and allow me to ask, why am I called upon to speak here today? What have I, or those I represent, to do with your national independence? Are the great principles of political freedom and of natural justice embodied in that Declaration of Independence, Independence extended to us? And am I therefore called upon to bring our humble offering to the national altar, and to confess the benefits, and express devout gratitude for the blessings, resulting from your independence to us?
>
> Would to God, both for your sakes and ours, ours that an affirmative answer could be truthfully returned to these questions! Then would my task be light, and my burden easy and delightful. For who is there so cold that a nation's sympathy could not warm him? Who so obdurate and dead to the claims of gratitude that would not thankfully acknowledge such priceless benefits? Who so stolid and selfish, that would not give his

voice to swell the hallelujahs of a nation's jubilee, when the chains of servitude had been torn from his limbs? I am not that man. In a case like that, the dumb my eloquently speak, and the lame man leap as a hart.

But, such is not the state of the case. I say it with a sad sense of the disparity between us. I am not included within the pale of this glorious and anniversary. Oh pity! Your high independence only reveals the immeasurable distance between us. The blessings in which you this day rejoice, I do not enjoy in common. The rich inheritance of justice, liberty, prosperity, and independence, bequeathed by your fathers, is shared by *you*, not by *me*. This Fourth of July is *yours,* not *mine*. You may rejoice, *I* must mourn. To drag a man in fetters into the grand illuminated temple of liberty, and call upon him to join you in joyous anthems, were inhuman mockery and sacrilegious irony. Do you mean, citizens, to mock me, by asking me to speak today? If so there is a parallel to your conduct. And let me warn you that it is dangerous to copy the example of a nation whose crimes, towering up to heaven, were thrown down by the breath of the Almighty, burying that nation and irrecoverable ruin! I can today take up the plaintive lament of a peeled and woe-smitten people.

By the rivers of Babylon, there we sat down. Yea! We wept when we remembered Zion. We hanged our harps upon the willows in the midst thereof. For there, they that carried us away captive, required of us a song; and they who wasted us required of us mirth, saying, "Sing us one of the songs of Zion." How can we sing the Lord's song in a strange land? If I forget thee, O Jerusalem, let my right hand forget her cunning. If I do not remember thee, let my tongue cleave to the roof of my mouth.

Excerpt from speech "What to the Slave is the Fourth of July?" by Frederick Douglass, 1852

37. What is the tone of the first paragraph of this passage?
  a. Exasperated
  b. Inclusive
  c. Contemplative
  d. Nonchalant

38. Which word CANNOT be used synonymously with the term *obdurate* as it is conveyed in the sentence below?

> Who so obdurate and dead to the claims of gratitude, that would not thankfully acknowledge such priceless benefits?

  a. Steadfast
  b. Stubborn
  c. Contented
  d. Unwavering

39. What is the central purpose of this text?
  a. To demonstrate the author's extensive knowledge of the Bible
  b. To address the feelings of exclusion expressed by African Americans after the establishment of the Fourth of July holiday
  c. To convince wealthy landowners to adopt new holiday rituals
  d. To explain why minorities often relished the notion of segregation in government institutions

40. Which statement serves as evidence for the question above?
   a. By the rivers of Babylon...down.
   b. Fellow citizens...today.
   c. I can...woe-smitten people.
   d. The rich inheritance of justice...*not by me*.

41. The statement below features an example of which of the following literary devices?

> Oh pity! Your high independence only reveals the immeasurable distance between us.

   a. Assonance
   b. Parallelism
   c. Amplification
   d. Hyperbole

42. The speaker's use of biblical references, such as "rivers of Babylon" and the "songs of Zion," helps the reader to do all EXCEPT which of the following?
   a. Identify with the speaker using common text
   b. Convince the audience that injustices have been committed by referencing another group of people who have been previously affected by slavery
   c. Display the equivocation of the speaker and those that he represents
   d. Appeal to the listener's sense of humanity

Questions 43–48 are based upon the following passage:

> "MANKIND being originally equals in the order of creation, the equality could only be destroyed by some subsequent circumstance; the distinctions of rich, and poor, may in a great measure be accounted for, and that without having recourse to the harsh ill sounding names of oppression and avarice. Oppression is often the consequence, but seldom or never the means of riches; and though avarice will preserve a man from being necessitously poor, it generally makes him too timorous to be wealthy.
>
> But there is another and greater distinction for which no truly natural or religious reason can be assigned, and that is, the distinction of men into KINGS and SUBJECTS. Male and female are the distinctions of nature, good and bad the distinctions of heaven; but how a race of men came into the world so exalted above the rest, and distinguished like some new species, is worth enquiring into, and whether they are the means of happiness or of misery to mankind.
>
> In the early ages of the world, according to the scripture chronology, there were no kings; the consequence of which was there were no wars; it is the pride of kings which throw mankind into confusion. Holland without a king hath enjoyed more peace for this last century than any of the monarchical governments in Europe. Antiquity favors the same remark; for the quiet and rural lives of the first patriarchs hath a happy something in them, which vanishes away when we come to the history of Jewish royalty.
>
> Government by kings was first introduced into the world by the Heathens, from whom the children of Israel copied the custom. It was the most prosperous invention the Devil ever set on foot for the promotion of idolatry. The Heathens paid divine honors to their deceased kings, and the Christian world hath improved on the plan by doing the same to

their living ones. How impious is the title of sacred majesty applied to a worm, who in the midst of his splendor is crumbling into dust!

As the exalting one man so greatly above the rest cannot be justified on the equal rights of nature, so neither can it be defended on the authority of scripture; for the will of the Almighty, as declared by Gideon and the prophet Samuel, expressly disapproves of government by kings. All anti-monarchical parts of scripture have been very smoothly glossed over in monarchical governments, but they undoubtedly merit the attention of countries, which have their governments yet to form. "Render unto Caesar the things which are Caesar's" is the scripture doctrine of courts, yet it is no support of monarchical government, for the Jews at that time were without a king, and in a state of vassalage to the Romans.

Near three thousand years passed away from the Mosaic account of the creation, till the Jews under a national delusion requested a king. Till then their form of government (except in extraordinary cases, where the Almighty interposed) was a kind of republic administered by a judge and the elders of the tribes. Kings they had none, and it was held sinful to acknowledge any being under that title but the Lord of Hosts. And when a man seriously reflects on the idolatrous homage which is paid to the persons of Kings, he need not wonder, that the Almighty ever jealous of his honor, should disapprove of a form of government which so impiously invades the prerogative of heaven.

Excerpt from "Common Sense" by Thomas Paine, 1776

43. According to the passage, what role does avarice, or greed, play in poverty?
  a. It can make a man very wealthy.
  b. It is the consequence of wealth.
  c. Avarice can prevent a man from being poor, but too fearful to be very wealthy.
  d. Avarice is what drives a person to be very wealthy

44. Of these distinctions, which does the author believe to be beyond natural or religious reason?
  a. Good and bad
  b. Male and female
  c. Human and animal
  d. King and subjects

45. According to the passage, what are the Heathens responsible for?
  a. Government by kings
  b. Quiet and rural lives of patriarchs
  c. Paying divine honors to their living kings
  d. Equal rights of nature

46. Which of the following best states Paine's rationale for the denouncement of monarchy?
  a. It is against the laws of nature.
  b. It is against the equal rights of nature and is denounced in scripture.
  c. Despite scripture, a monarchal government is unlawful.
  d. Neither the law nor scripture denounce monarchy.

47. Based on the passage, what is the best definition of the word *idolatrous*?
    a. Worshipping heroes
    b. Being deceitful
    c. Sinfulness
    d. Engaging in illegal activities

48. What is the essential meaning of the following lines?

> And when a man seriously reflects on the idolatrous homage which is paid to the persons of Kings, he need not wonder, that the Almighty ever jealous of his honor, should disapprove of a form of government which so impiously invades the prerogative of heaven.

    a. God would disapprove of the irreverence of a monarchical government.
    b. With careful reflection, men should realize that heaven is not promised.
    c. God will punish those that follow a monarchical government.
    d. Belief in a monarchical government cannot coexist with belief in God.

Question 49 is based on the following passage:

> Hand in hand with this we must frankly recognize the overbalance of population in our industrial centers and, by engaging on a national scale in a redistribution, endeavor to provide a better use of the land for those best fitted for the land. The task can be helped by definite efforts to raise the values of agricultural products and with this the power to purchase the output of our cities. It can be helped by preventing realistically the tragedy of the growing loss through foreclosure of our small homes and our farms. It can be helped by insistence that the Federal, State, and local governments act forthwith on the demand that their cost be drastically reduced. It can be helped by the unifying of relief activities which today are often scattered, uneconomical, and unequal. It can be helped by national planning for and supervision of all forms of transportation and of communications and other utilities which have a definitely public character. There are many ways in which it can be helped, but it can never be helped merely by talking about it. We must act and act quickly.
>
> Finally, in our progress toward a resumption of work we require two safeguards against a return of the evils of the old order: there must be a strict supervision of all banking and credits and investments, so that there will be an end to speculation with other people's money; and there must be provision for an adequate but sound currency.

President Franklin D. Roosevelt, Inaugural Address, March 4, 1933

49. Which of the following best describes President Roosevelt's underlying approach to government?
    a. Government must be focused on redistribution of land.
    b. Government must "act and act quickly" to intervene and regulate the economy.
    c. Government must exercise "strict supervision of all banking."
    d. Government must prevent the "growing loss through foreclosure."

Question 50 is based on the following passage:

> What, to the American slave, is your 4th of July? I answer: a day that reveals to him, more than all other days in the year, the gross injustice and cruelty to which he is the constant victim. To him, your celebration is a sham; your boasted liberty, an unholy license; your national greatness,

swelling vanity; your sounds of rejoicing are empty and heartless; your denunciations of tyrants, brass fronted impudence; your shouts of liberty and equality, hollow mockery; your prayers and hymns, your sermons and thanksgivings, with all your religious parade, and solemnity, are, to him, mere bombast, fraud, deception, impiety, and hypocrisy—a thin veil to cover up crimes which would disgrace a nation of savages. There is not a nation on the earth guilty of practices, more shocking and bloody, than are the people of these United States, at this very hour.

Excerpt from "What to the Slave is the Fourth of July?" by Frederick Douglass, 1852

50. What is the specific hypocrisy that Douglass repudiates?
   a. The Declaration of Independence declared that all men are created equal, but Thomas Jefferson owned slaves.
   b. Americans are free, but they do not value their freedom.
   c. The Fourth of July is a celebration about freedom, and slavery remained legal in the United States.
   d. The United States is a Christian nation, but American traditions contradict their faith.

Question 51 is based on the following passage:

May it please your honor, I shall never pay a dollar of your unjust penalty. All the stock in trade I possess is a $10,000 debt, incurred by publishing my paper—The Revolution—four years ago, the sole object of which was to educate all women to do precisely as I have done, rebel against your man-made, unjust, unconstitutional forms of law, that tax, fine, imprison and hang women, while they deny them the right of representation in the government; and I shall work on with might and main to pay every dollar of that honest debt, but not a penny shall go to this unjust claim. And I shall earnestly and persistently continue to urge all women to the practical recognition of the old revolutionary maxim, that "Resistance to tyranny is obedience to God."

An Account of the Proceedings on the Trial of Susan B. Anthony on the Charge of Illegal Voting, 1874.

51. What is the main idea presented in the excerpt?
   a. Taxation without representation is tyranny.
   b. Domestic abuse and violence against women is the cause of tyranny.
   c. Anthony cannot pay her fine due to debt accumulated from fighting for women's rights.
   d. Denying women the right to vote is tyranny and must be resisted.

52. Which of the following most accurately describes the platform of Ronald Reagan?
   a. Christianity, optimism, and preserving social safety nets
   b. Increased defense spending, deregulation, and tax cuts
   c. Moral majority, international cooperation, and compromise
   d. Conservatism, opposition to abortion, and organized labor

Question 53 is based on the following graph:

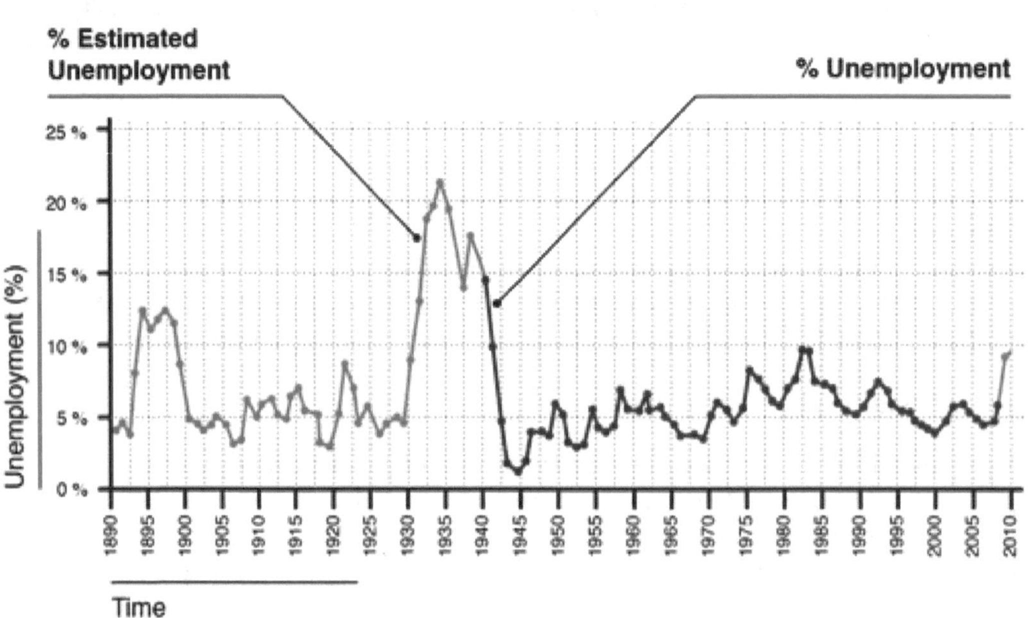

53. Which event caused the second largest increase in unemployment in American history?
    a. Panic of 1893
    b. Depression of 1920
    c. Depression of 1929
    d. Great Recession of 2007

Questions 54–55 are based on the following passage:

> I heartily accept the motto, "that government is best which governs least," and I should like to see it acted up to more rapidly and systematically. Carried out, it finally amounts to this, which also I believe—"that government is best which governs not at all," and when men are prepared for it, that will be the kind of government which they will have. Government is at best but an expedient; but most governments are usually, and all governments are sometimes, inexpedient. The objections which have been brought against a standing army, and they are many and weighty, and deserve to prevail, may also at last be brought against a standing government. The standing army is only an arm of the standing government. The government itself, which is only the mode which the people have chosen to execute their will, is equally liable to be abused and perverted before the people can act through it. Witness the present Mexican war, the work of comparatively a few individuals using the standing government as their tool; for, in the outset, the people would not have consented to this measure.
>
> This American government—what is it but a tradition, though a recent one, endeavoring to transmit itself unimpaired to posterity, but each instant losing some of its integrity? It has not the vitality and force of a single living man; for a single man can bend it to his will. It is a sort of wooden gun to the people themselves. But it is not the less necessary for this; for the people must have some complicated machinery or other, and hear its din, to satisfy that idea of

government which they have. Governments show thus how successfully men can be imposed on, even impose on themselves, for their own advantage. It is excellent, we must all allow. Yet this government never of itself furthered any enterprise, but by the alacrity with which it got out of its way. It does not keep the country free. It does not settle the West. It does not educate. The character inherent in the American people has done all that has been accomplished; and it would have done somewhat more, if the government had not sometimes got in its way. For government is an expedient by which men would fain succeed in letting one another alone; and, as has been said, when it is most expedient, the governed are most let alone by it. Trade and commerce, if they were not made of india-rubber, would never manage to bounce over the obstacles which legislators are continually putting in their way; and, if one were to judge these men wholly by the effects of their actions and not partly by their intentions, they would deserve to be classed and punished with those mischievous persons who put obstructions on the railroads.

But, to speak practically and as a citizen, unlike those who call themselves no-government men, I ask for, not at once no government, but at once a better government. Let every man make known what kind of government would command his respect, and that will be one step toward obtaining it.

Excerpt from Civil Disobedience by Henry David Thoreau, 1847

54. Which phrase best encapsulates Thoreau's use of the term *expedient* in the first paragraph?
    a. A dead end
    b. A state of order
    c. A means to an end
    d. Rushed construction

55. Which best describes Thoreau's view on the Mexican War?
    a. Government is inherently corrupt because it must wage war.
    b. Government can easily be manipulated by a few individuals for their own agenda.
    c. Government is a tool for the people, but it can also act against their interest.
    d. The Mexican War was a necessary action, but not all the people believed this.

Questions 56–57 are based on the following passage:

Christopher Columbus is often credited for discovering America. This is incorrect. First, it is impossible to "discover" somewhere where people already live; however, Christopher Columbus did explore places in the New World that were previously untouched by Europe, so the term "explorer" would be more accurate. Another correction must be made, as well: Christopher Columbus was not the first European explorer to reach the present-day Americas! Rather, it was Leif Erikson who first came to the New World and contacted the natives, nearly five hundred years before Christopher Columbus.

Leif Erikson, the son of Erik the Red (a famous Viking outlaw and explorer in his own right), was born in either 970 or 980, depending on which historian you seek. His own family, though, did not raise Leif, which was a Viking tradition. Instead, one of Erik's prisoners taught Leif reading and writing, languages, sailing, and weaponry. At age 12,

Leif was considered a man and returned to his family. He killed a man during a dispute shortly after his return, and the council banished the Erikson clan to Greenland.

In 999, Leif left Greenland and traveled to Norway where he would serve as a guard to King Olaf Tryggvason. It was there that he became a convert to Christianity. Leif later tried to return home with the intention of taking supplies and spreading Christianity to Greenland, however his ship was blown off course and he arrived in a strange new land: present day Newfoundland, Canada.

When he finally returned to his adopted homeland Greenland, Leif consulted with a merchant who had also seen the shores of this previously unknown land we now know as Canada. The son of the legendary Viking explorer then gathered a crew of 35 men and set sail. Leif became the first European to touch foot in the New World as he explored present-day Baffin Island and Labrador, Canada. His crew called the land "Vinland," since it was plentiful with grapes.

During their time in present-day Newfoundland, Leif's expedition made contact with the natives whom they referred to as Skraelings (which translates to "wretched ones" in Norse). There are several secondhand accounts of their meetings. Some contemporaries described trade between the peoples. Other accounts describe clashes where the Skraelings defeated the Viking explorers with long spears, while still others claim the Vikings dominated the natives. Regardless of the circumstances, it seems that the Vikings made contact of some kind. This happened around 1000, nearly five hundred years before Columbus famously sailed the ocean blue.

Eventually, in 1003, Leif set sail for home and arrived at Greenland with a ship full of timber. In 1020, seventeen years later, the legendary Viking died. Many believe that Leif Erikson should receive more credit for his contributions in exploring the New World.

56. Which of the following best describes how the author generally presents the information?
    a. Chronological order
    b. Comparison-contrast
    c. Cause-effect
    d. Conclusion-premises

57. Which of the following is an opinion, rather than historical fact, expressed by the author?
    a. Leif Erikson was definitely the son of Erik the Red; however, historians debate the year of his birth.
    b. Leif Erikson's crew called the land "Vinland," since it was plentiful with grapes.
    c. Leif Erikson deserves more credit for his contributions in exploring the New World.
    d. Leif Erikson explored the Americas nearly five hundred years before Christopher Columbus.

58. Which of the following most accurately describes the author's main conclusion?
    a. Leif Erikson is a legendary Viking explorer.
    b. Leif Erikson deserves more credit for exploring America hundreds of years before Columbus.
    c. Spreading Christianity motivated Leif Erikson's expeditions more than any other factor.
    d. Leif Erikson contacted the natives nearly five hundred years before Columbus.

59. Which of the following best describes the author's intent in the passage?
   a. To entertain
   b. To inform
   c. To alert
   d. To suggest

60. Which of the following can be logically inferred from the passage?
   a. The Vikings disliked exploring the New World.
   b. Leif Erikson's banishment from Iceland led to his exploration of present-day Canada.
   c. Leif Erikson never shared his stories of exploration with the King of Norway.
   d. Historians have difficulty definitively pinpointing events in the Vikings' history.

61. Regime types fall along a continuum between which two extremes?
   a. Constitutional and non-constitutional
   b. Military and judicial
   c. Federal and communist
   d. Authoritarian and democratic

62. Which political concept describes a ruling body's ability to influence the actions, behaviors, or attitudes of a person or community?
   a. Authority
   b. Sovereignty
   c. Power
   d. Legitimacy

63. The period of business and industrial growth from 1876 through the turn of the twentieth century was deemed by author Mark Twain as what?
   a. Manifest Destiny
   b. The Columbian Exchange
   c. The New Deal
   d. The Gilded Age

64. Which of the following statements would make the best conclusion to an essay about civil rights activist Rosa Parks?
   a. On December 1, 1955, Rosa Parks refused to give up her bus seat to a white passenger, setting in motion the Montgomery bus boycott.
   b. Rosa Parks was a hero to many and came to symbolize the way that ordinary people could bring about real change in the Civil Rights Movement.
   c. Rosa Parks died in 2005 in Detroit, having moved from Montgomery shortly after the bus boycott.
   d. Rosa Parks' arrest was an early part of the Civil Rights Movement and helped lead to the passage of the Civil Rights Act of 1964.

Questions 65 and 66 are based on the graphic that follows a brief introduction to the topic:

The United States Constitution directs Congress to conduct a census of the population to determine the country's population and demographic information. The United States Census Bureau carries out the survey. In 1790, then Secretary of State Thomas Jefferson conducted the first census, and the most recent U.S. census was in 2010. The next U.S. census will be the first to be issued primarily through the Internet.

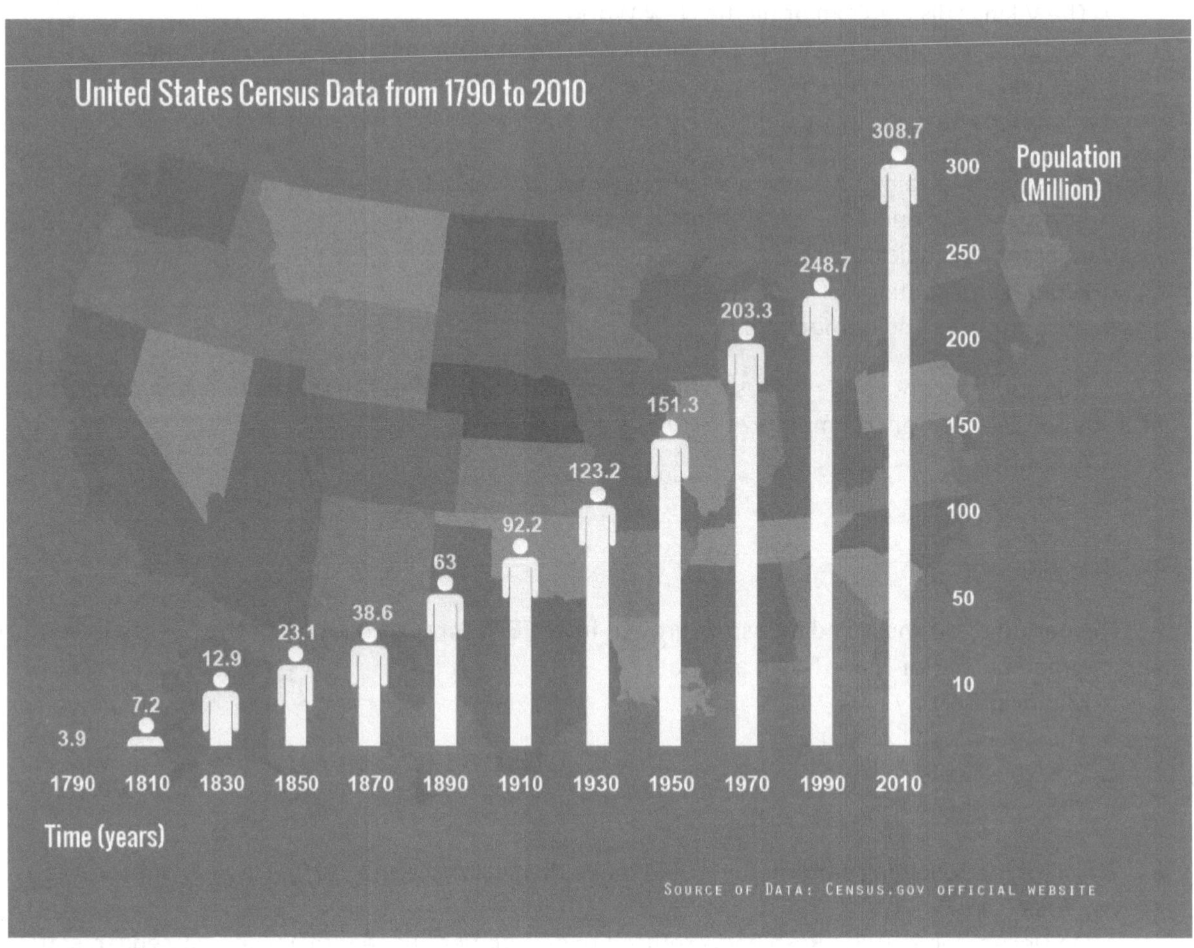

65. In which of the following years was the United States population less than it was in 1930?
    a. 1950
    b. 1970
    c. 1910
    d. 1990

66. In what year did the population increase the most during a twenty-year interval?
    a. From 1930 to 1950
    b. From 1950 to 1970
    c. From 1970 to 1990
    d. From 1990 to 2010

67. Latitudinal lines are used to measure distance
    a. from East to west
    b. from North to south
    c. Between two sets of coordinates
    d. In an inexact manner

68. Which best describes ethnic groups?
    a. Subgroups within a population who share a common history, language, or religion
    b. Divisive groups within a nation's boundaries seeking independence
    c. People who choose to leave a location
    d. Any minority group within a nation's boundaries

69. Which kind of market does not involve government interventions or monopolies while trades are made between suppliers and buyers?
    a. Free
    b. Command
    c. Gross
    d. Exchange

Questions 70–75 are based upon the following passage:

This excerpt is an adaptation from Abraham Lincoln's Address Delivered at the Dedication of the Cemetery at Gettysburg, November 19, 1863.

> Four score and seven years ago our fathers brought forth on this continent, a new nation, conceived in liberty, and dedicated to the proposition that all men are created equal.
>
> Now we are engaged in a great civil war, testing whether that nation, or any nation so conceived and so dedicated, can long endure. We are met on a great battlefield of that war. We have come to dedicate a portion of that field, as a final resting place for those who here gave their lives that this nation might live. It is altogether fitting and proper that we should do this.
>
> But, in a larger sense, we cannot dedicate, we cannot consecrate, we cannot hallow this ground.. The brave men, living and dead, who struggled here, have consecrated it, far above our poor power to add or detract. The world will little note, nor long remember what we say here, but it can never forget what they did here. It is for us the living, rather, to be dedicated here to the unfinished work which they who fought here have thus far so nobly advanced. It is rather for us to be here and dedicated to the great task remaining before us—that from these honored dead we take increased devotion to that cause for which they gave the last full measure of devotion—that we here highly resolve that these dead shall not have died in vain—that this nation, under God, shall have a new birth of freedom—and that government of people, by the people, for the people, shall not perish from the earth.

70. The best description for the phrase *four score and seven years ago* is which of the following?
   a. A unit of measurement
   b. A period of time
   c. A literary movement
   d. A statement of political reform

71. What is the setting of this text?
   a. A battleship off of the coast of France
   b. A desert plain on the Sahara Desert
   c. A battlefield in North America
   d. The residence of Abraham Lincoln

72. Which war is Abraham Lincoln referring to in the following passage?

> Now we are engaged in a great civil war, testing whether that nation, or any nation so conceived and so dedicated, can long endure.

   a. World War I
   b. The War of the Spanish Succession
   c. World War II
   d. The American Civil War

73. What message is the author trying to convey through this address?
   a. The audience should perpetuate the ideals of freedom that the soldiers died fighting for.
   b. The audience should honor the dead by establishing an annual memorial service.
   c. The audience should form a militia that would overturn the current political structure.
   d. The audience should forget the lives that were lost and discredit the soldiers.

74. In the following selection, what does the word *resolve* mean?

> . . . we here highly resolve that these dead shall not have died in vain—that this nation, under God, shall have a new birth of freedom—and that government of people, by the people, for the people, shall not perish from the earth.

   a. Foresee
   b. Request
   c. Prescribe
   d. Decide

75. What is the effect of Lincoln's statement in the following passage?

> But, in a larger sense, we cannot dedicate, we cannot consecrate, we cannot hallow this ground.. The brave men, living and dead, who struggled here, have consecrated it, far above our poor power to add or detract.

a. His comparison emphasizes the great sacrifice of the soldiers who fought in the war.
b. His comparison serves as a reminder of the inadequacies of his audience.
c. His comparison serves as a catalyst for guilt and shame among audience members.
d. His comparison attempts to illuminate the great differences between soldiers and civilians.

Populations of Countries of the European Union in 1998 and 2007 by percentage

1998

8 %
Poland
9 %
Spain
11 %
Italy
12 %
United Kingdom
30 %
All other countries
- 24 -
17 %
Germany
13 %
France

2007

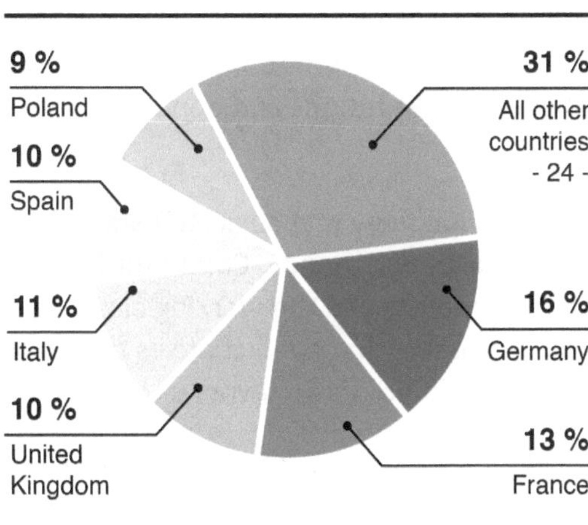

76. According to the pie charts above, how did the population of Germany change from 1998 to 2007?
   a. It decreased one percent
   b. It increased one percent
   c. It decreased three percent
   d. It increased three percent

77. First-hand accounts of an event, subject matter, time period, or an individual are referred to as what type of source?
   a. Primary sources
   b. Secondary sources
   c. Direct sources
   d. Indirect sources

78. Once the Constitution had been drafted, nine of the thirteen states had to ratify it. Vigorous debate erupted over whether or not the Constitution should be approved. Two different political factions emerged. The Federalists supported the Constitution because they felt a stronger central government was necessary in order to promote economic growth and improve national security. Several leading federalists published a series of articles urging voters to support the Constitution. However, the Anti-Federalists felt that the Constitution took too much power away from the states and gave it to the national government. They also thought there weren't enough protections for individual rights and lobbied for the addition of a Bill of Rights that guaranteed basic liberties. Ultimately, the Constitution was ratified in 1788 and the Bill of Rights was approved a year later.

Based on the passage above and your knowledge of social studies, which of the following people would most likely have agreed with the following statement:

> The Constitution should not be approved as is because it gives too much power to the national government.

   a. Alexander Hamilton
   b. James Madison
   c. Thomas Jefferson
   d. John Jay

Questions 79–80 are based on the following passage:

> In general, the orientations on the left emphasize social and economic equality and advocate for government intervention to achieve it. Orientations on the right of the spectrum generally value the existing and historical political institutions and oppose government intervention, especially in regard to the economy.
>
> **Communism** is a radical political ideology that seeks to establish common ownership over production and abolish social status and money. Communists believe that the world is split between two social classes—capitalists and the working class (often referred to as the proletariat). Communist politics assert that conflict arises from the inequality between the ruling class and the working class; thus, Communism favors a classless society.
>
> **Conservatism** is a political ideology that prioritizes traditional institutions within a culture and civilization. Conservatives, in general, oppose modern developments and value stability. Since Conservatism depends on the traditional institution, this ideology differs greatly from country to

country. Conservatives often emphasize the traditional family structure and the importance of individual self-reliance. Fiscal Conservatism is one of the most common variants, and in general, the proponents of fiscal Conservatism oppose government spending and public debt.

Progressivism maintains that progress in the form of scientific and technological advancement, social change, and economic development improve the quality of human life. Progressive ideals include the view that the political and economic interests of the ruling class suppress progress, which results in perpetual social and economic inequality.

Libertarianism opposes state intervention on society and the economy. Libertarians advocate for a weak central government, favoring more local rule, and seek to maximize personal autonomy and protect personal freedom. Libertarians often follow a conservative approach to government, especially in the context of power and intervention, but favor a progressive approach to rights and freedom, especially those tied to personal liberty, like freedom of speech.

Liberalism developed during the Age of Enlightenment in opposition to absolute monarchy, royal privilege, and state religion. In general, Liberalism emphasizes liberty and equality, and liberals support freedom of speech, freedom of religion, free markets, civil rights, gender equality, and secular governance. Liberals support government intervention into private matters to further social justice and fight inequality; thus, liberals often favor social welfare organizations and economic safety nets to combat income inequality.

Fascism is a form of totalitarianism that became popular in Europe after World War I. Fascists advocate for a centralized government led by an all-powerful dictator, tasked with preparing for total war and mobilizing all resources to benefit the state. This orientation's distinguishing features include a consolidated and centralized government.

Socialism is closely tied to an economic system. Socialists prioritize the health of the community over the rights of individuals, seeking collective and equitable ownership over the means of production. Socialists tend to be willing to work to elect Socialist policies, like social security, universal health care, unemployment benefits, and other programs related to building a societal safety net.

79. Using the information from the passages above and the introduction about left-axis and right-axis political orientations, which of the following correctly categorizes the orientations mentioned in the passage?

a. Left-axis ideologies: Socialism, Progressivism, Liberalism; Right-axis ideologies: Fascism, Libertarianism, Communism, Conservatism
b. Left-axis ideologies: Socialism, Progressivism, Liberalism, Communism; Right-axis ideologies: Fascism, Libertarianism, Conservatism
c. Left-axis ideologies: Socialism, Progressivism, Libertarianism, Liberalism; Right-axis ideologies: Fascism, Communism, Conservatism
d. Left-axis ideologies: Socialism, Progressivism, Libertarianism, Communism; Right-axis ideologies: Fascism, Liberalism, Conservatism

80. Which of the following correctly states one of the biggest differences between Fascism and Libertarianism?
    a. Fascists favor a powerful, centralized government, whereas Libertarians favor powerful local rule.
    b. Fascists prioritize governmental spending on strengthening the military, whereas Libertarians believe governmental involvement in terms of power and intervention should be minimal.
    c. Fascists favor a powerful localized government, whereas Libertarians favor a powerful, centralized government.
    d. Fascists believe governmental involvement in terms of power and intervention should be minimal, whereas Libertarians prioritize governmental spending on strengthening the military.

Questions 81–84 are based on the following passage:

> Immigrants and emigrants move for physical, cultural, economic, and political reasons. An immigrant is a person who comes from another country to the one currently being discussed, while an emigrant is a person who leaves their home country to settle elsewhere. Geographers traditionally separate reasons for migration into push and pull factors. Political push factors include war, government-induced violence and intimidation, genocide, or oppression. Economic push factors include economic depressions or panics, among other factors. Political pull factors include things like the lure of democracy, safety, and liberty. Economic pull factors include job creation, higher wages, and low unemployment rates. Environmental push factors include flooding, natural disasters, droughts, nuclear contamination, and water contamination. Environmental pull factors include more hospitable climates, low chances of natural disasters, and outdoor aesthetics.

81. Using the information from the passage, as well as your knowledge of social studies concepts, which of the following statements is correct?
    a. Refugees may immigrate from their country because of political push factors.
    b. Refugees may emigrate from their country because of political push factors.
    c. Refugees may immigrate from their country because of political pull factors.
    d. Refugees may emigrate from their country because of political pull factors.

82. During the 1960s–1980s, deindustrialization in cities in the Industrial North (now called the "Rust Belt"), including hubs like Buffalo, Cleveland, Chicago, and Milwaukee, would be considered an example of which of the following?
    a. Political push factor
    b. Political pull factor
    c. Economic push factor
    d. Economic pull factor

83. In the late 19th and early 20th centuries, millions of people immigrated to the United States from Europe because they were enamored by the purported freedoms in the United States. This would be an example of which of the following?
    a. Political push factor
    b. Political pull factor
    c. Economic push factor
    d. Economic pull factor

84. The relocation of many people from the Sahel region of North Africa to other areas because of intense droughts is an example of which of the following?

a. Political push factor
b. Political pull factor
c. Environmental push factor
d. Environmental pull factor

85. Which of the following is an example of how one main cause of a given effect can actually be subdivided into smaller factors or stretched out in a gradual process?

a. The way the invention of the telegraph caused changes to the way news traveled
b. The way the Japanese attack on Pearl Harbor in 1941 caused the United States to enter into World War II
c. The way Franz Ferdinand's death caused the start of World War I
d. The way slavery caused the Civil War

Please use the graphic below to answer Questions 86 and 87:

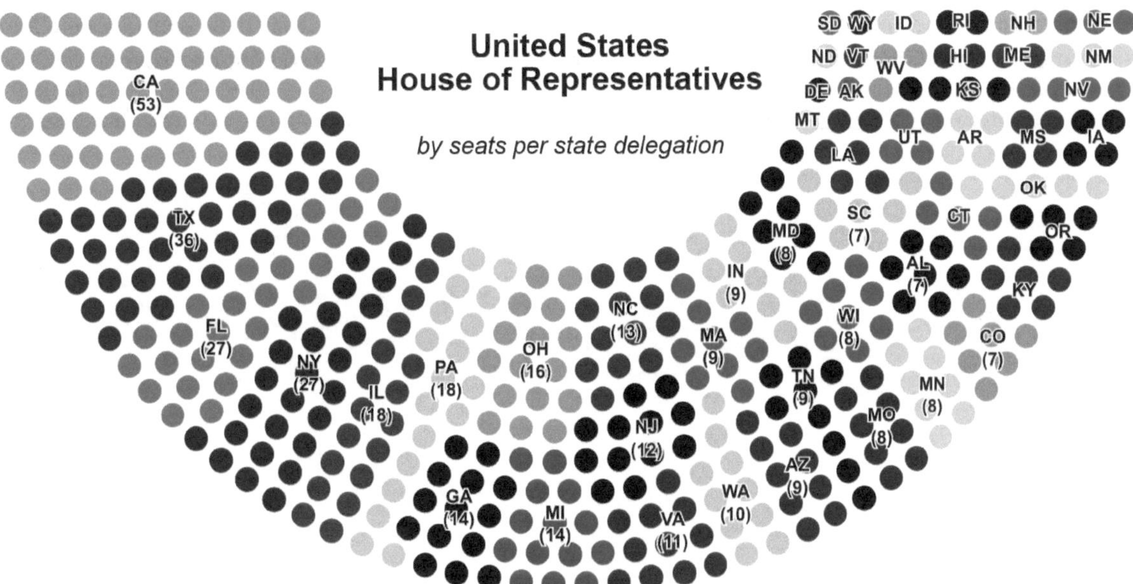

86. Which of the following statements is reflected in the graphic?

a. The ten least-populated states possess a greater collective representation than the two most-populated states.
b. The two most-populated states possess a greater collective representation than the ten least-populated states.
c. The two most-populated states and ten least-populated states possess an equal number of representation.
d. The ten most-populated states and two least-populated states possess an equal number of representatives.

87. Which of the following states would have the most votes within the Electoral College?
   a. Ohio
   b. Iowa
   c. Michigan
   d. South Dakota

Short-Answer Questions

Read the following passage and then answer the question that follows.

> In recent years there have been many signs of improvement, but only in proportion as the principles and practices that the white people of the state understand are those of Reconstruction are rejected or superseded. To the northern man Reconstruction probably meant and still means something quite different from what the white man of Alabama understands by the term. But as the latter understands it, he has accepted none of its essential principles and intends to accept none of its so-called successes.
>
> In destroying all that was old, Reconstruction probably removed some abuses; from the new order some permanent good must have resulted. But credit for neither can rightfully be claimed until it can be shown that those results were impossible under the régime destroyed.

Excerpt from Civil War and Reconstruction in Alabama (1905) by Walter L. Fleming, American historian

88. Based on the excerpt above, answer the following:

a) Briefly explain how ONE historical event or development undermined traditional Southern power structures during Reconstruction.

b) Briefly provide ONE historical example supporting the author's claim that Southern whites never accepted Reconstruction's "so-called successes."

c) Briefly provide ONE historical event or development to explain how the end of Reconstruction impacted African Americans' economic opportunities.

The image above is titled "The Gin House" (1879), unknown artist, published in The American Cyclopædia v. 5, p. 405

89. Based on the image above, answer the following:

a) Briefly describe ONE characteristic of late nineteenth-century agricultural production based on the image.

b) Briefly provide ONE example of how this method of agricultural production impacted the South's economic development.

c) Briefly explain ONE historical event or development triggered by the invention of the agricultural system expressed in the image.

90. Answer the following:

a) Briefly describe ONE specific historical difference between the American independence movement in the period 1750 to 1763 and in the period 1763 to 1776.

b) Briefly explain ONE specific historical consequence of British expansion on the American independence movement between 1750 and 1770.

c) Briefly provide ONE specific historical example of mass media contributing to the American independence movement during the 1770s.

91. Answer the following:

a) Briefly describe ONE specific historical similarity between American global power in the aftermath of World War I compared to American global power in the aftermath of World War II.

b) Briefly describe ONE specific historical difference between American global power in the aftermath of World War I and American global power in the aftermath of World War II.

c) Briefly describe ONE specific historical effect of American global power in either the aftermath of World War I or in the aftermath of World War II.

Document-Based Question

Evaluate and distinguish between the different perspectives on the causes of the American Civil War (1861–1865).

Document 1

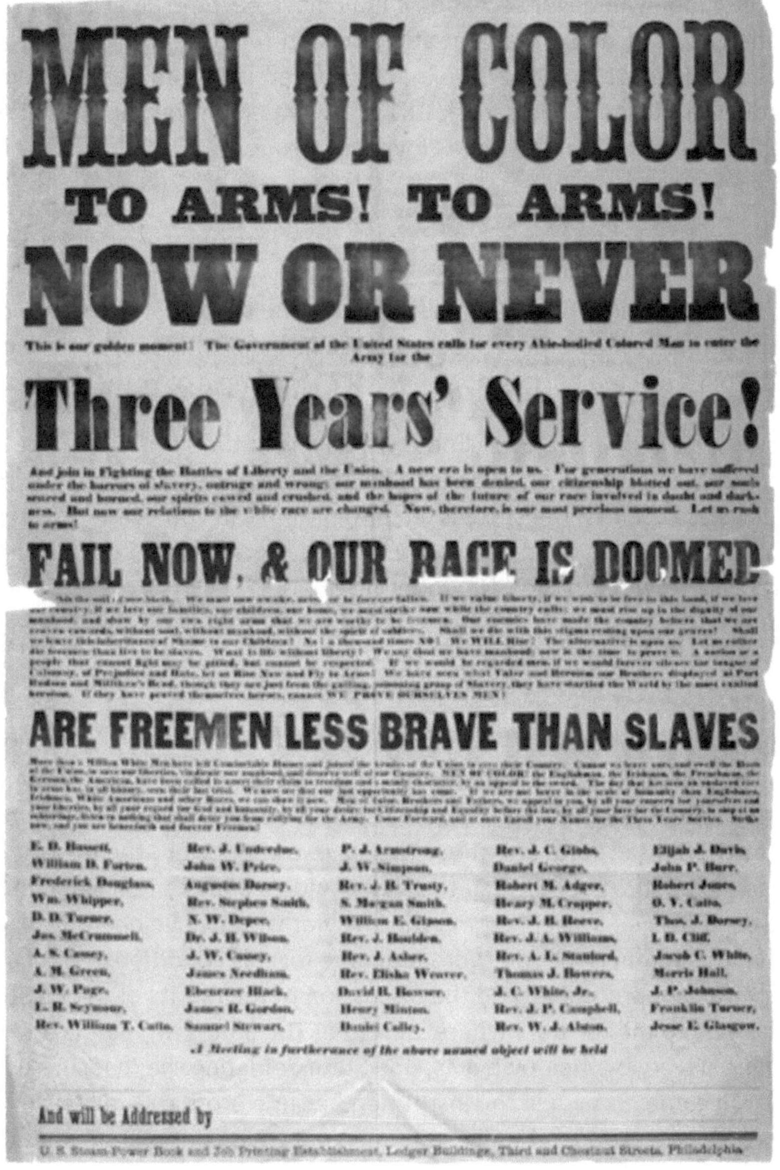

The image above is titled "Men of Color Civil War Recruitment Broadside" (1863), written by Frederick Douglass and signed by 54 African American community leaders

Document 2

States which claimed a sovereign right to secede from the Union naturally claimed the corresponding right to resume possession of all the land they had ceded to that Union's Government for the use of its naval and military posts. So South Carolina, after leading the way to secession on December 20, 1860, at once began to work for the retrocession of the forts defending her famous cotton port of Charleston. These defenses, being of vital consequence to both sides, were soon to attract the strained attention of the whole country...

The situation, here as elsewhere, was complicated by Floyd, President Buchanan's Secretary of War, soon to be forced out of office on a charge of misapplying public funds. Floyd, as an ardent Southerner, was using the last lax days of the Buchanan Government to get the army posts ready for capitulation whenever secession should have become an accomplished fact. He urged on construction, repairs, and armament at Charleston, while refusing to strengthen the garrison, in order, as he said, not to provoke Carolina. Moreover, in November he had replaced old Colonel Gardner, a Northern veteran of "1812," by Anderson the Southerner, in whom he hoped to find a good capitulator. But this time Floyd was wrong.

Excerpt from Captains of the Civil War: A Chronicle of the Blue and Gray, 1921, by William Wood, American historian

Document 3

Charleston, S. C., *November 8, 1860.*—Yesterday on the train, just before we reached Fernandina, a woman called out: "That settles the hash." Tanny touched me on the shoulder and said: "Lincoln's elected." "How do you know?" "The man over there has a telegram."

The excitement was very great. Everybody was talking at the same time. One, a little more moved than the others, stood up and said despondently: "The die is cast; no more vain regrets; sad forebodings are useless; the stake is life or death." "Did you ever!" was the prevailing exclamation, and some one cried out: "Now that the black radical Republicans have the power I suppose they will Brown[1] us all." No doubt of it.

Excerpt from A Diary from Dixie, 1906, by May Boykin Chesnut, Southern author and wife of influential Confederate leader

Document 4

There were two political parties, it is true, in all the States, both strong in numbers and respectability, but both equally loyal to the institution which stood paramount in Southern eyes to all other institutions in state or nation. The slave-owners were the minority, but governed both parties. Had politics ever divided the slave-holders and the non-slave-holders, the majority would have been obliged to yield, or internecine war would have been the consequence. I do not know that the Southern people were to blame for this condition of affairs. There was a time when slavery was not profitable, and the discussion of the merits of the institution was confined almost exclusively to the territory where it existed. The States of Virginia and Kentucky came near abolishing slavery by their own acts, one State defeating the measure by a tie vote and the other only lacking one. But when the institution became profitable, all talk of its abolition ceased where it existed; and naturally, as human nature is constituted, arguments were adduced in its support. The cotton-gin probably had much to do with the justification of slavery.

Excerpt from Personal Memoirs of U.S. Grant- Volume 1, 1885, by Ulysses S. Grant, Commanding General of the United States Army during the American Civil War and President of the United States during Reconstruction

Document 5

Our reliance is in the love of liberty which God has planted in us. Our defense is in the spirit which prizes liberty as the heritage of all men, in all lands everywhere. Destroy this spirit and you have planted the seeds of despotism at your own doors. Familiarize yourselves with the chains of bondage and you prepare your own limbs to wear them. Accustomed to trample on the rights of others, you have lost the genius of your own independence and become the fit subjects of the first cunning tyrant who rises among you. And let me tell you, that all these things are prepared for you by the teachings of history, if the elections shall promise that the next Dred Scott decision and all future decisions will be quietly acquiesced in by the people.

Excerpt of a campaign speech delivered by Abraham Lincoln on September 13, 1858, published in The Papers and Writings of Abraham Lincoln- Volume 5 (1865)

Document 6

As a mere historical fact, we have seen that African servitude among us—confessedly the mildest and most humane of all institutions to which the name "slavery" has ever been applied—existed in all the original States, and that it was recognized and protected in the fourth article of the Constitution. Subsequently, for climatic, industrial, and economical—not moral or sentimental—reasons, it was abolished in the Northern, while it continued to exist in the Southern States. Men differed in their views as to the abstract question of its right or wrong, but for two generations after the Revolution there was no geographical line of demarcation for such differences. The African slave-trade was carried on almost exclusively by New England merchants and Northern ships. Mr. Jefferson—a Southern man, the founder of the Democratic party, and the vindicator of State rights—was in theory a consistent enemy to every form of slavery...

The truth remains intact and incontrovertible, that the existence of African servitude was in no wise the cause of the conflict, but only an incident. In the later controversies that arose, however, its effect in operating as a lever upon the passions, prejudices, or sympathies of mankind, was so potent that it has been spread, like a thick cloud, over the whole horizon of historic truth.

Excerpt from The Rise and Fall of the Confederate Government, Volume 1, *1881*, by Jefferson Davis, President of the Confederate States

Document 7

Charleston was then a proud, aristocratic city, and assumed a leadership in the public opinion of the South far out of proportion to her population, wealth, or commerce. On more than one occasion previously, the inhabitants had almost inaugurated civil war, by their assertion and professed belief that each State had, in the original compact of government, reserved to itself the right to withdraw from the Union at its own option, whenever the people supposed they had sufficient cause. We used to discuss these things at our own mess-tables, vehemently and sometimes quite angrily; but I am sure that I never feared it would go further than it had already gone in the winter of 1832–'33, when the attempt at "nullification" was promptly suppressed by President Jackson's famous declaration, "The Union must and shall be preserved!" and by the judicious management of General Scott.

Still, civil war was to be; and, now that it has come and gone, we can rest secure in the knowledge that as the chief cause, slavery, has been eradicated forever, it is not likely to come again.

Excerpt from Memoirs of General W.T Sherman, Volume 1, *1875*, by William Tecumseh Sherman, General in the United States Army during the American Civil War

Long Essay Questions

1. Assess the extent to which the Spanish–American War (1899) transformed American foreign policy between 1890 and 1945.

2. Compare the similarities and differences between European colonizers' labor systems as practiced in the Americas between 1492 and 1800.

3. Evaluate the stances of American political parties and political movements in relation to civil rights during the Cold War (1947–1991).

Answer Explanations

Multiple-Choice Explanations

1. B: The American Revolution occurred first in 1775, and a number of European soldiers fought for the patriots. The American Revolution, in part, inspired the French Revolution. The Marquis de Lafayette came to America in 1777 and was wounded during the Battle of Brandywine. He returned to France after the American Revolution and became a leader in the French Revolution in 1789.

2. C: Although it can place a strain on some resources, population density is not a negative demographic indicator. For example, New York City, one of the most densely populated places on Earth, enjoys one of the highest standards of living in the world. Other world cities such as Tokyo, Los Angeles, and Sydney also have tremendously high population densities and high standards of living. High infant mortality rates, low literacy rates, and low life expectancies are all poor demographic indicators that suggest a low quality of life for the citizens living in those areas.

3. C: Opportunity cost. Opportunity cost can trade time, power, or anything else of value in exchange for something else. Economic systems determine what is being produced and by whom. Supply and demand refers to the quantity of goods and services that is produced or needed. Finally, inflation refers to how the cost of goods and services increases over time.

4. A: The atomic bomb was created during World War II (1939 – 1945). Scientists and engineers did develop a number of other weapons in order to break through the heavily entrenched front lines during World War I. Poison gas killed or injured millions of men between 1914 and 1918. Aircraft were used to observe enemy positions and bombard enemy troops. Armored tanks were able to crush barbed wire fences and deflected machine gun bullets.

5. A: Carolina is divided into two separate states—North and South. Maine was part of Nova Scotia and did not become an American territory until the War of 1812. Likewise, Vermont was not one of the original Thirteen Colonies. Canada remained a separate British colony. Finally, Florida was a Spanish territory. Therefore, by process of elimination, *A* is the correct list.

6. A: Most scholars already knew the world was round by 1492. On the other hand, the arrival of Europeans in North and South America introduced deadly diseases that killed millions of native peoples. Europeans had developed immunity to diseases such as smallpox, while Native Americans had not. In addition, Europeans introduced a number of new plants and animals to the New World, but they also adopted many new foods as well, including potatoes, tomatoes, chocolate, and tobacco. Finally, Europeans tried to convert Native Americans to Christianity, but Indians did not completely give up their traditional beliefs. Instead, they blended Christianity with indigenous and African beliefs to create new syncretic religions.

7. D: It is important to realize that the Cold War was never an official war and that the United States and the Soviet Union instead funded proxy conflicts. The Kyoto Protocol was signed by members of the United Nations, as the League of Nations was long since defunct. While Japan was a minor participant in World War I, it was not defeated by America until World War II. The correct answer is *D:* India's partition between Hindu India and Islamic Pakistan led to large outbreaks of religious violence.

8. B: A period of time. It is apparent that Lincoln is referring to a period of time within the context of the passage because of how the sentence is structured with the word *ago*.

9. C: Lincoln's reference to *the brave men, living and dead, who struggled here,* proves that he is referring to a battlefield. Choices *A* and *B* are incorrect, as a *civil war* is mentioned and not a war with France or a war in the Sahara Desert. Choice *D* is incorrect because it does not make sense to consecrate a President's ground instead of a battlefield ground for soldiers who died during the American Civil War.

10. A: The audience should perpetuate the ideals of freedom that the soldiers died fighting for. Lincoln doesn't address any of the topics outlined in Choices *B*, *C*, or *D*. Therefore, Choice *A* is the correct answer.

11. D: The word *resolve* means to make up one's mind or decide on something.

12. A: Choice *A* is correct because Lincoln's intention was to memorialize the soldiers who had fallen as a result of war as well as celebrate those who had put their lives in danger for the sake of their country. Choices *B* and *D* are incorrect because Lincoln's speech was supposed to foster a sense of pride among the members of the audience while connecting them to the soldiers' experiences.

13. B: As stated in the passage, left-axis political orientations typically favor social and economic equality and advocate for government intervention to achieve these goals. Communism, Socialism, Liberalism, and Progressivism are examples of political orientations on the left side of the spectrum that are discussed in the passage. Right-axis political orientations generally value the existing and historical political institutions and oppose government intervention, especially in regard to the economy. Libertarianism, Conservatism, and Fascism are the three orientations from the passage that are considered right-axis orientations. It is true that Libertarians have some progressive ideals; however, Libertarianism is still usually considered a right-axis orientation because the political ideals are conservative.

14. A: Fascists advocate for a strong, consolidated, centralized government led by an all-powerful dictator. They believe a key role of this centralized government is to prepare for war. While Libertarians still tend to maintain conservative approach to government, especially in the context of power and military intervention, they favor a weaker central government, with powerful local rule instead.

15. B: Emigration occurs when a person or entire group of people move *from* a location. Immigration occurs when a person or entire group of people move *to* a location. Push factors encourage (or force) people to move from their homes. Pull factors attract people to a location. As the passage mentioned, political push factors include war, government-induced violence and intimidation, genocide, or oppression. Refugees are those pushed from their home country because of such political factors. Refugees are often forcefully expunged from their home states when new countries are formed or when national boundaries are redrawn. For example, the unification of North Vietnam and South Vietnam after the Vietnam War brought hundreds of thousands of Vietnamese refugees to the United States during the 1970s. Choices *A* and *C* are incorrect because refugees *leave* their country, so they emigrate from their country; they immigrate *to* another country. Choice *D* is incorrect because refugees leave their country because of push factors, not pull factors.

16. C: Deindustrialization in cities in the Industrial North during the 1960s–1980s pushed away many residents from industrial hubs like Buffalo, Cleveland, Chicago, and Milwaukee because the number of jobs dropped significantly. Thus, people needed to move elsewhere to find employment. This is an example of an economic push factor—pushing people out of the area because of an economic downturn.

17. B: This scenario describes a political pull factor because it involves people moving to capitalize on the hopes of a better political situation; this enticement "pulls" them to the new location.

18. C: Environmental push factors include flooding, natural disasters, droughts, nuclear contamination, and water contamination, among others. In the Sahel region of North Africa, many people have found new lands due to the intense droughts. As another example, after Hurricane Katrina, many New Orleans residents had to relocate to Houston, Baton Rouge, or other cities to find refuge from the environmental and economic devastation.

19. D: Choice *D* is correct. Any territory gained via purchase is incorrect. Missouri and Nebraska became American territories through the Louisiana Purchase, and the United States purchased Alaska from Russia. In contrast, Mexico ceded Nevada as part of the peace agreement ending the Mexican-American War.

20. C: A participatory democracy in its truest form is a system in which everyone participates in the political system. Choice *A* describes an elite democracy, which was advocated by some of the Framers like James Madison. Choice *B* is a pluralist democracy—one where interest groups and advocacy for certain issues dominates the government. Choice *D* is the exact opposite of a democracy; it is what the colonies just fought a war to get themselves out of.

21. D: According to the system of checks and balances outlined in the Constitution, members of Congress debate and vote on legislation, although the president may request that legislators consider a certain proposal. The president may veto legislation that he or she disagrees with, but Congress can override the veto with a two-thirds majority in both chambers. The Supreme Court may review legislation and declare it unconstitutional.

22. B: According to the system of checks and balances, the Executive branch appoints federal judges, but the Legislative branch can impeach and remove judges. The Legislative branch must approve the appointment of federal judges.

23. A: Choice *A* is correct. John Stuart Mill was an English philosopher and political economist who advocated for utilitarianism and women's rights. In the excerpt, "utility" is defined as actions that are "right in proportion as they tend to promote happiness, wrong as they tend to produce the reverse of happiness." The excerpt then explains that happiness is measured by pleasure, and the reverse is pain. Therefore, Mill calls for actions to be evaluated based on the net total of pleasure. Choice *D* contradicts the definition provided in the excerpt. The excerpt doesn't support Choice *C*, as there's no evidence that pleasure-generating sacrifices merit special status. Choice *B* is incorrect because sacrifice can still be valuable if it leads to more pleasure than pain.

24. C: John Stuart Mills is best known for advocating for women's right to vote in Parliament. Mills believed in the philosophy of Utilitarianism, which suggests that whatever brings about the most positive effects is always the moral thing to do. He believed in the wellbeing of society and everyone in it.

25. C: Choice *C* is correct. Karl Marx, a philosopher, social scientist, historian, and revolutionary, is considered the father of communism. All the answer choices contain true statements or reasonable assumptions from the passage; however, Choice *C* best articulates the main idea—society is the history of class struggle, and working men must unite and fight a revolutionary battle like their historical ancestors.

26. B: Karl Marx was NOT considered a fascist. Karl Marx was a revolutionary, social scientist, historian, and philosopher, whose ideas contributed to the rise of Communism. A fascist regime is necessarily an authoritarian form of government. An example of a fascist regime is the leadership of Benito Mussolini in Italy from 1922 to 1943.

27. A: Choice *A* is correct. On the political spectrum, ideologies on the left side of the axis emphasize socioeconomic equality and advocate for government intervention, while ideologies on the right axis seek to preserve society's existing institutions and oppose government intervention. Therefore, the answer will be the farthest left on the axis, making Choice *A* correct.

28. C: Choice *C* is correct, as it most closely corresponds to the provided definition. Conservatism prioritizes traditional institutions. In general, conservatives oppose modern developments and value stability. Socialism and liberalism both feature the desire to change the government to increase equality. Libertarianism is more concerned with establishing a limited government to maximize personal autonomy.

29. D: Choice *D* is correct. The missing title is in the overlap between federal and state government powers. Concurrent powers are shared between federal and state governments. Reserved powers are the unspecified powers of the states not expressly granted to the federal government or denied to the state by the Constitution and left to the states by the Tenth Amendment. Implied powers are the unstated powers that can be reasonably inferred from the Constitution. Delegated powers are the specific powers granted to the federal government by the Constitution.

30. B: Implied powers are the unwritten powers that can be reasonably inferred from the Constitution. Choice *A* refers to delegated powers: the specific powers granted to the federal government by the Constitution. Choice *C* refers to inherent powers: the reasonable powers required by the government to manage the nation's affairs and maintain sovereignty. Choice *D* refers to reserved powers: the unspecified powers belonging to the state that are not expressly granted to the federal government or denied to the state by the Constitution.

31. D: Choice *D* is correct. The Federalists supported the expansion of the federal government, and the anti-Federalists feared that a stronger central government would weaken the states. *The Federalist Papers* argued for the ratification of the Constitution to establish a more powerful central government. The main idea of this excerpt is to argue that the Constitution establishes a central government powerful enough to rule, while also providing checks and balances to ensure the government doesn't abuse its power. Separation of powers is the concept behind checks and balances, so Choice *D* is the correct answer. Choices *A* and *C* are true statements, but they don't identify the main idea. Choice *B* references a theoretical assertion from the excerpt, but it's not the main idea.

32. A: The Federalist Papers were debates anonymously between the Federalists and the Anti-Federalists. Choice *B*, a document identifying basic liberties, is the bill of rights. Choice *C*, a document which articulated America's system of government, is the Articles of Confederation. Choice *D*, a document that required the colonists to pay a tax on legal documents, newspapers, magazines and other printed materials, is known as the Stamp Act.

33. C: Choice *C* is the correct answer. Checks and balances refer to the powers granted to ensure other branches don't overstep their authority. The other arrows in the diagram identify checks and balances, so the correct answer is the executive branch's checks and balances on the legislative branch. The executive branch can call special sessions of Congress and veto legislation, so Choice *C* is correct. Unlike the judicial and executive branches, members of the legislative branch cannot be impeached by another branch, though the legislative branch can expel its own members. The executive branch cannot refuse to enforce laws.

34. B: Choice *B* is correct. The Second Amendment states, "A well regulated Militia, being necessary to the security of a free State, the right of the people to keep and bear Arms, shall not be infringed." The First Amendment provides freedom of religion, speech, and the press, the right to assemble, and the right to petition the government. The Third Amendment establishes the right to refuse to house soldiers in times of war. The Fourth Amendment establishes a series of protections for citizens accused and charged with crimes.

35. B: Choice *B* is correct. The Electoral College determines the winner of presidential races, but if a candidate doesn't win a majority of electoral votes, the Twelfth Amendment requires the House of Representatives to decide the presidency, with each state delegation voting as a single bloc. The candidate with the most votes in the House wins the election. The table shows that Andrew Jackson won a plurality of electoral and popular votes, but he didn't receive a majority. John Quincy Adams received the most votes in the House of Representatives, so he won the presidency.

36. A: Choice *A* is correct. Electoral systems dictate how the members of the ruling body are selected, how votes translate into positions, and how seats are filled in the political offices at each level of government. In a majority system, a candidate must receive a majority of votes in order to be awarded a seat, but if none of the candidates reach a majority, a second round of voting occurs, commonly referred to as a runoff.

37. A: The tone is exasperated. While contemplative is an option because of the inquisitive nature of the text, Choice *A* is correct because the speaker is annoyed by the thought of being included when he felt that the fellow members of his race were being excluded. The speaker is not nonchalant, nor accepting of the circumstances which he describes.

38. C: Choice *C, contented,* is the only word that has different meaning. Furthermore, the speaker expresses objection and disdain throughout the entire text.

39. B: The main focus is to address the feelings of exclusion expressed by African Americans after the establishment of the Fourth of July holiday. While the speaker makes biblical references, it is not the main focus of the passage; therefore, Choice *A* is incorrect. The passage also makes no mention of wealthy landowners and doesn't speak of any positive response to the historical events, so Choices *C* and *D* are incorrect.

40: D: Choice *D* is the correct answer because it clearly makes reference to justice being denied.

41: D: It is an example of hyperbole. Choices *A* and *B* are unrelated. Assonance is the repetition of sounds and commonly occurs in poetry. Parallelism refers to two statements that correlate in some manner. Choice *C* is incorrect because amplification normally refers to clarification of meaning by broadening the sentence structure, while hyperbole refers to a phrase or statement that is being exaggerated.

42: C: Display the equivocation of the speaker and those that he represents. Choice *C* is correct because the speaker is clear about his intention and stance throughout the text. Choice *A* could be true, but the words "common text" is arguable. Choice *B* is also partially true, as another group of people affected by slavery are being referenced. However, the speaker is not trying to convince the audience that injustices have been committed, as it is already understood there have been injustices committed. Choice *D* is also close to the correct answer, but it is not the *best* answer choice possible.

43. C: In lines 6 and 7, it is stated that avarice can prevent a man from being necessitously poor, but too timorous, or fearful, to achieve real wealth. According to the passage, avarice does not tend to make a person very wealthy. The passage states that oppression, not avarice, is the consequence of wealth. The passage does not state that avarice drives a person's desire to be wealthy.

44. D: Paine believes that the distinction that is beyond a natural or religious reason is between king and subjects. He states that the distinction between good and bad is made in heaven. The distinction between male and female is natural. He does not mention anything about the distinction between humans and animals.

45. A: The passage states that the Heathens were the first to introduce government by kings into the world. The quiet lives of patriarchs came before the Heathens introduced this type of government. It was Christians, not Heathens, who paid divine honors to living kings. Heathens honored deceased kings. Equal rights of nature are mentioned in the paragraph, but not in relation to the Heathens.

46. B: Paine asserts that a monarchy is against the equal rights of nature and cites several parts of scripture that also denounce it. He doesn't say it is against the laws of nature, so Choice *A* is incorrect. Because he uses scripture to further his argument, it is not despite scripture that he denounces the monarchy. Therefore, Choice *C* is incorrect. Paine addresses the law by saying the courts also do not support a monarchical government; thus, Choice *D* is incorrect.

47. A: To be *idolatrous* is to worship idols or heroes, in this case, kings. It is not defined as being deceitful. While idolatry is considered a sin, it is an example of a sin, not a synonym for it. Idolatry may have been considered illegal in some cultures, but it is not a definition for the term.

48. A: The essential meaning of the passage is that the Almighty, God, would disapprove of this type of government. While heaven is mentioned, it is done so to suggest that the monarchical government is irreverent, not that heaven isn't promised. Thus, Choice *B* is incorrect. God's disapproval is mentioned, not his punishment. Therefore, Choice *C* is incorrect. The passage refers to the Jewish monarchy, which required both belief in God and kings. Therefore, Choice *D* is incorrect.

49. B: Choice *B* is correct. President Franklin D. Roosevelt introduced the New Deal, a series of executive orders and laws passed by Congress in response to the Great Depression. The excerpt describes how President Roosevelt intended to fight poverty by using the government's power to intervene and regulate the economy. Although the other answer choices correctly identify specific activities referenced in the excerpt, they are examples of the underlying philosophy in action. The underlying philosophy is an active role for government in the nation's economic affairs.

50. C: Choice *C* is correct. Frederick Douglass escaped from slavery and worked as an abolitionist for the rest of his life. The excerpt references the hypocrisy of the Fourth of July, as the holiday celebrates freedom in a country with millions of slaves. The other answer choices identify hypocritical aspects surrounding the slavery debate, but Choice *C* directly states the specific hypocrisy attacked in the excerpt.

51. D: Choice *D* is correct. Along with Lucy Stone and Elizabeth Cady Stanton, Susan B. Anthony was one of the most outspoken advocates for women's suffrage. Women couldn't vote in the United States until Congress passed the Nineteenth Amendment in 1920. Choice *D* accurately expresses the main idea of the excerpt. Denying women the right to vote is tyranny, so Anthony will not pay a fine for voting illegally. Choice *A* is the second-best answer, but it's too general to be the main idea of an excerpt specifically about women's suffrage.

52. B: Choice *B* is correct. Ronald Reagan won the presidential election of 1980 and promised to restore America's military power through defense spending, cutting government regulations, and reducing taxes. Evangelical Christians and the Moral Majority fiercely supported President Reagan's agenda, particularly his opposition to abortion and his conservative approach to social issues. The other answer choices include at least one mischaracterization. Choice *A* is incorrect because President Reagan generally opposed social programs. Choice *C* is incorrect because President Reagan valued American leadership more than international cooperation. In addition, his platform was far more radically conservative than compromising. Choice *D* is incorrect because President Reagan fought labor unions on several fronts, most notably when he broke a strike organized by an air traffic controllers' union.

53. A: Choice *A* is correct. The Depression of 1929, commonly referred to as the Great Depression, is the largest increase to unemployment, but the question stem asks for the second-largest increase. According to the graph, the Panic of 1893 increased unemployment by approximately ten percent; the Depression of 1920 increased unemployment by approximately six percent; the Depression of 1929 increased unemployment by approximately fifteen percent; and the Great Recession of 2007 increased unemployment by approximately four percent. Thus, the Panic of 1893 marks the second-largest increase to unemployment.

54. C: This is a tricky question, but it can be solved through careful context analysis and vocabulary knowledge. One can infer that the use of "expedient," while not necessarily very positive, isn't inherently bad in this context either. Note how in the next line, he says, "but most governments are usually, and all governments are sometimes, inexpedient." This use of "inexpedient" indicates that a government becomes a hindrance rather than a solution; it slows progress rather than helps facilitate progress. Thus, Choice *A* and Choice *D* can be ruled out because these are more of the result of government, not the intention or initial design. Choice *B* makes no logical sense. Therefore, Choice *C* is the best description of *expedient.* Essentially, Thoreau is saying that government is constructed as a way of developing order and people's rights, but the rigidness of government soon inhibits justice and human rights.

55. B: While Choice *D* is the only answer that mentions the Mexican War directly, Thoreau clearly thinks the war is unnecessary because the people generally didn't consent to the war. Choices *A*, *B*, and *C* are all correct to a degree, but the answer asks for the best description. Therefore, Choice *B* is the most accurate representation of Thoreau's views. Essentially, Thoreau brings to light the fact that the few people in power can twist government and policy for their own needs.

56. D: The passage does not proceed in chronological order since it begins by pointing out Christopher Columbus's explorations in America, so Choice *A* does not work. Although the author compares and contrasts Erikson with Christopher Columbus, this is not the main way in which the information is presented; therefore, Choice *B* does not work. Neither does Choice *C* because there is no mention of or reference to cause and effect in the passage. However, the passage does offer a conclusion (Leif Erikson deserves more credit) and premises (first European to set foot in the New World and first to contact the natives) to substantiate Erikson's historical importance. Thus, Choice *D* is correct.

57. C: Choice *C* is the correct answer because it is the author's opinion that Erikson deserves more credit. That, in fact, is the conclusion in the piece, but another person could argue that Columbus or another explorer deserves more credit for opening up the New World to exploration. Rather than being an indisputable fact, it is a subjective value claim. Choice *A* is incorrect because it describes facts: Leif Erikson was the son of Erik the Red and historians debate Leif's date of birth. These are not opinions. Choice *B* is incorrect; that Erikson called the land "Vinland" is a verifiable fact, as is Choice *D* because he did contact the natives almost 500 years before Columbus.

58. B: Choice *B* is correct because, as stated in the previous answer, it accurately identifies the author's statement that Erikson deserves more credit than he has received for being the first European to explore the New World. Choice *A* is incorrect because the author aims to go beyond describing Erikson as a mere legendary Viking. Choice *C* is incorrect because the author does not focus on Erikson's motivations, let alone name the spreading of Christianity as his primary objective. Choice *D* is incorrect because it is a premise that Erikson contacted the natives 500 years before Columbus, which is simply a part of supporting the author's conclusion.

59. B: Choice *A* is incorrect because the author is not in any way trying to entertain the reader. Choice *D* is incorrect because he goes beyond a mere suggestion; "suggest" is too vague. Although the author is certainly trying to alert the readers of Leif Erikson's unheralded accomplishments, the nature of the writing does not indicate the author would be satisfied with the reader merely knowing of Erikson's exploration (Choice *C*). Rather, the author would want the reader to be informed about it, which is more substantial (Choice *B*).

60. D: Choice *D* is correct because there are two examples of historians having trouble pinning down important dates in Viking history: Leif Erikson's date of birth and what happened during the encounter with the natives. Choice *A* is incorrect because the author never addresses the Vikings' state of mind or emotions. Choice *B* is incorrect because the author does not elaborate on Erikson's exile and whether he would have become an explorer if not for his banishment. Choice *C* is incorrect because there is not enough information to support this premise. It is unclear whether Erikson informed the King of Norway of his finding. Although it is true that the King did not send a follow-up expedition, he could have simply chosen not to expend the resources after receiving Erikson's news. It is not possible to logically infer whether Erikson told him.

61. D: Governmental regimes fall along a continuum between total authoritarianism and complete direct democracy. Most countries are neither totally authoritarian, nor a complete direct democracy, but they do all fall along this continuum. China and Iran would be towards the authoritarian end of the spectrum and the United States, United Kingdom, and Mexico would be towards the democratic end.

62. C: Power is the ability of a ruling body or political entity to influence the actions, behavior, and attitude of a person or group of people. Authority, Choice *A*, is the right and justification of the government to exercise power as recognized by the citizens or influential elites. Similarly, legitimacy, Choice *D*, is another way of expressing the concept of authority. Sovereignty, Choice *B,* refers to the ability of a state to determine and control their territory without foreign interference.

63. D: This period was called the Gilded Age since it appeared shiny and golden on the surface but was fueled by undercurrents of corruption led by big businessmen known as robber barons. Choice *A*, Manifest Destiny, is the concept referring to the pursuit and acquisition of new lands by the U.S., which led to the purchase of Alaska from Russia in 1867 and the annexation of Hawaii in 1898. The Columbian Exchange, Choice *B*, was an era of discovery, conquest, and colonization of the Americas by the

Europeans. The New Deal, Choice *C*, was a plan launched by President Franklin Delano Roosevelt to help rebuild America's economy after the Great Depression.

64. B: Choice *A*, Choice *C*, and Choice *D* all relate facts but do not present the kind of general statement needed for a conclusion.

65. C: The correct answer choice is C, *1910*. There are two ways to arrive at the correct answer. You could find the four answer choices on the graph, or you could have identified that the population never dips at any point. Thus, the correct answer needs to be the only answer choice that is earlier in time than the others, Choice *C*.

66. D: The population increased the most between 1990 and 2010. The question is asking you to identify the rate of change for each interval. Between 1930 and 1950, the population increased by approximately 28 million. Between 1950 and 1970, the population increased by approximately 52 million. Between 1970 and 1990, the population increased by approximately 45 million. Between 1990 and 2010, the population increased by approximately 60 million. Thus, Choice *D* is the correct answer. The slope is also the steepest in this interval, which represents its higher increase.

67. B: Lines of latitude measure distance North and South. The Equator is zero degrees, and the Tropic of Cancer is 23 ½ degrees north of the Equator. The distance between those two lines measures degrees North to South, as with any other two lines of latitude. Longitudinal lines, or meridians, measure distance East and West, even though they run north and south down the Globe. Latitude is not inexact, in that there are set distances between the lines. Furthermore, coordinates can only exist with the use of longitude and latitude.

68. A: Ethnic groups are simply a group of people with a religious, cultural, economic, or linguistic commonality. Additionally, ethnic groups don't always choose to leave places. Many have called certain locations home for centuries. Also, some ethnic groups actually make up the majority in some countries and are not always minority groups.

69. A: Free. A free market does not involve government interventions or monopolies while trading between buyers and suppliers. However, in a command market, the government determines the price of goods and services. Gross and exchange markets refer to situations where brokers and traders make exchanges in the financial realm.

70. B: A period of time. It is apparent that Lincoln is referring to a period of time within the context of the passage because of how the sentence is structured with the word *ago*.

71. C: Lincoln's reference to *the brave men, living and dead, who struggled here,* proves that he is referring to a battlefield. Choices *A* and *B* are incorrect, as a *civil war* is mentioned and not a war with France or a war in the Sahara Desert. Choice *D* is incorrect because it does not make sense to consecrate a President's ground instead of a battlefield ground for soldiers who died during the American Civil War.

72. D: Abraham Lincoln, the president of the United States when he gave that address, was referencing the Civil War.

73. A: The audience should perpetuate the ideals of freedom that the soldiers died fighting for. Lincoln doesn't address any of the topics outlined in Choices *B*, *C*, or *D*. Therefore, Choice *A* is the correct answer.

74. D: The word *resolve* means to make up one's mind or decide upon something.

75. A: Choice *A* is correct because Lincoln's intention was to memorialize the soldiers who had fallen as a result of war as well as celebrate those who had put their lives in danger for the sake of their country. Choices *B*, *C*, and *D* are incorrect because Lincoln's speech was supposed to foster a sense of pride, not shame, among the members of the audience while connecting them to the soldiers' experiences.

76. A: It decreased one percent. In the first pie chart, the percentage of the European Union population that lived in Germany was 17%. In the second pie chart, we can see that this percentage drops to 16%. Therefore, there was a one percent decrease.

77. A: Firsthand accounts are given by primary sources—individuals who provide personal or expert accounts of an event, subject matter, time period, or of an individual. They are viewed more as objective accounts than subjective. Secondary sources are accounts given by an individual or group of individuals who were not physically present at the event or who did not have firsthand knowledge of an individual or time period. Secondary sources are sources that have used research in order to create a written work. Direct and indirect sources are not terms used in literary circles.

78. C: The passage makes clear that the Anti-Federalists wanted the Constitution to be altered prior to its approval in a way that would give states and individuals more power rather than the national government. Of the listed men, Thomas Jefferson was the only Anti-Federalist. The other people listed were notable Federalists.

79. B: As stated in the passage, left-axis political orientations typically favor social and economic equality and advocate for government intervention to achieve these goals. Communism, Socialism, Liberalism, and Progressivism are examples of political orientations on the left side of the spectrum that are discussed in the passage. Right-axis political orientations generally value the existing and historical political institutions and oppose government intervention, especially in regard to the economy. Libertarianism, Conservatism, and Fascism are the three orientations from the passage that are considered right-axis orientations. It is true that Libertarians have some progressive ideals; however, Libertarianism is still usually considered a right-axis orientation because the political ideals are conservative.

80. A: Fascists advocate for a strong, consolidated, centralized government led by an all-powerful dictator. They believe a key role of this centralized government is to prepare for war. While Libertarians still tend to maintain a conservative approach to government, especially in the context of power and military intervention, they favor a weaker central government, with powerful local rule instead.

81. B: Emigration occurs when a person or entire group of people move *from* a location. Immigration occurs when a person or entire group of people move *to* a location. Push factors encourage (or force) people to move from their homes. Pull factors attract people to a location. As the passage mentioned, political push factors include war, government-induced violence and intimidation, genocide, or oppression. Refugees are those pushed from their home country because of such political factors. Refugees are often forcefully expunged from their home states when new countries are formed or when national boundaries are redrawn. For example, the unification of North Vietnam and South Vietnam after the Vietnam War brought hundreds of thousands of Vietnamese refugees to the United States during the 1970s. Choices *A* and *C* are incorrect because refugees *leave* their country, so they emigrate from their country; they immigrate *to* another country. Choice *D* is incorrect because refugees leave their country because of push factors, not pull factors.

82. C: Deindustrialization in cities in the Industrial North during the 1960s–1980s pushed away many residents from industrial hubs like Buffalo, Cleveland, Chicago, and Milwaukee because the number of jobs dropped significantly. Thus, people needed to move elsewhere to find employment. This is an example of an economic push factor—pushing people out of the area because of an economic downturn.

83. B: This scenario describes a political pull factor because it involves people moving to capitalize on the hopes of a better political situation; this enticement "pulls" them to the new location.

84. C: Environmental push factors include flooding, natural disasters, droughts, nuclear contamination, and water contamination, among others. In the Sahel region of North Africa, many people have found new lands due to the intense droughts. As another example, after Hurricane Katrina, many New Orleans residents had to relocate to Houston, Baton Rouge, or other cities to find refuge from the environmental and economic devastation.

85. D: An individual cause can be subdivided into smaller factors or stretched out in a gradual process. Although there were numerous issues that led to the Civil War, slavery was the primary cause. However, that issue stretched back to the very founding of the nation, and the existence of slavery was a controversial topic during the creation of the Declaration of Independence and the Constitution. The abolition movement as a whole did not start until the 1830s, but nevertheless, slavery is a cause that gradually grew more important over the following decades. In addition, opponents of slavery were divided by different motivations—some believed that it stifled the economy, while others focused on moral issues. On the other end of the spectrum, a single event can have numerous results. The rise of the telegraph, for example, had several effects on American history. The telegraph allowed news to travel much quicker and turned events into immediate national news, such as the sinking of the USS Maine, which sparked the Spanish-American War. In addition, the telegraph helped make railroads run more efficiently by improving the links between stations. The faster speed of both travel and communications led to a shift in time itself, and localized times were replaced by standardized time zones across the nation. Therefore, Choice *A* is incorrect. Choices *B* and *C* are incorrect because those are examples of single causes for the given effects.

86. B: The two most-populous states (California and Texas) possess a greater collective representation (eighty-nine representatives) than the ten least-populous states. All other answer choices do not reflect accurate comparisons of representation.

87. A: Ohio would have the most votes (seventeen) compared to Iowa (four), Michigan (fifteen), and South Dakota (one).

Short-Answer Explanations

88.

a) The author remarks that Reconstruction destroyed the former Southern regime, and few things did more to disrupt those traditional power structures than the Reconstruction Amendments. Prior to Reconstruction, the Southern economic and political systems had been extremely hierarchical and dependent on a large supply of the free labor forcibly taken from African slaves. The Reconstruction Amendments brought an end to the institution of slavery, and provided former slaves with political rights and civil liberty protections for the first time. While the South did ultimately move to roll back the Reconstruction Amendments, the Reconstruction Amendments permanently eliminated a major pillar of traditional Southern power structures.

b) Southern whites' dissatisfaction with Reconstruction was clearly illustrated by their fervent support of undermining and thwarting racial equality after the withdrawal of federal troops in 1877. Immediately after the end of Reconstruction, Southern states passed a series of legislation known as Jim Crow laws to prevent people of color from exercising their new constitutional rights. Because Southern white men were dominant in the racial caste system which they dominated, Southern white men were able to revive and sustain systemic white supremacy in economic, political, and social systems until the Civil Rights Movement in the 1960s.

c) Following the end of Reconstruction, Southern states passed Jim Crow laws to legally enforce white supremacy, and as a result, African Americans had extremely limited economic opportunities. The rise of the sharecropping industry underscores the economic plight of newly freed slaves. Without meaningful property rights and access to capital, most African Americans worked as sharecroppers, farming small parcels of land and paying white landowners a substantial share of the harvest. The system was highly exploitative due to the limited opportunities for advancement, and it deepened the generational poverty that dated back to slavery.

89.

a) The image depicts a complex cotton gin being operated by relatively few laborers. During the late eighteenth and early nineteenth centuries, the cotton gin greatly increased the efficiency and output of the cotton industry. Unlike earlier methods, the cotton gin offered a mechanical solution for harvesting and preparing cotton for export. Ever-increasing mechanization was a major characteristic of late nineteenth century agricultural production, and this trend accelerated as the North continued to industrialize, increasing the production of agricultural machinery and spare parts.

b) The cotton gin and other forms of mechanized agriculture contributed to the Southern states' continued dependence on agriculture. Many Southern leaders had hoped to build a New South after Reconstruction, largely based on mirroring Northern states' industrialization and urbanization. However, increasing yields sustained high profit margins, so plantation owners pursued large-scale production and sharecropping. Without the support of their wealthiest and most powerful citizens, the plans for a New South came to a halt.

c) The invention of the cotton gin increased sectionalism in the United States. Because the cotton gin increased the profitability of large-scale agriculture, it greatly strengthened Southern states' economic systems. This first occurred at a massive scale during the early nineteenth century when the Northern states were rapidly industrializing; in fact, the cotton gin spurred Northern industrialization because the larger supply of cotton led to the establishment of more factories and higher levels of textile production. While the economic differences between the North and South dated back to the era of the Thirteen Colonies, the cotton gin exponentially widened the economic divide.

90.

a) The American independence movement was significantly more aggressive in the period 1763 to 1776 as compared to the period 1750 to 1763. More Americans began discussing the need for greater unification in the early 1750s, but colonial leaders primarily lobbied for greater autonomy rather than independence. For example, Benjamin Franklin's Plan of Union (1754) called for a united colonial government, but it didn't renounce the authority of the British Crown. The French and Indian War (1756–1763) marked a major turning point for the independence movement. Americans believed they would be rewarded for their service, while the British Crown raised taxes to recover what it'd spent on protecting the colonies. Between 1763 and 1776, Britain passed a series of punitive measures intended to quash the growing rebellion, which only served to further fuel the American independence movement.

b) Britain acquired a staggering amount of North American territory after its victory in the Seven Years' War (1756–1763), annexing part of Spanish Florida and all of French Canada. While the new territory presented incredible profit potential, Britain faced issues balancing its conflicting problems with American Indian allies and American colonists. The British Crown decided to keep its agreement with the Iroquois, issuing the Royal Proclamation of 1763 to prohibit Americans from settling west of the Appalachian Mountains. Americans perceived this as a betrayal and increasingly sought to undermine British colonial rule. Over the next decade, the American independence movement rapidly gained popular support, allowing it to consolidate political and military power in the run-up to the American Revolutionary War (1775–1783).

c) During the 1770s, the most popular form of mass media was the publishing industry, particularly the widespread distribution of pamphlets. Thomas Paine's *Common Sense* (1776) was by far the most popular pamphlet of this period, and it was quickly distributed within the American independence movement. *Common Sense* denounced King George III for a variety of abuses, and it praised representative government for its emphasis on civic virtue. Overall, the American colonies' robust publishing industry represented the Patriots' best method of disseminating their revolutionary ideology and organizing mass actions against the British.

91.

a) The United States enjoyed a sizable boost in its relative global power in the aftermath of both World War I and World War II. Prior to World War I, the United States was an economic superpower, but European powers dwarfed America in terms of imperialism, military spending, and global influence. Afterward, the United States achieved parity with most global powers as reflected in its larger role in negotiating the Treaty of Versailles, arbitrating international disputes between major powers, and launching aggressive imperial interventions all over the world. World War II marked a similarly transformative movement for American power because the United States first established itself as the preeminent global superpower in its aftermath.

b) The United States was significantly more powerful relative to other global powers in the aftermath of World War II as compared to its relative hierarchical position after World War I. The United States had developed from a powerful country to one of the most powerful countries in the world. European states suffered considerable devastation after World War I, but most maintained their status as global powers with control over extensive amounts of foreign territory. In contrast, the United States was one of two remaining superpowers after World War II. No country could compete with American manufacturing and financial military power, and only the Soviet Union could pose any type of deterrent to the projection of American power overseas.

c) The United States' disproportionate amount of global power after the end of World War II resulted in the systematic destruction of Latin America. During the Cold War, the United States covertly and overtly provided material support to regime change in more than a dozen Latin American countries. This sometimes involved merely financing right-wing political movements, but material assistance was sometimes extended to known violators of human rights and death squads. American policymakers' fear of communism also led to the overthrow of democratically elected leaders, such as Chilean President Salvador Allende in 1973. Overall, the ascendance of American power at the end of World War II crippled the economic and political development of many Latin American states, particularly in regard to their long-term stability and self-sufficiency.

Index

Dear Customer,

We would like to start by thanking you for purchasing this history study guide. We hope that we exceeded your expectations.

Our goal in creating this study guide was to cover all of the topics that you need to know. We also strove to make our practice questions as similar as possible to what you will encounter on test day. With that being said, if you found something that you feel was not up to your standards, please send us an email and let us know.

Thanks Again and Happy Testing!
Product Development Team
info@studyguideteam.com

FREE Test Taking Tips DVD Offer

To help us better serve you, we have developed a Test Taking Tips DVD that we would like to give you for FREE. **This DVD covers world-class test taking tips that you can use to be even more successful when you are taking your test.**

All that we ask is that you email us your feedback about your study guide. Please let us know what you thought about it – whether that is good, bad or indifferent.

To get your **FREE Test Taking Tips DVD**, email freedvd@studyguideteam.com with "FREE DVD" in the subject line and the following information in the body of the email:

a. The title of your study guide.

b. Your product rating on a scale of 1-5, with 5 being the highest rating.

c. Your feedback about the study guide. What did you think of it?

d. Your full name and shipping address to send your free DVD.

If you have any questions or concerns, please don't hesitate to contact us at freedvd@studyguideteam.com.

Thanks again!

Made in United States
Troutdale, OR
06/20/2023

10701939R10164